1 & 2 Samuel

TEACH THE TEXT COMMENTARY SERIES

John H. Walton
Old Testament General Editor

Mark L. Strauss
New Testament General Editor

When complete, the TEACH THE TEXT COMMENTARY SERIES *will include the following volumes:*

Old Testament Volumes

New Testament Volumes

To see which titles are available, visit the series website at www.teachthetextseries.com.

TEACH the TEXT
COMMENTARY SERIES

1 & 2 Samuel
Robert B. Chisholm Jr.

Mark L. Strauss and John H. Walton
GENERAL EDITORS

Rosalie de Rosset
ASSOCIATE EDITOR

BakerBooks
a division of Baker Publishing Group
Grand Rapids, Michigan

Published by Baker Books
a division of Baker Publishing Group
P.O. Box 6287, Grand Rapids, MI 49516-6287
www.bakerbooks.com

Printed in the United States of America

Library of Congress Cataloging-in-Publication Data
Chisholm, Robert B.
    1 and 2 Samuel / Robert B. Chisholm Jr.
       p.   cm.   (Teach the text commentary series)
    Includes bibliographical references and index.
    ISBN 978-0-8010-9225-1 (cloth)
    1. Bible. O.T. Samuel—Commentaries. I. Title. II. Title: First & Second Samuel.
    BS1325.53.C49 2013
    222′.407—dc23   2012020200

13   14   15   16   17   18   19   7   6   5   4   3   2   1

Interior Design by Brian Brunsting

This commentary is dedicated with love and affection to my first four pastors, all of whom had a profound impact on my life:

The late Floyd Childs,
who introduced my father to the Savior
and radically altered the course of our family's history

The late Richard Prue,
who showed a young boy what it means
to love and serve Jesus with one's heart and soul

John Hunter,
who inspired a college graduate to go to seminary
rather than become a sportswriter

The late Richard Anderson,
who gave an inexperienced seminarian the opportunity
to preach and teach the Word of God on a regular basis

Contents

Welcome to the Teach the Text Commentary Series

Why another commentary series? That was the question the general editors posed when Baker Books asked us to produce this series. Is there something that we can offer to pastors and teachers that is not currently being offered by other commentary series, or that can be offered in a more helpful way? After carefully researching the needs of pastors who teach the text on a weekly basis, we concluded that yes, more can be done; this commentary is carefully designed to fill an important gap.

The technicality of modern commentaries often overwhelms readers with details that are tangential to the main purpose of the text. Discussions of source and redaction criticism, as well as detailed surveys of secondary literature, seem far removed from preaching and teaching the Word. Rather than wade through technical discussions, pastors often turn to devotional commentaries, which may contain exegetical weaknesses, misuse the Greek and Hebrew languages, and lack hermeneutical sophistication. There is a need for a commentary that utilizes the best of biblical scholarship but also presents the material in a clear, concise, attractive, and user-friendly format.

This commentary is designed for that purpose—to provide a ready reference for the exposition of the biblical text, giving easy access to information that a pastor needs to communicate the text effectively. To that end, the commentary is divided into carefully selected preaching units, each covered in six pages (with carefully regulated word counts both in the passage as a whole and in each subsection). Pastors and teachers engaged in weekly preparation thus know that they will be reading approximately the same amount of material on a week-by-week basis.

Each passage begins with a concise summary of the central message, or "Big Idea," of the passage and a list of its main themes. This is followed by a more detailed interpretation of the text, including the literary context of the passage, historical background material, and interpretive insights. While drawing on the best of biblical scholarship, this material is clear, concise, and to the point. Technical material is kept to a minimum, with endnotes pointing the reader to more detailed discussion and additional resources.

A second major focus of this commentary is on the preaching and teaching process itself. Few commentaries today help the pastor/teacher move from the meaning of the text to its effective communication. Our goal is to bridge this gap. In addition to interpreting the text in the "Understanding the Text" section, each six-page unit contains a "Teaching the Text" section and an "Illustrating the Text" section. The teaching section points to the key theological themes of the passage and ways to communicate these themes to today's audiences. The illustration section provides ideas and examples for retaining the interest of hearers and connecting the message to daily life.

The creative format of this commentary arises from our belief that the Bible is not just a record of God's dealings in the past but is the living Word of God, "alive and active" and "sharper than any double-edged sword" (Heb. 4:12). Our prayer is that this commentary will help to unleash that transforming power for the glory of God.

The General Editors

Introduction to the Teach the Text Commentary Series

This series is designed to provide a ready reference for teaching the biblical text, giving easy access to information that is needed to communicate a passage effectively. To that end, the commentary is carefully divided into units that are faithful to the biblical authors' ideas and of an appropriate length for teaching or preaching.

The following standard sections are offered in each unit.

1. *Big Idea*. For each unit the commentary identifies the primary theme, or "Big Idea," that drives both the passage and the commentary.
2. *Key Themes*. Together with the Big Idea, the commentary addresses in bullet-point fashion the key ideas presented in the passage.
3. *Understanding the Text*. This section focuses on the exegesis of the text and includes several sections.
   a. The Text in Context. Here the author gives a brief explanation of how the unit fits into the flow of the text around it, including refer-

ence to the rhetorical strategy of the book and the unit's contribution to the purpose of the book.
   b. Outline/Structure. For some literary genres (e.g., epistles), a brief exegetical outline may be provided to guide the reader through the structure and flow of the passage.
   c. Historical and Cultural Background. This section addresses historical and cultural background information that may illuminate a verse or passage.
   d. Interpretive Insights. This section provides information needed for a clear understanding of the passage. The intention of the author is to be highly selective and concise rather than exhaustive and expansive.
   e. Theological Insights. In this very brief section the commentary identifies a few carefully selected theological insights about the passage.

4. *Teaching the Text*. Under this second main heading the commentary offers guidance for teaching the text. In this section the author lays out the main themes and applications of the passage. These are linked carefully to the Big Idea and are represented in the Key Themes.

5. *Illustrating the Text*. Here the commentary provides suggestions of where useful illustrations may be found in fields such as literature, entertainment, history, or biography. They are intended to provide general ideas for illustrating the passage's key themes and so serve as a catalyst for effectively illustrating the text.

Abbreviations

ANET	James B. Pritchard, ed. *Ancient Near Eastern Texts Relating to the Old Testament*. 3rd ed. Princeton, NJ: Princeton University Press, 1969	ibid.	*ibidem*, in the same place
		KJV	King James Version
		LXX	Septuagint, ancient Greek version of the OT
ARAB	Daniel David Luckenbill. *Ancient Records of Assyria and Babylonia*. 2 vols. Chicago: University of Chicago Press, 1926–27	mg.	marginal reading/note
		MT	Masoretic Text; Hebrew reading or verse numbers
AT	author's translation	NASB	New American Standard Bible
b.	born	*NIDOTTE*	Willem A. VanGemeren, ed. *New International Dictionary of Old Testament Theology and Exegesis*. 5 vols. Grand Rapids: Zondervan, 1997
BDB	Francis Brown, S. R. Driver, and Charles A. Briggs. *The New Brown, Driver, Briggs, Gesenius Hebrew and English Lexicon*. Peabody, MA: Hendrickson, 1979		
		NIV	New International Version (2011)
ca.	*circa*, around, approximately	no.	number
cf.	*confer*, compare	NRSV	New Revised Standard Version
chap./chaps.	chapter/chapters	NT	New Testament
COS	William W. Hallo and K. Lawson Younger, eds. *The Context of Scripture*. 3 vols. Boston: Brill, 2003	OT	Old Testament
		¶	paragraph
		repr.	reprint
		rev.	revised, revised by
e.g.	*exempli gratia*, for example	*TDOT*	G. Johannes Botterweck and Helmer Ringgren, eds. *Theological Dictionary of the Old Testament*. 15 vols. Grand Rapids: Eerdmans, 1974–2006
esp.	especially		
HALOT	Ludwig Koehler and Walter Baumgartner. *The Hebrew and Aramaic Lexicon of the Old Testament*. Revised by W. Baumgartner and J. J. Stamm. Translated and edited by M. E. J. Richardson. 2 vols. Boston: Brill, 2001		
		v./vv.	verse/verses
		ZIBBCOT	John H. Walton, ed. *Zondervan Illustrated Bible Backgrounds Commentary: Old Testament*. 5 vols. Grand Rapids: Zondervan, 2009

Introduction to 1 & 2 Samuel

Canonical Importance

The books of 1–2 Samuel are at the core of the Bible's account of Israel's history. The book of Judges ends with the observation that Israel's lack of a king was responsible, at least in part, for the moral chaos that characterized the judges' period (Judg. 21:25; cf. 17:6). In 1 Samuel this problem is seemingly rectified, as the Lord gives Israel a king. But as Saul's reign goes from bad to worse, we discover all too quickly that not just any king will do. The rise of David, the man after God's "own heart" (1 Sam. 13:14), appears to right the ship, but his reign too is characterized by tragic failure and a return to the chaos that characterized the judges' period. Nevertheless, in contrast to his relationship to Saul, the Lord has committed himself to David by covenant and preserves him on Israel's throne, leaving readers with the hope that all is not lost after all. The Lord's covenant promise to David is a pivotal event in Israel's history and a guarantee that God's purposes for his people will be eventually realized. As 2 Samuel ends, one can forge ahead in the history with the confidence that the Lord has a plan for his people and will bring it to fruition through his chosen, albeit imperfect, servant David.

Literary Strategy

Three major characters, whose careers overlap, dominate the pages of 1–2 Samuel: Samuel (1 Sam. 1–16), Saul (1 Sam. 9–31), and David (1 Sam. 16–2 Sam. 24). David is the focal point of the story; literarily and historically, the other two characters function primarily in relation to David. As the Lord's chosen prophet, Samuel is the one who anoints both Saul and David. Saul is the king Israel desires and perhaps deserves, but in the end he is a foil for David, who is, at least when at his peak, the king Israel needs.

The narrator of 1–2 Samuel demonstrates David's superiority to Saul. He begins his defense of David's kingship by establishing Samuel's credentials as the Lord's prophet. This is important to his strategy since Samuel, the Lord's authorized spokesman, eventually denounces Saul and his dynasty, while anointing David as the new king. Samuel's support of David becomes foundational to the narrator's defense of David. After all, how can one argue with Samuel? In chapter after chapter, the narrator then establishes David's superiority to Saul, a fact that is recognized by virtually everyone, including Saul himself. The high point of this presentation is when the Lord makes a promise to David that secures his dynasty (2 Sam. 7). Of course, one might think that David's great sin will lead to his demise and the forfeiture of his special position, as it does with Saul. But even the account of David's failure contributes to the narrator's defense of his kingship. While certainly depicting the Lord's disciplinary measures in horrifying detail, the narrator makes it clear that the Lord's commitment to David remains firm. Indeed, a very tragic story concludes on an optimistic note as the thematically central poems of the epilogue celebrate David's status as the recipient of the divine promise (see 2 Sam. 22:51; 23:5).

Literary Connections to the Book of Judges

The Hebrew Bible is divided into three sections: the Torah (Law), the Prophets, and the Writings. The Prophets are divided into two parts: the Former and the Latter Prophets. First and Second Samuel are part of the Former Prophets, which include Joshua, Judges, 1–2 Samuel, and 1–2 Kings (Ruth is in the Writings in the Hebrew Bible). The Former Prophets record the history of Israel from their entry into the promised land under Joshua to their expulsion from the land in 586 BC. Though this history undoubtedly contains many literary sources written over this long period of time, in its final form it is a literary unit, complete with a macroplot, as well as several subthemes. In short, it is a story in every sense of the word, albeit one that displays great literary diversity.

As a story, the Former Prophets display the features one expects in a literary work, including foreshadowing and parallelism. This is especially true of 1–2 Samuel in relation to the book of Judges. The narrator employs patterns from Judges in his characterization of Samuel, Saul, and David.

From a literary standpoint, Samson (Judg. 13–16) and Micah (Judg. 17–18) are foils for Samuel. The accounts of all three

Fresco showing David's being anointed by Samuel, from the remains of the synagogue at Dura Europos (AD 245)

begin with a similar formula (Judg. 13:2; 17:1; 1 Sam. 1:1). Like Samson, Samuel is born to a barren woman. However, Samson's moral weakness and lack of wisdom led to his humiliation and death, while faithful Samuel becomes the catalyst for political and religious revival. Samson only began the deliverance of Israel from the Philistines (Judg. 13:5), but Samuel and the great king he eventually anoints complete this task (1 Sam. 7:14; 17:1–58; 2 Sam. 5:17–25; 8:1). In contrast to Micah, whose idolatry led to the rise of a renegade religious center that competed with the authorized sanctuary at Shiloh, Samuel's godly influence restores Shiloh to its rightful place (1 Sam. 3:21).[1]

As for Saul, though he is physically well endowed and empowered by the divine Spirit (1 Sam. 10:10; 11:6), he ends up a tragic failure who epitomizes all that is wrong with early Israel and many of its leaders. He resembles several of the characters that the narrator presents in a negative light earlier in the history. His initial hesitancy to take the responsibility of leadership (1 Sam. 10:22) is reminiscent of Barak (Judg. 4) and Gideon (Judg. 6–7), and his formal statements of self-commitment (1 Sam. 14:28, 44) are every bit as rash as those of Jephthah (Judg. 11:30–31) and the non-Benjamite tribes (Judg. 21:1). His failure to obey all the details of God's instructions regarding the destruction of Israel's enemies (1 Sam. 15) reminds one of Achan's sin (Josh. 7). Like Samson, Saul expires with a death wish on his lips and is publicly ridiculed

Israel was able to expand its borders under David's kingship because of the political weakness of the major powers across the ancient Near East. This map shows the empires of the ancient Near East in 900 BC.

by the Philistines (Judg. 16:21–30; 1 Sam. 31:1–10).

David's career likewise reflects patterns established earlier in the history. During his rise to power and the early years of his reign, he displays many of the admirable qualities of early Israel's great leaders. He completes the military conquests started by Joshua, in the process demonstrating faith and courage (2 Sam. 5). Like Joshua and Caleb, he trusts in God's power, even when confronted by giant warriors (cf. 1 Sam. 17 with Num. 13:22, 33; Josh. 11:21–22; 15:14). Like Othniel he wins the hand of a prominent leader's daughter through heroic military deeds (cf. Judg. 1:12–13 with 1 Sam. 17:25; 18:20–28). However, when he sees "a woman" and succumbs to lust (2 Sam. 11:2), he turns from being the new Joshua/Caleb/Othniel and becomes the new Samson. From this point onward in the story, David's family experiences the same sins that characterize the judges' period: rape, murder, and civil war (cf. Judg. 19–21 with 2 Sam. 13–20).

Structure

Perhaps the simplest way to outline 1–2 Samuel would be a three-part division corresponding to the three main characters. Samuel is the focal point of 1 Samuel 1–8, Saul of 1 Samuel 9–31, and David of 2 Samuel. However, because of the extensive overlapping of these characters' careers, this outline is too simplistic. Unlike the book of Judges, these books have no clear-cut structural markers at the macro-structural level, so perhaps the best we can do is outline 1–2 Samuel in light of its major plot movements, revolving around the theme of kingship:

Prelude to Kingship: The Lord chooses Samuel to lead Israel (1 Sam. 1–7)

Kingship Inaugurated: Saul becomes king of Israel (1 Sam. 8–12)

Kingship Fails: Saul forfeits his dynasty and throne (1 Sam. 13–15)

Kingship in Limbo: The Lord chooses and protects a new king (1 Sam. 16–31)

Kingship Revived: The Lord establishes David's throne and dynasty (2 Sam. 1–10)

Kingship Threatened and Preserved: The Lord punishes and preserves David (2 Sam. 11–20)

Epilogue: A microcosm of David's reign (2 Sam. 21–24)

The Focus and Approach of This Commentary

As indicated in the welcome to the series, this commentary is not designed as a reference work that provides exhaustive analysis of the text. There are plenty of these works available, many of which are cited in this volume's endnotes. The purpose of this commentary is to identify the major themes of each literary unit, to show how the text itself develops them, and to suggest how teachers can relevantly and accurately apply those themes to a modern audience. For this reason, readers should consult the reference commentaries for detailed discussions of higher-critical problems, background matters, and technical issues. This commentary focuses on the text's thematic and theological dimensions. Since the text's theological themes are often bound together with its literary features, this commentary is sensitive to the text's

This map shows the territory initially controlled by Saul, the large area conquered by David, and the expanded area ruled by Solomon.

MEDITERRANEAN SEA

Euphrates R.

°Damascus

Hazor°
Megiddo°
Joppa°
Gezer°

Syrian Desert

Ezion Geber°

Nile R.

Kingdom of Saul

Territory conquered by David

Area under Solomon's economic control

0   50   100 mi

0   50   100 km

literary dimension, especially intertextual connections within the Former Prophets and within 1–2 Samuel. Oddly enough, this literary dimension has been sorely neglected for the most part in the reference commentaries, which unfortunately and typically fail to the see the forest for the trees.

Moving from Text to Lesson

As stated above, the narrator's overriding concern is to demonstrate that David (not Saul) is the Lord's chosen king and the heir to a covenant promise that guarantees the realization of God's purposes for his people Israel. Throughout the commentary I show how each literary unit contributes to this strategy. For the most part, these observations appear in the sections titled "The Text in Context." Sound exposition of the book should keep this authorial intention before the modern audience. Granted, the interrelated themes of David's election and superiority to Saul may not seem as relevant today as they would have to an ancient Israelite audience, but it is important to recognize that the Davidic covenant is vital to biblical theology and, for that matter, to our understanding of Christology.

I am not suggesting that this strategic theme exhausts the application potential of 1–2 Samuel or that we should simply teach a series of lessons that repetitively assert David's election and the importance of the Davidic covenant. The Scriptures are too multidimensional to be squeezed into such a mold. Under the umbrella of David's divine election, the narrator weaves together the story of Israel in such a way that multiple and often interrelated themes emerge. Under the sections titled "Key Themes,"

I have tried to state these, as an ancient Israelite audience might have perceived them. In identifying the text's themes, I have taken my cue from the text itself. For example, in 1 Samuel 1–17, the major theme of almost every unit is stated in generalized form within discourse (quoted material) that appears within the episode (see 2:1–10, 30; 4:21–22; 5:7; 6:5–6, 20; 7:3, 12; 8:7; 9:16; 10:19; 11:13; 12:14–15, 22, 24–25; 13:14; 14:6, 29; 15:22–23; 16:7; 17:45–47).

In trying to surface the text's themes, I have consistently asked myself two questions: (1) How does God reveal himself in this passage? In other words, what does this passage teach us about God's character? (2) How does God relate to his people in this passage? In other words, how does God intervene in the story and/or respond to the actions of the human characters? I use a theocentric hermeneutical principle, focusing on what we learn about our sovereign, relational God in this story. Such an approach is foundational to sound exposition of the Scriptures, a primary purpose of which is to reveal the infinite God to his finite creatures.

Yet the actions and experiences of the characters in the story are also instructive and contribute to the text's message. True, the main characters in the story are leaders who occupy special positions in the covenant community at a particular time and place within Israel's history. For this reason we cannot simply assume that their actions and experiences are normative or paradigmatic. But at the same time, we dare not relegate their actions and experiences to their historical context as if they are completely time-bound. After all, the kings of Israel are to be spiritual leaders of the covenant community (Deut. 17:14–20). Indeed, the destinies of king and of community are linked (1 Sam. 12:13–15, 24–25). God's people can learn much from examining these kings' successes and failures, especially in cases where they obey or disobey covenant commands that apply to the entire community.

In developing the themes of the story, I have also tried to take account of the narrator's implied audience (the audience he envisions). Unfortunately, we do not know when 1–2 Samuel was written. We can safely assume that at least some of the source material originated as early as David's or Solomon's reign, because the pro-David apology, coupled with the anti-Saul polemic, would have been especially relevant in that setting. However, the book in its present form cannot be isolated to this one historical context. As noted above, it is part of a larger history known as the Former Prophets. The story of the Former Prophets culminates in the exile (2 Kings 25:27–30), so we can assume that the implied audience is the exilic or postexilic generation. With that in mind, as I sought to identify and develop the text's theme(s), I have asked myself: How would the literary unit under examination have affected the exiles? By including or retaining this particular episode in the larger story, what point is the narrator trying to make to his exilic audience? What lessons are there for them? My thoughts in this regard appear,

This stepped-stone structure, called the Millo, located in the ancient City of David in Jerusalem, may have supported a royal building, such as David's palace.

for the most part, under the sections titled "Theological Insights."

Finally, having derived themes from the text, I use them as the basis for the principles stated and developed in the sections titled "Teaching the Text." Here I develop so-called timeless truths from the text's themes and build a bridge from the ancient context to our contemporary situation. Hopefully, in this way the teaching points designed for a modern context are firmly rooted in the text's purpose in its ancient context and reflect the divine Author's intention for the passage. In this regard, the statements that appear under the "Big Idea" of each unit highlight the key timeless principle that emerges from that unit. Often this "Big Idea" synthesizes the themes into one concise statement.

Barren No More

Big Idea *The Lord, the incomparable King, vindicates his loyal followers.*

Understanding the Text

The Text in Context

The judges' period was a low point in Israel's history. God's people, without effective leadership, hit rock bottom morally, ethically, and spiritually. The final chapters of Judges contain alarming accounts of gang rape, civil war, mass slaughter of entire tribes and cities, and kidnapping. The book ends by declaring, "In those days Israel had no king; everyone did as they saw fit" (Judg. 21:25).

First Samuel is a fitting sequel to Judges. Samuel reverses the downward leadership trend depicted in Judges and eventually anoints David as king, giving the nation hope that the situation lamented at the end of Judges will be rectified. The book begins with an account of Samuel's birth. The key figure in the story is an oppressed, childless woman named Hannah. That this woman is suffering and oppressed comes as no surprise since the book of Judges ends with Israelite women being victimized by their own countrymen's misguided zeal and cruelty.

One of the central themes in 1–2 Samuel is David's God-given right to rule as Israel's king. The narrator demonstrates that God rejects Saul and chooses David. Though he does exhibit some political ambition, David does not usurp the throne and then claim divine authority to justify his power play. He respects Saul as God's anointed ruler and waits for God to remove Saul from the throne, rather than taking matters into his own hands. Samuel has an important role to play in this regard: after anointing Saul as king, Samuel with prophetic authority also pronounces God's rejection of Saul just before anointing David as his successor. It thus is important for the narrator to establish Samuel's credentials. This account of his divinely enabled birth (cf. 1 Sam. 1:19; 2:5) from a mother who demonstrates unwavering allegiance to the Lord contributes to this goal. It also links Samuel with the patriarchs Isaac and Jacob, who also were conceived by previously barren mothers, and suggests that Samuel will have a role in the outworking of the Lord's ancient promises to the patriarchs. The Lord's deliverance of Hannah from humiliation also foreshadows how he will deliver his people from their enemies through Hannah's son and the king he will anoint, as Hannah herself anticipates in her song of thanks (2:10).[1]

Historical and Cultural Background

The Canaanites (neighbors of ancient Israel) worshiped the fertility god Baal, believing him to be a mighty warrior king who controlled the elements of the storm. They counted Baal as responsible for both agricultural and human fertility. Baal's quest for kingship, under the ultimate authority of the high god El, is the main theme of their mythological texts. He defeats Yamm, the god of the unruly, threatening sea, but must then face the challenge of Mot, the god of the underworld and death. Mot initially defeats Baal, much to the dismay of El and the other gods. But then Baal returns to life and eventually engages in a violent conflict with Mot. Baal wins, but one suspects that the struggle for power is not over. The myth reflected the realities of nature. When the rains arrived at the proper time and the crops grew, Baal was in control. But when drought interrupted the natural cycle and brought starvation, Mot had defeated Baal.

In her song of praise following Samuel's birth, Hannah declares that the Lord is incomparable to all other so-called gods. Living at a time when many are worshiping the fertility god Baal (cf. Judg. 2:11–13; 6:25–32; 8:33; 10:6, 10; 1 Sam. 7:4), Hannah could be tempted to look to this popular god to deliver her from her childless condition. But she remains faithful to the Lord and is vindicated. She affirms that the Lord is sovereign, challenging the Canaanite belief that Baal is the incomparable king who ensures fertility. In contrast to Baal,

Key Themes of 1 Samuel 1:1–2:11

- The Lord begins a process of providing competent leadership for Israel.
- The Lord is the incomparable King, who protects and vindicates his loyal followers.

who periodically succumbs to the god of death, the Lord both kills and makes alive. The Lord, not Baal, is the one who thunders in the storm.[2]

Interpretive Insights

1:1 *There was a certain man from Ramathaim . . . whose name was Elkanah.* Hannah's story begins the same way as the stories of Samson (Judg. 13:2, "A certain man of Zorah, named Manoah") and Micah (Judg. 17:1, "Now a man named Micah from the hill country of Ephraim"). In contrast to Samson's unnamed mother, whose supernaturally conceived Nazirite son fails to recognize his role as the Lord's deliverer and never rises to the level of an effective leader, Hannah supernaturally gives birth to a son through whom the Lord restores effective leadership to Israel. Samson only begins the deliverance of Israel (Judg. 13:5), but Samuel and then David, whom Samuel anoints as king, defeat the enemies of Israel (1 Sam. 7:14; 17:1–58; 2 Sam. 5:17–25; 8:1). Micah's anonymous mother's obsession with idols contributes to the Danites' unauthorized worship system (Judg.

A god, perhaps Baal, is depicted as a warrior in this bronze figurine from Tyre (1400–1200 BC).

1 Samuel 1:1–2:11

17–18). But Hannah's allegiance to the Lord is the catalyst for the revival of true worship through the spiritual leadership of her son, Samuel.

1:5 *the Lord had closed her womb.* The narrator introduces an element of tension to the story by informing us that the Lord is responsible for Hannah's condition.[3] In the biblical world, events and circumstances that we might call natural occurrences are attributed to God. We probably would not think of a woman's inability to bear a child as being due to divine displeasure. But Hannah's family and even Hannah herself might wonder if God is displeased with her since she seems to be excluded from his promise of blessing (Exod. 23:25–26; Deut. 7:14). When the Lord answers her prayer for a child, Hannah's character is vindicated.

1:6 *her rival kept provoking her in order to irritate her.* We know from reading the patriarchal stories in Genesis that polygamy gives rise to domestic conflict, especially when one wife is barren. The same is true in Elkanah's home. The narrator identifies Peninnah as Hannah's *rival* because she ridicules Hannah's condition to the point where Hannah weeps and refuses to eat (v. 7). This portrait of Hannah's torment sets the

Hannah turned to the Lord in her despair over her barrenness. Other women in her situation may have used fertility figurines. Shown here is a pottery piece with an exaggerated female form. Referred to as "pillar figurines," hundreds have been found in Judah and date to the eighth and seventh centuries BC. Some think they may have been a type of talisman to bring about fertility and childbirth.

stage for her desperate plea for relief from her humiliation.

1:10 *In her deep anguish Hannah prayed to the Lord, weeping bitterly.* The expression "deep anguish" means severe depression and emotional torment (Job 3:20–22; 10:1; Prov. 31:6–7; Ezek. 27:31). Hannah's own words testify to her intense suffering. She speaks of her "misery" (v. 11) and "great anguish and grief" (v. 16); she describes herself as "deeply troubled" (v. 15). By emphasizing Hannah's suffering, the narrator sets the stage for the Lord's intervention. The Lord is not indifferent to the pain and oppression of the needy; he takes notice of them and lifts them from their affliction (2:3, 8).

1:11 *she made a vow.* In this culture, making a vow to a deity in a prayer for deliverance was a typical response to a crisis. Vows commonly offered the Deity a gift in return for granting the desired favor (cf. Num. 21:2).[4]

Lord Almighty. Hannah addresses the Lord with a title (traditionally, "Lord of Hosts" [KJV]) that highlights his sovereignty, envisioning him as one who sits enthroned above the cherubim of the ark of the covenant, the earthly symbol of his heavenly throne (1 Sam. 4:4; 2 Sam. 6:2). It makes sense that she would address the Lord in this way at Shiloh, for "the ark of God" is housed there (1 Sam. 4:3).

no razor will ever be used on his head. Though Samuel is never actually called a Nazirite, lengthy hair is one of the distinguishing characteristics of Nazirites (Num. 6:5; Judg. 13:5). This description facilitates the comparison with Samson (see the comments above on 1:1).[5]

1:13 *Eli thought she was drunk.* In this chapter the male characters misunderstand

Hannah.[6] Elkanah misunderstands the depth of Hannah's suffering and anguish, thinking that his assurances of his love should be enough to cheer her up (1:8). Eli fails to discern the depth of her sincerity and desperation, misinterpreting her intensity as drunkenness. The narrator begins to develop a portrait of Eli as being spiritually insensitive.

1:19 *the* L<small>ORD</small> *remembered her.* In her prayer Hannah asks the Lord to "remember" her by giving her a son (v. 11). As used here, the word does not refer to simple cognition or recall but carries the idea "remember and act." The repetition of the word draws attention to the fact that the Lord answers her prayer.

2:1 *my horn is lifted high.* The horn of an ox underlies the metaphor (Deut. 33:17; 1 Kings 22:11; Ps. 92:10), which depicts military strength. The idiom "exalt the horn" signifies military victory (Pss. 89:17, 24; 92:10; Lam. 2:17). In the ancient Near East powerful warrior kings would sometimes compare themselves to a goring bull using its horns to kill its enemies. Hannah views herself as the victor in her struggle with Peninnah.

2:2 *There is no one holy like the* L<small>ORD</small>. In the Ugaritic myths the assembly of the gods is called "sons of the Holy One" (COS, 1:246, 343). El, the high god, is the head of this assembly, but Baal has a prominent position. He is even depicted as standing beside El. The goddess Anat declares: "Mightiest Baal is our king, our judge, over whom there is none" (COS, 1:254–55). As if directly countering this claim, Hannah calls the Lord "holy" (that is, unique) and affirms that he is incomparable.

there is no Rock like our God. The term "Rock" refers to a rocky cliff, which is relatively inaccessible and provides protection for those being pursued by enemies. Consequently it depicts God as a place of refuge and safety.

2:6 *The* L<small>ORD</small> *brings death and makes alive; he brings down to the grave and raises up.* In the myths Baal engages in a struggle with death; he goes down to the grave, is pronounced dead, and later returns to life. In stark contrast, the Lord is sovereign over death. He can kill and make alive.

2:10 *The Most High will thunder from heaven.* The title "Most High" is used of Baal in the Ugaritic legend of Kirta, in a passage describing the storm-god as the source of rain (COS, 1:341). But Hannah affirms that the Lord is the one who will intervene in the storm as he defeats the enemies of his people.

and exalt the horn of his anointed. Though Israel has no king at this point, Hannah, reflecting the concern expressed in Judges 21:25, anticipates a time when the Lord will raise up a king for Israel like the one described in the law (Deut. 17:14–20).[7] The use of the horn metaphor here forms a thematic bracket (or inclusio) for the song.[8]

Theological Insights

Samuel's birth is a turning point in Israel's history. As Hannah acknowledges in her song of praise, her deliverance from her oppressed condition foreshadows what God will do for the nation in the years that immediately follow (2:10). Through Hannah's son, Samuel, God will once again reveal his word to his people, give them military victory over hostile enemies, and establish a king who will lead the nation to previously unrealized heights. The final canonical context of the Former Prophets is the exile (2 Kings 25). The exiles are enduring the consequences of their ancestors' and their own rebellious deeds and suffering oppression under foreign rule, but they can find hope in the realization that the Lord is just and eventually vindicates those who are loyal to him. They can confidently look to the future, anticipating God's intervention in the life of the covenant community and the arrival of an ideal Davidic king, through whom God will bring about the fulfillment of his ancient covenant promises.

Teaching the Text

This story has two main themes, the second of which has various dimensions:

1. *Even when the Lord's covenant community is spiritually deficient and plagued by a leadership void, his commitment to his people prompts him to provide leadership.* Ancient Israel needs a king (Judg. 21:25)—not just any king, but the kind of king envisioned in Deuteronomy 17:14–20. This king, in contrast to the typical king of the ancient world, is not to build a powerful chariot force, have a large harem, or accumulate great wealth. Instead, he is commissioned to promote God's covenant through his policies and practices. In response to Hannah's loyalty, the Lord gives her a son, Samuel, and sets in process a sequence of events that will culminate in the anointing of David, a man after God's own heart, as king of Israel.

In many ways David proves to be a tragic failure, and his dynasty fails to live up to God's standards. But God's covenantal commitment to David stands firm: eventually Jesus, the son of David par excellence, arrives on the scene as Israel's king (John 1:49; 12:13; 18:37). He eventually establishes his kingdom on earth, fulfilling God's promises to David (2 Sam. 7:16; Pss. 2:8–9; 72:1–19; 89:19–37) and completing what God has started with the birth of Samuel (Matt. 16:28; Rev. 17:14; 19:16).

2. *Though the sovereign Lord may allow his people to endure trials and even oppression, he is just and will eventually deliver them from distress when they cry out to him for vindication.* Hannah's story is a reminder to God's suffering people that (a) even though the reason(s) for trials may be shrouded in mystery, our sovereign God is just; (b) our compassionate God puts a light at the end of the tunnel, no matter how dark and terrifying that tunnel may be; and (c) our just God delivers those who trust him. Because the same God who intervenes on behalf of Hannah and Israel still reigns, we can be confident that he will

The kind of king envisioned in Deuteronomy was not a typical king of the ancient world, like Ramesses the Great (shown here). This thirteenth-century BC ruler of Egypt led his army into battle, had close to one hundred children, and commissioned many elaborate building projects.

vindicate his church when he establishes the rule of his Son, Jesus Christ.

This text does not promise or even imply that God will give children to a childless couple if they just pray hard enough or promise to God they will dedicate the child to his service. The text affirms that God is a just King, who vindicates his people. Hannah experiences that truth in a particular way that is relevant to her situation; others may experience it in different ways that are appropriate to their own circumstances. Though there is room for personal application of the text's theme, the passage is most naturally applied corporately to the covenant community: Hannah's experience foreshadows Israel's coming deliverance from foreign oppression and gives hope to the exiles, who are experiencing humiliation in a foreign land.

Illustrating the Text

There is mystery to trials and suffering.

Memoir: *A Stranger in the House of God*, by **John Koessler**. In this memoir (2007), Koessler, a professor and author, writes:

> My prayers felt like the petitions I sometimes made to my parents. The greater the request, the more ambiguous the response.
> "Mom, can I get a new bike?"
> "Mmm, we'll see."
> Such an answer occupied that mysterious no-man's-land between wish and fulfillment children know so well. This is a region where the atmosphere is a mixture of hope and disappointment—only as much hope as is needed to keep our wildest dreams at bay, and not enough disappointment to kill them altogether.[9]

The prayers of the persecuted are effective.

True Story: *The Story of Ruby Bridges*, by **Robert Coles**. Ruby came from a hardworking and deeply faith-reliant family. When a judge ordered the schools of New Orleans to be desegregated, Ruby was one of the first chosen to make this happen. Angry crowds gathered for her first school day, and for many days after. For months, Ruby was alone, escorted in and out by marshals. One day, Ruby uttered a prayer in front of the crowd, asking God to forgive those who had mistreated her because "they don't know what they're doing," just like people had said terrible things about Jesus "a long time ago."[10]

The justice of God identifies with and vindicates his oppressed people.

Poetry: **William Cullen Bryant.** The following poem by Bryant (1794–1878) was found (interleaved) at the opening of chapter 40 of Harriet Beecher Stowe's *Uncle Tom's Cabin*.

> Deem not the just by Heaven forgot!
> Though life its common gifts
>   deny,—
> Though, with a crushed and bleed-
>   ing heart,
> And spurned of man, he goes to die!
> For God hath marked each sorrow-
>   ing day,
> And numbered every bitter tear,
> And heaven's long years of bliss
>   shall pay
> For all his children suffer here.

Disrespect Can Be Deadly

Big Idea *The Lord opposes those who treat him with contempt and withholds his promised blessings from those who despise him.*

Understanding the Text

The Text in Context

Samuel's arrival at Shiloh (1:28; 2:11) provides a contrastive backdrop for the author's negative portrait of Eli and his sons. The narrator alternates between negative accounts of Eli's house (2:12–17, 22–25, 27–36) and brief positive observations about Samuel's growing relationship with the Lord (2:18–21, 26). This culminates in the account of how Samuel becomes the Lord's prophet and reiterates the earlier judgment announcement upon Eli's house (3:1–4:1a). The narrator's positive assessment of Samuel helps to establish the latter's credentials, which is an important part of his strategy in promoting David as God's chosen king (see the discussion above, under "The Text in Context" for 1 Sam. 1:1–2:11).

This account, along with the one that follows (3:1–4:1a), also contributes in another way to the narrator's goal of presenting David, not Saul, as God's chosen king. The rejection of Eli's house and the announcement of a new priestly dynasty establish a pattern that will be repeated with Saul and David. Just as God withdraws his promise of dynastic succession from Eli and gives it to another (2:30–36), so he will do with Saul (13:13–14). The house of Saul will not be able to appeal to God's election as unconditional, for Eli's experience demonstrates that disobedience can result in forfeiture of the divine promise. The Lord has the sovereign right to reject rebels and to accomplish his purposes through other and more-worthy instruments.

The account of Eli's rejection is important to the subsequent history in yet another way. When Solomon takes over the throne following his father's death, he replaces Abiathar, a descendant of Eli, with Zadok (1 Kings 2:26–27, 35). Solomon's decision, though motivated by Abiathar's decision to support Adonijah, is consistent with the prophetic proclamation recorded in 1 Samuel 2:27–36. One gets the impression

During Eli's day the tabernacle was in Shiloh, in the hills of Ephraim, making this an important religious center. Shown here is the tell at ancient Shiloh (modern Khirbet Seilun) with its visible Middle Bronze walls.

that the narrator of 1 Kings, by drawing attention to the fulfillment of the prophecy (cf. 2:27), is trying to absolve the house of David of any wrongdoing in the matter.

Interpretive Insights

2:12 *scoundrels.* In contrast to Hannah, whose trust in the Lord is exemplary, Eli's sons are depicted as those who dishonor God. Earlier Hannah pleads with Eli not to regard her as "wicked" (1:16), the same Hebrew word used of Eli's sons in 2:12. Eli's harsh initial response to her (1:14) suggests that he perceives her as such a woman, but ironically his own sons are really the ones who are wicked.[1] Eli is thus portrayed as a poor judge of what is evil or not, which calls into question his qualifications to serve as a judge in Israel. The narrator's characterization of Eli's sons as "scoundrels" is especially disconcerting when one realizes that the same expression is used of the men of Gibeah, who threaten to gang-rape a Levite and then violate and murder his concubine (Judg. 19:22).

they had no regard for the LORD. They surely know who the Lord is: they are serving at his sanctuary! But the verb translated "had no regard" means "did not acknowledge (as LORD)." Their actions demonstrate that they do not recognize the Lord's authority. Instead of following the procedure prescribed in the law (Lev. 7:28–36), they take the meat they want, even before the Lord is given his share (the fat; vv. 13–15).

2:17 *This sin . . . was very great in the* LORD's *sight.* This sin is considered to be as serious as adultery or idolatry (Gen. 20:9; Exod. 32:21, 30–31; 2 Kings 17:21). These other texts also mention a "great sin," but only here is the phrase emphasized by the

Key Themes of 1 Samuel 2:12–36

- The Lord expects his servants to treat him with the utmost respect.
- The Lord is not compelled to grant his promised blessing when his servants prove to be unworthy.

addition of "very." This assessment of their sin stands in stark contrast to the statement in verse 18 that Samuel is ministering in the Lord's sight.[2]

they were treating the LORD's *offering with contempt.* To treat the Lord or the things of the Lord with contempt usually results in severe punishment (Num. 14:23; 16:30; 2 Sam. 12:14; Pss. 10:13–15; 107:11–12; Isa. 1:4; 5:24).

2:22 *how they slept with the women who served at the entrance to the tent of meeting.* Here we read of another sin committed by Eli's sons. This particular statement is not mentioned, however, in the Qumran text of this passage, or in the Greek manuscript Codex Vaticanus. Some regard it as a later addition.[3] The narrator does not mention such a sin in his earlier account (2:13–17), nor does the prophet who confronts Eli menion it (2:27–29).

2:25 *God may mediate for the offender.* Eli's point is that a mediator is available to resolve a purely human conflict, but when someone sins against the Lord, there is no one who can successfully challenge his accusation against the wrongdoer. In short, Eli's sons have placed themselves in the unenviable and unviable position of being the opponents of God.

for it was the LORD's *will to put them to death.* Eli's warning to his sons falls on deaf ears because the Lord has already given them over to judgment and has determined to kill them. The statement is ironic in light of Hannah's earlier declaration that the Lord both kills and makes alive (v. 6).

2:29 *Why do you scorn?* The Hebrew verb occurs only here and in Deuteronomy 32:15, where it is used of an animal's kicking (a metaphor for Israel's rejection of God). The form here is plural, associating Eli with his sons.

Why do you honor your sons more than me? Though Eli confronts his sons about their behavior, albeit belatedly (vv. 23–25), apparently he still experiences the benefits of their actions and enjoys the food they take from the people. As far as the Lord is concerned, Eli's actions speak louder than his words and implicate him in their crimes.

2:30 *would minister before me forever.* The phrase translated "forever" refers to an indefinite period of time, with no immediate end in view (Deut. 23:3; 1 Sam. 1:22; 2 Sam. 12:10; Isa. 32:14; Jer. 17:4), and does not necessarily connote the concept of eternality. One might think that the use of "forever" in the Lord's promise would make it irrevocable, but this is clearly not the case here. The expression is used simply to emphasize the Lord's intention to bless

Eli. The actions of Eli and his sons cancel the conditional promise.

Those who honor me I will honor. In this case honoring the Lord means obeying him by offering the sacrifices properly and giving the Lord his proper share. The Lord would honor Eli by bestowing the promised blessings upon him (Ps. 91:15–16).

those who despise me will be disdained. To despise the Lord means to blatantly disobey him (2 Sam. 12:10; Prov. 14:2; Mal. 1:6–7). By honoring the enemies of the Lord (v. 29), Eli has despised the Lord. This is a key statement for understanding the primary theme of this chapter.

2:33 *to destroy your sight and sap your strength.* The language gives the impression that Eli will be around to see God's judgment on his descendants, but he is nearing one hundred years of age (1 Sam. 4:15) and will soon die (4:18). This is a dramatic rhetorical device and may also assume the principle of corporate solidarity, according to which an ancestor experiences later events through his offspring (Gen. 3:15; 28:14).

all your descendants will die in the prime of life. The prophecy seems to indicate that Eli will continue to have a priestly succession for a time, but that each successor will die prematurely (see vv. 31–32). According to many, the primary fulfillment of this prophecy is recorded in 1 Samuel 22 (see "Theological Insights" under 1 Sam. 22:6–23).

Offering sacrifices properly was part of honoring the Lord. Most cultures of the ancient Near East brought meat sacrifices to their gods. This relief from the Hatshepsut temple at Deir el-Bahari in Egypt shows an offering table before the Egyptian god Amon that includes whole cattle, cattle heads, and legs of beef (fifteenth century BC).

2:34 *they will both die on the same day.* This prophecy is fulfilled shortly afterward, when Hophni and Phinehas die in battle (4:11).

2:35 *I will raise up for myself a faithful priest.* This prophecy is fulfilled when Solomon demotes Eli's descendant Abiathar and appoints Zadok as priest in his place (1 Kings 2:26–27, 35).[4] Zadok is descended from Aaron through Eleazar (1 Chron. 6:3–8, 50–53), whereas Abiathar's father Ahimelek (1 Sam. 22:20) is a descendant of Aaron through Ithamar and Eli (1 Chron. 24:3). The descendants of Ithamar/Eli continue to serve, but in a subordinate role (24:4).

Aaron	
Eleazar	Ithamar
Phinehas	
Abishua	
Bukki	
Uzzi	
Zerahiah	Eli
Meraioth	Phinehas
Amariah	Ahitub
Ahitub	Ahimelek
ZADOK	ABIATHAR
Ahimaaz	Ahimelek

Note: See 1 Sam. 14:3; 22:9, 20; 2 Sam. 8:17; 1 Kings 2:26–27, 35; 1 Chron. 6:3–8, 50–53; 4:3, 6

2:36 *bow down before him for a piece of silver and a loaf of bread and plead.* The punishment fits the crime. Eli's sons are gorging themselves on food that belongs to the Lord and is being taken from the people by force (vv. 12–17), so Eli's descendants will someday need to beg for their food.[5]

Conditional Promises

More often than not, the Lord's promises in the Old Testament are conditional (whether explicitly or implicitly) and depend for their fulfillment on a proper response from the recipient.[a] Jeremiah 18 is a foundational text in this regard. Just as the potter improvises his design for the uncooperative clay, so the Lord can change his plans for Israel (vv. 5–6). If the Lord intends to destroy a nation, but it repents when warned of impending doom, the Lord will relent from sending judgment (vv. 7–8). Conversely, if the Lord intends to bless a nation, but it rebels, the Lord will alter his plan and withhold blessing (vv. 9–10). God announces his intentions, but the recipient's response can and often does affect God's decision as to what will actually transpire. In fact, contingent promises are designed to motivate a proper response to God's word so that a threatened judgment may be canceled or a promised blessing may be realized.[b] One finds the same phenomenon in Mesopotamia, where "most predictions were conditional."[c]

[a] Pratt, "Historical Contingencies"; Chisholm, "When Prophecy Appears to Fail."
[b] Clendenen, "Textlinguistics and Prophecy," 388–90.
[c] See Tiemeyer, "Prophecy as a Way of Cancelling Prophecy," 349.

We are not certain when and how this was fulfilled. First Kings 2:26–27 tells of Abiathar's demotion, but the subsequent narrative does not describe him or his offspring being reduced to poverty.

Theological Insights

The Lord does not tolerate those who dishonor his royal authority, including Eli, who passively endorses his sons' disrespect by failing to confront it forcefully enough. The Lord even cancels his conditional promise to Eli and announces that he will replace Eli's descendants with those who are more worthy. As noted above, this episode foreshadows God's rejection of Saul and election of David. In the passage's larger canonical context (the Former Prophets), it is a sobering reminder to the exiles that a privileged position before God does not insulate one from divine discipline and that disobedience can cause promised blessing to evaporate. At the same time, it serves as a challenge to the exiles not to repeat the sins of the past. They must respect the Lord's royal authority by obeying him.

Teaching the Text

1. *The Lord does not tolerate those who value their own selfish desires above honoring the Lord and thereby disrespect his royal authority.* In contrast to Hannah, who affirms the Lord's holiness (2:2), Eli's sons disrespect the Lord by disregarding his clearly revealed commands and depriving him of his proper portion of the people's offerings. Their attitudes and actions indicate that they value their own desires above honoring the Lord. In so doing they treat him as if he does not have authority over them. In a New Testament or modern context, disrespect for God's royal authority may take many specific forms, depending on one's circumstances. But at the most fundamental level, we disrespect God anytime we disregard his revealed moral will and by our attitudes and actions deny his authority over our lives. Now, as then, God will confront those who treat him with disrespect. In the case of Eli and his sons, they lose their lives and their priestly dynasty. In a New Testament or modern context, God's discipline may take a variety of forms (see, e.g., Acts 5:1–11; 1 Cor. 11:27–32; Heb. 11:15–17, 25), but one thing is certain: it can be unpleasant and even severe.

A corollary of this first principle may be stated as follows: the Lord expects total allegiance from his chosen servants. Eli warns his sons, albeit belatedly, about the consequences of their actions. Yet from God's perspective, this is not an adequate response. After all, apparently Eli is content to benefit from their misbehavior. Though he is old and weak, he has the authority to remove them from office, but he fails to do so. The Lord punishes Eli because he tolerates his sons' contempt, even though he does not approve of it or directly participate in it. In this case there is no middle ground. To participate in and tolerate the sons' sins in any way is to align oneself against the Lord. Eli serves as a reminder that God demands total allegiance from his servants. Halfhearted lip service without substantive action does not impress him.

2. *The Lord may withdraw his promised blessing from those who reject his authority.* The Lord is faithful and reliable, and he expects his servants to be loyal and obedient. Being called to a special position, as

Eli's sons dishonored the Lord by not following the sacrificial procedures described in the law. This life-size replica of the tabernacle located at Timna, Israel, shows the altar, with a shovel and three-prong fork leaning against it, in the courtyard of the tent of meeting.

Eli and his family are, does not insulate one from divine discipline. From everyone to whom much is given, much is required (Amos 3:2; Luke 12:48). God sometimes makes promises to those whom he chooses, but often these promises are contingent upon continued loyalty. Rather than being guarantees that give the recipients a license to act as they wish, these promises should motivate continued obedience.

This is not a text about parenting. One could use Eli's example to illustrate poor parenting *if* one were preaching from another passage that deals directly with the subject of parenting, such as a proverb. (The NT frequently uses OT characters and events for illustrative purposes, even when the OT text is not directly addressing the theme of the NT passage.) *But* if 1 Samuel 2:12–36 is one's base text for a sermon or lesson, then the themes outlined above, not parenting, should be the focus of the exposition.

Illustrating the Text

The importance of respecting God's authority cannot be overestimated.

History: During World War I, British soldiers understood that their leaders (military, political, and sovereign) expected them to fight even if it meant the loss of their lives, yet they entered the conflict. They knew that this was the only way for good to prevail. Even the overwhelming suffering of the war did not change their responsibility. Those who did succumb to their fears suffered the dire consequences of a court-martial or went before a firing squad. Among the first to experience this kind of military justice was Private Thomas Highgate. Revulsed by the deaths of thousands of British troops at the Battle of Mons, he escaped the scene and hid in a barn. Just a month after entrance into the war he was put to death, at the age of seventeen.[6]

Our uncompromising allegiance to God is crucial; halfhearted service is unacceptable.

Literature: *The Wise Woman*, by George MacDonald. This memorable story (1875; also called *The Lost Princess*) by nineteenth-century British author MacDonald (1824–1905) is about the character of God as represented in the Wise Woman. She possesses supernatural powers and visits two young girls, one the daughter of royalty, the other a shepherd's daughter. Both girls must be disciplined rigorously to be delivered from sins of pride, willfulness, and selfishness. The Wise Woman's relentless but loving approach tolerates no halfhearted change. The book, a quick read, is one of the stronger portraits in print of God's helping one to understand the consequences of incomplete submission.

To forfeit God's blessing is a tragedy.

Literature: *The Pilgrim's Progress*, by John Bunyan. In this well-known work (1678), Bunyan (1628–88) tells of a man locked up in an iron cage, full of despair. When asked how he came to be this way, unable even to repent, he replies, "I left off to watch and be sober. I laid the reins upon the neck of my lusts. I sinned against the light of the Word and the goodness of God. I have grieved the Spirit, and He is gone."[7]

The Lord Chooses a Prophet

Big Idea *The Lord is willing to revive his broken relationship with his people through those who honor him.*

Understanding the Text

The Text in Context

This account of God's choice of Samuel to be his prophet complements the preceding chapter, which tells of his rejecting the house of Eli. As noted above, chapter 2 contrasts Eli and his sons with Samuel. They were rejected, while Samuel grew in favor with the Lord (2:26). That contrast continues here. Samuel, earlier pictured in a priestly role (2:18), now also assumes a prophetic office. The Lord commissions him to reiterate the Lord's coming judgment of Eli's house and subsequently blesses his prophetic ministry, which all Israel recognizes as legitimate. As noted earlier, the narrator seeks to establish Samuel's prophetic credentials as part of his strategy to demonstrate the legitimacy of David's kingship. Through Samuel the Lord renews his self-revelation to Israel. This opening of the lines of communication foreshadows the renewal of national prosperity and security that the Lord will bring about through David.

Here the story displays a four-paneled structure. As is typical in such accounts, there is repetition yet also significant varia-tion, especially in the final panel.[1] In the first two panels (vv. 4–6), the Lord calls to Samuel, who goes to Eli, thinking his master has called him. Eli tells him to go back to sleep. To make sure that the reader does not wrongly conclude that Samuel is spiritually dull, the narrator points out that Samuel has never personally encountered the Lord and is inexperienced in such matters (v. 7). In the third panel Eli realizes that the Lord is calling Samuel and gives him instructions on how to respond if he is summoned again (vv. 8–9). In the fourth panel the Lord approaches and calls Samuel, who responds as instructed (v. 10). The Lord then delivers a prophetic revelation to Samuel (vv. 11–14). Through its structure and progression the story draws attention to the shift in authority in Samuel's life. Initially he goes to Eli, but then, as instructed by Eli, he speaks to the Lord, calling himself the Lord's servant. As Samuel delivers the prophetic message to Eli, one senses that their relationship will never be the same. Now Samuel is the Lord's spokesman, whose prophetic word has authority even over Eli. By the end of the chapter, "all Israel from Dan to Beersheba" (v. 20) recognizes Samuel, not Eli, as the Lord's chosen servant through whom he reveals his word to Israel. From this time forward, Samuel, not Eli, will lead Israel. The text makes it clear that Samuel does not represent a minority faction bent on imposing its will on the nation.

Interpretive Insights

3:2 *he could barely see.* Eli's blindness mirrors the situation in Israel under his and his sons' leadership; prophetic visions are rare (v. 1). By way of contrast, Samuel is depicted as close to the Lord; he even sleeps in the tabernacle near the ark, the earthly symbol of God's presence (v. 3).[2] The ark is kept in the inner sanctuary, at the rear of the tabernacle proper, while Samuel is sleeping in the nave, or main area.[3] There is a contrast between Samuel, who is "lying down" in his usual place near God's presence (vv. 2–3), and Eli's sons, who "slept" with the women serving at the tent of meeting (2:22). Both "lying down" and "slept" translate the same Hebrew verb (*shakab*).

3:3 *The lamp of God had not yet gone out.* According to Exodus 27:21, a lamp is to be kept burning in the tabernacle from evening until dawn. Perhaps the shining lamp in the vicinity of Samuel has a symbolic and foreshadowing function here. While Israel is in a spiritually dark period,

Key Themes of 1 Samuel 3

- The Lord begins to fill the void of spiritual leadership in Israel.
- The Lord honors those who honor him.

when divine revelation is rare, the lamp points to the dawning of a new day, when darkness will be dispelled through the one sleeping nearby.

3:4 *Here I am.* Samuel is depicted as one who is ready to obey his master, much like Abraham (Gen. 22:1, 11), Jacob (31:11; 46:2), Joseph (37:13), and Moses (Exod. 3:4) of old. He runs to his master as if eager to carry out his wishes (v. 5).

3:12 *everything I spoke against his family.* By repeating to Samuel the message he has spoken through the "man of God" (2:27), the Lord places Samuel on a par with that prophet. Furthermore, there is no indication that Samuel knows of the earlier judgment announcement. The essential repetition of that message through Samuel, who is obviously experiencing a theophanic encounter with the Lord, confirms Samuel's status to Eli, as

well as the inevitability of the announced judgment.

3:13 *his sons blasphemed God.* The traditional Hebrew text (MT) has "his sons made themselves contemptible," but it is more likely that the original reading, preserved in an ancient scribal tradition and in the Septuagint (LXX: ancient Greek version of the OT), is "his sons blasphemed God."[4] Normally this verb (*qalal*) refers to a verbal curse or, if God is the object, blasphemy (Exod. 22:28; Lev. 24:15). There is no indication that Eli's sons curse God verbally, but from the Lord's perspective, their blatant rebellion is serious enough to warrant such an accusation. According to the law, cursing God is a capital offense (Lev. 24:10–16).

he failed to restrain them. The meaning of the verb translated "restrain" (*kahah*) is uncertain. There is a verb *kahah* that means "grow dim, faint" (BDB, 462), and some understand the form here as meaning "weaken" in the sense of "restrain."[5] Others suggest that the term is a homonym meaning "scold, rebuke" (*HALOT*, 461). However, this proposal is problematic because Eli has scolded his sons (2:23–25). It is more likely that the verb refers here to forceful restraint, not merely a verbal rebuke. Eli possesses the authority to remove them from office but fails to do so.

3:14 *by sacrifice or offering.* The punishment is appropriate. Those who scorn the Lord's "sacrifice and offering" (2:29) will not be able to make atonement for their sins by sacrifices and offerings. It may seem surprising or even shocking that the Lord leaves no room for forgiveness in this case, but sometimes the Lord does formally and unconditionally decree judgment, precluding restoration. Indeed, the Lord's rejection of Eli foreshadows what will happen to Saul (see 15:28–29). With regard to the gravity of Eli's sin, Boda observes: (1) "sin against the sacred precincts has most serious consequences"; (2) "such direct sin against the Deity is inexpiable—that is, no sacrifice or offering is adequate to make atonement for this sin"; and (3) "there are intergenerational implications for sin, and thus patriarchal figures must pay close attention to the behavior of those within their family units."[6]

3:18 *He is the LORD; let him do what is good in his eyes.* Eli's resignation to God's judgment bears out the truth of what he has told his sons: one cannot appeal to a higher authority when the Lord pronounces sentence (2:25). His resignation also shows that he understands the Lord's message to be irrevocable, as one suspects from the oath formula used to introduce it (v. 14).

3:19 *The LORD was with Samuel.* The narrator goes out of his way to establish Samuel's credentials as the Lord's prophet. He makes four important points: (1) The Lord is "with Samuel," just as he was present with Isaac (Gen. 26:3), Jacob (31:3), Moses (Exod. 3:12), Joshua (Josh. 1:5), and Gideon (Judg. 6:16). (2) The Lord does not allow any of Samuel's prophecies to fail, for such failure would call Samuel's authority into question (cf. Deut. 18:17–22). (3) All Israel, from the far north (Dan) to the far south (Beersheba), recognizes his authority (v. 20) and receives his prophetic word (4:1a). (4) The Lord continues to reveal himself to Samuel at Shiloh (v. 21).

3:20 *Samuel was attested as a prophet of the LORD.* Here the word translated "attested" (*ne'eman*) means "confirmed" or "validated" (Gen. 42:20; 1 Kings 8:26).

Later the Lord promises David that he will make his dynasty "endure forever" (2 Sam. 7:16). The term translated "endure" is the same one used of Samuel in verse 20. This is yet another link binding Samuel, the Lord's chosen prophet, to David, whom Samuel will anoint as the Lord's chosen king and with whom the Lord will make a binding covenant.

Theological Insights

As noted above, this chapter complements the previous one and further develops the theme stated in 2:30: The Lord honors those who honor him but rejects those who despise him. The Lord's rejection of Eli's house is reiterated in 3:11–14, but the focus of chapter 3 is on the Lord's choice of Samuel. The Lord honors loyal Hannah by choosing her son as his prophet, the one through whom he renews his relationship with Israel. Youthful Samuel represents the renewed Israel of the future, whom Samuel will lead to victory (chap. 7). Aging, blind Eli and his sinful sons represent the corrupt Israel of the judges' period, which will soon experience humiliating defeat (see chap. 4). In the larger canonical context of the Former Prophets, the story challenges the exiles to honor the Lord so that they, as God's covenant community, may experience a renewed relationship with their King, culminating in the restoration of the nation under the authority of an ideal human king.

Teaching the Text

1. *The Lord is willing to renew his relationship with his covenant community through*

The small plateau shown in this photo, on the ancient site of Shiloh, is one possible area where the tabernacle may have stood. The mention of doorposts (1 Sam. 1:9) and doors (1 Sam. 3:15) seems to indicate that the tent structure had been replaced by something more permanent. The Lord continued to appear at Shiloh and reveal himself to Samuel (1 Sam. 3:21).

those who honor him. In Samuel's time the Lord renews this relationship by once again providing prophetic revelation and eventually by giving Israel a king. In our day spiritual renewal of God's people comes through different means. When the covenant community is alienated from God by sin, repentance is essential (for more on this theme, see 1 Sam. 7). Yet it is also vital that we honor God and trust him to reward our loyalty. One of the ways God does this is by establishing leaders who will honor him.

2. *The Lord honors those who honor him*. In his pronouncement of judgment upon Eli, the Lord declares: "Those who honor me I will honor" (2:30). The story of Samuel's rise to the prophetic office fleshes out this statement by showing how the Lord honors Hannah's allegiance. She looks to the Lord alone for relief and justice and then dedicates her son to him out of gratitude for answered prayer. The Lord honors her loyalty by choosing her son to be a prophetic voice in Israel and to eventually anoint the king, whose arrival and success Hannah anticipates (2:10).

Jesus warns the religious leaders of his day that honoring God is not mere lip service and adherence to human rules, but rather heartfelt loyalty (Matt. 15:8; Mark 7:6). No one can honor the Father without honoring Jesus (John 5:23). Those who serve and therefore honor Jesus will be honored by the Father (12:26).

More specifically, we honor the Lord by abstaining from sexual immorality (1 Cor. 6:12–20) and by generously sharing our material wealth with those who are in need (2 Cor. 8:19; Gal. 6:10).

This is a story about honoring God and experiencing spiritual renewal, not about how God reveals himself to people. New Testament believers reading this story should not expect to be visited by God in the night or to receive prophetic visions about impending judgment. Samuel's experience was not normative in his day, and the New Testament gives us no reason to expect it to be in ours.

Illustrating the Text

God will honor those who honor him.

Literature: *Jane Eyre*, **by Charlotte Brontë.** In this beautifully written and principled

Samuel served the Lord as both priest and prophet. In his priestly role he would have worn a special linen ephod. In this scene from a fourteenth-century Egyptian text, the scribe appears before the Egyptian god in a linen garment.

novel (1847), the lead character, Jane, learns restraint over her anger at the way people have treated her in her past and present. Jane has been orphaned young, then severely mistreated by extended family, and finally placed in an orphanage where the children are abused; she survives because of the building strength of her character. Eventually she becomes a governess (often a difficult job in Victorian England, a subservient position that can be as pleasant or horrific as the employer wants to make it). Jane soon meets Rochester (her employer), and they fall deeply in love, a love with intellectual as well as emotional motivation. On their wedding day, however, Jane learns of circumstances that make it morally impossible for her to continue with the marriage.

Deeply grieved, the heroine nevertheless does the right thing and leaves Rochester, fleeing temptation. Without resources, she endures more suffering and deprivation, but God honors her obedience as she calls upon him. She reasons with herself:

> Which is better? To have surrendered to temptation; listened to passion; made no painful effort—no struggle—but to have sunk down in the silken snare; fallen asleep on the flowers covering it; wakened in a southern clime amongst the luxuries of a pleasure villa; to have been now living in France, Mr. Rochester's mistress. . . . Whether is it better, I ask, to be a slave in a fool's paradise—fevered with delusive bliss one hour—suffocating with the bitterest tears of remorse and shame the next—or to be a village schoolmistress, free and honest, in a breezy mountain nook in the healthy part of England? Yes, I feel now that I was right when I adhered to principle and law, and scorned and crushed the insane promptings of a frenzied moment. God directed me to a correct choice: I thank His providence for the guidance.[7]

With this declaration, Jane exemplifies the significance of honorable decisions before God, and in time she experiences God's honoring of her obedience. A recent film version (2011) earned critical acclaim.

God brings spiritual renewal through those who honor him.

Christian Biography: Billy Graham. It has often been said that there is no explanation for Graham's (b. 1918) success as a worldwide evangelist who has preached to 215 million people in more than 185 countries, founded the Billy Graham Association, and had an audience with a number of presidents, starting with Harry Truman. Despite his worldwide success and his access to the halls of power, Graham is widely recognized for his humility and his deep desire to honor the Lord. He did indeed bring the salvation message and spiritual renewal to tens of thousands in his preaching career.

Defeat, Death, and Departure

Big Idea *The Lord's decree of judgment is certain of fulfillment, bringing tragedy in its path.*

Understanding the Text

The Text in Context

This chapter records the initial fulfillment of the Lord's decree of judgment prophesied by the man of God (2:27–36). The Lord has warned that Eli's sons would "both die on the same day" (2:33–34). This would be the "sign," or guarantee, that the prophecy would eventually be fulfilled in its entirety (2:34).

The ark of the covenant, mentioned just once in the book to this point (3:3), becomes a focal point in chapter 4 and continues to occupy the narrator's interest in chapters 5 and 6. The Israelites take the ark into battle, thinking it will assure them of victory. Yet they experience a humiliating defeat, and the ark is captured. But this is not what it may appear to be, as the Philistines later discover (see chap. 5).

The news of the ark's capture so shocks aging Eli that he falls over dead. One tragedy leads to another. When his pregnant daughter-in-law hears that the ark is captured and that her father-in-law and husband are dead, she goes into labor and dies in childbirth. It is no surprise to see an Israelite woman suffering death as a result of the foolish actions of Israelite

men: this same pattern is apparent in the book of Judges.

The description of her death contributes to the ongoing contrast between Samuel and Eli. When Hannah gave birth to Samuel, it was a jubilant event that prompted Hannah to praise the Lord as her Savior and to anticipate future Israelite victories through a king (2:1–10). But for Eli's daughter-in-law, the birth of a son brings death and transforms one of life's greatest joys into mourning: she dies while lamenting the disappearance of God's "Glory . . . from Israel" (4:22). Once more we see that Samuel represents the Israel of the future, whom he will lead to victory (chap. 7), while Eli and his sons represent the corrupt Israel of the judges' period, which is passing away.

Historical and Cultural Background

The ark of the covenant serves as the visible earthly symbol of the Lord's heavenly throne and as a tangible reminder of the Lord's presence as King among his people. But Israel is not to view it as an image of God in the way the Philistines view the image of Dagon in the Ashdod temple (cf. chap. 5). The Lord promises to meet his people at the ark (Exod. 25:22;

Lev. 16:2; Num. 7:89; 2 Sam. 6:2), but he does not reside in the ark. Walton explains: "The ark mediated the presence of Deity in a limited fashion, but not in the same way that an image did. It did not contain the divine essence. Furthermore, it did not mediate revelation or worship."[1]

In this chapter the Philistines are mentioned for the first time in 1 Samuel. Genesis indicates that Philistines were already present in Canaan in the time of the patriarchs, but the majority of the biblical references to them occur in Judges and 1–2 Samuel.[2] This reflects the fact that more Philistines arrived in Canaan after the patriarchal period. In about 1200 BC a coalition of the Sea Peoples invaded Canaan. Ramesses III, who was able to prevent them from conquering Egypt, mentions several groups by name, including the Peleset, or Philistines. They settled along the Mediterranean coast, occupying three coastal towns (Ashdod, Ashkelon, and Gaza) and two towns further inland (Ekron and Gath). They ruled over Israel prior to and during the time of Samson (Judg. 13:1), roughly 1190–1130 BC. Major conflicts between the Philistines and Israel continued during the days of Samuel, Saul, and David, covering roughly 1130–970 BC.[3]

Key Themes of 1 Samuel 4

- The Lord's reliable decree is fulfilled.
- The Lord refuses to be manipulated into granting victory when judgment has been decreed.

answer to this question is "Someone has sinned" (cf. Josh. 7:8–11). Instead, the elders think they can ensure, or at least encourage, the Lord's intervention by bringing the tangible symbol of his presence into the camp. They apparently view the ark as a palladium or relic that can be used to compel God to intervene on their behalf. After all, God's powerful presence is closely associated with the ark (Exod. 25:22; Num. 10:33–36; 2 Sam. 6:2), and the ark seemed to play a key role in the defeat of Jericho (Josh. 6:6–13). When the Canaanites and Amalekites defeated Israel in the days of Moses, the ark was conspicuous by its absence (Num. 14:42–45).[4] So one can see why some might think of it as a guarantee of victory, but such a notion is fundamentally pagan. The Lord cannot be manipulated or coerced into intervening for his people, and we should not view the Lord as being like a rabbit's foot or four-leaf clover.

4:4 *And Eli's two sons, Hophni and Phinehas, were there with the ark of the covenant of God.* One might think that

Interpretive Insights

4:3 *Why did the* LORD *bring defeat on us today?* The obvious

Sea Peoples captured by Ramesses III, which include Philistines, are shown in this Egyptian relief from Medinet Habu (twelfth century BC). They are identified by their distinctive headdress.

Israel's prospects are promising since "the LORD Almighty [LORD of armies]" sits enthroned above the cherubim of the ark. But this reference to Hophni and Phinehas being there "with" the ark is ominous and casts a cloud over the story. By mentioning their names here, the narrator reminds us of the real reason for Israel's defeat.[5] We know that they do not acknowledge the Lord's authority (2:12). On the contrary, they despise the Lord (2:30), who has determined to kill them and has decreed their sudden demise (2:25, 34).

4:8 *Who will deliver us?* The Philistines share the Israelites' view of the ark. They believe "a god" has come into the Israelite camp (v. 7) and expect to face an assault by the "gods" that have delivered Israel from Egypt (note their polytheistic perspective). They anticipate defeat but courageously resolve to fight (v. 9). Implicit in their words is the belief that Israel's gods are superior. Yet the Philistines win the battle, causing one to wonder how and why they are able to prevail when they themselves expect to lose. The answer comes in verse 11: in one breath we are told that the ark is captured and Eli's sons are killed. The two events are inextricably linked.[6] As in verse 4, herein lies the solution to the dilemma of Israel's defeat. The Lord's focus is on killing the sons of Eli (2:25), not on cooperating with their pagan effort to manipulate him into giving Israel a victory.

4:13 *there was Eli sitting on his chair.* In this final scene of Eli's life, he is pictured as sitting on his chair, just as he is in the very first scene in which he appears in the story (1:9). The chair (*kisse'*, sometimes translated "throne") may signify his authority, and we expect him to be in a sitting posture, given his advanced age (4:15).[7] But there may be more here than meets the eye. The narrator depicts Eli as one who only belatedly understands what is going on around him: (1) he initially misjudged Hannah's character (1:14); (2) he heard about, rather than saw for himself, his sons' sins and then made only a halfhearted attempt to stop their behavior (2:22–25); (3) he did not immediately recognize that the Lord was calling young Samuel, probably because prophetic revelation was rare in those days (3:1–9); and (4) now he is one of the last in the town to discover the news of Israel's defeat (4:12–14). His blindness (3:2; 4:15) may epitomize the fact that he is continually "in the dark" about people and events. In the same way, the references to his sitting on

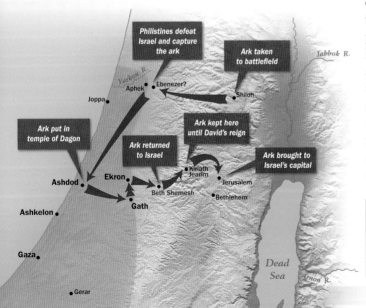

Philistines defeat Israel and capture the ark

Ark taken to battlefield

Jabbok R.

Yarkon R.

Aphek • Ebenezer?

Joppa •

Shiloh

Ark put in temple of Dagon

Ark kept here until David's reign

Ark returned to Israel

Ark brought to Israel's capital

Kiriath Jearim

Ashdod •

Ekron •

Jerusalem •

Beth Shemesh • Bethlehem •

Ashkelon •

Gath

Gaza •

Dead Sea

Arnon R.

• Gerar

Map shows the major Philistine cities (in bold) and the territory the Philistines controlled (in green). The ark of the covenant will make its way from Shiloh to Jerusalem as the narrative of 1–2 Samuel unfolds.

his chair at both the beginning and end of the story epitomize the fact that he is a relatively passive and ineffective leader, always waiting to receive information from others. There is irony here—his is a passive authority in which his passivity emasculates his authority.

his heart feared for the ark of God. Eli's sole concern appears to be the ark, not his sons (see v. 18 as well). This seems to be commendable and suggests that he has his priorities straight, but actually his obsession with the ark is tragically ironic. His lack of concern about his sons has been the problem all along (2:29; 3:13).

4:21–22 *The Glory has departed from Israel.* Phinehas's dying wife names her newborn son Ichabod, meaning either "no glory" or "Where is the glory?" (that is, "Where has the Glory gone?"). Verse 21 suggests that she is referring to the ark, as well as to Eli and Phinehas, while verse 22 focuses only on the ark. Yet it seems more likely that "Glory" refers to the Lord's glorious presence (Deut. 5:24). Her point is clear: the Lord's glorious presence has departed from Israel because the symbol of that presence, the ark, has been taken away, and because God's priests, the caretakers of the ark, are dead. Her actual quoted words mention only the ark, but in verse 21 the narrator gives us insight into her thinking.

Theological Insights

God's decree of judgment begins to fall upon Eli's house, just as God has announced (cf. 1 Sam. 2:34 with 4:11). This "sign" is a guarantee that the decreed judgment will be realized in its entirety and a vivid reminder that God's decree is reliable. God's conditional promise of blessing to Eli was revoked because of disobedience (2:30), but his decree of judgment, sealed by divine oath (3:14), is certain of fulfillment. This story resonates with the exiles, for they too have experienced the consequences of sin and the outworking of God's decree of judgment. As Firth points out, "The authenticity of the prophetic word" also "demonstrates the authority of YHWH over the people of Israel."[8]

This story also illustrates the folly of the pagan notion that God can be manipulated into granting success. When the ark enters the Israelite camp, the Philistines declare, "A god has come into the camp" (4:7). Apparently the Israelites view the ark in a similar manner. By associating the Lord too closely with the ark, Israel reduces the Lord to the level of the pagan gods, who can be represented by idols. This faulty thinking explains in part why Eli and his daughter-in-law are so horrified at the news of the ark's capture. When the Lord gave Israel the ark, he was contextualizing his self-revelation to Israel's cultural expectations. The nations worshiped images of their gods. The Lord prohibited idolatry in Israel, but he did give Israel a tangible reminder of his royal presence. Unfortunately, Israel, perhaps due to the religious environment of its world, had a propensity toward idolatry (cf. Exod. 32:2–6; 1 Kings 12:28–33) and a tendency to treat symbols as objects of worship (cf. Judg. 8:27; 2 Kings 18:4).

On this occasion Israel's attitudes and actions foreshadow those of Saul, who will demonstrate a preoccupation with the formal elements of religion in a manipulative attempt to secure divine favor. Thus the story contributes to the author's strategy of demonstrating David's superiority to

Saul. While David is linked literarily with Samuel, Saul proves to be like Eli and his sons. God rejects the houses of both Eli and Saul.

This story is instructive for the exiles. Before the exile, Israel takes God's presence for granted, thinking that Jerusalem will never be destroyed because God lives in the city (Jer. 6:13–14; 8:11; 14:13; 23:17). This so-called Zion theology is rooted in the faulty notion that God's protective presence can be guaranteed by proper cultic ritual apart from obedience (Isa. 1:11–20). As the exiles look to the future and wonder how to be reconciled to God, they need to remember that loyalty and obedience are the only guarantees of divine favor and that God cannot be manipulated into bestowing favor upon those who disrespect him.

Teaching the Text

1. *The Lord's word is reliable.* This story shows how God's decree of judgment begins to fall inexorably upon the house of Eli. Like so many passages in the Bible, it illustrates the truth that God's word is reliable and must be taken seriously. In the case of decrees of judgment, this principle is terrifying: it means that those who are the recipients of such decrees are doomed, with no hope of escape (Matt. 13:49–50; Luke 16:26; Heb. 9:27; Rev. 20:11–15). Such a frightening prospect should motivate all people to respond properly to God now, before it is too late (2 Cor. 6:2). But not all of God's decrees pertain to judgment: some are promises of salvation. The recipients of these can take great comfort in knowing that such promises are reliable and trustworthy (1 Pet. 1:22–25).

2. *The Lord cannot be manipulated into granting his favor.* Israel too closely identifies the Lord with the symbol of his presence. They think that by bringing the ark to the battle, they can manipulate God into granting a victory. Surely God will protect himself! He will never allow himself to be hauled away into captivity! But such thinking is foolish and betrays a pagan notion. God is not a good-luck charm and should never be treated as such. Obedience is the key to experiencing God's favor, as the ancient covenant list of blessings and curses makes clear (Deut. 28) and as Jesus teaches his disciples (John 15:1–17).

The ark of the covenant may have been similar in size to the gilded box on which the Egyptian god Anubis, in his jackal form, sits. Like the ark, this box has carrying poles. It was found in King Tutankhamen's tomb at the entrance to the treasury (fourteenth century BC).

Illustrating the Text

God's word is reliable and must be taken seriously.

Film and Television: For decades there have been movies and television series in which the main character becomes an avenger (some less righteous and heroic than others), bringing "judgment" to the evil characters and "salvation" to the innocently victimized. Audiences delight in the satisfaction of such justice but also expect that these will be reliable avengers; onlookers know they will do as they promise. Some movie examples are *Batman*, *Superman*, and *Terminator*; particularly powerful in presence is Clint Eastwood in *Dirty Harry*. Televised avengers include the older *The Incredible Hulk*, later *The Avengers* (British series), and more recently Jack Bauer in *24*. The audience knows that the central character who brings justice means business, is someone to be feared by wrongdoers, and is to be loved by the injured. These characters are often godlike figures. But, even though these stories remind us of our longing for justice, we are reminded in the discussion of 1 Samuel 24 below that vengeance ultimately belongs to the Lord.

God cannot be manipulated, and to try to do so is dangerous.

Bible: Matthew 6:7. "And when you pray, do not keep on babbling like pagans, for they think they will be heard because of their many words."

Nonfiction: *Teaching a Stone to Talk*, **by Annie Dillard.** In this collection of essays (1982), the Pulitzer Prize–winning author Dillard (b. 1945) asks:

Why do people in churches seem like cheerful, brainless tourists on a packaged tour of the Absolute? On the whole I do not find Christians, outside the catacombs, sufficiently sensible of the conditions. Does anyone have the foggiest idea what sort of power we so blithely invoke? Or, as I suspect, does no one believe a word of it? The churches are children playing on the floor with their chemistry sets, mixing up a batch of TNT to kill a Sunday morning. It is madness to wear ladies' straw hats and velvet hats to church; we should all be wearing crash helmets. Ushers should issue life preservers and signal flares; they should lash us to our pews. For the sleeping god may wake some day and take offense, or the waking god may draw us out to where we can never return.[9]

Television: *The Paper Chase*. This series (1978–79) is based on a novel by John Jay Osborn Jr. The short-lived series had a devoted following and is often quoted in classrooms and among students. Hart, a freshman law student at Harvard, faces the stern and larger-than-life law professor Charles Kingsfield. Haughty, with unrelenting expectations, Kingsfield asserts, "You teach *yourselves* the law. I train your *minds*. You come in here with a *skull full of mush*, and if you survive, you'll leave *thinking like a lawyer*." Kingsfield always knows when a student is unprepared and is able to see the smallest bit of laziness or manipulation in the would-be lawyer. Every student knows that Kingsfield means what he says. He will have the final word.

The Ark Does Some Damage

Big Idea *Even when the Lord appears to be defeated, he remains sovereign and invincible.*

Understanding the Text

The Text in Context

This chapter focuses on the ark, which was captured when the Philistines defeated Israel (4:22). Though one suspects Israel's defeat was due to the Lord's judgment upon Eli's sons, the capture of the ark creates tension in the story and raises questions: How could the Lord allow the visible symbol of his presence to be taken away? Have the Philistines and their god actually defeated the Lord? What are the implications for Israel's relationship with the Lord and for the future of the nation? This chapter addresses these questions and shows that God's power remains active and invincible, even if enemies have captured the symbol of his presence.

During the period of the judges, the Israelites worshiped the gods of the neighboring peoples, including those of the Canaanites, Aramaeans, Sidonians, Moabites, Ammonites, and Philistines (Judg. 10:6). But Israel's idolatry consistently brought defeat and humiliation. Some might misinterpret Israel's defeats as being due to the Lord's weakness or to the strength of the foreign gods. So in this section of the Former Prophets (Judges and 1 Samuel),

the narrator affirms that Israel's defeats are punitive, not due to some deficiency on the Lord's part.[1]

As part of his strategy, the narrator demonstrates the Lord's superiority to foreign gods, in particular Baal, the Canaanite god of the storm, and Dagon, the god of the Philistines. The Song of Deborah depicts the Lord as sovereign over the storm as he defeats the Canaanite armies (Judg. 5:4–5). The Gideon account, along with its sequel about Abimelek, contains a strong anti-Baal polemic, showing how Baal is unable to fully avenge Gideon's (Jerubbaal's) attack on his altar.[2] The polemical dimension takes a different turn in the Samson story, where Samson burns the grain supposedly provided by the Philistine grain-god Dagon (15:4–5), who is viewed as Baal's father. Though Dagon seems to win the conflict (16:23–24), in the end Samson brings Dagon's temple to the ground (16:30).

The polemic against both of these gods continues in 1 Samuel. As noted above, Hannah celebrates the Lord's ability to give fertility (1 Sam. 2:1–10) in terms that echo the Baal myths. Now chapter 5 tells how the ark of God humiliates Dagon in the latter's very own temple and then continues to assault him and his people as long as it remains in Philistine territory. The polemic against these foreign gods culminates in 1 Samuel 7, which records how the Lord thunders against the Philistines. In light of the Lord's absolute superiority, it makes no sense for the Israelites to worship these gods and perfect sense for them to follow the Lord.[3]

Historical and Cultural Background

The text describes Dagon as being present in the temple of Ashdod (5:2–4). The referent here is an idol of the deity, complete with face, head, and hands. Walton observes that in the ancient Near East "the deity's presence was marked by the image of the deity." He explains that the "image functioned in the cult as a mediator of the divine presence. As such it represented the mystical union of transcendence and immanence." The god takes up residence in the image and in this way reveals himself to his worshipers and gives them a tangible object to worship.[4]

Dagon appears to be the chief deity of the Philistines. Though an older interpretation understood him to be a fish-god, it is more likely that he was a weather-fertility deity responsible for crops. Scholars debate whether he was fundamentally a storm-god

or a god of vegetation, but in either case he was associated with fertility. In Ugaritic the cognate word *daganu* means "grain," and the storm-god Baal is called Dagon's son. In the Ugaritic texts both Dagon and El are identified as Baal's father. This does not mean that these two deities should be equated, nor does it indicate that there were competing traditions.[5] The most likely explanation is that Dagon was considered to be Baal's literal father, but that El could also be called Baal's father because he was the patriarch of the gods, who stood at the head of the divine genealogical tree. El may have been viewed as Baal's grandfather.[6]

The Old Testament does not deny the existence of the pagan gods and promote monotheism in a modern, Western philosophical sense. But it does declare and assume that Yahweh, the God of Israel, is the incomparable God and the only Deity deserving of worship (Exod. 15:11; 18:11; 20:2–5; Deut. 10:17; Pss. 86:8; 95:3; 96:4–5; 97:7, 9; 135:2; 136:2). Regarding the first of the Ten Commandments, Walton states,

This relief shows Assyrian soldiers carrying the gods of a defeated enemy. In the ancient world it was assumed that if a city or army was vanquished, the god was too weak to protect them. The relief is from the palace at Nimrud, eighth century BC.

Although it does not state explicitly that no other gods exist, it does remove them from the presence of Yahweh. If Yahweh does not share power, authority, or jurisdiction with them, they are not gods in any meaningful sense of the word. The first commandment does not insist that the other gods are non-existent, but that they are powerless; it disenfranchises them. It does not simply say that they should not be worshiped; it leaves them with no status worthy of worship.[7]

Interpretive Insights

5:1 *they took it from Ebenezer to Ashdod.* There is tragic irony in these words. In 4:3 the Israelites said, "Let us bring [or, "take"] the ark of the LORD's covenant from Shiloh." But now we read that the Philistines "took" it away to Ashdod.[8] Ancient battles between human armies were also battles between their gods. The winning army assumed its god(s) to be superior. This explains why the Philistines take the ark to Dagon's temple and place it before their god (v. 2).

5:3 *fallen on his face on the ground.* The expression "fall on the ground" often refers to an act of submission and/or fear (Gen.

44:14; Josh. 5:14; 7:6; Judg. 13:20; Ruth 2:10; 1 Sam. 28:20; 2 Sam. 1:2; 14:4, 22; 2 Kings 4:37; Job 1:20), but it can also be used of military defeat and death (Judg. 3:25; 1 Sam. 17:49; 2 Chron. 20:24). The first nuance fits well in verse 3, where Dagon's image falls before the ark without being damaged. But the second nuance makes better sense in verse 4, where Dagon's image has been broken.[9]

5:4 *His head and hands had been broken off.* The decapitation of Dagon should probably be viewed as a military act, since conquerors sometimes decapitated their defeated enemies (1 Sam. 17:51; 31:9). The cutting off of the hands may also be interpreted in this light, since hands were sometimes cut off and counted following a battle. In a scene in an Ugaritic myth, the warrior goddess Anat ties the decapitated heads of her defeated foes into a necklace and attaches their disembodied hands to her belt (COS, 1:250).[10]

5:6 *The LORD's hand was heavy.* This reference to the Lord's hand being "heavy" upon the Philistines (see also vv. 7, 9, 11) is ironic, humorous, and perhaps even sarcastic. Dagon has lost his hands (v. 4), but the Lord's hand is wreaking havoc among Dagon's worshipers.

tumors. The term translated "tumors" should probably be understood here as "swellings." The Lord struck the Philistines with a disease, perhaps bubonic plague, one of the chief symptoms of which is inflamed lymph glands in the armpit and groin. In

Dagon's broken head and hands were reminiscent of the hands and heads that were routinely cut off fallen enemies. This relief from the mortuary temple of Ramesses III shows scribes recording the number of severed hands and therefore the number of defeated enemies (twelfth century BC).

favor of this interpretation is the fact that the Philistines make golden rats (or mice) and tumors as a guilt offering to the Lord (6:4). Rats are carriers of bubonic plague, a fact recognized in the ancient world. Some ancient textual witnesses even make the connection between rats and the plague in verse 6.[11] Another tradition, perhaps preserved in the margin of the Hebrew Bible, understands these "tumors, swellings" as anal ulcers or hemorrhoids. In this case the Lord strikes the Philistines with dysentery, which produces anal sores.[12]

5:10 *the people of Ekron cried out.* As the story progresses, the narrator pictures ever-increasing panic among the Philistines. Verse 6 speaks of the devastation and affliction in Ashdod, which prompts the Ashdodites to request that the ark be removed from their city. As it moves to Gath, there is "a great panic" (v. 9). When the ark arrives in Ekron, the people object, for death has "filled the city with panic" (v. 11). Furthermore "God's hand [is] *very* heavy on it" (v. 11, emphasis added), and now there is an "outcry" that goes "up to heaven" (v. 12).

Theological Insights

Israel identifies the Lord too closely with the ark, thereby reducing him to the level of the pagan gods. Consequently they are horrified when the ark is captured. But events in Philistine territory demonstrate that the Lord cannot be imprisoned or rendered impotent by the capture of the ark. This is a profound story for the exiles to recall, for they have experienced the loss of the ark. (We cannot be sure if it was taken to Babylon with the temple treasures [2 Kings 24:13] or destroyed when the temple was burned [25:9].) This tragic event is one of the negative consequences of the Lord's broken relationship with his people. But it does not mean that God has been defeated or that he is now powerless. Nor does it mean that the future holds no hope. Indeed, Jeremiah anticipates a time of restoration and renewal when the ark will be forgotten, for the Lord will make his royal presence known in Jerusalem in an even more tangible fashion than before (Jer. 3:16–17).

The history of the ark's exile and return actually provides a pattern for the exiles to understand both their past and future. As Walton observes, Israel's disobedience, capped off by the failure of the priesthood under Eli, prompts God to undertake "a self-imposed exile" in which he allows the ark, the symbol of his presence, to go into captivity (Ps. 78:56–64). This begins "a transitional period," which extends from the ark's capture (1 Sam. 4) to its arrival in Jerusalem (2 Sam. 6; cf. Ps. 78:65–72). God then makes his covenant with David, which marks the beginning of a new era for Israel, promising blessing and security (2 Sam. 7).[13] But Israel's sin throughout the period of the kingdom, capped off by the pollution of the temple, God's dwelling place, prompts God to take another "self-imposed exile" (Ezek. 8–11) from his earthly worship center. The exiled people are now in a transitional period, but they can look forward to a time when God's presence will return to Jerusalem and he will inaugurate a new covenant (Isa. 40–55; Jer. 30–33; Ezek. 36–37).

Teaching the Text

1. *The Lord is more powerful than the pagan gods.* Even though the Philistines have

captured the symbol of the Lord's presence, they have not captured the Lord himself, as events in Ashdod and the other Philistine cities clearly demonstrate. But the Lord does accommodate himself to the Philistine mindset. They identify the ark with Israel's "gods" (4:8), so the

Fresco showing the ark of the covenant leaving the temple of Dagon with the statue of Dagon broken behind it, from the remains of the synagogue at Dura Europos (AD 245)

Lord works in conjunction with the ark to impress upon the Philistines his incomparability and power. The Lord will not allow the ark to sit beside Dagon's image in Dagon's temple. When Dagon falls before the ark, the Philistines do not seem to get the point. But when Dagon then ends up decapitated and dismembered, they apparently do. Wherever the ark goes, the Lord brings death and destruction, demonstrating his superiority to Dagon. This episode demonstrates that the power of Israel's God transcends territorial boundaries and is unimpeded, even when the symbol of his presence is in a foreign land or another god's temple.

The Lord's superiority to the gods of the nations is a persistent theme in the Old Testament. Through his servant Moses he defeats and humiliates the gods of Egypt (Exod. 12:12). When the Canaanites hear the news, they recognize that Israel's God is "God in heaven above and on the earth below" (Josh. 2:11). God demonstrates his power over other gods on several occasions during the judges' period (see our discussion above under "The Text in Context"). In the days of Elijah he sent his prophet to Phoenicia, Baal's backyard, and demonstrated his power to give food and life during a time of drought (1 Kings 17). According to the mythological texts, drought is a consequence of Baal's death and imprisonment in the underworld. Then on Mount Carmel, as Elijah confronts the Baal prophets imported by Jezebel, the Lord proves his power to send the lightning and rain (1 Kings 18).[14] Against the backdrop of the exile, God challenges the idol-gods of the nations to demonstrate their power, lampoons their inability to do so, and declares his incomparability and right to exclusive worship (Isa. 40:18–20; 41:5–7, 21–29; 44:9–20; 45:5, 16; 46:1–2, 6–7; 48:5, 14).

2. *The Lord's power transcends any mere tangible reminder of his presence.* This story highlights the Lord's power and makes it clear that his spiritual essence

(John 4:24) cannot be equated with a mere physical token of his presence. Although the Philistines capture the ark, it does not imprison or weaken God. When God's people are defeated, this hardly means that God himself has been defeated. One should never misinterpret God's willingness to contextualize his self-revelation, as he did when he gave Israel the ark, to mean that God is finite. While God may reveal himself in anthropomorphic ways and even temporarily impose limitations on himself to accommodate human freedom and to facilitate divine-human relationships, he remains the infinite God who may be challenged, but never defeated.

Illustrating the Text

The one true God is superior to the so-called gods of the nations.

Literature: *The Last Battle*, by C. S. Lewis. In this, Lewis's (1898–1963) last volume (1956) in The Chronicles of Narnia, an ape named Shift has persuaded a well-meaning but simple donkey called Puzzle to dress in a lion's skin and pretend to be the great lion, Aslan. Shift, using Puzzle as his pawn, convinces the Narnians that he speaks for Aslan. King Tirian and others at first believe the rumors of Aslan's return, but they see the lie when Shift tells the Narnians that Aslan and the Calormene god Tash are one and the same.

> But now, as Tirian looked round on the miserable faces of the Narnians, and saw how they would all believe that Aslan and Tash were one and the same, he could bear it no longer. "Ape," he cried with a great voice, "you lie. You lie damnably. You lie like a Calormene. You lie like an Ape."

> He meant to go on and ask how the terrible god Tash who fed on the blood of his people could possibly be the same as the good Lion by whose blood all Narnia was saved.[15]

When Tirian accuses the ape of lying, the Calormenes bind the king to a tree. Tirian calls on Aslan for help, and some of the other characters who have populated the Narnian chronicles come to his aid. A fight ensues, and finally Aslan appears. All the people and animals, including those who previously died, gather outside the barn and are judged by Aslan. Those loyal to Aslan or the code upheld by the Narnians join Aslan in Aslan's Country. Those who have opposed or deserted him become ordinary animals and vanish to an unmentioned place.

There is a distinction between God's essence and the mere symbols of his presence.

Human Experience: We all understand the difference between photographs and the person or place they represent. Almost everyone has had the experience of travel, the excitement of looking at the pictures later and knowing that there is a profound difference between the two: nothing can really capture the full sensory dimension of being at that place, feeling the air, tasting the food, taking in the color, sitting in the physical landscape. The same is true of a photograph of a person one loves: it is simply a representation, not the actual person one cares about or wants to be with. So it is with the Lord: his spiritual essence cannot be equated with a mere physical token of his presence.

The Ark Heads Home

Big Idea *The holy God must be treated with respect.*

Understanding the Text

The Text in Context

This chapter continues the story of the ark. In the aftermath of the Israelite defeat at Ebenezer, the Philistines captured the ark and took it to Ashdod. But it brought death and destruction wherever it went in Philistine territory. Finally the people of Ekron insisted that it be sent back to its homeland (5:11). Chapter 6 tells how the ark returns to Israelite territory, but not without incident! The ark does not make it back to Shiloh or another major worship center. This leaves the story hanging until it resumes much later, when David decides to bring the ark to Jerusalem (2 Sam. 6). The fact that the ark does not go to a worship center upon its return to Israelite territory is important because it proves that David does not violate a sanctuary to retrieve it. One gathers the impression that the ark is waiting to be taken to its proper place.

On a more negative note, the incident at Beth Shemesh, where the ark is not treated with proper respect and several people die as a result (1 Sam. 6:19–20), foreshadows the Uzzah incident (2 Sam. 6:6–7). Both stories are stern reminders to Israel that the Lord must be treated with the utmost respect, for he is holy (1 Sam. 6:20). This is a lesson the Philistines have learned the hard way. The appeal of the Philistine leaders to honor the Lord (1 Sam. 6:5) serves as a foil in this chapter to the flippant way the Israelites later treat the ark. It also anticipates Samuel's calls for Israel to repent in following chapters of the unfolding history (1 Sam. 7:3; 12:20–25).

Historical and Cultural Background

When the Philistines need advice concerning what to do with the ark, they call for their priests and "diviners" (1 Sam. 6:2). The Mosaic law prohibits divination in Israel (Deut. 18:10); in the ancient Near East it was a popular form of discerning the divine will and receiving guidance for life (cf. Deut. 18:14). There were two main categories of "divination" in the ancient world: (1) "Inspired divination is initiated in the divine realm and uses a human intermediary."[1] This type of divination takes the forms of official and informal prophecy, as well as dreams. (2) "Deductive divination" also originates in the divine realm, "but its revelation is communicated through events and phenomena that can be observed." It is this deductive type of divination that the law prohibits.[2] Deductive divination involves the interpretation of omens, which includes examining the internal organs of animals, casting lots, and observing celestial, terrestrial, and physiognomic patterns.[3]

Magic also played an important role in ancient Near Eastern religion. Walton explains its relationship to divination: "While divination is concerned with gaining knowledge, magic involves exercising power." Magic involves the use of incantations and rituals designed "to manipulate cosmic forces in pursuit of self-interest" and to ward off the danger associated with bad omens.[4]

The priests and diviners described in chapter 6 advise the Philistines with regard to both divination and magic. Their suggestion regarding the two cows and the cart is an ad hoc form of divination designed to determine if Israel's God really is the source of the calamity they have suffered.[5] The reparation offering, in the form of golden tumors and rats, appears to be a type of sympathetic magic designed to draw off the plague and to appease the Israelite deity.

Interpretive Insights

6:3 *guilt offering.* This refers to a reparation offering that makes compensation for offenses involving the desecration of sacred space or property.[6] Certainly the Philistines are guilty of such an offense, for they have mishandled the ark, which has sacred status. In this case the offering takes the form of five gold tumors and five gold rats (v. 5). The gold objects have great monetary value and communicate that Israel's God is worthy of honor. The tumors and rats respectively mirror the disease afflicting the Philistines (5:4–5) and its immediate source

Key Themes of 1 Samuel 6

- Even though the ark is only a symbol of the Lord's presence, it is to be treated with honor because it represents the holy God.
- Those who have offended the Lord must honor him rather than harden their hearts.

The Philistines, like other surrounding Near Eastern peoples, practiced divination. In this Assyrian relief from the palace at Nimrud (865–860 BC), a priest, wearing the flat hat, stands over a slaughtered animal. Its entrails would be studied and the omen literature consulted to receive answers to yes-or-no questions.

(see the earlier note on 5:6 about tumors). Apparently they expect these objects to draw off the disease and to appease the Lord (cf. Num. 21:8–9).[7]

6:5 *give glory to Israel's god.* The Philistine leaders' exhortation sounds almost prophetic as they urge their people to show "Israel's god" the proper respect and chastise them for hardening their hearts as Pharaoh and the Egyptians did.[8] They seem aware of the exodus event and even use language from that story.[9] They also exhibit respect for the Lord's sovereignty by using the word "perhaps" (v. 5). They do not presume upon his mercy or assume that they can force him to lift his judgment. There is wordplay in the Hebrew text: the Philistines are to give "glory" (*kabod*) to the Lord and not "harden" (the verb *kabed* is related to *kabod*) their hearts. The wordplay draws attention to the reversal that is needed in the Philistines' attitude.[10]

The language plays off three earlier statements: (1) Israel's priest Eli (cf. 1 Sam. 1:9) has honored (*kabed*) his sons (who are also priests, 1:3) more than the Lord and has failed to give the Lord the respect he deserves (2:29–30).[11] But here, ironically, we hear the Philistine priests exhorting their people to honor the Lord! (2) The glory (*kabod*) may have departed from Israel when the ark was captured (4:21–22), but this hardly incapacitates the Lord, whose mighty deeds prompt the Philistines to ascribe glory (*kabod*) to him. (3) The Lord's hand is "heavy" (*kabed*) upon the Philistines (5:6, 11) because they have hardened (*kabed*) their hearts (6:6).

This is not the only instance in the Old Testament where foreigners make insightful statements about the proper way to think about and relate to the Lord. Prime examples include Balaam (Num. 23–24), Rahab (Josh. 2:8–11), Naaman (2 Kings 5:15–18), the sailors and the Ninevite king in the book of Jonah (1:14; 3:7–9), Nebuchadnezzar (Dan. 4:34–35), and Darius the Mede (Dan. 6:26–27).

6:14 *sacrificed the cows as a burnt offering.* The appearance of the Levites in the next verse gives the impression that the ark is being handled properly. After all, the Levites are the authorized custodians of the ark (Num. 3:31; Deut. 10:8). However, despite the presence of Levites, all is not well. The people sacrifice the cows as a burnt offering, but the law says to use a male animal (bull, ram, goat) for such an offering (Lev. 1:3, 5; 22:18–19).

6:19 *seventy of them.* The Hebrew text and the ancient versions read "50,070 men," a number that is impossible to accept as original. The site of ancient Beth Shemesh could not have accommodated this many people.[12] A few medieval Hebrew manuscripts and Josephus support the smaller number seventy, as read by the NIV.

they looked into the ark. The standard interpretation of this text is that some of the people looked *into* the ark (which implies that someone touched it) and were struck down because of their lack of respect. How-

This is an aerial view of Beth Shemesh, modern Tell er-Rumeliah. It was a prosperous Israelite town located in the Sorek Valley at the edge of Philistine territory.

ever, this view is problematic. The Hebrew expression used here (ra'ah, "see," followed by the preposition b-, "in") more commonly means "look at," not "look into." But it seems unlikely that the Lord would strike the people down for simply looking *at* the ark. The Septuagint preserves a different tradition of what happens: "But the sons of Jeconiah did not join in the celebration with the men of Beth Shemesh when they saw the ark of the Lord."[13] In this case the Lord struck down some of the people because one group neglected to celebrate the ark's return. The standard interpretation is preferable for two reasons: (1) The phrase ra'ah b- never occurs elsewhere with "ark" as the object, so we cannot assume that the normal idiom applies here. (2) In the two other passages (one here in chap. 6) where people look *at* the ark, the direct-object marker 'et, not the preposition b-, precedes the object (Josh. 3:3; 1 Sam. 6:13), suggesting that this use of the preposition b- conveys a different idea than simply "look *at*."

heavy blow. A better reading might be "great slaughter" (KJV) since elsewhere the expression refers to heavy casualties, the loss of human life (Josh. 10:10, 20; Judg. 11:33; 15:8; 1 Sam. 4:10; 19:8; 23:5; 1 Kings 20:21; 2 Chron. 28:5). The appearance of the phrase here is ironic, for in 1 Samuel 4:10 it describes how the Philistine army devastated the Israelites ("the slaughter was very great"). In that case the enemy inflicted a "great slaughter" upon Israel, but the ark of the Lord can do the same if it is treated with disrespect.

6:20 *Who can stand in the presence of.* The Hebrew expression can mean "attend to" (Judg. 20:27–28), but it can also carry the nuance "withstand, resist" (Exod. 9:11; Judg. 2:14; 2 Kings 10:4).[14] The latter nuance fits nicely here as an affirmation of God's invincible and potentially destructive power.

this holy God. In its primary sense "holy" refers to someone or something that is distinct from what is commonplace or ordinary. Here the nuance may be "off limits, unapproachable," since touching and peering into the ark causes the death of the people.

Theological Insights

The Philistine religious leaders advise their people to give glory (*kabod*) to Israel's god and warn them not to harden (*kabed*) their hearts. As noted above, the wordplay highlights the reversal that is necessary in the Philistines' attitude toward Israel's God. The leaders, who apparently are familiar with the Israelite exodus tradition, point out that Pharaoh and the Egyptians initially resisted Israel's God but eventually relented and allowed the Israelites to leave their land. Their command to ascribe glory to the Lord echoes the Lord's stated agenda in the exodus story, where he declares that he will bring glory to himself (Exod. 14:4, 17–18).

The narrator undoubtedly includes the leaders' exhortation in the story because their advice to their own people is pertinent to Israel. They too must ascribe glory to the Lord and not harden their hearts. In the larger exilic setting of the Former Prophets, this story is not directly applicable, for the ark has been lost. However, the broader principle is relevant. The holy God must be treated with respect. Israel's failure to honor God has brought about the exile, but reconciliation is still possible (see

Deut. 30:1–10). The advice of the Philistine priests and diviners is as relevant for the exiles as it was hundreds of years before. Rather than hardening their hearts, they are to repent and honor their God (see Ezek. 18).

Teaching the Text

1. *The holy God must be treated with respect.* Though the Lord is not to be identified with the ark, the people are not to disrespect it by treating it as an object of curiosity. The ark is a symbol of the Lord's holy presence and is to be treated with honor. For the people of Beth Shemesh, the Lord's holiness is cause for fear because they have witnessed firsthand the effect of violating it (6:20). Before this, the word "holy" has appeared only twice in the Former Prophets. For Joshua, God's holiness is cause for pessimism, for he knows Israel's propensity to violate God's standards and thereby offend his holiness (Josh. 24:19). Hannah employs the term when describing the Lord as absolutely sovereign and unique in his capacity to protect his people (1 Sam. 2:2). For Hannah, the Lord's holiness is cause for celebration, for his incomparability assures his loyal followers of vindication. The contrast between Hannah and the people of Beth Shemesh is particularly striking. Those who disrespect the holy God find him terrifying,

while those who honor him find his holiness to be reassuring and cause for hope.

2. *Those who have offended the Lord must honor him rather than harden their hearts.* When Israel violates God's holiness and experiences the punishment that inevitably results, they have two options before them: stubborn resistance or humble repentance. Both the Philistine religious leaders and the narrator of our story recommend the second of these as the appropriate response. Both Deuteronomy (see 30:1–10) and the Former Prophets hold out the possibility of repentance for Israel, even when they have blatantly rebelled against God and experienced his punishment in full measure (see esp. Judg. 2; 1 Sam. 12; 1 Kings 8). The Latter Prophets urge the exiled nation to respond in repentance and experience the renewal that God offers (see esp. Isa. 55; Ezek. 18). The author of Hebrews, using the wilderness generation as a negative example, also warns God's people of the danger of hardening their hearts (3:8, 15; 4:7).

As noted above, the Philistine religious leaders urge their people to ascribe glory to Israel's god. Giving God the honor due him is surely at the heart of genuine worship (cf.

The Philistines honored Israel's God by preparing a guilt offering and returning the ark of the covenant. They made sure that the God of the Israelites was controlling the return of the ark by putting it on a cart pulled by mother cows, whose natural inclination would be to return to their calves. This relief from El-Lisht shows cattle following a calf as an Egyptian herds them through a swamp.

Pss. 29:1–2; 96:7–8), for the incomparable God refuses to share his glory (Isa. 42:8; 48:11). Genuine repentance culminates in genuine worship when the repentant ones ascribe to God the glory he deserves. Paul points out that the pagan world has "exchanged the glory of the immortal God" for idols (Rom. 1:23), but John foresees a day when survivors of God's eschatological judgment will proclaim God's glory (Rev. 11:13). Indeed, he tells how an angel will proclaim the gospel, announce impending judgment, and call the nations to worship, exhorting them to "fear God and give him glory" (Rev. 14:7).

Illustrating the Text

Disrespect and respect for God are visible in specific ways in our lives and others' lives.

Quote: *The Trivialization of God*, by Donald McCullough. McCullough argues that the way we worship matters greatly in forming our attitude toward God; we must be thoughtful about how we present ourselves before him. He writes,

> We dare not leave things we value most to vagaries of whim. . . . The choice, therefore, is not between structured or unstructured worship, but between thoughtful or unthoughtful structure. . . . Rituals of public worship deeply influence us, imprinting themselves on our subconscious minds and thus shaping the pattern of our personal spirituality. What we do corporately tends to set up boundaries and create an ethos for what we do privately.[15]

Culture: Today there is little respect for sacred space. More and more we observe people in churches pulling out smart phones and similar forms of technology during all parts of a service. One might also observe attenders leaving any part of the church service to answer a phone call. This is a serious absence of respect for God that is going unaddressed. Patrons frown on this in concert halls and even movie theaters! In church we seem to be able to do anything, and the disrespect is seldom addressed from the pulpit. If we cannot respect sacred space, how soon will we forget God in our private lives?

We honor God by refusing to harden our hearts, by living in a posture of repentance.

Film: *Dead Man Walking.* This movie (1995) is based on a true story by Sister Helen Prejean (b. 1939) about her relationship with Matthew Poncelet, a convicted murderer on his way to the electric chair. The convict is manipulative, self-defensive, and defiant, refusing to confess his role in the brutal attack on a young couple (he and an accomplice raped the woman and murdered the man). At one point, Prejean says to him, "You blame him, the government, drugs, blacks, the Percys [parents of one of the victims]. You blame the kids for being there. What about Matthew Poncelet? Where's he in this story? What, is he just an innocent? A victim?" Prejean passionately urges Poncelet to admit his guilt, to stop excusing himself, to soften his hardened heart and repent, which he finally does. This moving scene near the end of the movie could be shown, illustrating the work of repentance.

Repentance and Victory

Big Idea *Repentance and renewed allegiance to the Lord are foundational to a restored relationship with him.*

Understanding the Text

The Text in Context

This chapter depicts Samuel as a spiritual and military leader. He revives Israel spiritually and politically and delivers them from Philistine bondage. This positive portrait of Samuel continues the contrast with Eli's house so evident in chapters 2–4. Israel's defeat was closely linked with the death of Eli and his sons. The text even seems to indicate that it was their sin that brought about the loss of the ark (see 4:4). But Samuel is linked with the military success and renewed security that his mother anticipated in her thanksgiving song (2:10). This contrast between Samuel and Eli is facilitated by the fact that both Israel's earlier defeat and the victory described in chapter 7 occur at places named Ebenezer (see the note on 7:12 below). Samuel's victory also foreshadows greater victories to come under the king he will anoint. Since his victory shows that he enjoys God's favor, it contributes to his

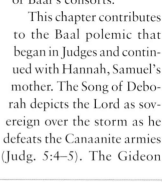

Astarte Plaque found at Tel Dan, fourteenth to thirteenth century BC

credentials as the one who will anoint kings and eventually elevate David over Saul.

Historical and Cultural Background

According to verses 3–4, the Israelites are worshiping the Baals and Ashtoreths at this time. The plural forms likely refer to various local manifestations and idols of the deities Baal and Astarte, respectively, though it is also possible that the phrase refers in a general way to Canaanite male and female deities.[1] Astarte appears as a female consort of Baal in the mythological texts from Ugarit, sometimes in association with Anat, another of Baal's consorts.

This chapter contributes to the Baal polemic that began in Judges and continued with Hannah, Samuel's mother. The Song of Deborah depicts the Lord as sovereign over the storm as he defeats the Canaanite armies (Judg. 5:4–5). The Gideon account, along with its sequel about Abimelek, contains a strong anti-Baal polemic, showing how Baal is unable to fully avenge Gideon's (Jerubbaal's) attack on his altar. Hannah celebrates the Lord's ability to give fertility (1 Sam. 2:1–10) in terms that echo the Baal myths. This polemic against Baal culminates in 1 Samuel 7, which records how the Lord thunders in battle against his enemies. The Lord's self-revelation in the storm is particularly significant and appropriate here because the Israelites, in response to Samuel's exhortation, have just thrown away their Baal idols and renewed their commitment to the Lord (7:2–4). As if to confirm the wisdom of their decision, the Lord reveals himself in a Baal-like manner, proving that he, not the Canaanite storm-god, controls nature and possesses the capacity to bless Israel with fertility.[2]

The description of the Lord's thundering against his enemies has parallels in the broader culture. Warrior kings often compared their battle cry to the thunder of the storm-god.[3] The Assyrian kings Sargon II and Ashurbanipal both report that the storm-god Adad himself thundered against their enemy during battle.[4]

Interpretive Insights

7:3 *If you are returning . . . with all your hearts.* The reference to the Israelites' "hearts" emphasizes the need for sincere motives as a foundation for action. The idiom "return with the heart" focuses on the internal dimension of repentance as the foundation for appropriate actions (see 1 Kings 8:48; 2 Kings 23:25; Joel 2:12).

rid yourselves of the foreign gods. Joshua used this same expression when he commanded the Israelites to put away their

Key Themes of 1 Samuel 7

- Repentance and renewed allegiance to the Lord open the door to deliverance.
- The Lord is the one true God and the only genuine source of his people's security.

idols (Josh. 24:14, 23). By reporting that Samuel addresses Israel in this same way, the narrator may be casting him in the role of Joshua and suggesting that he has become the spiritual leader of the nation.

serve him only. "Serve" carries connotations of worship and loyalty. The addition of "only" emphasizes the exclusivity that is intended. (Only here and in v. 4 is the Hebrew verb translated "serve" used with the phrase translated "only.")[5] It is likely that Israel is worshiping the Lord *along with* other gods, but there is no room for polytheism or syncretism in the worship of the one true God. In this regard Samuel's demand is countercultural, for such exclusivism did not characterize religion in the ancient Near East.

7:4 *So the Israelites put away their Baals and Ashtoreths, and served the LORD only.* The repetition of Samuel's command ("rid yourselves" [v. 3] and "put away" translate the same Hebrew verb) in the report of Israel's response highlights the people's sincerity and obedience. Apparently this is a firm decision on the part of Israel, for we do not read of the people as worshiping the Baals again until the time of Ahab (1 Kings 16:31), who ruled in 874–853 BC.[6] If we date Samuel's victory to roughly 1070 BC, then it appears that Israel did not worship Baal for close to two hundred years.

7:5 *I will intercede . . . for you.* Prior to this, the expression "intercede for" is used only of Abraham (Gen. 20:7 AT; "pray for,"

NIV) and Moses (Num. 21:7; Deut. 9:20). Here (1 Sam. 7:6) and in Numbers 21:7 the people confess their sins with the simple statement "We have sinned," and the leader prays on behalf of the people (intercession for an individual is in view in Gen. 20:7 and Deut. 9:20). A similar account appears in 1 Samuel 12:19, 23 (AT), where the expression "intercede for" is used once more in the context of communal confession of sin.

7:6 *they drew water and poured it out.* The significance of this action is unclear. Perhaps it symbolizes their repentant spirit (see Lam. 2:19),[7] indicates their willingness to deprive themselves of the bare essentials of life (thus fasting in v. 6),[8] and/or symbolizes purification of guilt.[9]

they fasted. Their fasting apparently expresses their sincere sorrow over their past sins (see Judg. 20:26; 1 Sam. 31:13; 2 Sam. 1:12).

7:9 *the LORD answered him.* The narrator again establishes Samuel's credentials as the Lord's chosen spiritual leader and intercessor. The Lord responds (v. 10) to his prayer. This theme of the Lord's answering (or not answering) prayer becomes important in 1 Samuel. The Lord responds to Samuel's prayer here and to David's at Keilah (23:4), but Samuel warns that the Lord will not respond to the cries of disobedient Israel (8:18), nor does he answer the rejected Saul (28:6).

7:10 *the LORD thundered.* See above, under "Historical and Cultural Background."

and threw them into such a panic. The use of this verb (*hamam*) links this event with earlier instances of the Lord's supernatural intervention on behalf of Israel (Exod. 14:24; Josh. 10:10; Judg. 4:15). By linking this victory with the exodus and conquest, the narrator makes the point that the God of Israel, who has won great victories in the past, is alive and well. He may be depicting Samuel, the Lord's human instrument on this occasion, as a new Joshua (see 7:3).

they were routed. The narrator uses this verb (*nagap*) to highlight the contrast between the Israelites' earlier defeat under

This stele depicting the storm-god Baal was found in the temple of Baal at Ras Shamra (ancient Ugarit) and is dated to the eighteenth to fifteenth century BC. In the typical pose of ancient Near Eastern storm-gods, Baal has his right arm raised above his head and grips a weapon in his right hand as if to call down the storm. The spear in his left hand presses into the ground and sprouts leaves, perhaps illustrating the fertility of the land that rain brings.

Eli's sons and their victory under Samuel. In 4:2 the narrator describes how "Israel was defeated by [or perhaps more accurately, "before"] the Philistines" (see also 4:10). But here the tables are turned as the Philistines are "routed before the Israelites."

7:12 *Ebenezer*. The name means "stone of help." It is a reminder that the Lord has helped his people by giving them a liberating victory. The name is ironic because it was at a (different) place named Ebenezer that Israel lost an earlier battle to the Philistines (4:1; 5:1). On that first occasion, Israel took the ark into battle but still lost despite God's presence. On this second occasion, they do not take the ark into battle, yet God is with them, and they win a great victory. This also contributes to the contrast between Samuel and the house of Eli. When associated with the house of Eli, the name Ebenezer recalls defeat and humiliation, but for spiritually renewed Israel under Samuel's leadership, the name becomes a reminder of God's saving intervention.

Theological Insights

The use of the verb "thundered" (7:10) links this event with Hannah's prayer (1 Sam. 2:10), recorded near the beginning of 1–2 Samuel, and with David's prayer (2 Sam. 22:14), recorded near the end of these books. The Lord's self-revelation in the storm to deliver his people partly fulfills Hannah's vision of divine intervention on behalf of Israel's anointed king. But Samuel is not the anointed king of Israel; his victory is anticipatory and in turn foreshadows the experience of David, who poetically depicts the Lord as coming in the storm to deliver him from his powerful enemies. By linking Samuel and David with Hannah's song in this way, the narrator suggests that David is the rightful king anticipated by Hannah and anointed by her son, Samuel.

Another important theological theme in this chapter is the emergence of Samuel as Israel's intercessor. Moses told Israel that the Lord would establish a prophet like him (Deut. 18:15–18). In his prophetic role Moses revealed God's will to the people and interceded on behalf of the nation to God (Num. 21:7). Samuel fulfills this promise in part.[10] Not only does he reveal God's word to Israel (1 Sam. 3:19–4:1a), but here he also intercedes for the people (7:5, 9). The narrator presents Samuel as a new Moses, thereby establishing his credentials as the mediator between God and Israel who possesses the authority to anoint kings on behalf of God. It is no surprise that the Lord, when speaking to Jeremiah, mentions Moses and Samuel in the same breath when recalling intercessors from Israel's past (Jer. 15:1; see also Ps. 99:6).

From the unique perspective of the exiles, repentance is perhaps the most relevant theme of this chapter.[11] Israel's response to Samuel's prophetic exhortation provides a paradigm of repentance for the exiles. Like Samuel's generation, they find themselves alienated from God, just as Moses anticipated (Deut. 30:1–10). They too must repudiate the idolatry of their fathers and renew their allegiance to the Lord.

Teaching the Text

1. *Repentance and renewed allegiance to God open the door to deliverance.* This account is instructive for understanding the nature of repentance. Several observations are in order:

a. God's wayward people can initiate repentance. In describing Israel's reconciliation to God, Moses stresses the exiled people's responsibility to make the first move (Deut. 30:1–2, 10). The Lord will then respond in compassion (vv. 3–6). This balance between human responsibility and divine sovereignty is apparent in Jeremiah 29:10–14 (cf. Ezek. 18:30–32; 36:26–27) and in Jesus's parable of the prodigal son. The wayward son, exasperated by the consequences of his sin, decides to return home to his father, who rushes to meet him and greets him with open arms and great rejoicing (Luke 15:11–32).

b. Repentance can have a corporate dimension when the individual members of the covenant community have participated together in the same sins.

c. Repentance begins with sincere motives, but it also involves actions, not just emotion. The substance of repentance is changed behavior, often involving a radical repudiation of one's former behavior and allegiances. Symbolic rituals and confession of sin may accompany repentance, but these formal expressions have significance only if supported by changed behavior. This focus on actions as the genuine fruit of repentance is also apparent in the New Testament (Matt. 3:8; Luke 3:8; Acts 26:20; 2 Cor. 7:9–11).

d. Repentance results in exclusive worship of the one true God.

e. Repentance does not insulate one from trouble. On the contrary, when the Philistines hear about Israel's assembly at Mizpah, they attack (1 Sam. 7:10). But repentance and reconciliation to God do bring divine support amid trying circumstances and protection from one's enemies.

2. *The Lord is the one true God and his people's only genuine source of security.* As noted earlier, the Lord's self-revelation in the storm confirms the wisdom of Israel's decision to worship the Lord alone. In light of the Lord's incomparability, it makes no sense for the Israelites to worship foreign gods and perfect sense for them to follow the Lord, for in him alone can they find genuine security.

The truth that the incomparable God is fully capable of providing security for his

Before the Israelites' military confrontation, Samuel offers a sacrifice and cries out to the Lord, recognizing that only with the Lord's gracious help will the Israelites be victorious over the Philistines. Military success in the ancient Near East was attributed to the relative strength of the gods. This Assyrian relief (Nineveh, 700–692 BC) shows a fortified army camp where, in the upper left-hand quadrant, priests are engaged in a ritual to assure the favor of their god.

people is comforting, but it also challenges the Lord's people to genuine faith. If the Lord really is the only true God and his people's only genuine source of security, then he deserves and demands their exclusive worship. There is no room for syncretism or polytheism in genuine worship.

Illustrating the Text

Radical repentance is what God requires.

Biography/Autobiography: Many individuals have been radically changed by the power of God. These range from familiar stories, like John Newton's, to more recent accounts, such as Jim Cymbala's anecdotes in *Fresh Wind, Fresh Fire* (1997; with Dean Merrill), appropriately subtitled *What Happens When God's Spirit Invades the Heart of His People*, or David Wilkerson's *The Cross and the Switchblade* (1963).

Film: *The Mission.* This award-winning film (1986) is based on the tragic story of political mishandling of the Jesuit mission settlements in Paraguay during the seventeenth and eighteenth centuries. The repentant sinner in the film is Rodrigo Mendoza, a Spanish adventurer played by Robert De Niro. He has enslaved Indians, capturing them in the most loathsome ways; he even killed his brother in a duel over a woman, similar to the Cain-and-Abel story. Arrested for the murder of his brother, Mendoza becomes filled with self-loathing and molders in a prison cell until a priest (played by Jeremy Irons) comes to talk to him firmly and persistently. He begins to move beyond his self-hatred and wants forgiveness. As a sign of his repentance, he drags a bag of heavy armor, a symbol of his past life, up a cliff above the Iguaçú Falls. When the bag falls, he goes down and starts over, repeatedly. Awaiting him at the top are the Indians whom he enslaved. This man's radical repentance is followed by his devotion to the same Indians he has so wronged.

God is superior to pagan gods.

See also the "Illustrating the Text" section of 1 Samuel 5.

Greek Mythology: Greek pagan gods, as well as all pagan gods, were notoriously fickle, abusive, immoral, and volatile, utterly different from the God of the Bible. An example is Zeus, the child of Cronus, a cruel Titan. Zeus had two brothers, Poseidon and Hades; the three brothers overthrew their father, then drew lots to see who would become the supreme ruler of the gods. Zeus won and reigned as leader of the gods. He married his sister Hera, although he is probably best known for his scandalous affairs. Zeus was known as the god of the sky; his weapon was the thunderbolt, something he wielded randomly and without resort to noble reasoning.

Christian Nonfiction: *The Trivialization of God,* **by Donald McCullough.** In this book (1995), author McCullough argues that today we have trivialized the Holy God into the "god of my comfort" and the "god of my success," a resort to personal narcissism, which can only fail us. These culturally created gods are also pagan gods.

Israel Demands a King

Big Idea *Even when the Lord regards his people's lack of faith as a rejection of his authority, he warns them of the negative consequences of their rebellion.*

Understanding the Text

The Text in Context

Israel demands to have a king like the nations that live around them. They complain about the injustice of Samuel's sons (1 Sam. 8:4–5), but the underlying reason for their demand is their desire to have a military leader who will ensure national security (v. 20). The request is surprising because the Lord has demonstrated his capacity to protect his people by defeating the Philistines (1 Sam. 7). However, this is not the first time Israel has made such a request (Judg. 8:22).

Long before this the Lord anticipated that the people would make a request like this, and he made provision for it (Deut. 17:14–20). However, a close look at the Deuteronomic regulations indicates that the Lord did not intend to give Israel a king like other nations (see fuller discussion below, under "Theological Insights"). Yet here in 1 Samuel 8 he seems to accede to the people's request as he instructs Samuel to give them what they demand (vv. 7–9, 22a). What is even more baffling is Samuel's response. Rather than obeying the Lord, he sends the people home (v. 22b). The issue is left unresolved at the end of the chapter. Will the Lord actually give them what they want?

Historical and Cultural Background

Israel wants a king who will ensure social justice and national security (1 Sam. 8:4–5, 19). Ancient Near Eastern kings were responsible for providing both of

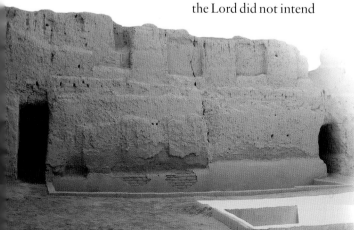

Royal prerogatives and the bureaucracy involved in a monarchy are explained by Samuel and attested by both archaeological and literary sources in the ancient world. A small portion of the remains of the palace of King Zimri-Lim of Mari, in modern Syria, is shown here (eighteenth century BC). Archaeologists have uncovered an elaborate structure with two large courtyards, which acted as welcoming halls, the king's house, and the House of the Women. These contained the throne room, stores, second-floor royal apartments, servants' quarters, kitchens, administrative offices, and bathrooms.

these benefits. Yet there is a downside to kingship. A royal bureaucratic institution inevitably grows and needs to be subsidized by those whom it protects. As it gains more and more power, this royal bureaucracy can easily became oppressive. This is exactly the picture that Samuel paints for the people as he describes what the typical king will be like. Eventually they will view their king as a tyrant, not a protector. Too late they will discover that having a king like other nations is not as desirable as they expect it to be. Second-millennium BC evidence from Syria-Palestine, particularly the sites of Alalakh, Mari, and Ugarit, supports Samuel's argument.[1]

Interpretive Insights

8:3 *accepted bribes and perverted justice.* Samuel's sons, in contrast to their father (v. 5; 12:3–4), violate the cardinal principles of the Mosaic law pertaining to the ethical conduct of judges (Deut. 16:19; 27:19, 25).[2] When Samuel's sons fail to follow their father's example, the people, without rejecting the dynastic principle, decide that a different arrangement is preferable. They want a king to "lead" (v. 6; or "judge") them, not judges like Samuel and his sons.

8:7 *Listen to all that the people are saying to you.* The Hebrew expression "listen to" ("hear the voice of") also occurs in verses 9 and 22 with the nuance "accede to" (in v. 22 the next command is "give them a king"). The statement in verse 7 is slightly different in that it adds "all." Essentially the same expression occurs in 1 Samuel 12:1, where Samuel says he has acceded to their request by giving them a king. It is probable that the Lord's statement in verse 7 is

a command to accede to their request and give them the king they desire.

they have rejected me as their king. Though the Lord has anticipated that Israel will make such a request (Deut. 17:14), he regards this particular demand as a rejection of his kingship (see 1 Sam. 12:17, 19). The reason for his response comes into clearer focus in verse 20: the people apparently do not fully trust the Lord to protect them but feel they need a human king to lead them in battle. Perhaps we should see the people's request against the background of the loss of the ark (1 Sam. 4). The Israelites, led by Eli's sons Hophni and Phinehas, seem to view the ark as a palladium or relic that can be used to compel God to intervene on their behalf. The ark's failure to bring victory and then, even worse, its capture may have led to the belief that it is ineffective. The people possibly feel that a surrogate palladium is needed to do the job they expected the ark to do. So they request a king to lead them into battle, as the ark has done at Jericho. Since the surrounding nations believe that their deity leads in battle through the person of the king, this request is consistent with their desire to have a king like the nations around them. From the people's perspective, they are not asking for a king *instead* of God, but they do want a king *as a means to compel* God.[3] From God's perspective, this is a rejection of his rule, because they want to

be in direct control of their destiny and of God himself. Their request is contrary to the kind of submission and faith that God demands from them.

8:8 *so they are doing to you.* On the surface this seems to contradict the Lord's statement in verse 7 that the people have rejected him, not Samuel. However, it is possible that the statement in verse 7 is exaggerated for effect. Sometimes Hebrew uses the idiom "not *x*, but *y*" to mean "not so much *x* as *y*" (see, e.g., Hosea 6:6). In other words, the Lord is not denying that the people have rejected Samuel, but he is helping Samuel put this rejection into proper perspective. They have not so much rejected Samuel as they have rejected the Lord himself.[4] After all, Samuel is the Lord's representative.

8:9 *warn them solemnly.* Though the Lord appears to be willing to give in to the people's demand for a king, he instructs Samuel to warn the people of the consequences of such an unwise decision. The term translated "warn" has a formal, legal connotation. Thus the Lord is absolved of any wrongdoing in granting their request: in refusing to listen, the people incriminate themselves.[5]

what the king who will reign over them will claim as his rights. The Hebrew text refers to the "custom [*mishpat*] of the king." Here *mishpat* refers to the royal custom of the time, the typical manner in which a king rules (vv. 11–18). There is irony here, for *mishpat* often refers to "justice," but the typical king brings just the opposite.

8:11 *He will take your sons.* Samuel goes out of his way to emphasize that the king will take away what rightfully belongs to the people. In the Hebrew text the verb "take" appears four times in the speech (vv. 11, 13–14, 16). Even more striking is the repetition of the possessive pronoun "your" twelve times in the Hebrew text of verses 11, 13–17, suffixed to a noun referring to someone or something belonging to the people. The second-person forms emphasize that the king will take away what rightfully belongs to the people.

8:18 *you will cry out for relief from the king you have chosen.* The verb "cry out" is ironic, for it is used earlier to describe humiliated Israel's cries for divine relief (Exod. 2:23; Judg. 3:9, 15; 6:6–7; 10:10, 14; 1 Sam. 4:13). Israel thinks a king will bring relief from injustice (vv. 3–5), but instead they will experience oppression at his hand. Samuel has just "cried out" to the Lord on behalf of the people (1 Sam. 7:8–9), and the Lord has "answered" by thundering against the enemy and delivering his people (7:10). But he will not "answer" rebellious Israel when they will cry out under the burden of this king they insist on having.

8:19 *But the people refused to listen.* Again the narrator stresses the people's insistence, thereby highlighting their culpability and absolving the Lord of any wrongdoing in this matter. There is irony in that the Lord three times instructs Samuel to listen to the people (vv. 7, 9, 22), but the people refuse to listen to Samuel.[6]

8:20 *and fight our battles.* The underlying reason for the people's demand emerges here. They want a king to lead them in battle as a replacement for the ark, which, from their perspective, has been ineffective. The military threat posed by Nahash causes the people to panic (12:12). Yet the Lord has recently demonstrated his ability to defeat their enemies (7:10). In fact, from the very beginning of Israel's history, the Lord has led them to victory in battle (Exod. 14:14, 25; Deut. 1:30; 3:22; 20:4; Josh. 10:14, 42; 23:3).

8:22 *Everyone go back to your own town.* Rather than acceding to the people's request as instructed by the Lord, Samuel dismisses them. Perhaps the people assume he will summon them once he has found a king (see 10:17).[7] But then again, Samuel does delay, perhaps hoping the Lord will change his mind.[8] Earlier intercessors reason with the Lord in an effort to change his mind (Gen. 18:23–33; Exod. 32:9–14); Samuel speaks no words, but his refusal to

carry out the Lord's instructions, at least immediately, may have the same intent. Perhaps his "silent" intercession has some effect, for the Lord does alter his plan to some degree, as we shall see.

Theological Insights

In this chapter kingship is presented in a negative light. The people's demand to have a king like the surrounding nations displeases Samuel, and the Lord views it as a rejection of his authority. This raises at least two problems:

1. From Israel's perspective, the people do not view the request for a king as a rejection of the Lord. Like other nations, which claim that a god gives victory to their king, Israel wants a king who is supported by God and represents God in battle. So why does the Lord view their request as a rejection of his authority? It is obvious that Israel is dissatisfied with the arrangement under the judges, where God in response to a crisis raises up a leader who summons the people for war. There is no standing army or chariot force. By Samuel's time they decide that they want what the other nations have.[9] They are not asking for a king in place of God, but they do want to see tangible evidence of their military strength, able to be called upon immediately in a crisis and serve as a deterrent to foreign attack. But the Lord demands radical faith on Israel's part that is counter to the cultural norm and expectation. The typical arrangement can too easily cause people to trust in the tangible, rather than in the God behind it. Earlier in Israel's story we see God's concern in this regard. He commands Joshua to burn the Canaanite chariots (Josh. 11:4–11); he makes Gideon

dismantle the bulk of his army lest the people think they have defeated the Midianites by their own strength (Judg. 7:2). In Deuteronomy 17:14–20, which anticipates Israel's request for a king like other nations, the Lord refuses to give them such a king. They may have a king, but he is not to build a chariot force, form political alliances through marriages, or accumulate wealth—all of which are typical of foreign kings, who count them as essential for national security. Moses tells Israel that they are not to fear when they see the chariotry and army of their enemies; they are to trust in the Lord to fight for them (Deut. 20:1–4). Joshua reminds them that the Lord has supernaturally annihilated the Egyptian chariots and horsemen and that the Lord, not the Israelites' swords and bows, have defeated the Amorites (Josh. 24:6–7, 12).

2. How does one harmonize this negative view of kingship with the epilogue of Judges, which views the institution positively? The narrator of Judges suggests that the moral anarchy of the period could have been avoided if Israel had only possessed a king (Judg. 17:6; 21:25). However, this does not mean that any king will do. The statement in Judges reflects the Deuteronomic ideal of a king who promotes the law by his teaching and example (Deut. 17:18–20).[10] This will entail regulating the cult, ensuring social justice, and unifying the nation.[11] As noted above, the Deuteronomic model of kingship differs in several respects from the cultural model of kingship that the people are demanding.

Israelite kingship may seem like a thing of the past for the exiles. After all, they are under the rule of a powerful empire. Yet the prophets have kept the hope of a future Davidic king before the people, and many must anticipate his arrival when they hear the predictions of Haggai (2:20–23) and Zechariah (12:8). However, this account (in 1 Sam. 8) reminds them that their future security will not be found in a human ruler like other nations have. To follow such a king will bring only oppression and enslavement. They must submit to God's rule as King and look for his chosen human king in accord with the Davidic covenant (cf. Zech. 4:6).

Teaching the Text

1. *God's people are prone to ignore his self-revelation, reject his authority, and conform to the thinking of the world around them.* The Lord expects Is-

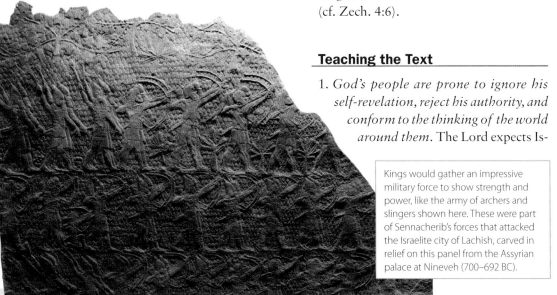

Kings would gather an impressive military force to show strength and power, like the army of archers and slingers shown here. These were part of Sennacherib's forces that attacked the Israelite city of Lachish, carved in relief on this panel from the Assyrian palace at Nineveh (700–692 BC).

rael to be distinct from the surrounding nations (Lev. 18:2–5; 19:2; 20:23–24, 26; Josh. 23:7–12) because he wants his people to be a model society that will be a beacon of justice and truth in the world (Deut. 4:5–8). But Israel is prone to reject the Lord's authority and conform to the viewpoints and practices of the surrounding nations (Judg. 2:10–3:5), as illustrated by their request to have a king like the other nations. The New Testament also demands that God's covenant community be distinct (see esp. 1 Pet. 2:9–10, as well as Rom. 12:1–2; Eph. 1:4; 5:3; Col. 3:12; 1 Thess. 4:3–8; 1 Pet. 1:13–16).

2. *When God's people decide to act self-destructively, he warns them of the consequences of their rebellion.* God is the sovereign Creator and King of the world, but he has granted freedom to human beings and allows them to exercise that freedom within the limits of his sovereign rule and providence. When God's people choose to act against his moral will, God warns them of the consequences of their behavior so that they have no excuse when those consequences materialize.

Illustrating the Text

God's people may be influenced by the world's self-destructive thinking.

Quote: *No Place for Truth*, by David Wells. In this book (1993), theologian Wells (b. 1939) describes the trend to self-centered religion and away from objective truth.

> Theology becomes therapy. . . . The biblical interest in righteousness is replaced by a search for happiness, holiness by wholeness, truth by feeling, ethics by feeling good

about one's self. The world shrinks to the range of personal circumstances; the community of faith shrinks to a circle of personal friends. The past recedes. The church recedes. All that remains is the self.[12]

God warns his people about the consequences of sin.

Literature: *The Pilgrim's Progress*, by John Bunyan. Bunyan (1628–88) provides many scenes of warning in this classic allegory (1678). When Christian and Hopeful leave the Delectable Mountains, the shepherds (divinely appointed by God) warn them, "Beware of the Flatterer." By sad experience, the pilgrims learn the foolishness of neglecting this advice. They come to a place where two roads run parallel, both seeming straight. As they think what to do, a man "very black of flesh but covered with a very light robe" (a flatterer metaphorically) asks them why they are there. They tell him they are on the way to the Celestial City but do not know which way to take. "Follow me," he says, and little by little he leads them away from the city, until they fall "within the compass of a net in which they [are] both so entangled" that they do not know what to do. Then the man's white robe falls off, and they lie there crying, unable to help themselves. Spurgeon observes that this is not a picture of temptation, nor "did they go blundering on, but consulted with each other." They just did not follow the warning given by the shepherd; they failed to consult their Book. Hopeful actually says, "Here David was wiser than we; for, saith he, concerning the works of men, 'By the word of Thy lips I have kept me from the paths of the destroyer.'"[13]

Meet Israel's New King

Big Idea *Even when his people's faith falls short of his expectations, the Lord remains faithful and makes provision for their deliverance.*

Understanding the Text

The Text in Context

Israel demanded to have a king like the nations that lived around them (1 Sam. 8). They wanted a leader who would ensure national security (8:19–20) through an army and alliances. Despite how they may have viewed this request, the Lord regarded it as a rejection of his authority (8:7): it showed that the people were not willing to demonstrate the radical, countercultural faith the Lord demanded from them. The Lord anticipated that the people would make this request (Deut. 17:14–20). But the Deuteronomic regulations do not authorize Israel to have a king *like other nations*, for the king is not to build a chariot force, secure political alliances through marriage, or accumulate wealth. Surprisingly, God initially acceded to the people's request: three times he instructed Samuel to give them what they demanded (1 Sam. 8:7–9, 22a). However, Samuel seemed to balk at this and sent the people home (v. 22b), leaving the matter unresolved. This plot tension reaches its resolution in chapters 9–10. The Lord providentially brings his chosen king to Samuel to be anointed, but it becomes apparent that the Lord, despite his earlier instructions, is not going to give Israel the kind of king they want. Yet, recognizing the people's concern for security as legitimate, he does intend to deliver them from their enemies through this ruler.

Interpretive Insights

9:1 *There was a Benjamite . . . whose name was Kish.* This story begins the same way as the stories of Samson (Judg. 13:2), Micah (Judg. 17:1), and Samuel (1 Sam. 1:1) do. Though it might appear to be a standard way of beginning a story, a closer look reveals that this introductory formula occurs only in these three passages and here in 1 Samuel 9:1, where Saul's family is introduced. The parallels between these texts indicate that the formula links the stories together by design. For further discussion, see the commentary on 1 Samuel 10:9–27, "The Text in Context."

9:2 *named Saul.* The name Saul means "asked for, requested." This is ironic in that the narrator has already described the people as "asking" the Lord for a king (1 Sam. 8:10). Later, in his so-called farewell address to the nation, Samuel twice refers to Saul as the one the people "asked for" (1 Sam. 12:13, 17), and the people acknowledge that they have sinned by "asking for a king" (12:19). Saul's very name is a reminder of the people's sin of rejecting the Lord: it suggests that he has been chosen according to their standard, not the Lord's. For more on this, see the commentary on 1 Samuel 10:9–27, "Theological Insights."

9:3 *Now the donkeys belonging to Saul's father Kish were lost*. The account of Saul's search for his father's lost donkeys has a twofold function in the story. On a positive note, it illustrates how God in his providence manipulates circumstances to accomplish his purposes. Saul's quest to find the donkeys leads him to Samuel, seemingly by chance, but it is really the Lord who sends him to the prophet (v. 16). On a more negative note, the episode begins to paint a portrait of Saul that is less than flattering (see the comment on v. 5 below).

9:5 *Come, let's go back*. In contrast to his servant, Saul appears hesitant and passive. He is a follower, not a leader. The first words out of his mouth portray him as one who is ready to quit without accomplishing the task his father has sent him to do (v. 3). When the servant, who knows of Samuel and his reputation, sug-

Key Themes of 1 Samuel 9:1–10:8

- Despite the people's rejection of the Lord, he does not reject them.
- The Lord decides to deliver his people through his chosen ruler.

gests that they inquire of the prophet, Saul initially raises an objection (v. 7). He tends to impede action rather than move it along.[1] Furthermore, the story depicts Saul as one who is spiritually insensitive: he seems ignorant of Samuel's presence, he does not take initiative in seeking divine guidance, and then he views such insight as something that must be purchased.[2]

9:6 *everything he says comes true*. The narrator allows the servant to declare Samuel's reputation as a respected and reliable prophet of God. Samuel's reliability has already been made evident (chaps. 3–4) and will be demonstrated again, when his prophecies of Saul's rejection and death are fulfilled (13:13–14; 15:28–29; 28:16–19). Those hearing the story for a second time, knowing how Saul's career has ended, will pick up on the tragic irony of the servant's statement.[3]

9:13 *he must bless the sacrifice*. The girls' words, like the servant's (see v. 6), have a foreshadowing function: their statement

Donkeys were valuable livestock in the ancient Near East. They were used as beasts of burden, like those shown in this Egyptian relief. They were used in agriculture for plowing. Travelers used them for transportation, and the kings of Israel rode them when they journeyed on official business. The relief is from the tomb of Seshemnefer IV, Sixth Dynasty (2345–2181 BC), Giza.

anticipates Saul's failure to obey Samuel (see 10:8; 13:8–14).

9:16 *Anoint him ruler.* The word translated "ruler" (*nagid*) differs from the term translated "king" (*melek*) in chapter 8. The sudden appearance of this word, which is not used in chapter 8, and the total absence of "king," which is used nine times in chapter 8 (vv. 5–6, 9–11, 18–20, 22), indicates that the Lord is not going to give his people what they want after all, despite his apparent decision to do so in chapter 8.[4] The term *nagid* is used elsewhere of leaders in a variety of contexts, including tribal leaders, military officers, religious officials, and palace officials. When used of the leader of the nation in Samuel–Kings, it views the king as one officially chosen and appointed by the Lord to serve as the Lord's viceregent over his covenant people (1 Sam. 9:16; 10:1; 13:14; 25:30; 2 Sam. 5:2; 6:21; 7:8; 1 Kings 14:7; 16:2; 2 Kings 20:5). First Kings 1:35 may appear to be an exception, but here David, who knows he is God's *nagid* (2 Sam. 6:21), transfers the right to sit on his throne to Solomon, and Be-

Samuel anointed Saul as God's chosen leader for the Israelites. This horn-shaped jar from the Philistine period may have been used for anointing.

naiah responds with a blessing clarifying that the Lord must confirm David's decision (1 Kings 1:36–37).

my people Israel. In verses 16–17 the Lord calls Israel "my people" four times, whereas in chapter 8 he refers to them simply as "the people" (v. 7). This is an additional signal that the Lord, who regards their request as a rejection of his kingship (8:7), is not going to reject them.[5]

he will deliver them from the hand of the Philistines. In the second half of the verse this promise of deliverance is linked with the Lord's merciful response to their cry for help, implying that this leader will be operating as the Lord's instrument of salvation, not independently from him. The expression "deliver from the hand of" reminds us of the judges (cf. Judg. 2:16, 18; 8:22; 13:5) and Samuel, through whom the Lord delivers his people (Judg. 10:12; 1 Sam. 7:8).[6] This may be another signal that Saul's kingship will not be patterned after that of other nations.

their cry has reached me. The people's desire for national security has motivated them to demand a king like all the other nations (8:20). While the Lord views their proposal as a rejection of his rule (8:7), he recognizes their need for security as legitimate. He promises to provide for this need through his chosen instrument of salvation, just as he has done through the judges and Samuel (7:7–10).

9:17 *he will govern my people.* The verb translated "govern" (*'atsar*) is not used in chapter 8. One might have expected the verb "reign" (*malak*) to appear here, since it is used in chapter 8 to describe the rule of the king (vv. 9, 11). Its absence here is striking, supporting the idea that the Lord is not intending to give the people exactly what they want.[7] The verb '*atsar* means "restrain, detain, withhold," suggesting that the appointed leader will hold the people in check. (Note esp. the use of the verb in 1 Sam. 21:5; Job 12:15; 29:9.) Perhaps this means he will hold them in check by binding them together and keeping them from going their separate ways, as was sometimes the case in the judges' period. The verb is not describing rulership per se but is characterizing Saul's rule. In this context it appears to have a positive connotation, perhaps alluding to the role of the king as described in Deuteronomy 17:14–20.[8]

9:21 *Why do you say such a thing to me?* Apparently aware of Israel's demand for a king, Saul understands the implications of Samuel's statement that the "desire of Israel" is directed toward him (v. 20). Sounding like Gideon, another reluctant individual called by God to be a deliverer (Judg. 6:15), Saul protests that he is unqualified to lead Israel, because he is from an insignificant clan within the smallest Israelite tribe. While one could interpret this response as commendable for its humility, the parallel with Gideon suggests otherwise. Like Gideon before him, Saul should recall that God is able to take the youngest and seemingly insignificant and elevate them to great prominence (see Gen. 25:23; 48:13–20). He will eventually prove this with David (1 Sam. 16:11–12).

10:1 *Has not the LORD anointed you ruler over his inheritance?* The Hebrew text, upon which the NIV is based, has been shortened by an accidental scribal error of omission. In this case the Septuagint preserves the original text. The text should read: "Has not the LORD anointed

you as ruler over his people Israel? You will govern the LORD's people, and you will deliver them from the hand of their enemies who surround them. This will be your sign that the LORD has anointed you as ruler over his inheritance." Within this quotation, as reconstructed from the Greek into Hebrew by Klein, Saul is twice called the "ruler" (*nagid*), not "king," of Israel (cf. 9:16); the verb "govern" ('*atsar*), not "reign," is used (cf. 9:17); and three times the people are identified as belonging to the Lord (cf. 9:16–17).[9]

Saul's commission is clear: the Lord has chosen him to lead the people and, more specifically, to deliver them from their enemies. This is consistent with the Lord's earlier announcement to Samuel, where the focus was on the deliverance of oppressed Israel from the Philistines (9:16–17).

10:2–6 Samuel gives Saul a threefold sign to verify the authenticity of his election as Israel's anointed leader and of the commission that Samuel has just delivered to him. The first two signs will demonstrate God's providential control of events, and the third will demonstrate that God has chosen Saul to be his special instrument, empowered by the divine Spirit for the task at hand.

10:7 *do whatever your hand finds to do.* Once the signs are fulfilled and Saul is convinced of God's presence and enabling power, he is to do what is appropriate. Though this command may seem a bit vague, it appears from the context that Samuel has a military action in mind.[10] After all, Saul's commission is to deliver Israel from its enemies (10:1, see above; cf. 9:16), and Samuel makes a point of reminding him that there is a Philistine garrison (or perhaps the Hebrew word refers to a prefect) at Gibeah (v. 5).[11] The promise that the Lord's Spirit will "come upon" Saul (v. 6) may also hint at military action. This verb (*tsalah*) is used of the Spirit only three times before this, and in each case the Spirit empowered Samson to perform extraordinary physical deeds in conflict with a lion (Judg. 14:6) and with Philistines (14:19; 15:14).[12] In Saul's case, the empowerment with the Spirit is associated with the capacity to prophesy (v. 6), but this need not rule out a military purpose, for prophecy is sometimes a prelude to military action (1 Kings 22:10; 2 Kings 3:14–19).[13]

The third sign to Saul was the empowerment by the Spirit of the Lord after he encountered a procession of prophets. They would have been playing musical instruments, like the drum or tambourine and harps shown on this relief from eighth-century BC Zincirli. Music was often used in a prophetic context, where it helped to bring forth an ecstatic state.

Theological Insights

In chapter 8 it appears that the Lord is ready to authorize a king like all the nations, dooming the people to oppression and eventual enslavement. However, here it is apparent that he has decided not to do this, even though he views their demand for such a king as a rejection of his authority (8:7; cf. 10:19). He will give the people the security they legitimately desire by raising up a leader who will defeat their enemies. The pattern is similar to what we see in Judges, especially in the Gideon and Samson accounts, where the focus is on what the Lord will accomplish through an individual, not necessarily an army. In this regard the intertextual connections to these accounts in 1 Samuel 9:16 and 10:7 (see comments above) are significant and contribute to our understanding of the kind of king God intends Saul to be.

How do the exilic readers of the Former Prophets respond to this story? The Lord's decision to maintain his relationship with rebellious Israel and to deliver them from their enemies should encourage the exiles. It demonstrates the Lord's patience with and commitment to his covenant people, even when they act foolishly and seek to reject his authority, as the exiles and their parents have done. It is still another example of his great mercy and compassion.

Teaching the Text

1. *Even when God regards his people's lack of faith as a rejection of his authority, he maintains his commitment to them.* In their

legitimate desire to experience national security, Israel seeks to follow the pattern of the nations. The Lord regards this as a rejection of his authority. Yet he does not abandon his people to their foolishness. Initially, he is ready to accede to their request, but then he decides not to do so. (For further discussion, see the commentary on 10:9–27 below.)

2. *The Lord recognizes his people's legitimate need for security and mercifully intervenes to prevent their destruction.* Sometimes God's people develop foolish solutions to their legitimate needs. Such is the case when Israel asks for a king like other nations. But God does not ignore their legitimate need. He determines to deliver them from oppression through a ruler whom he will choose and empower for the task. One sees this same pattern during the wilderness wanderings. Due to weak faith, Israel complains to God about legitimate needs for food and water, and the Lord supplies those needs (Exod. 15:24–27; 16:1–36; 17:1–7; Num. 11:1–35; 20:1–11).

As in the case of Gideon (Judg. 6), the granting of signs to Saul (10:1–6) should not be viewed as normative. On the contrary, it may be an accommodation to Saul's hesitancy and weak faith. This is a special occasion in which the Lord intervenes in a special way to get Saul's attention. Though divine enablement is always necessary for carrying out God's will, verse 6 should not be understood as paradigmatic. Modern preachers cannot expect the Lord's Spirit to rush upon them and change them into a different person. There is no warrant for assuming such a broader application in this context or in the New Testament.

Illustrating the Text

In his mercy, God sometimes withholds what the faithless think they need.

Literature: *Robinson Crusoe*, by Daniel Defoe. In this work (1719), one of the first modern novels written, Defoe (1660–1731) tells the story of Robinson Crusoe, who has an addiction to travel, a wanderlust. Against the wishes of his parents, he joins sailing expeditions, some disastrous. He survives them all, but on a later trip he is shipwrecked off an island he calls Despair. His companions die; he is left alone with three animals and the remnants of the ship. Though not the most courageous or resourceful of men, he begins to adapt. Then he reads his Bible, is marvelously converted, and gives thanks for having been shipwrecked, because of what he has begun to learn. He journals, "'Now,' said I aloud, 'My dear father's words are come to pass: God's Justice has overtaken me, and I have none to help or hear me: I rejected the Voice of Providence.'" And again, "Thus we never see the true state of our condition till it is illustrated to us by its Contraries; nor know how to value what we enjoy, but by the want of it."[14] This is a great study of God's sovereignty.

In his mercy, God often provides the legitimate needs of the faithless.

Literature: *Robinson Crusoe*, by Daniel Defoe. One could continue illustrating the text in Samuel by using this novel by Defoe. Just as God withholds company and travel from the wandering pagan Robinson Crusoe, so too he mercifully provides all that Crusoe needs, including the company of animals (significant in the book) and finally the friendship of the cannibal turned Christian: "Friday."

Be Careful What You Ask For

Big Idea *The Lord decides the form of leadership for his covenant community, yet he sometimes gives his people a taste of what they want as a form of discipline.*

Understanding the Text

The Text in Context

In response to the people's request, the Lord decided to give them a king, but he reserved the right to set the pattern for kingship. Recognizing the people's need for security, he chose and commissioned a ruler to deliver them from their enemies. The plot tension of chapter 8 appears to be resolved, but new plot tensions appear in the story. Though Samuel presents Saul to the people as a qualified king based on superficial physical appearances (10:23–24; see 9:2), the narrator's presentation of Saul reveals a serious character flaw that was foreshadowed in deficient leaders of the judges' period. Despite his divine commission, Saul is hesitant to carry out the Lord's purposes. Furthermore, some of the people, observing his hesitancy and realizing this is not the kingship arrangement for which they have asked, refuse to recognize Saul as king (10:27). These tensions will be resolved, ultimately in tragic fashion, as the story continues to unfold.

As noted above (see comments on 9:1), the stories of Samson, Micah, Samuel, and Saul all begin with the same formula. This formal linking appears to be by design, because there are parallels between the stories. There are several parallels between Samson and Saul: (1) The Lord intends to use both individuals to deliver Israel from the Philistines (Judg. 13:5; 1 Sam. 9:16). (2) The Lord's Spirit rushes on both, empowering them for physical conflict (Judg. 14:6, 19; 15:14; 1 Sam. 11:6). (3) The Lord removes his enabling presence from both of them following disobedience (Judg. 16:20; 1 Sam. 16:14). (4) Both expire with a death wish on their lips (Judg. 16:30; 1 Sam. 31:5–6) and are humiliated by the Philistines, Samson before his death and Saul afterward (Judg. 16:21, 25; 1 Sam. 31:9–10).[1] The parallels cast Saul in the role of a second Samson. Both are physically impressive and seemingly possess great promise, but both die tragic deaths after disobeying the Lord.

As commented earlier (on 1:1), the narrator contrasts Samuel and Samson. In contrast to Samson's unnamed barren mother, whose son failed to recognize his role as the Lord's deliverer and never rose to the level of an effective leader, barren Hannah gives birth to a son through whom the Lord restores effective leadership to Israel. Samson only began the deliverance of Israel (Judg.

13:5), but Samuel and then David, whom Samuel anoints as king, defeat the enemies of Israel (1 Sam. 7:14; 17:1–58; 2 Sam. 5:17–25; 8:1). By linking Saul with Samson, the narrator distances Samuel, who is unlike Samson, from Saul and paves the way for linking the prophet with David. This is a literary feature of the story that facilitates the narrator's goal of presenting David, not Saul, as God's chosen king.

The negative portrayal of Saul also contributes to the narrator's goal of presenting David, not Saul, as God's chosen king. Saul, ostensibly chosen because of his physical attributes, proves unfit to rule for a variety of reasons. As the story unfolds, it becomes clear that the Lord chooses Saul by using the people's standard, perhaps to discipline them for their rebellion (see 10:17–19; cf. Hosea 13:10–11) and in the process to demonstrate the limitations of the human perspective they embrace when they demand a king like other nations. However, when it comes time to replace Saul, the Lord picks David on the basis of his own standard, which gives priority to inner character rather than physical attributes (1 Sam. 16:7). When the time comes to act decisively on the Lord's behalf, David demonstrates no hesitancy (1 Sam. 17).

Historical and Cultural Background

Verses 23–24 focus on Saul's physical attributes, especially his height (cf. 9:2). This stands in marked contrast to the account of David's anointing, where the Lord focuses on David's inner qualities (16:7). It also suggests that the choice of Saul reflects the people's, not the Lord's, standard, for human beings tend to judge on such a su-

perficial basis (see 16:6–7 and "Theological Insights" below).

In the ancient Near Eastern ideal of kingship, a premium was placed on physical attributes (cf. *ZIBBCOT*, 311). One of the most vivid examples of this is the description of Ramesses, depicted as "a beautiful youth who was well developed" and was "strong of arms."[2] He was said to be adept at horsemanship, rowing, and archery, and his physical prowess is highlighted. He could outrow all others, and he allegedly shot an arrow through a thick copper shield.[3] Though one must make room for hyperbole, Lichtheim points out that "his mummy is that of an exceptionally tall and strongly built man."[4]

Interpretive Insights

10:13 *he went to the high place.* It appears that this high place, or worship center, is located in Saul's hometown of Gibeah, since the next verse describes a conversation between Saul and his uncle.

This statue of Ramesses II stands in Memphis, Egypt (thirteenth century BC).

Apparently Saul's purpose in going there is to worship. This brief, matter-of-fact description of Saul's actions is disturbing, not so much for what it says, but because of what follows. One might expect Saul to worship before fighting, but Samuel has encouraged him to launch a military action against the Philistine garrison in Gibeah and then proceed to Gilgal (v. 8). Saul does neither. This sets the pattern for what will transpire in later chapters. Saul engages in religious acts that are typical and might even be commendable, but in Saul's case the timing of such actions becomes problematic.

10:16 *But he did not tell his uncle what Samuel had said about the kingship.* Saul's refusal to obey Samuel (see v. 13 above) shows that he is reluctant to fulfill his divine commission and become Israel's king. His conversation with his uncle, recorded in verses 13–16, confirms this. He speaks only of the quest for the lost donkeys and says nothing about the matter of kingship.

10:19 *you have now rejected your God.* When Samuel summons Israel to the formal presentation of their new king, he presents the Lord's perspective on their request for a king (cf. 8:7) and accuses them of rejecting the Lord's royal position and authority. (For a discussion of the contrast between the Lord's and the people's perspectives, see the commentary on chap. 8 under "Theological Insights.") As noted earlier (see 8:20), the people's primary concern in asking for a king is to have a military leader to provide tangible, immediate security and perhaps even compel the Lord to intervene on their terms. They have made this request even though the Lord has recently demonstrated his ability to defeat their enemies (7:10). As the Lord reminds them (10:18), from the very beginning of Israel's history he has led them to victory in battle (Exod. 14:14, 25; Deut. 1:30; 3:22; 20:4; Josh. 10:14, 42; 23:3). He regards their refusal to exhibit radical, countercultural faith in his power to deliver as a rejection of his authority.

So now present yourselves. Samuel's speech up to this point is quite negative in tone and resembles a prophetic judgment speech. After quoting the Lord's own synopsis of salvation history (v. 18), Samuel accuses the people of rejecting the Lord by asking for a king (v. 19a). At this point one expects the announcement of judgment, but instead Samuel summons the people for the purpose of selecting the king. The substitution of the selection process for an

Located in the territory of Benjamin, one of the possible sites for Mizpah is Tell en-Nasbeh, shown here. It is about eight miles north of Jerusalem, located on a main road from Jerusalem to the northern hill country. Although there is much erosion on the site, archaeologists have uncovered the remains of walls, gates, and towers from the Iron Age II period. This is the second time that Samuel has called the Israelites to assemble here.

announcement of judgment suggests that the selection of the king is a disciplinary or even punitive act.[5] The Lord has decided to regulate kingship in accord with the Deuteronomic policies (see v. 25 below), but ironically in time kingship in Israel will evolve into an institution that operates much like the description given by Samuel earlier (8:10–18).

10:24 *Do you see the man the* LORD *has chosen?* Samuel avoids using the word "king" in describing Israel's new leader. The people use the term in acclaiming Saul (v. 24b), and Samuel does use the term in quoting the people's earlier demand (v. 19), but the prophet prefers to draw attention to the fact that this leader is chosen by the Lord. In doing so, he hints that the king will rule under the authority of the Lord and be responsible to the Lord. The statement contrasts with Samuel's earlier reference to "the king you [the people] have chosen" (8:18). It echoes Deuteronomy 17:15, where Moses instructs Israel: "Be sure to appoint over you the king whom the LORD your God chooses."

10:25 *the rights and duties of kingship.* At first glance one might identify the "rights and duties of kingship" (*mishpat hammelukah*) with the "rights" of the king (*mishpat hammelek*) mentioned in 8:9, 11 (where NIV paraphrases, "will claim as his rights"). In this case the scroll mentioned in verse 25 would be a perpetual reminder of the Lord's earlier warning—a sort of "I told you so" document to be brought out when the people complain about the king they once wanted so badly. However, in light of the allusion to Deuteronomy 17:15 in the previous verse, as well as the emphasis in chapters 9–10 on the Lord's continuing

authority over Israel and the king, it is more likely that the "regulations" mentioned here are the rules governing kingship as outlined in Deuteronomy 17:14–20. In this case the regulations are placed before the Lord as a reminder that he will hold the king and the nation accountable for obeying them.[6]

10:27 *They despised him.* Perhaps these "scoundrels" are skeptical about Saul's ability to rule because of his hesitant behavior. But there is more here than meets the eye. They want a king like other nations, but the Deuteronomic regulations imposed on the king (v. 25) place limitations upon the king and should prevent him from being like the typical foreign king. More specifically, Israel's king is not to build a chariot force, form alliances through marriage, or accumulate wealth.

Theological Insights

In chapter 8 the Lord seems ready to give Israel a king like all the other nations, dooming them to oppression and eventual enslavement. By the end of chapter 10, however, it is apparent that he has decided not to give Israel a king like other nations, even though he views their demand for such a king as a rejection of his authority (10:19; cf. 8:7). One senses this is the case in 9:16–17 (see comments above), and then it becomes clear in 10:24–25 (see above). This comes into even sharper focus in chapter 11, where Saul, even though he is now a king/ruler, functions more as the judges did. When the news of the Ammonite threat arrives, he is working in a field (11:5), not sitting in a palace, and must summon citizen soldiers from the tribes (11:6–8), as the judges did. Yet there is a dark side to this. The king whom the Lord chooses has obvious flaws, and one senses from Samuel's rhetoric that there may be a disciplinary or punitive dimension to the granting of a king. Later prophetic reflection on this event seems to bear this out (cf. Hosea 13:10–11).

How do the exilic readers of the Former Prophets respond to this story? In addition to encouraging them with the Lord's continuing commitment to his people (see commentary on 9:1–10:8, under "Theological Insights"), the story should challenge them to focus on the Lord as their King and not to place their faith in human leaders, especially those with only superficial qualifications. Failure to keep their eyes focused on their true King can lead only to more painful discipline.

Teaching the Text

1. *When God's people foolishly embrace cultural norms and reject his authority, he exercises his right to rule his covenant community in a way that is best for them.* As in the previous literary unit, we see God protecting his people from themselves. Samuel warns the people that kingship after the pattern of the nations will ultimately prove to be oppressive (8:11–18), yet Israel insists on having such a king. After initially telling Samuel to give them what they want, the Lord decides to give them a king who is directed to rule in accordance with the Lord's standards (Deut. 17:14–20), which run counter to the cultural norm and are designed to limit the power of the king.

2. *When God's people foolishly seek false security and reject his authority, he may discipline them by letting them experience the consequences of their behavior.* While the Lord protects the people from their lack of foresight, he also decides to discipline them for their lack of commitment. As the story unfolds, it becomes clear that he employs their superficial standard in choosing a king, one that focuses on outward appearances rather than inner qualities. The structure of Samuel's speech suggests that the granting of a king is actually a disciplinary punishment for the people's rejection of God's rule (10:17–19). Saul, the "one asked for," will prove to be a disappointment, and his reign will jeopardize Israel's security and bring the nation precariously close to

The Israelites had a misguided view of kingship. They would have been pleased with attributes such as those represented in the later Assyrian king, Shalmaneser III (858–824 BC), who is depicted in this statue. He was successful in his military excursions to expand the Assyrian Empire and was able to protect its northern borders from the advances of the kingdom of Urartu. In the process, through gathering spoils and collecting tribute, he gathered wealth and resources for the Assyrian Empire, which supported his continued military campaigns and extensive building projects.

disaster. The story illustrates the saying "Be careful what you ask for, because you just might get it!" Even when God displays his mercy, he sometimes disciplines his people for their ultimate good (cf. Heb. 12:7–11). Forgiveness does not necessarily eliminate the need for discipline (see, e.g., Num. 14:17–25; 2 Sam. 12:13–14).

Illustrating the Text

God extends his mercy to those who reject him.

Bible: The Parable of the Prodigal Son, a story of waste, purposelessness, jealousy, and love (Luke 15:11–32); **Hosea and Gomer,** a tale of degradation and restoration. As Jean Fleming puts it in a book called *The Homesick Heart,*

> Neither Gomer nor the prodigal son could see how good they had it at home. It was some craving within that drove them wantonly on. This is the human condition. . . . The high point of these stories . . . is that just when I expect God to lob in hand grenades, he runs to His son, falls on his neck with kisses, and kills the fatted calf for a dinner celebration. When I expect Him to say, Serves you right, or, Fry in hell, He buys Gomer out of slavery and makes her a bride again. . . . [He] Drapes the robe around my shoulders. / Slips the ring on my finger. / And turns *me* toward Home.[7]

Christian Biography: John Newton. This familiar story is, nevertheless, powerful. Though born into a godly home, Newton (1725–1807) sank to the lowest depths of sin—living, he says, a life of "continual godlessness and profanity." His life was spared over and over, but he always forgot the mercy of God. He became a slave trader and then, ironically, a slave himself, sold to a powerful black woman, who tossed him crusts under the table.

Later, Newton feared for his life during a terrible storm. Surrounded by "black, unfathomable despair," he sought enduring mercy and found it. "My prayer for mercy," he wrote, "was like the cry of the ravens, which yet the Lord Jesus does not disdain to hear." He went on to have a great Christian ministry, providing spiritual leadership for England; he wielded power for good in the best of ways and had influence on such great men as Wilberforce and Cowper. He wrote many great hymns, including "How Sweet the Name of Jesus Sounds," "Glorious Things of Thee Are Spoken," and "Amazing Grace."

In the words of the old proverb, "Be careful what you ask for, because you just might get it."

Famous Gaffe: "Everybody was saying we must have more leisure. Now they are complaining they are unemployed." Said by Prince Philip of England at the height of the recession in 1981. This famous gaffe perfectly encapsulates the human dilemma. When we want something and go after it tenaciously or ask for it insistently, we are sometimes very undiscerning about the consequences of what we ask for. We often live to regret the answer to our requests.

Saul's Finest Hour

Big Idea *The Lord alone is his people's Savior and source of security.*

Understanding the Text

The Text in Context

In chapter 10 we read of how the Lord gave Israel a king yet placed limitations on him (v. 25). However, not everyone was pleased with this arrangement or with the Lord's choice of a king (v. 27). Indeed, hesitant Saul appeared to be an unlikely candidate for the job; his apparent qualifications were only superficial. The chapter ends in tension. Would Saul be an effective leader and deliver Israel from their enemies? Would Israel support Saul, or would troublemakers create problems within the nation? Chapter 11 appears to resolve the tension positively: the Lord energizes Saul and enables him to lead Israel to victory. The people wholeheartedly support their new king and renew their allegiance to him. But this initial success proves to be short lived and eventually becomes a tragic reminder of what could have been.

Historical and Cultural Background

The Philistines, who lived along the Mediterranean coast to the west, were certainly a major threat to Israel's security at this time, as chapters 4–7 illustrate (see also 9:16). But there were other threats as well, including the Ammonites, who lived east of the Jordan River. The Ammonites were descendants of Lot by his incestuous relationship with one of his daughters (Gen. 19:38). When Israel approached the promised land, the Lord did not allow them to invade or conquer Ammon; he expected Israel to respect Ammon's territorial boundaries (Deut. 2:19). However, during the judges' period the Ammonites did make war with Israel on occasion. They allied with the Moabite king Eglon (Judg. 3:13) and later crossed the Jordan and threatened the tribes of Judah, Benjamin, and Ephraim (10:9). They also claimed territory east of the Jordan that Israel had taken from the Amorites, arguing that it originally belonged to them (11:13). Now in Saul's time the Ammonites are again creating problems as their king, Nahash (cf. 1 Sam. 12:12), besieges the Israelite Transjordanian town of Jabesh Gilead.[1]

In the scroll of Samuel found in cave 4 at Qumran, an entire additional verse is included at the beginning of 1 Samuel 11. It reads: "Nahash, king of the Ammonites, was oppressing the Gadites and Reubenites severely, and he was boring out every right eye, allowing no one to save Israel. There was no one left among the Israelites across the Jordan whose right eye Nahash, king of the Ammonites, had not bored out. Seven thousand men had escaped from the power of the Ammonites, however, and had come to Jabesh Gilead."[2] Josephus was also aware of this tradition (*Antiquities* 6.68–71). The verse may have been omitted from the original text by accidental scribal error.[3] If it is a reliable historical tradition, then Nahash is engaging in an aggressive imperialistic campaign in Transjordan, designed to bring the entire region under his rule. Indeed, Samuel's speech in chapter 12 declares that it is specifically the military threat posed by Nahash that has prompted Israel to ask for a king in the first place (1 Sam. 12:12).

Interpretive Insights

11:2 *I will . . . gouge out the right eye of every one of you and so bring disgrace on all Israel.* The men of Jabesh Gilead are willing to submit to Nahash's rule by agreeing to a treaty (v. 1). But Nahash is not satisfied with this: he wants to humiliate Israel and incapacitate their warriors by depriving each man of his right eye. There are other instances in the Bible of mutilating (Judg. 1:6) or blinding a defeated enemy (Judg. 16:21; 2 Kings 25:7), but in the latter case both of the victim's eyes are blinded. Nahash wants to humiliate Israel yet at the same

Mutilation of captured prisoners or defeated enemies was common practice in the ancient Near East. Here we see a soldier with his sword poised to cut off his victim's head, while another victim has already lost his hands and feet. These scenes are from the bronze bands that were part of the gates of the palace of Shalmaneser III at Balawat, 858–824 BC.

Key Themes of 1 Samuel 11

- The Lord again demonstrates his ability to deliver his people from their enemies.
- The Lord's supernatural enablement is the key to effective leadership.

time leave his subjects capable of producing tribute for him.[4]

11:3 *Give us seven days.* It may seem peculiar that Nahash agrees to let the men of Jabesh Gilead send for help. However, his decision to do so is probably practical. Rather than conducting a time-consuming siege against the town, he undoubtedly welcomes the opportunity to end this campaign in a mere week and add Jabesh Gilead to his list of subjects. His decision surely presupposes his belief that no one will be willing or even able to organize an

army so quickly and come to the aid of the city. If the longer Qumran text is taken as reliable (see above under "Historical and Cultural Background"), this belief is well founded, for Nahash has already defeated all of the surrounding towns.

11:4 *When the messengers came to Gibeah of Saul.* There apparently is an ancient connection between Jabesh Gilead and Gibeah. After the Israelites defeated Benjamin in the civil war that occurred in the judges' period, they almost wiped out the entire tribe. Only six hundred Benjamite men were left, and the Israelites vowed they would not give their daughters to the survivors as wives. However, when they discovered that Jabesh Gilead had not sent men to the battle, they wiped out the city, kidnapped four hundred virgins, and gave them to the Benjamite survivors as wives (Judg. 21:6–14). So by Saul's time many of the Benjamites could trace their roots to Jabesh Gilead. Surely some of the residents of Jabesh Gilead escaped the earlier atrocity perpetrated against them. Their descendants will still recognize some of the Benjamites as distant relatives.

11:5 *Saul was returning from the fields.* Saul is farming at the time the messengers arrive. It is apparent that he is not serving as a typical king, living in a palace surrounded by a royal court and servants. His actions in this chapter resemble those of the judges, whom God raised up for special occasions. One recalls how Gideon, when he met the Lord, was threshing wheat in a winepress (Judg. 6:11).

11:6 *the Spirit of God came powerfully upon him.* For the second time in the story, God's Spirit comes upon Saul (cf. 1 Sam. 10:10). The same verb (*tsalah*) is used to describe how the Lord's Spirit rushed upon Samson and energized him for conflict (Judg. 14:6, 19; 15:14).

11:7 *and sent the pieces by messengers throughout Israel.* The language is reminiscent of the account in Judges 19–20, the only other place in the Hebrew Bible where the verbs "cut" (*natah*) and "sent" (*shalah*) are used together (Judg. 19:29; 20:6). The author may very well intend that we compare the two stories, especially since Jabesh Gilead plays a significant role in both. Such a comparison yields thematic correlations. In contrast to the Levite, Saul cuts up and sends to the tribes the body parts of a team of oxen, not a murdered woman. He is rallying Israelites to rescue fellow Israelites, rather than to kill their brothers. Furthermore, this event will end with the residents of Jabesh Gilead being delivered, not murdered and kidnapped. The point of the contrast seems to be that a new era has arrived, one in which the nation will be united, not torn apart.[5]

together as one. Again the language (NIV paraphrases MT's "as one man") echoes the account in Judges 20, and again a contrast may be intended. In Judges 20 the tribes unified "as one man" against Gibeah in order to fight against their own brothers (vv. 1, 8, 11 AT). But here Saul, a resident of Gibeah, musters the Israelites "as one man" in order to fight against a foreign enemy and deliver their brothers.[6]

11:13 *the LORD has rescued Israel.* Israel has demanded a king to lead them into battle. As in Gideon's day, the people may be tempted to focus on the Lord's human instrument and forget that ultimately the Lord's power is the key to victory and security (cf. Judg. 7:2; 8:22). To Saul's credit, he does not let this happen. Turning attention away from himself, he acknowledges that the Lord has given the victory. This is a key statement for understanding the primary theme of this chapter. His critics have questioned his ability to "save" Israel (10:27), but Saul's statement is an appropriate response because it reminds them, and everyone, that the Lord, not a human leader (no matter how impressive or unimpressive his appearance), is Israel's defender.[7]

11:14 *renew the kingship.* Contrary to what some source critics have assumed, this is not an alternate Gilgal tradition of Saul's anointing that contradicts the Mizpah tradition recorded in chapter 10. Here Samuel refers to reaffirming, or renewing, the kingship.[8] Elsewhere the Hebrew verb refers to rebuilding or reconstructing what has been marred and describes an action that repeats an earlier one (see 2 Chron. 15:8; 24:4, 12; Job 10:17; Pss. 51:10; 104:30; Isa. 61:4; Lam. 5:21). In Saul's case it is necessary to "renew" the kingship because of the

This map shows the kingdom of Saul (with gold shading), the surrounding territories, and the location of the battle at Jabesh Gilead.

less-than-unanimous support he received after the first ceremony at Mizpah (10:27; 11:12).[9]

Theological Insights

In this chapter the Lord once more displays his ability to deliver his people (see esp. v. 13), just as he has done throughout the judges' period (see 1 Sam. 12:11). Despite Saul's flaws, God empowers him for battle by granting him the enablement of his Spirit, just as he has done for Samson. Though the chapter ends with Saul's being reaffirmed as king, it is apparent that Israel really does not need a king like other nations in order to be secure from their enemies. The threat of Nahash has prompted the people to ask for such a king, but the Lord proves he is capable of protecting them apart from a standing army. He is Israel's true Savior and King, and the people must remember that, no matter how impressive or successful his human instruments may be. For the exiles, this account is yet another reminder that the Lord is fully capable of delivering them and making them secure, even when they have no human king. Victory and security are accomplished "not by might nor by power," but by the Lord's Spirit (Zech. 4:6).

Teaching the Text

1. *The Lord is fully capable of delivering his people from their enemies and must be the sole object of his people's trust.* We human beings have a tendency to walk by sight rather than faith. When faced with imposing, tangible enemies, we are inclined to seek tangible, flesh-and-blood solutions and look to human leaders for deliverance and security. But Israel's history shows that this is foolish. Beginning at the Red Sea, Israel was almost always militarily inferior to the nations who threatened them. Yet the

Lord repeatedly delivered them from their enemies, proving his infinite superiority to kings and their armies. He is a mighty warrior King who devastates human rulers and armaments (Exod. 15:3–4; Judg. 5:19–21; Pss. 48:4–7; 68:12; 76:6; 136:17–18; Prov. 21:31). When Israel faces the threat of Nahash the Ammonite, they think they need a human king with a standing army to protect them, but the Lord proves he can defeat the enemy, working through a Spirit-empowered farmer (1 Sam. 11:5–6, 13). The principle is clear: the Lord alone is the Savior of his people (Ps. 20:7), and he is able and willing to deliver his faithful servants (Ps. 33:10–22). Israel needs to remember this in the time of Samuel and later when they find themselves in exile. But the principle is timeless, and God's covenant community in the present era will also do well to appropriate it.

2. *God's supernatural enablement is the key to effective spiritual leadership.* While the Lord is always the true King and Savior of his people, he often uses human instruments to accomplish his purposes and protect his people. Like ancient Israel, we are prone to focus on the human instrument and choose leaders according to our superficial, human standards. As Saul's example illustrates, the key to effective leadership is not one's outward appearance or some other quality that impresses or attracts us. Rather, it is God's supernatural enablement. Saul has been acclaimed king (10:24), but he hardly seems up to the task. He has failed to initiate military action against the Philistines, and he tries to avoid being publicly selected as king. When the messengers arrive from Jabesh Gilead, we find him doing the work of a farmer, not a king, much like

Gideon of old (Judg. 6:11). But once God's Spirit energizes him, he acts decisively, uniting the people and displaying impressive military strategy. The key to his success is God's supernatural enablement, not his physical attributes or his status as the newly acclaimed king. Unfortunately, Saul will soon get out of step with the divine Spirit and forfeit God's enabling power (1 Sam. 16:14). That power will be transferred to another, whose inner character is predisposed to obey God (13:14).

Illustrating the Text

The Lord is capable of delivering his people from threatening enemies.

Quote: *Real Presences*, by George Steiner. Steiner (b. 1929) is an influential American literary critic, essayist, philosopher, novelist, and translator. In this book (1991) he expresses the powerful reality that no matter what evil befalls God's people, there is hope. Though experiences may leave them feeling abandoned, as in the Saturday after Good Friday, yet God's people await the liberation, rebirth, and deliverance that will follow. "Ours is the long day's journey of the Saturday. Between suffering, aloneness, unutterable waste on the one hand and the dream of liberation, of rebirth on the other."[10]

God supernaturally enables weak and unlikely instruments.

Christian Biography: **Samuel Kaboo Morris.** Morris (1873–93), a nineteenth-century Liberian prince, converted to Christianity when he was about fourteen. Sometime after his conversion but before he left for the United States, he was captured by a tribe who cruelly tortured him. Knowing he would likely die if he stayed there, he managed a miraculous escape and was taken in by another former slave.

The young man's dream was to go to America, to learn more about God and the Holy Spirit—a particular interest—so that he could return to Liberia to teach. Finally he was hired on board a trading ship as a sailor, where he was again abused cruelly. By the time the ship reached America, because of his influence, the crew was praying and singing hymns. Samuel Morris's prayer life was legendary, and his effective witness for Christ was notable, even in a very racist time. Through a series of circumstances, he ended up at Taylor University in Indiana, but within two years he died of complications of a respiratory infection. His life has been the subject of five novels, over a dozen biographies, and a 1954 film. Taylor University has named numerous buildings, scholarships, and a society in his honor. A great deal of information about him is available on the web, including pictures and film clips.

Samuel Confronts the People

Big Idea *The security of God's covenant people depends on their allegiance to the Lord, who remains committed to them.*

Understanding the Text

The Text in Context

This chapter provides a fitting conclusion to the story of Saul's accession to kingship. Facing a serious military threat from the Ammonites (12:12), Israel demanded a king like all the nations, for they thought such a king, supported by a standing army, would give them the security they so desperately needed (8:19–20). When the time came to choose this king, the Lord made it clear he was not going to give them what they wanted. He would give them a leader to deliver them from their enemies (9:16–17), but the king would be subject to the "regulations of kingship" provided in the law (10:25 AT; cf. Deut. 17:14–20). Saul, the Lord's chosen king, appeared qualified by superficial, human standards, but his failure to take military action against the Philistine garrison (10:1–13) and his hesitancy to accept his divine calling (10:22) were cause for alarm and skepticism (10:27). Yet the divine Spirit energized Saul for battle, and he defeated the Ammonites (11:6–11). Saul gave the Lord credit for the victory, and the people, led by Samuel, reaffirmed Saul's kingship (11:13–14).

Though chapter 11 ends with a great celebration complete with fellowship offerings, Samuel recognizes that much remains to be said. Although Saul makes it clear that the Lord has rescued the people (11:13), Israel is prone to attribute God's great deeds to his human instruments (see Judg. 7:2; 8:22) and trust in the latter for their security. Furthermore, the people, who are simply thinking according to the cultural norm of the surrounding nations, have not yet come to grips with the fact that they have rebelled against God's authority in asking for a king. So it is necessary to clarify these issues. Samuel confronts the people in a formal, legal manner and challenges them to renew their covenantal relationship with the Lord.

Historical and Cultural Background

The Lord verifies Samuel's prophetic authority and message by sending thunder and rain at the time of the wheat harvest (vv. 17–18). Wheat is harvested in May–June, after the winter rains. A thunderstorm during harvest is such a rare occurrence that the people are forced to recognize it as a sign. Furthermore, it is an ominous sign, for a storm can ruin the crop, especially if accompanied by hail (see Prov. 26:1).[1] The Hebrew terms translated "thunder" and "rain" appear together elsewhere only in Exodus 9:23, 33, a passage that tells how the Lord sent thunder, rain, and hail to destroy the Egyptians' crops.

Interpretive Insights

12:1 *have set a king over you.* The Lord has instructed Samuel to "listen" to all that the people are demanding (8:7) and to "give" them the king they want (8:22). On the surface, one might think that Samuel is claiming here that he has done this ("set a king" in 12:1 and "give . . . a king" in 8:22 translate the same verb). However, in chapter 9 the Lord makes it clear he is not going to give them the *kind* of king they want, complete with an institutionalized state structure and standing army (vv. 16–17). On the contrary, the Lord makes the king subject to regulations designed to prevent him from being like foreign kings (10:25). In chapters 9–10 both the Lord and Samuel avoid using the verb *malak*, "to rule," or the noun *melek*, "king," in referring to this ruler (9:16–17; 10:1, 24), except when Samuel quotes the people (10:19). But here Samuel uses these terms, reflecting the perspective of the people (8:5, 19–20; 10:24), just as the narrator does in 11:15.

However, there is a telling omission here: Samuel does not say that he has given them a king "like all the nations." Surely the people know that the Lord has only partially acceded to their original request, for Samuel has explained the regulations of kingship to the people (10:25). So perhaps we should understand "everything" in verse 1 as overstated for the purpose of Samuel's legal self-defense, or as assuming the qualifications placed on the king by the Lord. Perhaps we could paraphrase: "Within the limitations placed on kingship by the LORD, I have fully acceded to your demand for a king."

12:5 *you have not found anything in my hand.* Samuel's self-defense, with which the people readily agree, is important in the narrator's strategy of presenting Samuel as the Lord's chosen leader and as one who is fully qualified to anoint Israel's king.

12:11 *and he delivered you.* Samuel reminds the people that the Lord has delivered them from their enemies "all around." In so doing, he drives home the

Harvesting wheat is still done by hand in parts of Israel today.

point, already made by Saul in 11:13, that the Lord is ultimately Israel's Savior. Their national security depends on him, not on a human leader, institutionalized state, or standing army.

12:12 *even though the LORD your God was your king.* The Lord assumed kingship over Israel at Sinai (Deut. 33:5). He led his people into the land of Canaan with the intention of ruling over them forever (Exod. 15:18). As their king, the Lord has proved his ability to deliver them from their enemies (1 Sam. 12:11). And as their history demonstrates, their national security depends solely on their allegiance to the Lord (v. 10).

12:13 *here is the king you have chosen.* When Samuel earlier presented Saul to the people, he described him as the one whom the Lord had chosen (10:24), echoing the language of Deuteronomy 17:15. But here the language echoes Samuel's earlier

statement, when he spoke of the "king" whom the people chose (8:18). There is something foreboding about this. While the Lord intended to place limitations on kingship (10:25; cf. Deut. 17:14–20), in Saul he gives them the impressive-looking king who fits their criteria. Furthermore, despite the Lord's restraints, kingship will eventually evolve into something much like Samuel's description in 8:11–18.

12:14 *If you fear the LORD and serve.* The combination of the verbs "fear" and "serve" echoes the commands of Moses (Deut. 6:13; 10:20) and Joshua (Josh. 24:14). The words are repeated as a double command in verse 24, with added emphasis (see the note below). It is apparent that the Lord, despite granting Israel a king, remains sovereign over his covenant people and expects them to renew their covenantal allegiance to him.

and do not rebel. This command recalls the rebellion of Moses, Aaron, and Israel that prevented all the concerned parties from entering the land of promise (Num. 20:24; 27:14; Deut. 1:26, 43; 9:23). If this new generation rebels against the Lord,

In Samuel's speech to the Israelites, he reminds them of God's faithful deliverance through Barak after they had been oppressed by the Canaanite army and the chariots of Sisera. The plain below Mount Tabor (shown here) was the setting for God's victory as he sent a mighty rainstorm, rendering the chariots useless and providing Barak's forces with the upper hand and military success.

they too will experience his punishment (vv. 15, 25).

12:15 *his hand will be against you.* Prior to this the Lord's "hand" (power) has been directed against the Philistines (5:9; 7:13), but rebellion against his commands will thrust Israel into the role of his enemy, and they will experience his opposition.

12:16 *stand still and see.* Before this the only time these two Hebrew verbs have been juxtaposed is in Exodus 14:13, where Moses, just before dividing the water of the Red Sea, commands the people to pay attention and witness the Lord's mighty saving power. On this occasion as well, the Lord will display his great power.

12:18 *So all the people stood in awe of the Lord and of Samuel.* By stating that the people fear both the Lord and Samuel, the narrator once more establishes Samuel's credentials as the Lord's representative.[2] The point of the sign is to verify the truth of Samuel's accusation (vv. 12, 19–20).

12:19 *Pray to the Lord your God.* The narrator enhances Samuel's credentials by portraying him as the nation's intercessor (see the note at 7:5). By using the words "your God," the people acknowledge Samuel's close relationship to God and express their sense of alienation from the Lord.

12:21 *nor can they rescue you.* Earlier Samuel used this same verb (*natsal*) when he promised Israel that the Lord would "deliver" his people from their enemies if they put away the foreign gods they were serving (7:3). He also quoted the Lord as saying that he had "delivered" Israel from Egypt and their other enemies (10:18). Now he reminds the people that useless idols cannot save them. The word translated "useless" (*tohu*) is used elsewhere of an empty

wasteland or desert. It refers to that which is nonfunctional and nonproductive; as such it is an appropriate term to describe idols.

12:23 *far be it from me that I should sin.* Again the narrator casts Samuel in a positive light as one who fulfills his responsibility as intercessor by praying for the people and instructing them in "the way that is good and right." As far as Samuel is concerned, to do anything less is sin.

12:24 *But be sure to fear the Lord and serve him faithfully with all your heart.* Samuel again urges the people to fear and serve the Lord (see v. 14), but here he adds emphasis by attaching the words "faithfully with all your heart." The words "serve faithfully" echo Joshua's command to Israel (Josh. 24:14), and the idea of serving with all of one's heart (or will) is expressed in Deuteronomy (10:12; 11:13) as well as by Joshua (Josh. 22:5).

Theological Insights

The kingship crisis is resolved—the Lord gives the people a king, but not like the kings of the other nations. They do not really need a king in order to be secure, for the Lord has demonstrated his ability to deliver them from their enemies throughout their history, including the most recent threat. The people have violated their covenant with the Lord at the most fundamental level by not believing in him in the radical, countercultural manner he expects. Yet the Lord does not reject them and is willing to restore his covenantal relationship with them. His prophetic agent, Samuel, challenges the nation to obey the Lord and warns the people of the consequences of disobedience. The Lord even gives them a vivid sign to validate Samuel's accusation against them, prompting them to confess their sin in asking for a king. They appeal to Samuel as the nation's intercessor, and he promises to pray for them and to instruct them in the ways of the Lord. The narrator further enhances Samuel's credentials as the Lord's representative and makes it clear that the people and their king remain subject to Samuel's authority, which is derived from the Lord. This sets a pattern for the future: Israel's kings are to be subject to the Lord's prophetic revelation.

For the exiles this account is of supreme importance, for their fathers, like ancient Israel in the time of Samuel, have rejected God and broken the Mosaic covenant. They have experienced the fulfillment of Samuel's prophetic warning: both they and their king have been swept away into exile. But this account demonstrates God's unswerving covenantal commitment to his people. In combination with prophetic messages such as Isaiah 40–55, it encourages them by reminding them of the Lord's faithfulness. As a nation that is subject to foreign rule and no longer has a human king sitting on David's throne in Jerusalem, they can still find encouragement, because this account reminds them that the Lord, not a human ruler, is the one who provides security for his people. Yet Samuel's speech makes it clear that security is not automatic. Like Israel in Samuel's time, the exiles need to renew their allegiance to God by confessing their sin, obeying the Lord's commands, and rejecting the worthless idols of the nations.

Teaching the Text

1. *Even when his people rebel, the Lord offers them security in exchange for their re-* *newed covenantal allegiance to him.* God's people often sin against him and need restoration. The Lord offers cleansing from sin in exchange for repentance (1 John 1:9). He expects those who have received his mercy to demonstrate their loyalty by obeying his commandments, the greatest of which is to love one another (John 15:9–17).

2. *The Lord remains faithful to his covenantal commitment, even when his people prove unworthy.* The Lord's willingness to forgive his people and restore them to a covenantal relationship derives from his faithful character. Samuel indicates that the Lord will not reject his people, because his reputation as a faithful God is at stake (1 Sam. 12:22). One sees this theme elsewhere in the Old Testament. The most famous psalm of all affirms that God providentially guides and protects his people "for his name's sake" (Ps. 23:3). When the Lord threatened to destroy Israel, Moses interceded for the nation, reminding the Lord that his reputation as a covenant-keeping God was at stake and could be harmed if he followed through on his threat (Exod. 32:9–14). The Lord relented. In addressing the exiles, the Lord promises he will deliver them for his "own name's sake," despite their rebellion (Isa. 48:9, 11). Indeed, the Lord has shown mercy to Israel throughout their rebellious history for the sake of his own name (Ezek. 20:9, 14, 22; cf. Ps. 106:8) and promises to continue to do so in the future (Ezek. 20:44). In interceding for the people, Jeremiah appeals to the Lord's concern for his own reputation (Jer. 14:7, 21). Several psalms appeal to God on the basis of his reputation (Pss. 25:11; 31:3; 79:9; 109:21; 143:11).

Illustrating the Text

The Lord is willing to restore his relationship with those who have rebelled against him.

Poetry: "Hymn to God the Father," by John Donne. The biography and poems of Donne (1572–1631) are worth perusing. Having earlier in his life made a religious commitment, he fell away and spent some time in open rebellion against God before becoming a devout Christian, a prominent metaphysical poet, and an eloquent preacher. This experience is reflected in this poem, found in his *Poetical Works* (215).

> Wilt Thou forgive that sin where I
>   begun,
>   Which was my sin, though it
>   were done before?
> Wilt Thou forgive that sin, through
>   which I run,
>   And do run still, though still I do
>   deplore?
>   When Thou hast done, Thou
>   hast not done,
>   For I have more.
> Wilt Thou forgive that sin which I
>   have won
>   Others to sin, and made my sin
>   their door?
> Wilt Thou forgive that sin which I
>   did shun
>   A year or two, but wallowed in a
>   score?
>   When Thou hast done, Thou
>   hast not done,
>   For I have more.
> I have a sin of fear, that when I have
>   spun
> My last thread, I shall perish on
>   the shore;
> But swear by Thyself, that at my
>   death Thy Son
> Shall shine as he shines now, and
>   heretofore;
> And having done that, Thou hast
>   done;
> I fear no more.

The Lord is faithful to his people even when they go astray.

Literature: *The Lion, the Witch and the Wardrobe*, by C. S. Lewis. One episode in Lewis's (1898–1963) familiar children's tale (1950), which is also completely delightful for adults, is memorable as an instance of God's faithfulness to sinners. Edmund, one of the four children who make their way into Narnia, is a disgruntled child, a condition that makes him vulnerable to the seductions of the evil White Witch, who has taken charge of Narnia. "She could make things look like what they aren't" (152). Consumed with himself, Edmund falls prey to her deceit (in chap. 4). Eventually he sees that the seduction is just that—empty and dangerous, not only to him but also to his siblings. He begins to see his selfishness, and his heart softens; in the mercy of Aslan (the Christ figure), he is brought back to his siblings; his temperament is transformed. Finally we read that Edmund is "looking all the time at Aslan's face" (156) and has "got past thinking about himself" (155). Aslan kindly takes him aside and speaks to him, but no one ever knows what was said. However, Edmund is forever afterward a wise and good king.[3]

Saul Forfeits a Dynasty

Big Idea *God's people can forfeit their privilege and blessing by foolishly disobeying the Lord's word.*

Understanding the Text

The Text in Context

As chapter 12 concludes, one hopes and may even expect that Saul will succeed. After all, empowered by the Lord's Spirit, he defeated the Ammonites, and the rebellious people responded positively to Samuel's call to covenantal renewal. Yet there was unfinished business. The Ammonites have been defeated, but the Philistine problem remains. The Lord announced to Samuel that the new king would deliver Israel from the Philistine threat (9:16). When Samuel commissioned Saul, he indicated that Saul, once empowered by the Lord's Spirit, should take action against the Philistines, then proceed to Gilgal and wait for Samuel to arrive and give him further instructions (10:5–8). But Saul aborted the plan by *not* attacking the Philistines (10:13). So one wonders if Saul, emboldened by his success against the Ammonites, will now initiate a campaign against the Philistines.

In chapter 13 the scenario envisioned by Samuel back in chapter 10 begins to unfold. Saul's son Jonathan attacks the Philistine outpost,[1] prompting Saul to gather his troops at Gilgal while the Philistines prepare to launch an attack against Israel. Suddenly Saul finds himself in the situation foreseen by Samuel, waiting for the prophet to come to Gilgal. Samuel's command has been clear: Saul is to wait seven days for Samuel to arrive, when the prophet will offer the appropriate sacrifices and give the king further instructions (10:8). Though some time may have passed, Saul realizes he is in the very situation foretold by Samuel (13:8, 11). But when Samuel delays his coming, Saul goes ahead and offers the sacrifice, bringing divine judgment upon himself. This account ends with the prophet's announcing the termination of Saul's dynasty and the Lord's choice of a new leader. For the first time, the narrator reveals his pro-David agenda in a direct manner, though the name of Saul's successor is withheld for the present.

As noted above (see 2:12–36), the rejection of Saul's dynasty has been foreshadowed in the story of the fall of Eli's house. The rejection of Eli's priestly dynasty in favor of a new one established a pattern that is repeated with Saul. Just as God withdrew his promise of dynastic succession from Eli and gave it to another (2:30–36), so he will do with Saul (13:13–14). The house of Saul will not be able to appeal to God's election as unconditional, for Eli's experience has demonstrated that disobedience can result in forfeiture of the divine promise. The Lord has the sovereign right to reject rebels and to accomplish his purposes through other and more-worthy instruments.

Historical and Cultural Background

The Hebrew text of verse 1 is notoriously difficult and probably textually corrupt.[2] It reads, "Saul was a son of a year [one year old!] when he became king, and he reigned for two years over Israel." Some ancient Greek textual witnesses omit the entire verse. How old was Saul when he became king? According to 1 Samuel 9:2, he was a "young man" when he met Samuel. The Syriac version indicates he was twenty-one years old when he became king, while some Greek witnesses read "thirty years old," perhaps on analogy with David (see 2 Sam. 5:4). How long did Saul reign? The

NIV has "reigned . . . forty-two years," appealing for support (see the margin) to Acts 13:21, which says he reigned for forty years (a figure that finds support from Josephus, though he says forty years in one place but twenty in another). The NIV has apparently taken the figure given in Acts as a rounded number and then combined it with the "two" in the Hebrew text.

Interpretive Insights

13:3 *Jonathan attacked the Philistine outpost.* To appreciate what happens here, we must go back to chapter 10. See above, under "The Text in Context."

13:5 *chariots . . . charioteers.* The mention of the Philistines' numerous chariots

The Philistine army camped at Mikmash, perhaps located at the modern Arab village of Mukhmas. This photo shows the area around modern Mukhmas.

and charioteers recalls the Red Sea crossing, when the Lord destroyed Pharaoh's many chariots and charioteers and demonstrated his ability to deliver his people (Exod. 14:9, 17–18, 23, 26, 28; 15:19; Josh. 24:6).

as numerous as the sand on the seashore. The description of the Philistine army is reminiscent of the Canaanite coalition that attacked Joshua (Josh. 11:4) and the Midianite horde that opposed Gideon (Judg. 7:12). In both of those cases, the Lord gave Israel a complete victory (Josh. 11:8; Judg. 7:22).

13:6 *they hid in caves.* This reaction by the Israelite army recalls Judges 6:2, which describes a similar reaction to the Midianite invaders.

13:7 *were quaking with fear.* This appears to be yet another allusion to the Gideon story. The description of Saul's fearful army is reminiscent of Gideon's troops (Judg. 7:1, 3).

13:8 *He waited seven days, the time set by Samuel; but Samuel did not come to Gilgal.* Some argue that Samuel does arrive within the specified time,[3] but this seems unlikely. By using the precise wording of 10:8 ("wait seven days") and then identifying this as "the time set by Samuel," the narrator seems to emphasize that Saul does indeed wait for the specified period. Saul's statement in verse 11, which uses the same term (*mo'ed*) for the set time, appears to be technically correct, even though Samuel arrives just as Saul finishes the offering. Saul's sin is not that he offers the sacrifice prematurely (because he does wait until the time set by Samuel is up). His sin is that he disrespects Samuel's authority by offering the sacrifice himself. In 10:8 Samuel makes it clear that he himself is the one who will offer the sacrifice and give Saul his orders. Samuel's earlier statement does not imply that a tardy arrival gives Saul the authority to do as he pleases. That is sheer presumption, born out of panic (see vv. 11–13).

13:12 *So I felt compelled to offer the burnt offering.* The longer Saul waits, the more men are deserting (vv. 8, 11). The Philistine troops are massed for battle and can attack at any moment. If that happens, Saul does not want to be in a position where he has not "sought the LORD's favor" (the Hebrew word may carry the idea of "appease" here; see *HALOT*, 317). On closer inspection, Saul's viewpoint is flawed in at least three important ways: (1) His concern about his dwindling forces reveals a belief that human armies, not the Lord, will decide the battle (in this regard recall Judg. 7). (2) His concern with offering a sacrifice reveals a faulty theology that elevates ritual above obedience (see 15:22–23) and tends to think that ritual can in some way guarantee divine favor. (3) Saul oversteps his bounds.[4] He is the king, but he is under the authority of the prophet-priest Samuel, who is the intercessor for the nation (cf. 7:7–11; 12:18–19, 23).[5] In Deuteronomy 17–18, where the regulations of Israelite kingship are given (17:14–20; cf. 1 Sam. 10:25), the king's role is clearly distinguished from that of the priests (Deut. 18:1–13) and the prophets (18:14–22). As noted above, Samuel has made it clear that he will offer the sacrifices (cf. 10:8) and that he, in his prophetic capacity, will give the king instructions. Even the girls whom Saul met when he entered Samuel's town recognized Samuel's authority in this regard (9:13). Ironically, their statement that "the people will not begin eating until" Samuel the man

of God / seer (cf. 9:10–11) arrives to "bless the sacrifice" anticipates Saul's failure to obey Samuel. This lack of respect for the prophetic office subsequently becomes a major issue in Israel and a prominent theme in the Former Prophets.

13:13 *You have done a foolish thing.* Samuel charges Saul with foolish behavior. The verb used here can refer to unwise actions (2 Sam. 15:31), but it can also describe, as here, sinful behavior (1 Sam. 26:21; 2 Sam. 24:10).

You have not kept the command. Samuel accuses Saul of disobeying the Lord's command that he should wait for Samuel to offer the sacrifices and give him instructions (10:8). The importance of keeping (obeying) the Lord's command(s) is a prominent theme in Deuteronomy (4:2; 5:10, 29; 6:17; 7:9, 11; 8:2, 6, 11; 10:13; 11:8, 22; 13:18; 19:9; 26:17–18; 27:1; 28:9, 15, 45; 30:10, 16); it also appears in Joshua 22:3, 5.

13:14 *a man after his own heart.* The new leader appointed by the Lord is described as "a man after [or, "according to"] his [the Lord's] own heart." In light of the contextual emphasis on Saul's disobedience, this expression probably means "like-minded," that is, "committed to obey the Lord's commands" (cf. Acts 13:22). Long shows that the statement "You have acted foolishly" is balanced by and contrasted with "sought out a man after his own heart" in the structure of verses 13–14.[6] This suggests that the latter refers to a character quality of the new king. Furthermore, the phrase "according to your heart" is used in 14:7 by Jonathan's armor-bearer to emphasize that he is "with" Jonathan in "heart and soul," that is, loyal to Jonathan and committed to whatever Jonathan decides to do.[7]

appointed him ruler. The Lord announces that he will terminate Saul's royal dynasty and replace him with another whom he has "appointed." The verb translated "appointed" (*tsiwwah*) is also used in verse 13 to describe the command that the Lord "gave" (or "commanded") to Saul, and in verse 14 of the command that Saul has "not kept." (The last statement in v. 14 reads, "for you have not kept that which the LORD commanded you" [AT].) The irony is apparent. Because Saul did not obey what the Lord commanded, the Lord has commanded (or decreed) that someone else should occupy the position of ruler over Israel.[8] The use of the word "ruler" (*nagid*), rather than "king," harks back to the Lord's announcement to Samuel in 9:16 and Samuel's commission to Saul (10:1; see "Theological Insights" under 1 Sam. 9–10 above). The use of the term here is rhetorically charged: it should remind Saul that the king is under the Lord's (and his prophet's) authority and is not permitted to freelance.

Theological Insights

In the face of what seems like overwhelming odds against him, Saul panics. As the Philistines assemble for battle and 80 percent of Saul's army deserts because of fear (13:5–7),[9] he apparently fails to recall how the Lord delivered Israel at the Red Sea, again in the time of Gideon, more recently at Ebenezer (1 Sam. 7), and in his own campaign against the Ammonites (1 Sam. 11).

Saul fails to respect Samuel's authority. He disobeys Samuel's prophetic word and oversteps his bounds by assuming Samuel's prophetic-priestly office. This conflict between prophet and king will escalate throughout Israel's history. By disregarding the prophetic command and office, Saul forfeits the royal dynasty that could have been his (13:13–14). This was already foreshadowed by the rejection of Eli's house and the announcement of a new priestly dynasty. God rejected Eli's priestly dynasty and transferred leadership to another (2:30–36); he will do the same to Saul. Saul's descendants should not assume that God's choice of Saul is unconditional, becaus God's rejection of Eli proved that rebels can forfeit God's promise. The Lord has the authority and right to set aside those who disobey and replace them with those who are more worthy.

This account of the rejection of Saul's royal dynasty is relevant to the exiles. As they anticipate a time when the Lord will restore their nation, this account confirms the prophets' message that the Davidic dynasty will be restored and a Davidic king will be the rightful ruler of Israel. At a more fundamental level the account also reminds the exiles of the importance of obeying the Lord's commands. Their forebears, like Saul, have indeed disobeyed the law and have forfeited, at least for a time, the privileged position they have enjoyed as God's covenantal people and the blessings that he has promised in exchange for their loyalty and obedience (see Deut. 28).

Teaching the Text

1. *The Lord expects his chosen leaders to obey his prophetic command.* Israel's king is to be a model of obedience to God's law (Deut. 17:18–20; see also Ps. 101). He, of all people, is responsible to keep God's command to the letter. In the same way, leaders in the New Testament church are to be beyond reproach (Titus 1:5–9; 1 Pet. 5:1–4). However, this passage is not limited to leaders in its application. Leaders then and now are paradigms for the covenant community. God's people are to follow their example of faith and obedience (Phil. 3:17; 1 Tim. 4:11–16; Titus 2:7–8; 1 Pet. 5:2–3).

2. *Disobedience can result in the loss of privilege and blessing.* As we saw with Eli (see 2:12–36 above), the Lord expects his servants to be loyal and obedient. Being called to a special position, as were Eli and Saul, does not make one immune from di-

vine discipline. From everyone to whom much is given, much is required (Amos 3:2; Luke 12:48). God sometimes makes promises to those whom he chooses, but often these promises are contingent upon continued loyalty. Rather than being guarantees that give the recipients a license to act as they wish, these promises should motivate continued obedience.

Illustrating the Text

Strong leaders can influence the people under their authority positively or negatively.

History: Jim Jones. Jones (1931–78) was the founder and leader of a group called the People's Temple, best known for its November 18, 1978, mass suicide of more than nine hundred of its members in Jonestown, Guyana, an event that shocked the world. Five other people, including a US congressperson leading a delegation to investigate the camp, were also killed at a nearby airstrip. Jones was born in Indiana, where he started the Temple in the 1950s. The group later relocated to California and gained notoriety with the move of the headquarters to San Francisco in the mid-1970s. The tragedy in Guyana ranks among the largest mass murders/suicides in history.

Christian Biography: D. L. Moody. Moody (1837–99) started from humble roots (he was poor, fatherless, minimally educated), became a shoe salesman early in life, was converted, then moved to Chicago. There he went into business and also became a lay pastor. Eventually he gave up business to go into full-time ministry. Moody was one of the great personalities of the nineteenth century, Christian and secular; his Christian influence was widespread, and his name continues to be remembered through the institutions of which he was a part. He knew many of the prominent Chicago businessmen of his time, and some of them contributed to his ministry. He carried on notable revival meetings in England and America and organized training for men and women, paying special heed to those who had little opportunity to succeed. Finally, he led in the founding of Moody Bible Institute in Chicago.

Deficient faith coupled with a faulty/pagan view of the Lord robs God's people of his blessing.

Quote: A. W. Tozer. "Christianity is so entangled with the world that millions never guess how radically they have missed the New Testament pattern. Compromise is everywhere. The world is whitewashed just enough to pass inspection by blind men posing as believers, and these same believers are everlastingly seeking to gain acceptance with the world. By mutual concessions men who call themselves Christians manage to get on with men who have for the things of God nothing but quiet contempt."[10]

Church History: As an example of this principle, one could address a particular heresy invading the church in the guise of orthodoxy—one contemporary with the preaching of this passage.

Jonathan's Faith Ignites a Victory

Big Idea *Faith in the Lord's great power can be the catalyst for his saving intervention.*

Understanding the Text

The Text in Context

After announcing the demise of Saul's dynasty, Samuel departs, leaving Saul alone with a mere six hundred troops to face the Philistine army (1 Sam. 13:15). The situation appears to be bleak, especially when the narrator informs us that the Israelite troops are ill equipped for battle due to a Philistine monopoly on iron (vv. 19–22). But sometimes crisis is the seedbed for heroism. Saul's son Jonathan, empowered by his faith in the Lord's ability to deliver his people, steps forward and ignites the battle (14:1–14). The Lord causes the Philistines to panic and gives Israel a great victory (vv. 15–23). While inspiring, the account is tragically ironic. Jonathan possesses unhesitating, courageous faith and would make a fine king for Israel, but we know from the preceding account that Saul has already forfeited his dynasty, and we suspect that Jonathan

will never realize his full potential. Furthermore, Saul continues to display his flawed character (vv. 18–19), which quickly dilutes the victory and even jeopardizes his son's life (vv. 24–46), much like Jephthah has done (see Judg. 11). Despite his heroism and faith, Jonathan ends up being a mere literary foil for his father and never ascends to the role of a main character in the narrative or to the throne of Israel.[1] Though he is

> Archaeological excavations at Tel Qasile in Tel Aviv have uncovered a Philistine settlement dated to the Iron Age (twelfth to tenth century BC). Two clay smelting crucibles were found near the circular kiln shown in this photo, evidence of a bronze-casting workshop. This supports the observation in 1 Samuel 13:19–21 that the Philistines had established metalworking facilities during the time of Saul.

superior to Saul in character, his destiny is linked with his father's, and they eventually die together on the battlefield (1 Sam. 31).

Interpretive Insights

13:16 *Saul and his son Jonathan.* The reference to Jonathan as Saul's son is ironic in light of the fact that the Lord has just rejected Saul's dynasty (vv. 13–14). Earlier in the chapter, Jonathan is mentioned twice (vv. 2–3) but not identified as Saul's son. The narrator waits to identify him as such until after Samuel's announcement, as if to draw attention to the tragic dimension of Saul's sin. Jonathan has proved (v. 3) and will again prove (14:1–14) that he would make a worthy successor to his father, but sadly this will never be.[2]

14:3 *Ahijah, who was wearing an ephod.* Jonathan prepares to ignite a battle against the Philistines (v. 1), but Saul remains inactive, apparently waiting for an oracle from God (v. 3 refers to the ephod).[3] It is ironic that a priestly descendant of Eli is with Saul, for we have here a king whose dynasty is doomed (13:13–14) collaborating with a priest whose dynasty was doomed (2:30–36).[4]

14:6 *Perhaps the LORD will act in our behalf.* Jonathan respects the Lord's sovereign freedom, but he still takes the initiative to act, with the confidence that the Lord is capable of delivering with even a few. Saul panics when his troops are dwindling, but Jonathan has unwavering, contagious faith in the Lord's power (v. 7).

14:10 *that will be our sign.* The narrator's earlier description of both the Philistine army and Israel's response to it invites us to recall the Midianite crisis faced by Gideon (see the comments on 13:5–7). But

Key Themes of 1 Samuel 13:16–14:23

- In response to Jonathan's faith, the Lord once more demonstrates his ability to deliver Israel from their enemies.
- The Lord is an invincible warrior and can deliver by many or by a few.

unlike Gideon, who needs a sign to buttress his wavering faith before he engages the enemy (Judg. 7:13–14), Jonathan is eager to engage the enemy. His waiting for a sign reflects his desire not to be presumptuous (see v. 6), yet we can tell that Jonathan is just itching to spring into action. Furthermore, his choice of a sign reflects his faith: he assumes that God will be in this business even if the task seems impossible (vv. 8–10).[5] From a human perspective, two men climbing up a cliff to fight with several soldiers waiting for them when they arrive at the top appears to be the height of foolishness, but Jonathan is assessing the situation from the perspective of faith.

the LORD has given them into our hands. Jonathan uses a perfect verbal form, indicating completed action, to describe what the Lord *will* do. This rhetorical use of the verb highlights his certainty of victory because of his faith in God's power. It also echoes the battle cry of Ehud (Judg. 3:28), as well as Deborah's assuring word to Barak (Judg. 4:14) and Gideon's charge to his troops once he received assurance of victory (Judg. 7:15).

14:15 *It was a panic sent by God.* In the Hebrew text the noun translated "panic" occurs twice and its verbal root once. The repetition emphasizes the supernatural fear that the Lord sends upon the Philistines and also highlights the reversal that the Lord has produced. Before the battle, the Israelites are "quaking with fear," but when the Lord intervenes, the Philistines are overcome with terror. ("Quaking with fear" in 13:7 translates the verb *harad*, reused in 14:15 as a verb and in its noun form as "panic.")

14:16 *saw the army melting away.* Prior to this the verb translated "melting away" appears only in Exodus 15:15 and Joshua 2:9, 24, where it describes the fear of the Canaanites at the news of the Lord's great victory over the Egyptians at the Red Sea. Its use here may emphasize the extent of the Lord's victory, placing it in the category of the exodus event. (The depiction of the Philistine army is reminiscent of the description of Pharaoh's army; see the comment on 13:5 above.)

14:18 *Bring the ark of God.* Saul's hesitant inactivity contrasts with Jonathan's aggressive attack. His preoccupation with what he perceives to be proper prebattle ritual causes an unnecessary delay. Saul's behavior is true to form. Apparently he feels the need to consult the Lord before attacking, even though it is obvious that the Lord is already at work (v. 16). As noted above (see 13:1–15, under "The Text in Context"), this account is literarily linked to 10:7–8. Saul is in the situation described by Samuel at the time of his commissioning and has had the opportunity to carry out Samuel's earlier orders (10:7). Now his son Jonathan has already set in motion the attack envisioned by Samuel. Though ordinarily it is proper to consult the Lord, here it is unnecessary, for Saul already has his marching orders.

According to the Hebrew text, he asks for the ark to be brought, but it is more likely that we should read "ephod" here (with the LXX and Josephus). Unless it has been temporarily transported to the battle, the ark is in Kiriath Jearim, located about six miles to the west (see 1 Sam. 7:2), too far away to bring to Saul in time to launch an attack. It is more likely that

The ephod was a special garment worn by the high priest. It is shown here as the purple, red, and gold striped fabric coming down from the shoulders and twisted around the waist. Exodus 28 gives some idea of how it might have looked, also noting that the breastplate that housed the Urim and Thummim was fastened to it. The Urim and Thummim were used to make inquiries of the Lord. This reproduction of the ephod and breastplate of the high priest is from the life-size tabernacle model at Timna, Israel.

Ahijah's ephod, mentioned in verse 3, is in view here, since an ephod is used to consult the divine will. The use of the verb "bring" supports this, for it appears with "ephod" as an object elsewhere (1 Sam. 23:9; 30:7).[6]

14:23 *on that day the LORD saved Israel.* The use of the verb "saved/rescued" (*yasha'*) may echo the exodus (cf. Exod. 14:30) and Gideon's victory over the Midianites (Judg. 7:7), two events alluded to already in the account (see the comments on 13:5–7 above). It also recalls what the people ask Samuel to pray for (1 Sam. 7:8) and Jonathan's assuring word to his armor-bearer before the battle (1 Sam. 14:6).

Theological Insights

With its allusions to earlier events in Israel's history, especially the exodus and Gideon's victory over the Midianites, this account demonstrates that the God of Moses and Gideon is still alive and well, fully capable of accomplishing great victories for his people. Like the Egyptians at the Red Sea, the Philistines come against Israel with chariots, but the Lord rescues his people. Like the Midianites in Gideon's day, the Philistines are as numerous as the sand on the seashore, causing the Israelites to tremble in fear. But working in conjunction with Jonathan's courageous act of faith, the Lord throws the Philistine army into a panic. This story, like many others in the Former Prophets before and after this, illustrates the point that the Lord does not need a powerful army to win battles and deliver his people. As Jonathan declares, he can save "by many or by few." What is important is the presence of faith, which can serve as a catalyst for divine interven-

tion. For the exiles, this account, like the story of Saul's victory over the Ammonites, is yet another reminder that the Lord is fully capable of delivering them and making them secure, even when they feel weak and powerless before the foreign nations.

Teaching the Text

1. *Faith in the Lord's great power can be the catalyst for his saving intervention.* This account is related thematically to the stories of the Lord's victories recorded in chapters 7 and 11. Chapter 7 focuses on Israel's repentance as a prerequisite for divine intervention, while chapter 11 highlights divine enablement as the key to victory. In chapter 14 the narrator emphasizes Jonathan's faith as a catalyst for divine intervention. Like Ehud before him, he has unwavering faith that prompts him to courageously ignite a conflict with the enemy. Neither Ehud nor Jonathan is mentioned in Hebrews 11, but they too "through faith conquered kingdoms" (Heb. 11:33).

2. *The Lord is an invincible warrior and can deliver by many or by a few.* The Lord's ability as a mighty warrior has been affirmed and amply illustrated earlier in 1 Samuel (2:10; 7:10; 11:13; 12:11), but this account stresses his capacity to deliver even in the face of seemingly impossible odds. This theme surely highlights Israel's history, beginning at the Red Sea, when the Lord rescued his defenseless people by miraculously drowning Pharaoh's charging charioteers in the surging water. It is particularly prominent in Judges. Ehud ignited a war of liberation by assassinating the oppressive Moabite king Eglon in the royal palace while the royal bodyguards

waited in a nearby room. The Lord reduced Gideon's army to a meager three hundred men, armed with torches and trumpets, and then gave this small force a supernatural victory over the vast Midianite army. And the Lord's Spirit empowered Samson to defeat a thousand Philistines single-handedly. One of the greatest expressions of this theme appears in the noncanonical, intertestamental book of 1 Maccabees. As Judas Maccabeus leads a small force out to face the powerful Syrian army, his men ask, "How can we, few as we are, fight against so great and so strong a multitude?" (3:17 NRSV). But Judas responds: "It is easy for many to be hemmed in by a few, for in the sight of Heaven there is no difference between saving by many or by few. It is not on the size of the army that victory in battle depends, but strength comes from Heaven" (vv. 18–19 NRSV). Judas then attacks the Syrians and routs them (vv. 23–24).[7]

Illustrating the Text

The Lord can accomplish great things for his people when they have strong faith in his power.

Christian Nonfiction: *Fresh Wind, Fresh Fire*, by Jim Cymbala. In this moving and much-read account (1997), Cymbala tells of the evolution of Brooklyn Tabernacle in New York City, where he became the pastor in 1971, a "woeful church that my father-in-law had coaxed me into," he says. He has worked there ever since. The church, which initially met in a broken-down building in an area of Brooklyn sometimes called one of America's meanest neighborhoods, now numbers in the thousands and is, as the book cover states, "a testament of what God can do when men and women begin to pour their hearts out before God." From the beginning Cymbala realized the key ingredient to a vital church was prayer. He states in the book that Christians often "think lukewarm is normal." With prayer and love for those who enter the doors (the homeless, drug addicts, prostitutes), Cymbala and his wife (leader of the interracial and world-renowned Brooklyn Tabernacle Choir) faced and still face inevitable hardships. Included was a period of time when they had serious difficulties with their daughter but saw God work miraculously in her life. Cymbala writes in this inspiring story,

The cliff up which Jonathan climbed to reach the Philistine outpost may have been along the Wadi Swenit where it narrows into a gorge. In the foreground you can see the modern town of Mukhmas, which may be the site of ancient Mikmash, with the steep cliff down to the wadi behind the town.

Let us never accept the excuse that God cannot work in *our* situation, . . . that our particular people are too rich, or too poor, . . . too inner-city or too suburban, . . . too traditional or too avant-garde. That kind of thinking is never found in the Word of God. . . . We can see God do things just as he did in the book of Acts since he has never changed.[8]

The Lord can deliver his people in the face of seemingly impossible odds.

History: "Letter from a Birmingham Jail," by Martin Luther King Jr. King (1928–68), who was a minister and civil rights leader, worked tirelessly and passionately with a core message of nonviolence until his assassination in Memphis in 1968. In this eloquent letter (April 16, 1963), written while he was in jail and sent to white Christian leaders, he pleads for them to stop the delay in righting the wrongs against the black populace. King eloquently shows how the Lord's deliverance must be depended upon in the face of indifference or refusal. He writes,

> Whenever the early Christians entered a town, the people in power became disturbed and immediately sought to convict the Christians for being "disturbers of the peace" and "outside agitators." But the Christians pressed on, in the conviction that they were a "colony of heaven" called to obey God rather than man. Small in number, they were big in commitment. They were too God-intoxicated to be "astronomically intimidated."[9]

Saul Dilutes a Victory

Big Idea *A preoccupation with one's own honor can dilute divine blessing.*

Understanding the Text

The Text in Context

The preceding account ended with the Lord's giving Israel a great victory, despite Saul's hesitant actions. In this next story we see Saul continue to retard the action rather than advance it. This account highlights one of Saul's major weaknesses and leadership flaws—one that has already emerged in earlier accounts and will prove fatal in the next chapter. Saul is preoccupied, perhaps even obsessed, with religious formalism. Certainly ritual and formalism have their place, and perhaps we can view Saul as simply naive. However, the narrator seems to view this tendency in a more negative light. Saul's preoccupation with worship does not result in his attacking the Philistine outpost (cf. 10:7–8 with 10:13–16) after the threefold sign has been fulfilled. Thus his worship, something commendable when viewed in isolation, seems to replace military action: *instead* of beginning the deliverance of Israel from the Philistines, Saul goes up to the high place (apparently to worship). Later his concern for ritual prompts him to offer up sacrifices, rather than waiting for Samuel to arrive as he has been instructed (13:8–10). Here in chapter 14 his preoccupation with formalism first causes him to delay the attack against the Philistines as he seeks a divine oracle (14:18–19) and then leads to a series of rash oaths (vv. 24, 39, 44). As stated above, this account is literarily linked to 10:7–8. Saul now has the opportunity to carry out Samuel's earlier orders (10:7–8). In fact, his son Jonathan has set in motion the attack envisioned by Samuel. While ordinarily it is proper to consult the Lord, it is unnecessary to do so in this case: Saul already has his marching orders. To make matters even worse, the turmoil within the Israelite army allows the Philistines to escape and prevents Israel from winning a total victory (14:6). The report in verse 46 becomes tragically ironic when we read shortly after this of the Philistines' mustering their troops to attack Israel yet again (17:1).[1]

This account includes a summary of Saul's career that mentions his military successes after he assumes kingship (vv. 47–48) and provides information about his family and royal court (vv. 49–51). Long says that there are "dark shadows" here, "cast not so much by what is said as by what is not said." He adds: "Specifically, the lack of any mention of Yahweh or his involvement with Saul is disturbing" (contrast David in 2 Sam. 8:6, 14).[2]

This section concludes with a brief note (v. 52) about Saul's ongoing struggles with the Philistines and reminds us that the Lord's expectation for Saul has not been completely realized (see 9:16). This concluding statement also informs us that Saul, as a matter of policy, is always looking for brave men to add to his army. While this observation seems relatively minor, it opens the door (13:14 unlocked the door) for David, who will eventually enter Saul's court as one of these brave warriors (see 16:18).

Historical and Cultural Background

It is uncertain how the lot casting (14:41–42) operates. However, if we reconstruct the original text on the basis of the Septuagint, we get a better idea of what may be happening. Verses 41–42 should read as follows (italic words from LXX):

> Saul said to the Lord God of Israel: "*Why have you not answered your servant today? If this iniquity is in me or in Jonathan my son, O Lord God of Israel, give Urim. But if this iniquity is in your people Israel*, give Thummim." And Jonathan and Saul were taken by lot, and the men were cleared. (v. 41)
>
> Saul said: "Cast the lot between me and Jonathan my son! *Let him whom the Lord takes die!" And though the soldiers said to him, "Let it not be so*,"

The Israelite battles with the Philistines would have involved hand-to-hand combat similar to that shown in this relief from Medinet Habu, Egypt (twelfth century BC). Here the Egyptians under the command of Ramesses III are fighting the Sea Peoples (which may have included Philistines), who have invaded Egypt.

Saul prevailed upon them, and they cast lots between him and Jonathan his son. And Jonathan was taken. (v. 42)[3]

Interpretive Insights

14:24 *the Israelites were in distress that day, because Saul had bound the people under an oath.* As translated by the NIV, "distress" refers to the army's fatigue due to the fact that Saul's oath deprives them of the nourishment and strength they need. However, the subject-fronted disjunctive clause at the beginning of verse 24 may signal a flashback to events before the battle. In this case Israel's distress is its fear of the Philistines (see 13:6). One could then translate verse 24b, "so Saul bound" (there is no causal connector "because" in the Hebrew text). In this case the distress is not the result of the oath, but the distress precipitates the oath.[4] So while Jonathan

Egyptian tomb relief showing cattle being butchered (2350 BC)

is igniting a battle with his heroic act of faith, Saul is playing mind games with his army and trying to frighten them into action through a self-serving curse. Perhaps he is even trying to draw God into battle rather than following God into battle (as Jonathan and later David do).

I have avenged myself on my enemies! The emphasis on personal vengeance (v. 24) is reminiscent of Samson (see Judg. 15:7; 16:28) but may also echo the actions of Gideon (8:4–21), Abimelek (9:31–50), and Jephthah (12:1–6).[5] Saul's self-serving motivation stands in contrast to the perspectives of Jonathan (v. 10) and the narrator (v. 23), both of whom view this as the Lord's battle. The oath is the latest in a line of foolish vows and oaths (Josh. 9:15; Judg. 11:30–31; 21:1, 5, 18) and casts Saul in a very negative light.

14:29 *My father has made trouble.* The Hebrew word translated "made trouble" (*'akar*) is used to describe the effect of disobedient Achan's sin on Israel (Josh. 7:25; cf. 6:18). Jephthah also uses it in accusing

his daughter of bringing trouble upon him when she greets him after his victory (Judg. 11:35). Both Jephthah and Saul make rash formal statements of personal obligation that affect their children.[6] In Jephthah's case, he accuses his daughter of troubling him and then offers her up as a whole burnt offering in fulfillment of his vow (v. 39; cf. vv. 30–31). In Saul's case, the situation is similar but plays out differently.[7]

14:32 *and ate them, together with the blood.* The weary and hungry men butchered the animals on the ground and failed to drain the blood from the meat in accordance with the Mosaic law (see Lev. 19:26; Deut. 12:23–27; also Gen. 9:4; Lev. 17:11). When informed of this cultic violation, Saul accuses the men of violating the covenant, but it is his rash oath that has brought them to the point of such desperation.

14:37 *Will you give them into Israel's hand?* Saul's request is ironic in light of the fact that the Lord has already handed the Philistines over to Israel (vv. 10, 12).

But God did not answer him that day. The Lord's silence in response to Saul's inquiry foreshadows the final days of Saul's life, when the Lord will cut off all communication with him (1 Sam. 28:6, 15). The divine silence also contrasts Saul with Samuel, who receives a divine response before engaging the Philistines in battle (7:9), and with David, who receives an assuring oracle that the Lord will give the Philistines into his hand (23:4).

14:39 *he must die.* The original oath pronounces a curse on the violator (v. 24) but does not specifically mention execution or death. In verse 39 Saul may be expanding the oath to include death. Saul's willingness to sacrifice his own son casts him in the role of a new Jephthah and is entirely consistent with what has occurred in chapter 13, where Saul ruins his son's future (13:13–14).

14:45 *So the men rescued Jonathan.* The men's oath (see "as surely as the LORD lives") trumps Saul's oath (v. 39). They state that Jonathan has accomplished his exploits "with God's help": "He has worked with God this day" (AT). Their argument is reminiscent of Saul's after his victory over the Ammonites (cf. 11:13). But now Saul is ready to kill his own son for unknowingly violating Saul's rash oath. The deterioration in Saul's leadership capacity is striking.

Theological Insights

The narrator's pro-David/anti-Saul agenda begins to gain momentum: he depicts Saul as being preoccupied with religious formalism and his own interests. After his earlier victory over the Ammonites, Saul is very much aware that the Lord has rescued Israel (11:13). But he views this battle against the Philistines primarily as an opportunity

Did Jonathan Sin?

How are we to interpret this incident? Does Jonathan actually "sin" (v. 38)? Can Jonathan be responsible for keeping the oath that Saul imposes on the army, even though he does not know about it or swear to it personally? In this case we may also assume, with Saul, that the Lord's silence is due to the violation of the oath. Verses 40–42 seem to favor the view that Jonathan has sinned, for the Lord causes the lot to isolate him in response to Saul's request, which in its original form (see the LXX) mentions "iniquity."[a] If so, even though the men save Jonathan, Saul's curse, especially in its expanded form (v. 39), continues to hang over Jonathan's head, unless "rescued" in verse 45 implies that they "redeemed" Jonathan by "paying off" the Lord. The term translated "rescued" (*padah*) may simply mean "delivered, rescued," but it could indicate that they paid a price to redeem Jonathan from the consequences of the oath (see Exod. 21:30; Lev. 27:1–8). In this case Jonathan escapes the curse, but if so, does that mean that Saul now stands in a precarious position due to his self-imposed curse (v. 44)?[b]

[a] One might be inclined to say that the Lord's silence is due to the sin of the army in eating meat that still contains blood (vv. 33–34). But if this were the case, one would expect the lot to indicate the people, not Saul and Jonathan. See v. 41 in its original, expanded form, as reflected in the LXX.

[b] In this regard see Cartledge, *1 and 2 Samuel*, 186.

for personal vengeance (14:24). Though the Lord has given the Philistines into Israel's hand (vv. 10, 12), Saul seems unaware of that fact (v. 37). In the end he tries to execute the hero of the day, prompting his entire army to oppose him (vv. 44–45). He hardly appears to be a quality leader. In fact, he resembles several of the judges. A preoccupation with one's own interests and with pursuing vengeance also plagues Gideon (Judg. 8:4–21), Jephthah (12:1–6), and Samson (see Judg. 15:7; 16:28), as well as the rogue antijudge Abimelek (9:31–50). Saul's foolish oath, like Jephthah's rash vow, demonstrates a woeful lack of foresight and brings nothing but trouble in its wake. For the exiles, the lesson of this story is clear: Israel needs leaders who will pursue the Lord's work rather than their own agenda, as Saul does.

Teaching the Text

1. *God desires to bless his people, but they may dilute his blessing if they become preoccupied with their own honor.* By his hesitant, cautious behavior and his preoccupation with his own honor, Saul turns what could have been total victory into something far less. He allows the priest to divert him from completing the God-given victory (cf. vv. 15, 20, 23); he delays and tries to kill his own son, God's cowarrior (v. 45), and he allows the enemy to escape and fight another day (v. 46; cf. 17:1). Saul's obsession with personal honor dilutes the victory and brings nothing but trouble to Israel.

Saul perpetuates a pattern that was set in place in the judges' period, where a preoccupation with personal honor invariably led to death for either the would-be avenger or others and diluted the work of God (cf. Judg. 8:8–21; 12:1–6). Samson never viewed himself as Israel's savior, but he pursued vengeance against the Philistines to the point where he pronounced a death wish upon himself (16:28, 30). In the book's final

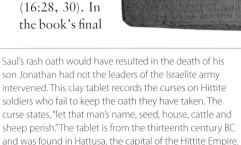

Saul's rash oath would have resulted in the death of his son Jonathan had not the leaders of the Israelite army intervened. This clay tablet records the curses on Hittite soldiers who fail to keep the oath they have taken. The curse states, "let that man's name, seed, house, cattle and sheep perish." The tablet is from the thirteenth century BC and was found in Hattusa, the capital of the Hittite Empire.

chapters, the Israelite tribes are so obsessed with carrying out vengeance against Benjamin that they make a foolish oath and almost end up exterminating an entire tribe (21:1–7). This leads to the murder and kidnapping of hundreds of innocent victims (21:8–23).

2. *God desires to bless his people, but they may inhibit his work if they become too preoccupied with religious formalism.* The story also warns its audience, whether ancient or modern, about the dangers of a preoccupation with religious formalism. For Saul, this takes the form of making rash oaths (1 Sam. 14:24, 39, 44), offering ill-advised sacrifices (vv. 34–35), and seeking unnecessary oracles (v. 37; cf. vv. 18–19). In any given modern culture, one needs to determine what might correspond to these actions. While seeking oracles and offering animal sacrifices are not a part of modern Christian religious expression, people today sometimes become paralyzed while waiting on the Lord or seeking the Lord's "will" when it is obvious what God is doing, and it is clear that they need to get involved in his work.

In the Old Testament, oaths are a normal part of life and are even regulated by the Old Testament law (see, e.g., Num. 30:2). The third commandment assumes they will be made and emphasizes that they must be kept (Exod. 20:7; Deut. 5:11). Exodus 22:10–11 even commands that an oath be taken under certain circumstances, and the Lord himself takes an oath on occasion to give emphasis to his word or promise (Num. 14:21–23). Religious oaths were commonplace in Jesus's time. They are solemn, formal statements designed to emphasize the truth of one's words or the certainty that one's promises will be fulfilled. However, the Old Testament principles regulating oaths were being badly neglected and abused. For this reason, Jesus goes so far as to tell his disciples not to use them at all (Matt. 5:33–37), a command with which James concurs (James 5:12). Does this mean Christians should never take an oath, even when the law requires it? At his trial before the religious authorities, Jesus allows the high priest to place him under oath (Matt. 26:62–64). On several occasions Paul uses an oath formula to emphasize the truth of his words (Rom. 1:9; 2 Cor. 1:23; 11:11; Gal. 1:20; Phil. 1:8; 1 Thess. 2:5, 10). Jesus and Paul are affirming either present truths about themselves or the truthfulness of past events, not making promises about the future. It seems permissible, then, to appeal to God as witness when testifying to the truth of present realities or past events, but in deference to God's sovereignty, one should avoid emphatic oaths when making promises.

Illustrating the Text

Preoccupation with one's honor can divert attention from God.

Quote: *Mere Christianity*, by C. S. Lewis. In book 4 (chap. 8), Lewis (1898–1963) addresses self-preoccupation, essentially pride.

The terrible thing, the almost impossible thing, is to hand over your whole self—all your wishes and precautions—to Christ.

But it is far easier than what we are all trying to do instead, . . . to remain what we call "ourselves," to keep personal happiness as our great aim in life, and yet at the same time be "good." We are all trying to let our mind and heart go their own way—centred on money or pleasure or ambition—and hoping, in spite of this, to behave honestly and chastely and humbly. And that is exactly what Christ warned us you could not do.[8]

Preoccupation with religious formalism diminishes the work of God and brings trouble to the people of God.

Film: *Babette's Feast*. This Danish film (1987) is based on a story by Isak Dinesen. In this unforgettable winner of the Foreign Film Oscar, the effects of and redemption from religious formalism are explored. Two pious Christian sisters, daughters of the founder of a strict Christian sect, live in a village on the remote coast of Jutland. After their father's death, the sect stagnates, but the aging sisters preside lovingly over their brood of disgruntled believers, who woodenly keep the religious formalities. Into their midst comes Babette, a refugee (and one of the finest chefs in Europe) from a Paris revolution. She spends fourteen years as their cook, easing everyone's lives, her only link to her former life being a lottery ticket renewed yearly by a friend in Paris. When Babette wins ten thousand francs, she could return to Paris. Instead, she spends her entire earnings to prepare a sumptuous dinner for the congregation on the founder's hundredth birthday, a lavish outpouring of self-sacrifice with eucharistic echoes. The deliverance from formalism, pride, and dead spirituality in this congregation is a delight. Scenes of the meal where the congregants begin to mellow, enticed into righteousness, could be shown.

Obedience Is Better Than Sacrifice

Big Idea *The Lord gives greater priority to obedience than to religious formalism.*

Understanding the Text

The Text in Context

In this account the narrator's pro-David/anti-Saul agenda continues to gain momentum. In chapter 13 Samuel announced that Saul would have no royal dynasty, placing the king on thin ice. Chapter 14 did nothing to ease our concerns about Saul, as he exhibited a preoccupation with his own honor and an obsession with religious formalism, particularly oaths. He was ready to execute his own son, and he deprived Israel of total victory as he placed his army under an unrealistic restriction and retarded the action with his delays. In chapter 15 Saul's situation now becomes even more precarious. He exhibits pride and disobeys the Lord's clear command; this brings serious repercussions (see vv. 23–35).

Historical and Cultural Background

The Lord tells Saul to wipe out the Amalekites, killing all of the people and even their animals (v. 3). The reason for this is clearly stated: the Lord intends to "punish the Amalekites for what they did to Israel when they waylaid them as they came up from Egypt" (v. 2; cf. Exod. 17:8–16). Moses announces that "the LORD will be at war against the Amalekites from generation to generation" (Exod. 17:16). Later, as Moses speaks to a new generation that is ready to enter the land, he urges them to remember how the Amalekites attacked the Israelites when they were tired and vulnerable (Deut. 25:17–18). He commands them to "blot out the memory of Amalek from under heaven" and emphatically urges them, "Do not forget!" (v. 19).

The Amalekites are descendants of Esau through his wife Adah (Gen. 36:16), who is called a woman of Canaan and more specifically identified as a Hittite (v. 2). One of Esau's sons, Eliphaz, fathered Amalek through his concubine, Timna (Gen. 36:12). The Amalekites eventually settled in the south of Canaan in the Negev (Num. 13:29), though some also lived in the hill country of Ephraim (Judg. 12:15). They have opposed Israel from its beginning (Exod. 17:8–16) and continue to be a thorn in Israel's side on into the period of David (Num. 14:43–45; 24:20; Judg. 3:13; 6:3; 10:12; 1 Sam. 14:48; 30:1; 2 Sam. 8:12; Ps. 83:5–7). Moses expected Israel to wipe out the Amalekites as soon as they secured their place in the land; Israel's failure to do so comes back to haunt them many times.

The use of the verb "totally destroy" (*haram*) in verse 3 shows that this is an instance of the so-called ban.[1] God earlier told Israel to exterminate the Canaanites in order to preserve the covenant community's holy standing before him (Deut. 7:1–6). The victims are regarded as "devoted" to the Lord himself (cf. Josh. 6:17, 21), perhaps in part as an offering of gratitude for the Lord's help (cf. Num. 21:2–3). In the case of Jericho, the articles of gold, silver, bronze, and iron are also devoted to the Lord by being placed in his treasury (Josh. 6:17–19; the related *herem* [thing/person devoted] appears in Lev. 27:21, 28; Num. 18:14; Ezek. 44:29). When Achan takes some of the devoted items, he makes the whole camp subject to the ban (Josh. 7:12; cf. 6:18; 22:20) and must be executed to avert the divine anger. The ban thus fulfills God's command and also has a sacrificial nature: people and/or objects are offered up to the Lord as a token of gratitude and/or an offering to appease God.

This concept of the ban is also attested on the Moabite Stone (Mesha inscription), where Mesha of Moab boasts that he devoted to his god Chemosh seven thousand Israelite captives (COS, 2:137–38). In 1 Samuel 15 it appears that Saul views the Lord's instructions along these lines, for he intends to offer up the best of the Amalekite plunder as a formal sacrifice to the Lord (*herem* appears in v. 21). However, Niditch suggests that in this case the ban is viewed not as a sacrifice but rather as a punishment.[2] Yet, as Niditch points out, Samuel's execution of the Amalekite king Agag

Key Themes of 1 Samuel 15:1–22

- Saul's pride and preoccupation with religious formalism cause him to disobey God's command.
- The Lord gives greater priority to obedience than to sacrifice.

"before the LORD at Gilgal" (v. 33) has a sacrificial flavor to it.

Interpretive Insights

15:2 *I will punish.* The Lord's use of the first person indicates that this is *his* campaign. Saul is simply his instrument and has no right to improvise in carrying out the Lord's decree of judgment.

The Moabite Stone (ninth century BC)

15:9 *But Saul and the army spared.* In verse 3 the Lord clearly commands, "Do not spare them." The simple repetition of the verb here in verse 9 highlights Saul's disobedience yet also implicates the army.

they were unwilling to destroy completely. The use of the verb "be willing" (*'abah*) stresses the fact that sparing the king and the best animals is a deliberate act of their will.

15:11 *because he has turned away from me.* The Hebrew expression translated "turned away from" is used elsewhere of serious rebellion against the Lord (Num. 14:43; 32:15; Josh. 22:16, 18, 23, 29).

and has not carried out my instructions. The Hebrew text reads, "And my words he has not established." When used of human beings' "establishing" God's word or covenant, the expression means obeying the word that God has commanded (see Deut. 27:26; 2 Kings 23:3, 24; Jer. 34:18).

Samuel was angry, and he cried out. The content and purpose of Samuel's cry to the Lord are not stated, nor is the object of his anger. Elsewhere the verb "cry out" (*za'aq*) describes a cry of distress or pain (1 Sam. 12:8, 10). In 1 Samuel 7:8–9 it is used of Samuel's intercessory cry on behalf of Israel (note esp. "on Israel's behalf" in v. 9), but no such prepositional phrase is used here in verse 11. There is no indication that Samuel intercedes with the Lord on Saul's behalf. It seems more likely that he is lamenting Saul's actions and the potential damage they can cause for Israel.

15:12 *he has set up a monument in his own honor.* Saul likely sets up this monument

Saul's monument may have been a stele similar to ones erected by or to honor later Assyrian kings. This stele of King Adad-Nirari III, king of Assyria (810–783 BC), describes his military campaigns into Palestine. The end of the inscription reads, "At that time I had an image of my royal self made. The power of my might, the deeds of my hands, I inscribed thereon."

The Problem of Genocide

The Lord's command to Saul in verses 2–3 raises ethical questions. How can the Lord authorize genocide that includes the slaughter of women, children, and even animals? How can the Lord hold this generation of Amalekites responsible for the sins of their ancestors, committed over three hundred years earlier?

God's decree to implement genocide against the Amalekites must be examined within the larger context of his decision to exterminate the Canaanites. Granted, this is philosophically problematic, because we rightly view genocide as one of the most heinous of human crimes. However, we remember that Israel's invasion of Canaan was not a purely imperialistic landgrab victimizing morally neutral peoples. Israel was God's instrument of judgment against the Canaanites, whose sins became repulsive to him (see Gen. 15:16; Lev. 18:28; Josh. 11:20; Judg. 1:7; 1 Kings 21:26; 2 Kings 16:3). The Canaanites had to be exterminated; otherwise, like a moral and spiritual cancer, they would contaminate Israel (Deut. 7:1–6; 20:16–18). As the sovereign King over all peoples, God has the right to remove nations from the face of the earth when they violate his moral standards to an excessive degree.

As for the Amalekites, they are not typically included in the lists of nations to be exterminated, but they are closely associated with these peoples in Numbers 13:29 and 14:25, 43, 45. Because of their merciless hostility toward Israel, they are placed under a customized order of execution (Exod. 17:14; Deut. 25:17–19).[a]

We also recognize that corporate thinking underlies the Lord's command. In our modern Western world, we emphasize individual rights, but much of the world today looks at individuals primarily as parts of corporate units. Such corporate thinking is pervasive in the Bible.[b] Even God often deals with people corporately. For example,

children many times are punished for the sins of their parents. The Lord warns his enemies that their sin will have negative consequences for their family throughout their lifetime (Exod. 20:5; 34:7; Num. 14:18). Dathan's, Abiram's, and Achan's innocent children die along with their sinful parents (Num. 16:27, 32 [Korah's sons are apparently spared: Num. 26:11]; Josh. 7:24), and David, with the Lord's approval, allows the Gibeonites to execute seven of Saul's descendants because of Saul's crimes against that city (2 Sam. 21:1–9, 14). The Lord also takes the lives of four of David's sons because of his sin against Uriah (2 Sam. 12:5–6, 10; cf. 12:14–15; 13:28–29; 18:15; 1 Kings 2:25). Though Jeremiah anticipates a day when God's judgment will operate on a strictly individual basis, he seems to assume that God has judged the children for their parents' sins in the past (31:29–30; cf. Lam. 5:7).

Thus in a patriarchal culture, as here in 1 Samuel 15, the Amalekites' wives, children, and animals are their possessions and must be destroyed along with the males. Even though centuries have passed since the Amalekites attacked Israel, the later generations of Amalekites are merely an extension of their ancestors (1 Sam. 15:2–3) and continue to carry on their legacy of violence (cf. 15:18, 33).

On a more positive note, we see the corporate way of thinking also reflected in 1 Samuel 15:6, where Saul warns the Kenites to move away from the Amalekites so that they will not be destroyed along with them. The reason for this is that the ancestors of the Kenites, with whom this later generation is identified (note "for you"!), showed Israel kindness when they came out of Egypt (see Judg. 1:16).

[a] McCarter, *I Samuel*, 266.
[b] See Kaminsky, *Corporate Responsibility*.

---

to honor his victory and perpetuate his fame (cf. Absalom in 2 Sam. 18:18),[3] as kings sometimes did in the ancient Near East. Initially Saul was hesitant to take the throne, despite prophetic affirmation and divine confirmation through signs. But now, drunk with success, he seeks to elevate himself in the nation's eyes, ironically, just before receiving a prophetic rebuke and divine rejection notice.

15:13 *I have carried out the Lord's instructions.* The Lord does not share Saul's view (v. 11). The verbal repetition draws attention to Saul's naïveté and spiritual insensitivity. Seemingly oblivious to what he has done, he pronounces a blessing on Samuel and boasts that he has carried out the Lord's command.

15:15 *they spared the best . . . , but we totally destroyed the rest.* When Samuel asks about the animals he hears, Saul responds in a subtle, self-defensive manner. Undoubtedly recalling the Lord's command, he states that *the army* has spared the animals, albeit for a worthy purpose: sacrifice. But when describing the total destruction of the rest, he includes himself in the action.

15:19 *and do evil in the eyes of the* Lord. The expression describes the sinful behavior of the Israelites in the wilderness (Num. 32:13; Deut. 9:18) and later in the judges' period (Judg. 2:11; 3:7, 12; 4:1; 6:1; 10:6; 13:1). It is often associated with idolatry (Deut. 4:25; 17:2–3; 31:29; Judg. 2:11; 3:7; 10:6). Saul is not guilty of idolatry, but his "rebellion" is just as serious in the Lord's eyes (v. 23).

15:20 *and brought back Agag.* Saul deliberately uses the word "brought back" rather than "spared," perhaps to sidestep the fact that he has disobeyed the Lord's command (v. 3). His choice of words contrasts sharply with the narrator's assessment of his actions (v. 9).[4]

15:21 *The soldiers took sheep and cattle.* Just in case Samuel will not step back from his accusation against those who have spared the livestock, Saul wants to distance himself from the people. But in case he is unable to make that distinction, he wants to emphasize that the people's motives are pure and that they are pursuing a higher good.

Theological Insights

See "Theological Insights" for 1 Samuel 15:23–35.

Teaching the Text

The Lord places greater priority on obedience than he does on religious formalism. Saul labors under the faulty notion that God places a priority on formal religious acts. But a proper relationship with God cannot be guaranteed through formal religious behavior such as sacrifice or prayer (see esp. Isa. 1:11–15). As Samuel tells Saul, religious formalism is meaningless apart from obedience. One can have a vibrant, healthy relationship with God only if one is submissive to his moral will, as demonstrated by obedience to his moral and ethical standards.

Even though the spoils of war often included the livestock, when Saul spared the best livestock of the Amalekites, he disobeyed God's command. In this Assyrian relief, sheep and goats are being led away after a successful siege (palace at Nimrud, 728 BC).

Although sacrifice is not as much of an issue in the New Testament, the basic principle is still present there, though perhaps applied a bit more pointedly. The New Testament makes it clear that all the law can be summarized in the simple commands to love God and to love one's neighbor (Mark 12:29–31). One cannot do the former without doing the latter. A meaningful relationship with God (the vertical plane) is not possible unless one obeys God's command to love one's fellow human beings in tangible, practical ways (the horizontal plane). So James (1:27) makes caring for those who are vulnerable and needy (epitomized by the widow and orphan) one of the twin pillars of genuine religion, because it fulfills the "royal law" of love for one's neighbor (2:8). Jesus teaches that one cannot expect to receive God's forgiveness if one is not willing to forgive others (Matt. 6:14–15). Reconciling differences with a brother or sister must be given priority over formal religious acts (5:23–24). Withholding one's material goods from a needy brother is proof that one does not have a genuine relationship with God (1 John 3:17). Treating one's wife with disrespect can hinder one's prayer life (1 Pet. 3:7). These examples illustrate the basic principle that obedience (to the royal law of love in a NT context) has priority over sacrifice (or formal religious acts, such as offerings and prayer, in a NT context). In genuine biblical "religion," obedience is foundational to having a vital relationship with God, in contrast to pagan religion, which seeks such a relationship through religious formalism.

Illustrating the Text

Obedience is more important to God than formal religious manifestations.

Lyrics: "To Obey Is Better Than Sacrifice," by Keith Green. In this song, Green tells us that God wants us more than our ritualistic church attendance, more than our perfunctory prayers offered dutifully, more than our money given mechanically. God wants our hearts, our devotion, our thoughtful, focused, living obedience.

A meaningful relationship with God is possible only if one loves fellow human beings in tangible, practical ways.

Literature: "Where Love Is, God Is," by Leo Tolstoy. This short story was made into a wonderful Claymation called "Martin the Cobbler" (1977). Martin, an old cobbler, has lost his family and all interest in life. He lives now only for his work. But one day in a dream, Martin hears a voice, which he assumes is the Lord's, promising to come and visit him the next day. The following day, various people in need arrive at Martin's door, and he helps each one of them. By evening Martin is disappointed that his "special guest" has not arrived. Shortly after this, an extraordinary vision reveals to him that in caring for others he has met his "special visitor." When Martin begins to understand that "where love is, God is," he looks at life in a new way.

Saul Forfeits His Throne

Big Idea *The disobedient may forfeit the special privilege the Lord has granted to them.*

Understanding the Text

The Text in Context

In these verses, Samuel announces that Saul will forfeit his throne. Earlier the Lord announced that Saul would have no dynasty (13:13–14), but now he also takes Saul's position as king from him.[1] Though Saul begs for forgiveness, Samuel makes it clear that the divine decision is final. At this point we expect the account of Saul's demise to follow and his successor, the "one better" than Saul (15:28), to emerge from anonymity. This is exactly what happens in chapter 16.

Historical and Cultural Background

In verse 23 the Lord states that rebellion is as evil as divination. For a discussion of divination, see above under 1 Samuel 6, "Historical and Cultural Background."

Interpretive Insights

15:23 *For rebellion is like the sin of divination.* The Lord characterizes Saul's behavior as rebellion. The noun translated "rebellion" (*meri*) is related to the verb "rebel" (*marah*), which was used earlier by Samuel when he warned Israel and their king not to rebel against the Lord (12:14–15). The relationship of rebellion to divination is unclear. The Hebrew text lacks a comparative, but translators typically add "like" because the context does not indicate that Saul actually engages in divination, at least on this occasion. The statement may be emphatic and is surely ironic. Saul expects to please the Lord through the proposed sacrifice, which he regards as perfectly legitimate and appropriate. But from the Lord's perspective, Saul disobeys the divine command in order to make this sacrifice, so it is an act of rebellion, no different than divination or idolatry. By equating Saul's rebellion with divination, the Lord makes the point in a more rhetorically forceful way than by drawing a formal comparison.

and arrogance like the evil of idolatry. The Hebrew form translated "arrogance" (*haptsar*; a Hiphil infinitive, as a verbal noun) occurs elsewhere (in the Qal stem) with the meaning "urge, coerce," so the NIV's translation is questionable. Coercion or compulsion seems to be a more likely meaning. In this context it may refer to Saul's stated intention to offer a sacrifice (cf. v. 21), perhaps with the motivation to compel or manipulate God to act in a favorable manner. The word translated "idolatry" is *terapim*, a type of idol apparently used in divination. (See comments on 1 Sam. 19 below, under "Historical and Cultural Background.") That would explain why it appears here in parallel with "divination" (cf. v. 23a). Once again the Hebrew text lacks a comparative, but since Saul does not seem to have engaged in idolatry or divination here, translators typically understand an implied comparison. Perhaps the idea is that Saul's intention to compel or manipulate God through sacrifice is tantamount to idolatry from God's perspective and deserves the same punishment.

Because you have rejected the word of the LORD, he has rejected you as king. The repetition of the verb "rejected" highlights the Lord's poetic justice and the appropriate nature of the judgment. The use of the verb echoes the Lord's earlier accusations against Israel (8:7; 10:19).

15:24 *I have sinned.* Twice in this passage Saul confesses that he has sinned (see v. 30). This self-incrimination is important to the narrator's portrayal of Saul as one who disobeys God and forfeits his right to the throne. Ironically, it puts him in the same category as the "wicked" Amalekites. (See v. 18, where *hatta'im*, "wicked people" in NIV, is used of the Amalekites. This term is related to the verb "to sin" [*hata'*], used by Saul in vv. 24 and 30.)[2] Saul's confession

Key Themes of 1 Samuel 15:23–35

- Saul's pride and preoccupation with religious formalism cause him to forfeit his special position of king over Israel.
- When the Lord decrees unconditional punishment, he will not retract his word.

may echo that of Achan, who also sinned in the matter of spoil that belonged to the Lord and confessed his sin with these words (Josh. 7:20–21). If so, the parallel is omi-

When Saul accidently tears the hem of Samuel's robe, Samuel reiterates the Lord's rejection of Saul by saying, "The LORD has torn the kingdom of Israel from you today" (1 Sam. 15:28). Samuel's robe was probably an outer garment with loose, wide sleeves worn only by royalty or priests. The edge of the cloth was probably elaborately fringed, like this robe that Bar-rakib, king of Zincirli, is wearing in this eighth-century BC relief from his palace.

nous (see the comment below on 1 Sam. 31:12).

I was afraid of the men and so I gave in to them. Saul's confession of sin is not entirely sincere. He implies that his disobedience was due to pressure from his men. At the same time, his words are self-incriminatory. He confesses that he "gave in to" them. The Hebrew text reads, "I obeyed them." Earlier, when Samuel accused him of disobedience (v. 19), Saul claimed to obey the Lord (v. 20), but now he acknowledges that he has obeyed the people, not the Lord (cf. v. 11).

15:29 *for he is not a human being, that he should change his mind.* To make sure there is no doubt in Saul's mind, Samuel formalizes the announcement of God's rejection. By saying that God will not change his mind in this case, Samuel marks his announcement about Saul's demise as an unconditional decree. It is necessary to declare this since God typically is willing to relent from sending calamity.

15:30 *please honor me.* Apparently recognizing that Samuel has decreed his doom, Saul retracts his request for forgiveness. (The words "forgive my sin" [v. 25] are omitted in v. 30.) He again acknowledges his sin and requests that Samuel return with him to worship. This time Samuel agrees, for the request is no longer coupled with a prayer for forgiveness. Before the announcement's being formalized, Saul might have misinterpreted Samuel's compliance as a sign of divine forgiveness; now that this matter has been clarified and Saul has withdrawn his request for forgiveness, Samuel can go with Saul without sending any false signals.

before the elders of my people and before Israel. Saul identifies with the people (note "*my* people"), but he distances himself from the Lord when he says to Samuel, "Come back with me, so that I may worship the LORD *your* God" (as also in v. 15). Having just heard that the kingdom has been irrevocably torn from him (vv. 28–29), he is concerned with his standing before the people. This foreshadows what will transpire in the chapters to follow. God's choice of David is readily apparent, even to

Because Saul did not obey the Lord's command to totally destroy the Amalekites and all that belonged to them, Samuel had to complete the task by killing the Amalekite king, Agag. This relief shows an Assyrian preparing to kill an Elamite officer after the Assyrian victory at Til-Tuba (645–635 BC).

Saul (24:20), yet Saul hangs on to his royal position and seeks to kill David.

15:31 *So Samuel went back with Saul, and Saul worshiped the LORD.* Saul's primary concern is to be *seen* as worshiping the Lord (see also v. 25, 30) rather than to fulfill his commission by executing Agag. This is reminiscent of what happened at the beginning of Saul's career. Rather than attacking the Philistine garrison, as Samuel indicated he should do (10:5–7), he simply went to the high place, presumably to worship (10:13).

Here in 15:31 the text gives no indication that Samuel worships with Saul. Samuel has more important matters to attend to. Before departing (v. 34), Samuel does what Israel should have done earlier. He executes the Amalekite king, making it clear that the deed is one of divine justice (v. 33; note Samuel's statement, as well as the phrase "before the LORD").

Theological Insights

The most important theological theme of this chapter is the priority of obedience over sacrifice (v. 22). This principle, articulated here by the prophet Samuel, is especially prominent in the prophetic literature (Isa. 1:11–17; Jer. 7:21–26; Hosea 6:6–7; Amos 5:7, 10–12, 21–24; Mic. 6:6–8). It is fundamental to God's covenant with Israel and is at the heart of genuine religion. Israel's failure to observe it has resulted in the exile (Isa. 1:19–20; Amos 5:27; Mic. 6:16). As the exiles anticipate returning to the land and renewing their covenantal relationship with the Lord, it is a principle that needs to be foremost in their thinking and to be evident in their behavior.

Does God "Change His Mind"?

As noted earlier (see the sidebar in the unit on 2:12–36), more often than not the Lord's promises in the Old Testament are conditional (whether explicitly or implicitly) and depend for their fulfillment on a proper response from the recipient.[a] Jeremiah 18 is a foundational text in this regard. Consistent with this are the texts asserting that God typically relents in response to human repentance (Jer. 18:5–10; Joel 2:13; Jon. 4:2), describing his doing so (Exod. 32:14; Amos 7:3, 6; Jon. 3:10), or at least assuming that he might (Jer. 26:3; Joel 2:14; Jon. 3:9). On the other hand, a handful of passages affirm that God will not relent once he has decreed a course of action (Num. 23:19; 1 Sam. 15:29; Ps. 110:4). However, these texts, rather than stating a theological universal, mark particular divine announcements as unconditional decrees. This is necessary because normally his announcements are conditional, whether explicitly or implicitly.[b]

The verb *niham* has the nuance "change [his] mind" or "retract" (a pronouncement) in verse 29. In verses 11 and 35, this same verb is used of how the Lord regrets or is grieved that he has made Saul king. These statements do not contradict each other; the verb has a different nuance of meaning in verses 11 and 35, namely, "to experience emotional pain, feel regret" (over a past action). Even though the same Hebrew verb is used in all three passages, this need not mean that it has the same sense of meaning or connotation in each case. God's and the narrator's statements pertain to a past action (God's making Saul king), which God now regrets. Samuel's statement pertains to God's future course of action with respect to Saul. By saying that God will not change his mind in this case, Samuel marks his announcement about Saul's demise as an unconditional decree. There is irony here: God regrets (or "changed his mind" [AT]) that he has made Saul king and consequently decides that he will not "change his mind" (retract his decree) about removing Saul from kingship.[c]

[a] Pratt, "Historical Contingencies," 182–203.
[b] For fuller discussion, see Chisholm, "Does God 'Change His Mind'?," 387–99; idem, "How a Hermeneutical Virus Can Corrupt," 270n18.
[c] See Long, *The Reign and Rejection of Saul*, 163.

This principle counters the typical view of religion in the ancient Near East, in which humans were responsible for meeting the needs of the gods by providing food (sacrifices), housing (temples), clothing, worship, and even privacy. In exchange for this service, the gods would protect their worshipers and provide for them. Within such a framework, religious formalism is of the utmost importance. In the biblical covenantal model, humans serve God, but he does not need their service. He desires a relationship with them in which he provides for their needs in exchange for covenantal faithfulness demonstrated by obedience.[3] Saul's actions suggest that he does not fully understand the covenantal model and is operating in accordance with the cultural norms of surrounding nations; this explains his preoccupation with sacrifice.

Teaching the Text

1. *Disobedience can deprive one of special privilege granted by God.* This principle has already appeared in the story of Eli and his sons (1 Sam. 2:12–36), who forfeited their special priestly position and dynasty because of disobedience, and in chapter 13, where Saul forfeited his dynasty due to disobedience. The Lord expects his servants to be loyal to him, for he is faithful to them. A special calling from God does not make one exempt from God's discipline. From everyone to whom much is given, much is required (Amos 3:2; Luke 12:48).

2. *When God announces judgment unconditionally, he will not alter his decree.* This theme has also appeared earlier in the story (see chap. 4). As illustrated in the account of the fall of Eli and his sons, God's unconditional decree of judgment cannot be averted. As the story continues, Saul meets his demise in an inexorable manner, facilitated by God's sending an "evil spirit" to torment him and make it clear to all that he has been rejected by God. Both Eli's and Saul's stories demonstrate

that God's word is reliable and must be taken seriously. In the case of decrees of judgment, the recipients are doomed, with no hope of escape (Matt. 13:49–50; Luke 16:26; Heb. 9:27; Rev. 20:11–15). This reality should motivate all people to respond properly to God now, before it is too late (2 Cor. 6:2). But not all of God's decrees pertain to judgment; some are promises of salvation. The recipients of these can take great comfort in knowing that they are reliable and trustworthy (1 Pet. 1:22–25).

Illustrating the Text

To forfeit blessing is a tragedy.

See also the "Illustrating the Text" section of 1 Samuel 2:12–36.

Personal Stories: Anyone who has been in ministry for even a short time has encountered situations in which individuals have disobeyed the Lord and through that disobedient decision have made a turn in their lives that cannot be reversed. Any preacher or teacher can tell stories of students who married against the advice of those who counseled them otherwise; who didn't finish school because they "had peace" about doing some other project; who chose the wrong companions, thinking they were strong enough to sustain their witness among them. These decisions often lead to a detour from which the individual never recovers fully. The unwise marriage may distract them from the Christian vocation to which they have been called; they may never return to school and the education that would have guided life; the companions may persuade them to disobey the Lord even more. As a result, they may never return to a path of living wholeheartedly for God;

even if there is recognition and recovery, grace does not eliminate the scars of the disobedience or restore the blessing that was originally intended.

Literature: *The Lord of the Rings,* by J. R. R. Tolkien. This novel (1954–55) by Tolkien (1892–1973) has been adapted into a trilogy of movies, *The Fellowship of the Ring, The Two Towers,* and *The Return of the King.* Observe the powerful contrast between Frodo Baggins, who ultimately wins against the seduction of the ring and becomes a hero; and Gollum, who while at times seeing the evil, finally surrenders to obsession and avarice and forfeits all good.

God's word is trustworthy and must be taken seriously; his unconditional decrees are reliable.

Quote: *The Trivialization of God,* by Donald McCullough.

> The fire of holiness, as it burns against unholiness, first purges. The grace of God's commitment not to be separate includes the judgment of God's opposition against all that creates the separation.
>
> Judgment is not a popular notion today—especially the thought of *God's* judgment. We prefer to imagine a deity who happily lets bygones be bygones, who winks at failures and pats us on the back to build our self-esteem. But according to Scripture, "God is love." And love devoid of judgment is only watered-down kindness.

Divine Regret

The statements of divine regret in 1 Samuel 15:11, 35 and Genesis 6:6–7 may seem inconsistent with the Lord's omniscience, but this is not the case. They express his emotional response to relational situations in space and time and do not imply that the developments have taken him by surprise or that he admits to making a mistake. If we think in terms of language function, the statements may be understood as expressive (they express God's emotional response to what has happened) and as performative (they are speech acts that officially pronounce the termination of God's relationship with the party in view).[a] Even human experience tells us that just because we regret some action, it does not mean that we have acted wrongly or would do differently if given the choice again. For example, a father might regret disciplining a child because he wishes it had been unnecessary, even though it was totally appropriate. In this case the father's regret does not suggest he should or would have done differently.

[a] Tsumura, *The First Book of Samuel,* 395–96.

> The holy God is not "kind." Love is something far more stern and splendid than mere kindness.[4]

Here McCullough quotes C. S. Lewis:

> Kindness . . . cares not whether its object becomes good or bad, provided only that it escapes suffering. . . . If God is Love, He is, by definition, something more than kindness. And it appears from all records, that though He has often rebuked us and condemned us, He has never regarded us with contempt. He has paid us the intolerable compliment of loving us, in the deepest, most tragic, most inexorable sense.[5]

The Lord Chooses a New King

Big Idea *When choosing his servants, the Lord gives priority to inner character, not outward appearances.*

Understanding the Text

The Text in Context

In the previous chapters Saul lost his dynasty (13:13–14) and then his position as king (15:26–28). Chapter 16 is a turning point in the story: the process of Saul's actual removal from kingship begins. God withdraws his Spirit and sends another spirit to torment Saul and undermine his kingship. Prior to this, the Lord announced that he would raise up "a man after his own heart" (13:14) to be the new king, one who is a "neighbor of Saul" and "better than" Saul (15:28). In chapter 16 that individual is now introduced by name. Samuel anoints him (v. 13), and then one of Saul's servants describes him as "a brave man and a warrior," with whom the Lord is present in a special way (v. 18). The narrator's pro-David apology reaches its peak when the Lord's Spirit comes upon David (v. 13) and leaves Saul (v. 14). David's superiority to Saul is evident. Saul becomes dependent upon David for even his sanity. David helps Saul and supports him, as he does throughout the ensuing story. In this way the narrator exonerates David from any charges of fomenting a rebellion against Saul.

Interpretive Insights

16:1 *How long will you mourn for Saul?* The previous chapter ended with Samuel's mourning over Saul, and the Lord's grieving over the fact that he has made Saul king. But as this chapter opens, the Lord confronts Samuel and urges him to move on. When used in this verbal stem (Hitpael) of humans' mourning for other humans, the verb translated "mourn" (*'abal*) refers to mourning for the dead (Gen. 37:34; 1 Sam. 6:19; 2 Sam. 14:2; 19:1 [2 MT]; 1 Chron. 7:22; 2 Chron. 35:24) or, in one instance, to grieving over a lengthy separation from a loved one (2 Sam. 13:37). Samuel's remorse is deep and painful. It is clear that Samuel is not part of some conspiracy against Saul, who eventually loses his throne because of divine disapproval, not human betrayal.

16:4 *the elders of the town trembled.* The elders' fear at Samuel's arrival comes as no surprise to the reader, for the previous two times that Samuel arrived on the scene in the story, it was to pronounce judgment (13:10; 15:13). The elders' timid question to Samuel stands in stark contrast to Saul's bold, confident reaction to the prophet's arrival in the previous story (15:13) and his brazen attempt to correct Samuel (15:20). The new king comes from a town where people give the Lord's prophet the respect he is due.

16:7 *People look at the outward appearance, but the* LORD *looks at the heart.* The heart is viewed as the seat of the emotions (1 Sam. 1:8; 4:13; 17:32; 25:36; 28:5), will (6:6; 7:3), motives (17:28), reason (21:12), and conscience (25:31; 2 Sam. 24:10). A person's "heart," or mind, is relatively inaccessible to human beings, but the Lord is able to probe people's innermost regions and assess one's true character (Jer. 11:20; 20:12).

When God chose Saul as king, he gave the people the kind of physically imposing individual that they, like other nations, would find desirable (1 Sam. 8:5; 9:2; 10:23–24). Samuel himself falls into this superficial way of thinking when he reasons that Jesse's son Eliab, who apparently is physically impressive (v. 7), is God's chosen king (see

Key Themes of 1 Samuel 16

- The Lord bases his choice of a king on quality of character, not on outward appearances.
- Once he rejects Saul, the Lord undermines Saul's effectiveness.

as well his words in 10:24). Humans tend to look on the outward appearance when evaluating someone's suitability for a task, but God is more concerned about what is on the inside. He accommodated himself to the people's wishes and standards when he selected Saul, but he will choose Saul's replacement in accordance with his own standards.

To get from Ramah to Bethlehem, Samuel would have traveled the Central Ridge Route, passing Gibeah and Jerusalem. Bethlehem was a small village adjacent to fertile regions for agriculture and more-arid regions suitable for raising goats and sheep. Flocks still graze in the area below the modern city of Bethlehem, as shown here.

16:13 *the Spirit of the LORD came powerfully upon David.* Earlier the Spirit came upon (*tsalah*) Saul in this fashion (10:6, 10; 11:6), but now David is the recipient of this special divine empowerment. In the narrator's pro-David strategy, this signals that David has replaced Saul as God's king, a fact that becomes crystal clear in the next verse, where we are told that the Spirit has abandoned Saul.

Yet there is also an ominous sound here if one reflects more carefully on the language used (see the sidebar). Earlier the Spirit came upon (*tsalah*) Samson (Judg. 14:6, 19; 15:14) and, as just noted, Saul (1 Sam. 10:6, 10; 11:6). Both accomplished great things in the Spirit's power, but this special empowerment did not prevent them from experiencing great tragedy. David too will ultimately fail, a development that is already foreshadowed here when one reads the story a second time. (See the comments below on 2 Sam. 11:2.)

16:14 *an evil spirit from the LORD tormented him.* The departure of the Lord's Spirit signals that Saul is no longer the Lord's chosen king and will no longer enjoy the Lord's enablement in battle (cf. 10:6, 10; 11:6). The arrival of this "evil spirit" signals that Saul now is an object of God's judgment and an enemy of God (cf. 28:16–18). Rather than describing the spirit's essential character, the term "evil" probably refers to his mission as one of

judgment.[1] The Hebrew word translated "evil" can refer to disaster or calamity sent as punishment by God. In this case the spirit is sent to undermine Saul's effectiveness and make the Lord's rejection of Saul apparent. The only other instance in the Old Testament of God's using an "evil spirit" in judgment is in Judges 9:23, where he sends such a spirit to bring about Abimelek's demise. This is not the only parallel between Saul and Abimelek (cf. Judg. 9:54 with 1 Sam. 31:4), suggesting that the narrator is casting Saul in a negative light by associating him with a villain from the past.

16:18 *And the LORD is with him.* Through the mouth of Saul's servant, the narrator emphasizes David's many positive qualities. Perhaps most important, the Lord is "with him," a fact that links David with Samuel (3:19). The reality of God's presence with David reappears in the story (18:12, 14, 28; 2 Sam. 5:10; 7:3), while it also becomes apparent that the divine presence has departed from Saul (18:12; 20:13).

16:21 *Saul liked him very much.* The Hebrew text does not specifically identify the subject or object of the verb "liked" (or "loved"). The usual assumption, reflected in the NIV, is that Saul is the subject and David the object. This interpretation is supported by some ancient

David is summoned to Saul's service because of his skill in playing the harp. The Hebrew word used probably describes a lyre strung with four to eight strings, which may have been similar to the one painted on this pottery jug from Megiddo (eleventh century BC).

Greek textual witnesses, by the following verse (in which Saul declares that he is pleased with David), and by the fact that the narrator later depicts David as the object of others' love. Jonathan, all Israel and Judah, Michal, and all Saul's servants love David (18:1, 16, 20, 22, 28; 20:17). However, here in verse 21 David is the subject of the two preceding verbs (came, entered) and the one that immediately follows (became), so it would be consistent with the context to understand David as the subject of "loved" and Saul as the object.[2] In this case, the verb "love," rather than emphasizing an emotional attachment, probably suggests the commitment of a subject to his king, as it does in several ancient Near Eastern texts.[3] If this interpretation is correct, the narrator from the outset stresses David's loyalty to Saul (see the note on v. 22 below). In either case, it is apparent that David enjoys God's favor. Indeed, Saul is helpless without David's soothing music (16:23).

16:22 *I am pleased with him.* This expression is used elsewhere when one is the recipient or object of another's kindness. The kindness extended is offered freely and without obligation (Gen. 19:19; 47:25; Ruth 2:2), but it can be prompted by the recipient's character or actions (Gen. 6:8–9; 39:3–4; Ruth 2:10–12), as is the case here (see vv. 21, 23). The narrator allows Saul to testify to David's character. This demonstrates that from the very beginning David is a faithful servant and tries to help the king.[4]

Theological Insights

As noted above, the dual themes of David's election and Saul's rejection are highlighted in this chapter. God's choice of David is based on David's inner charac-

Divine Deception?

Samuel is concerned that Saul will kill him if he finds out that the prophet has gone to Bethlehem to anoint a new king. To complicate matters, the ten-mile trip from Ramah (Samuel's hometown, 1 Sam. 15:34) to Bethlehem will take the prophet right through Gibeah (Saul's hometown, 1 Sam. 15:34). To protect his prophet, the Lord tells Samuel to go to Bethlehem under the pretense of offering a sacrifice. This half-truth will serve to protect Samuel and to veil the Lord's intentions. God is not above using deception when he judges rebels (see, e.g., 1 Kings 22:19–22; Jer. 4:10; Ezek. 14:9). The Lord is a God of truth, whose word is reliable, but he may very well deceive his enemies when they have, by their actions, forfeited their right to know the truth (see 2 Sam. 22:26–27; 2 Thess. 2:11–12).[a]

[a] For more on the subject of divine deception, see Chisholm, "Does God Deceive?"

ter (16:7) and predisposition to obey him (13:13–14), not his outward appearance, as impressive as it happens to be. The rejection of David's brother Eliab, who apparently is tall (16:7a), is an implicit rejection of Saul, whose height was highlighted by Samuel when he publicly anointed Saul (10:23–24). The narrator allows key characters to testify of David's qualifications. Saul's servant speaks of David's abilities (16:18), and Saul himself expresses his pleasure with David (16:22).

In contrast to David's election is the divine rejection of Saul. Not only is the divine Spirit taken from him (16:14); the Lord also sends an "evil spirit" to torment him. This spirit makes Saul afraid and even causes him to try to murder David, who is, ironically, his only source of comfort and relief from the spirit's torment. Any objective observer can see that Saul has been abandoned by God and is unfit to rule. Eventually David himself comes to suspect that Saul's hostility toward him is engineered by God as a form of divine judgment upon the king (see the comments on 26:19 below).

For the exiles reading the history, this account serves as a reminder of what genuine leadership entails and a challenge to them to choose and evaluate leaders from God's perspective. As they anticipate the arrival of the ideal Davidic king, they need to realize that he will not necessarily be outwardly impressive (cf. Isa. 53:1–3). Instead, he will be one who reflects and models God's character by promoting justice (Isa. 11:1–5) and reaching out to the downtrodden (Isa. 42:1–4, 7; 61:1–3; cf. Luke 4:16–21).

Teaching the Text

1. *When choosing his servants, the Lord gives priority to inner character, not outward appearances.* Scripture teaches that the omniscient God knows human thoughts and motives and is able to evaluate a person's inner character (Gen. 18:12–15; Ps. 44:21; Prov. 17:3; Acts 1:24; 15:8; Heb. 4:12). The Lord desires his people to have pure hearts and rewards those who possess godly inner character (Ps. 147:10–11; Prov. 21:2–3; Jer. 17:9–10; Matt. 5:8; Eph. 6:5–6; 1 Tim. 1:5; 2 Tim. 2:22; Heb. 10:22; 1 Pet. 1:22). Human beings have a tendency to evaluate leadership potential on a super-ficial basis, but the Lord looks beyond the surface and chooses those whose hearts are inclined to obey his will (1 Sam. 16:7; cf. 13:13–14). While human beings cannot probe and evaluate a person's inner character as the omniscient God is able to do, they can look for evidence of godly character in one's words and deeds (Matt. 12:34). Paul exhorts the church to give priority to spiritual qualities when evaluating and choosing leaders (1 Tim. 3:1–13; Titus 1:5–9).

2. *The Lord sometimes actively undermines the effectiveness of those whom he rejects.* The story of Saul's rejection is tragic; one who possesses the divine Spirit and has the potential to lead God's covenant community into a new era of security and prosperity fails miserably. But the story exceeds tragedy: it also has a frightening dimension to it. God does more than simply reject Saul and withdraw his enabling Spirit. He actively opposes him by sending an "evil spirit" to torment him and undermine his rule, demonstrating to all objective witnesses that Saul is now an object of his displeasure and no longer his chosen king. God's opposition to rebels can take various forms. Sometimes God gives sinners over to evil desires that in turn prompt divine anger (Rom. 1:18–32). At other times he may harden or even deceive the objects of his judgment (Rom. 9:18; 2 Thess. 2:11–12).[5] As the author of Hebrews declares, it is indeed "a dreadful thing to fall into the hands of the living God" (10:31).

Although the Lord had rejected him as king, Saul was still attempting to rule from his home in Gibeah. Several sites have been proposed for the biblical Gibeah of Saul. One possibility is Tel-el Ful, which is this hilltop surrounded by a modern neighborhood.

Illustrating the Text

Godly character is the foundation of good leadership.

Quote: *Prophetic Untimeliness: A Challenge to the Idol of Relevance,* **by Os Guinness.** In this passage, British author and speaker Guinness (b. 1941) addresses the difference between older great leaders and the trend today:

> The faith-world of John Wesley, Jonathan Edwards, John Jay, William Wilberforce, Hannah More, Lord Shaftesbury, Catherine Booth, Hudson Taylor, D. L. Moody, Charles Spurgeon, Oswald Chambers, Andrew Murray, Carl Henry, and John Stott is disappearing. In its place a new evangelicalism is arriving in which therapeutic self-concern overshadows knowing God, [and] spirituality displaces theology, . . . marketing triumphs over mission, . . . opinion polls outweigh reliance on biblical exposition, concerns for power and relevance are more obvious than concern for piety and faithfulness."[6]

God opposes those who rebel against him.

Literature: *Paradise Lost,* **by John Milton.** In this classic poem (1667), Milton (1608–74) represents rebellion profoundly and vividly in describing the fall of Satan, the favored angel of God. The rebellion is dramatic, larger than life, and runs the range from stunning to terrifying. God announces that the Son has been appointed to reign over all the angels: "To Him shall bow / All knees in Heav'n" (5.607–8). Satan is jealous of the Son's rank, believing himself to be equally worthy. Even after he has been defeated by the Son and cast into Hell, Satan utters these now-familiar lines: "Here at last / We shall be free. . . . Better to reign in Hell than serve in Heaven!" (1.258–59, 263). Satan's plans to get revenge will backfire; God will oppose him and have the last word. Satan's "malice" does exactly the opposite of what he wants, because it serves to "bring forth / Infinite goodness." He will experience "treble confusion." God changes him and his followers into serpents. "Who aspires must down as low / As high he soared" (9.169–70).

Why Does the Author Focus on David's Good Looks?

The narrator describes David as "glowing with health and . . . a fine appearance and handsome features" (or, in the Hebrew text, "ruddy, with beauty of eyes and goodness of appearance"; 16:12). Perhaps David's good looks are a sign of divine favor (see v. 18), but this focus on David's appearance seems to run counter to the theme of the story. The Lord has just declared that "people look at the outward appearance" (Hebrew, "look to the eyes"), as opposed to the heart (v. 7). In light of this, we do not expect the narrator to draw attention to the beauty of David's eyes. Perhaps the description is foreboding and reflects the human perspective, just illustrated in Samuel's reaction to Eliab's appearance. While the Lord looks at the heart, people (including even someone as spiritually astute as Samuel) have a tendency to look on the outward appearance.

Though David is not as obvious a candidate for king as his older brother Eliab, he nevertheless is physically appealing. Though he apparently has a "heart" that impresses God (1 Sam. 13:14), he will be, because of his special physical qualities, susceptible to the temptations that inevitably face those who are so endowed (see Gen. 39:6). Perhaps it is not coincidental that Bathsheba is called "beautiful [or "good"] of appearance" (2 Sam. 11:2 AT), a description that is quite similar to the phrase "handsome [or "good"] of appearance," used of David in verse 12.[a] When human beings are involved, the potential for failure is always latent, even in one as impressive (even to God!) as David.

[a] See Brueggemann, *David's Truth,* 20.

David's Faith Ignites a Victory

Big Idea *Faith in the Lord's power to save can be the catalyst for victory.*

Understanding the Text

The Text in Context

In the previous chapter, Samuel anointed David as the new king. Having departed from Saul, the Lord's Spirit came upon David, and the Lord sent an "evil spirit" to torment Saul.[1] Through God's providence, David has arrived in Saul's royal court and relieved Saul's fears with his music. Now the stage is set for David to replace Saul. In chapter 17 the narrator continues to demonstrate David's superiority to Saul. In the face of the enemy, Saul is paralyzed by fear and cannot see beyond the surface. But David is concerned with the Lord's honor and convinced that the Lord will give Israel the victory.

The people requested a king to lead Israel's armies in battle. Their focus was on the tangible: they wanted a standing army like other nations had. Here David demonstrates that battles are fought in God's strength and for God's honor. Though warriors may show skill and daring, "the living God" is the victor. David models for Israel what a king should believe and how a king should act.

Yet David's success sets the stage for Saul's jealousy, which prompts him to plot David's demise. Beginning in the next chapter, the story will focus on Saul's relentless efforts to kill David and the Lord's providential protection of his chosen king.

Historical and Cultural Background

The encounter between Goliath and David is an ordeal of divine judgment.[2] David treats the Philistine's words as an insult against Israel's God (1 Sam. 17:26, 36) and regards himself as the Lord's representative on the field of battle (vv. 37, 45–47). Likewise, the Philistine calls upon his gods to destroy David (v. 43). There are other examples of single combat in ancient Near Eastern literature (*COS*, 1:79, 201).[3]

Interpretive Insights

17:4 *His height was six cubits and a span.* When presenting Saul to Israel, Samuel drew attention to his height (10:23–24). But now the enemy produces a champion who is even taller than Saul and so impressive that Saul is paralyzed with fear. However, great physical stature does not impress God (16:7), nor does it frighten David.[4]

17:5 *He had a bronze helmet.* The narrator gives a lengthy description of Goliath's armor and weapons, to paint a vivid picture of just how formidable a foe he appears to be.[5] This has the literary effect of increasing the tension of the plot, but in the end it also has the effect of highlighting the faith of David, who is not intimidated by this imposing and seemingly invincible warrior.[6]

17:8 *servants of Saul*. Unless this is part of his rhetorical strategy, the Philistine champion, like the Israelites (see v. 11), does not see beyond his senses. He characterizes the Israelite army as simply "the servants of Saul," when in reality they are the "armies of the living God" (vv. 26, 36). He defies the "armies of Israel" and asks for a mere man to meet him in battle (v. 10), when in reality he is facing and defying the "LORD Almighty" (v. 45). David, however, understands the full implications of the Philistine's challenge and responds with extraordinary theological insight (vv. 26, 36, 45–47).[7]

17:11 *On hearing the Philistine's words, Saul and all the Israelites were dismayed and terrified*. Israel's response is antithetical to the prebattle exhortations of Moses, Joshua, and the Lord himself (Deut. 1:21; 31:8; Josh. 1:9; 8:1; 10:25). Their response also marks a sad reversal of an earlier event when the people respond to the Lord's self-revelation in the storm with great fear (12:18).[8]

17:24 *they all fled from him in great fear*. In the reference to Israel's fleeing from the Philistine, there may be an echo of the defeat at Aphek, when the ark was captured (1 Sam. 4:10, 16–17), and an ironic contrast with Jonathan's earlier victory over the Philistines (14:22).

17:33 *you are only a young man*. Once more Saul assesses the situation strictly on the basis of what he perceives with his senses (cf. v. 11), without factoring God into the equation.

17:34 *When a lion or a bear came*. The verbal sequence in verses 34–35 (conjunction with perfect form) indicates that these actions are customary. David is not describing an isolated incident. As a shepherd he has encountered predators on several occasions, and on each occasion he has followed

Goliath is described as carrying a javelin, spear, and sword and wearing a bronze helmet, a coat of scale armor, and bronze greaves (shin armor). The javelin was a medium-range weapon meant to be thrown, while the sword and spear were used for slashing or stabbing in hand-to-hand combat. The soldiers on this warrior vase from Mycenae (twelfth century BC) are outfitted in a similar manner. They are wearing helmets, armor, and greaves and carrying javelins and shields.

1 Samuel 17

the described procedure. These experiences have taught him to act quickly, skillfully, and decisively.

17:37 *The* Lord *. . . will rescue me*. David's declaration echoes the speeches of Samuel, who on two occasions reminded the people how the Lord is able to deliver them from the hand of their enemies (1 Sam. 7:3; 10:18).

17:38 *Then Saul dressed David in his own tunic*. Saul has heard David's confession of how the Lord has delivered him, and he has even prayed that the Lord will be with David. Yet his focus remains limited: he tries to dress David in his own armor. He even puts a "bronze helmet" on David's head, as if to make him a little Goliath (cf. v. 5). But David has not specifically mentioned armor or weapons in relating his exploits: his focus is on the Lord's enablement (v. 37), and he has a more creative plan in mind for defeating Goliath.

17:40 *approached the Philistine*. The narrator depicts David as being unhesitating and courageous. David's aggressive forward advance expresses his unflinching faith in the Lord's power to deliver and stands in sharp contrast to the Israelites, who fled from Goliath when they saw him (v. 24).

17:42 *He looked David over and saw . . . a boy*. Consistent with this chapter's pattern, Goliath, like Saul, cannot see beyond his senses. He sees only David, a mere boy, who seems poorly armed; he does not recognize the Lord, who is with David (cf. v. 8).

17:46 *the* Lord *will deliver you into my hands*. While Goliath's focus is his personal honor and prowess (vv. 43–44), David focuses attention upon the Lord. David will act to bring glory to God, not to himself.

17:49 *taking out a stone, he slung it*. David demonstrates great courage, born of his faith in the Lord; he also displays ingenuity and cunning. The scene shows that everyone expects this battle to be fought at close quarters: (1) Goliath's weaponry (javelin [or perhaps scimitar],[9] spear, and sword; cf. vv. 6–7, 47, 51) is designed for fighting at close quarters. (2) Saul tries to outfit David with his armor and sword, as if expecting a hand-to-hand struggle. (3) David's reference to fighting wild animals at close range hints that he might fight Goliath in the same way. (4) Goliath's movements (v. 41) and challenge, "Come to me" (v. 44), suggest that he is expecting a close-range conflict. The text makes it clear that Goliath does not see David (v. 42) until after David has chosen his stones (v. 40).[10] When he mentions David's weapons, he speaks only of "sticks" (v. 43; cf. v. 40) and says nothing about the sling, which David uses to deck the giant in one swift, deadly moment. King and Stager estimate that one can propel a sling stone at a speed of 160–240

> The confrontation between David and Goliath occurred in the Valley of Elah, pictured here.

kilometers per hour (ca. 100–150 miles per hour).[11] In the hands of a well-trained slinger, this weapon can be deadly accurate (Judg. 20:16).

he fell facedown on the ground. The language echoes that used for the fall of Dagon in 1 Samuel 5:3–4. Just as the Philistine god Dagon fell on his face before the ark of the Lord with his head cut off, so the Philistine champion falls on his face before the Lord's warrior, who then cuts off his head (v. 51).[12] The parallels to the earlier text attest to the accuracy of David's perspective: he is merely the Lord's instrument in defeating the enemy, and the Lord, in contrast to the decapitated Philistine deity, is the living God.

Theological Insights

In the narrative typology of the Former Prophets, David emerges as a new Caleb/Joshua. Those heroes of the conquest period fearlessly confronted and defeated the gigantic Anakites, who had paralyzed Israel with fear (Num. 13:26–33; Josh. 11:21–22; 14:12–15; 15:13–14; Judg. 1:10, 20). Following the paradigmatic judges Othniel and Ehud, there was a visible decline in the quality of Israelite leadership. Barak, Gideon, Jephthah, and Samson were plagued by weak faith and deficient wisdom. The situation took a turn for the better as Samuel assumed leadership. When David steps forward to face the Philistine giant (who may have been related to the Anakites; cf. Deut. 2:11 with 1 Chron. 20:4–8), he demonstrates the same courage born of faith that Joshua and Caleb exhibited. Like them, he focuses on God's enablement, not the strength of the enemy (Josh. 14:12).

David's portrayal of God is indeed theologically rich. David twice calls the Lord the "living God" (vv. 26, 36). This title is not just an affirmation of God's existence (alive, as opposed to nonexistent or dead). It also focuses on his active presence, self-revelation, power, authority, and ongoing involvement in history.[13] He is the living God in the sense that he actively intervenes for his people. He rescues his people (v. 37), saves them (v. 47), and hands their enemies over to them (vv. 46–47). He is a mighty warrior king, who is "the Lord Almighty, the God of the armies of Israel" (v. 45). In this context the title "Lord Almighty" (traditionally, "Lord of Hosts" [KJV]) depicts the Lord as the one who leads his "hosts" (here the Israelite army) into battle. He is an invincible warrior. In fact, the battle belongs to him; he determines its outcome regardless of how well equipped the combatants may be (v. 47).[14]

For the exiles, David's example, in both word and deed, is an encouragement and inspiration. Though they have been defeated and are under the authority of a foreign king, David's experience is a reminder that faith in God's power is rewarded, for he is the living God and is active in the life of his people. As the one who is sovereign over battles and their outcome, he has allowed his people to experience defeat and exile, but he also has the capacity to rescue and save his people. This is a message that the exiles need to embrace as they look ahead to what must appear to be an uncertain future (see Isa. 40).

In contrast to Goliath's weapons, David arms himself with a sling and sling stones for a long-range offensive attack. Slings were used not only by shepherds but by armies, as shown in this Assyrian relief from Nineveh (700–692 BC).

Teaching the Text

1. *The Lord's power is determinative in battle, and faith in that power can be the catalyst for victory.* David's faith is exemplary. In the face of a physically imposing, seemingly invincible enemy, he refuses to focus on what he hears and sees on the battlefield. He places his faith in the living God, who has proved himself trustworthy in David's experience. As frail human beings, who are so easily influenced by our physical senses, we are prone to let the challenges of the present swallow up what we have learned in the past and paralyze us. David's faith does not allow this to happen. He remembers how God has delivered him from powerful predators, and he is convinced that the past will be repeated in the present. David is obviously skilled with the weapons of a shepherd, including the deadly sling. But he does not brag about those skills and place false confidence in them. He realizes that it is the Lord who empowers him for battle and gives him the nerve and presence of mind to use his training and weapons effectively (see as well 2 Sam. 22:30–46 = Ps. 18:29–45). For David, the Lord is worthy of complete trust, for he is the living, active God, who determines the outcome of battles and gives his people victory and salvation. In teaching this passage, we should follow David's lead and highlight the Lord's power rather than David's heroism or skill.

2. *Focusing on outward appearances rather than the Lord's power can obscure reality, stifle faith, and produce paralyzing fear.* In this account, Saul and the Israelites

serve as a literary foil for David. David's faith is impressive, but especially so when seen against the backdrop of their fear. One expects that Saul, as the leader of Israel's armies, will be the champion, going out in the Lord's power and representing God and Israel in single combat. But Saul and the army are unable to see beyond their senses. When they hear the Philistine's arrogant challenge, they are overcome by fear (v. 11). When they see him, they literally run in fear (v. 24). When David asks for Saul's permission to fight the Philistine, Saul sees only David's youth and inexperience (v. 33). Israel's obsession with that which is tangible obscures the reality that David's faith allows him to see. The Lord is sovereign over the battle and fully capable of delivering his people and giving them the victory. Walking by sight stifles faith and brings paralyzing fear. All Israel can do is stand, wait, and tremble, while the Philistine defies them and, indirectly, their God. When God's people respond in this way, they send the wrong message to the watching world. The Lord is a living God, but the world fails to see his active presence if his people do not activate his intervention through their faith. David wants all observers to recognize God's sovereignty and God's commitment to his people (vv. 46–47).

Illustrating the Text

Walking by faith and not by sight assures the believer of God's intervention and of his power to deliver.

Quote: *Reaching for the Invisible God*, by **Philip Yancey.** Yancey (b. 1949) reflects on a public television series based on interviews with World War II survivors. In one interview, the soldiers recount how they spent a particular day. Each one had done some small thing: played cards, watched a tank go by while engaged in firefights. Soon, however, they discovered they had just been part of one of the most crucial parts of the war, the Battle of the Bulge. As Yancey puts it,

> It did not *feel* decisive to any of them at the time; . . . None had the big picture of what was happening elsewhere. Great victories are won when ordinary people execute their assigned tasks—and a faithful person does not debate each day whether he or she is in the mood to follow the sergeant's orders. . . . We exercise faith by responding to the task . . . before us, for we have control only over our actions in the present moment.[15]

Lyrics: **"I Still Believe," by Jeremy Camp.** For a young audience, Jeremy's testimony and the words to this song are meaningful. Jeremy lost his young wife to ovarian cancer shortly after they were married; her faith has deeply influenced his spiritual walk.

Church History: *Foxe's Book of Martyrs,* **by John Foxe.** This is an account (1563) of Christian martyrs throughout Western history from the first century through the early sixteenth century, emphasizing the sufferings of English Protestants. This classic book is an invaluable resource for stories of the faithful.

Walking by sight stifles faith and produces paralyzing fear, obscuring the reality of God's presence and power.

Bible: Matthew 14:22–33. This is the account of Peter walking on the water.

The Lord Is with David

Big Idea *The Lord protects and grants success to his chosen servants.*

Understanding the Text

The Text in Context

The tension between Saul and David has been building in the story line. At first, Saul's successor was described as one who is in touch with God and superior to Saul (13:14; 15:28), but he was not named. In chapters 16 and 17 he appears and quickly demonstrates his qualifications by bringing the king relief from his distress and then leading Israel to a great victory. All seems to be well. Impressed by David's prowess and success, Saul made him a full-time member of the royal court and gave him a promotion within the army. Divine providence has moved David even closer to the throne he is destined to possess.

However, the narrator quickly informs us that the road to the throne will not be easy. David's popularity prompts Saul's jealousy. The narrator depicts Saul as one who acts contrary to Israel's best interests and who opposes God's chosen ruler. The conflict that bursts to the surface in chapter 18 will consume the story until Saul's death and even then will not be completely resolved. Yet there is no conflict in the narrator's mind. Through his description of events, he makes it clear that David is God's chosen king. Everyone comes to love David (vv. 3, 16, 20), even Saul's own son and heir apparent, Jonathan, and his own daughter Michal. Throughout the chapter, the narrator emphasizes that the Lord is with David, granting him success (vv. 5, 12, 14, 28, 30), while he characterizes Saul as angry, jealous, emotionally unstable, and increasingly fearful (vv. 8–12, 15, 29). There should be no doubt that David, not Saul, is the rightful king. The following chapters only serve to drive home that point.

Historical and Cultural Background

In this chapter we are told that Jonathan "loved" David (v. 1) and that all Israel and Judah "loved" him as well (v. 16). In this case the verb carries the connotation "was loyal to" (cf. vv. 1, 3). This idiom is attested in the broader culture.[1] In the Amarna letters (fourteenth century BC) cities are said to "love" a leader; the term refers to loyalty. For example, in one letter (no. 138) the king of Byblos, writing to Pharaoh, says, "Behold the city! Half of it loves the sons of Abdi-ashirta [a rebel] and half of it loves my lord [Pharaoh]."[2]

Interpretive Insights

18:1 *he loved him as himself.* Here the word "loved" refers primarily to devotion and allegiance (cf. 20:16–17) that prompts Jonathan to make a covenant with David (v. 3).[3] Following Jonathan's death in battle, David remarks that his love surpassed that of women (2 Sam. 1:26). This does not suggest that David and Jonathan have a homosexual relationship. David's point is that Jonathan's allegiance to him is even stronger and more enduring than the romantic love between a man and woman or that Jonathan's loyalty means more to him than even the romantic love he experiences from women.

18:7 *and David his tens of thousands.* The second poetic line makes an advance on and intensifies the first,[4] and the shift in subject from Saul to David expresses a contrast between them.[5] This prompts suspicious (paranoid?) Saul to keep a close eye on David (v. 9). It is likely that Samuel's words (see 1 Sam. 15:28) are echoing loudly in Saul's mind at this point.

18:8 *Saul was very angry.* These Hebrew words are also used of Saul when he hears of the Ammonite threat against Jabesh Gilead (11:6). On that occasion he displays righteous anger on behalf of his fellow Israelites. But on this second occasion his anger is self-centered, prompted by a per-

Key Themes of 1 Samuel 18

- Despite Saul's attempts to kill David, the Lord protects him and grants him success.
- Saul's ambition produces jealousy, fear, and opposition to the Lord's chosen king.

ceived threat to his honor. The reversal in circumstances and motives highlights how far Saul has fallen.

18:10 *came forcefully on Saul.* The verb (*tsalah*) was used of the Lord's Spirit rushing upon Saul on two earlier occasions (10:6, 10; 11:6). On the first occasion, possession of the Spirit was a sign that the Lord had chosen and empowered Saul (see note above on 10:2–6). On the second occasion, the Spirit energized Saul to rally his troops and deliver Jabesh Gilead from the Ammonites. The repetition of this verb in 18:10 draws attention to the tragic irony of what has happened to Saul. Having been abandoned by the Lord's Spirit, he is now victimized by this evil spirit.

He was prophesying. We might be tempted to think of prophesying in a positive

In 1 Samuel 18:6 the women of the Israelite towns celebrate the defeat of Goliath by greeting the returning Saul with singing and dancing accompanied by musical instruments. This type of response was common in the cultures of the ancient Near East, as shown on this section of an Assyrian relief (Nineveh, 660–650 BC). Here the remaining residents of a recently defeated Elamite town welcome their new ruler with musicians playing harps and pipes, followed by women and children clapping and singing.

sense, as a means of divine revelation. But in this case Saul's behavior is a prelude to violence and wrongdoing. We should not assume that his prophesying involves any revelation from God. Saul's prophesying is a sign to those around him that the evil spirit is once more tormenting him.

18:12 *Saul was afraid.* Fear is attributed to Saul on two prior occasions (1 Sam. 15:24; 17:11). On both of these occasions, Saul's fear is unwarranted and inappropriate. Now, ironically, he fears David, even though David is loyal to him. This fear will escalate as God's favor upon David becomes more and more apparent (vv. 15, 29).

but [the LORD] had departed from Saul. In 16:14 we are told that the Lord's Spirit has "departed" from Saul. Here it is the Lord himself who has left Saul, suggesting a close relationship between the Lord and his Spirit. In 28:16 Samuel likewise refers to the Lord's departing from Saul and adds an additional idea: the Lord has actually become Saul's enemy.

18:16 *all Israel and Judah loved David.* This need not mean that they have transferred their official allegiance from Saul to David, but it does suggest that they are drawn to David as a military leader and willingly follow him into battle (cf. vv. 13–14).

18:17 *I will give her to you in marriage.* Saul has already promised his daughter to Goliath's killer (cf. 17:25), but apparently he has not kept his side of the bargain. Perhaps this causes David to be skeptical of the king's trustworthiness. The spear-throwing incident makes David wary about getting too close to Saul. It comes as no surprise that David respectfully declines Saul's offer (vv. 18–19).

18:22 *his attendants all love you.* This argument is especially devious on Saul's part for it is designed to tempt David to seek power. Saul's attendants are his court officials (cf. 1 Sam. 16:15), whose loyalty would give David "a natural base of power at court."[6]

18:25 *a hundred Philistine foreskins.* Thinking that David might be concerned that he would have to pay an exorbitant bride-price, Saul assures David that all he wants are the foreskins of one hundred Philistines.[7] For David, such an offer is appealing because he can do this in the course of carrying out his responsibilities as a military commander without needing to diminish his own personal wealth in any way. Agreeing to the deal, David brings two hundred foreskins to Saul,

Saul's unusual bride-price request was not as strange as it might sound. Body parts were often collected as war trophies, and piles of heads and hands are often pictured on ancient Near Eastern reliefs. Normally the bride-price would be set at some monetary amount, which the groom would pay in silver. Shown here is a coil of silver, which would be cut into shekel-weight pieces for payment.

giving him twice what he has demanded (vv. 26–27a).[8]

18:28 *When Saul realized.* In verse 15 Saul sees how successful David is and fears him. Here his recognition deepens: he not only sees but also realizes (or, "knows") that the Lord is with David.

Theological Insights

As noted above, in this chapter the narrator continues to mount his case that David is God's chosen king, even though he also refuses to whitewash David. The Lord is with David and grants him success (vv. 5, 12, 14, 28, 30). The narrator presents contrasting responses to God's chosen king. Desperate to hold on to his position in spite of Samuel's prophetic announcement of his coming demise as king, Saul grows jealous and afraid of David and tries to kill him. Everyone else comes to love David (vv. 3, 16, 20), including Saul's daughter and his son Jonathan.

Jonathan is a literary foil for Saul. God has chosen David to be king and has rejected Saul. Jonathan knows what God has decreed for Saul and his family (1 Sam. 13:13–14; 15:26–29). Though apparently unaware of what has taken place at Jesse's house (16:1–13), he senses David's destiny. Saul, due to his pride and his lust for power, resists God's program in his quest to destroy David, but Jonathan, who stands in line to inherit his father's throne, rejects personal ambition and is loyal to David.[9]

For exilic readers anticipating a time when the Lord will restore their nation, this account supports the prophets' message that the Lord will reestablish the nation through an ideal Davidic king. It also provides a model of what this king will

The "Evil Spirit" and Saul

This is the second time that the narrator has told us that the "evil spirit" comes from God (cf. 16:14–15). It appears that this spirit prompts Saul to try to kill David, which seems against God's purposes. The key to resolving the issue is to note the repetition of the statement "The LORD was with" David (vv. 12, 14, 28). The Lord is protecting David from danger and is not about to let Saul kill him. The Lord's purpose in sending the spirit is not to harm David but to torment Saul and, by prompting him to attempt such a heinous deed, demonstrate to everyone that Saul has been abandoned by the Lord and is unfit to rule Israel. As when he later tries to kill his own son Jonathan, he acts contrary to Israel's best interests and opposes one whom God has obviously favored.

look like. He will, like David, experience the empowering presence of the Lord in a special way. The Lord's presence is vital to success. Furthermore, the tragic example of Saul reminds them of what can happen to those who, out of self-interest, oppose God's program and chosen leader: they are swept downward in a spiral of anger and fear that consumes them and ultimately destroys them. In stark contrast to his father, Jonathan models the proper response to the Lord's chosen: loyalty.

Teaching the Text

1. *The Lord protects those whom he chooses and grants them success.* In this chapter the narrator emphasizes that the Lord is "with" David, granting him success in his military endeavors, while protecting him from Saul's attempts to kill him. The Lord's provision for David is paradigmatic of the way he protects and blesses all whom he chooses. Sometimes, as with David, the Lord provides physical protection (Acts 18:9–10), but this is not always the case, as the pages of Scripture and the record of the church's martyrs remind us. However, Jesus does

promise his chosen servants his powerful presence as they carry out his commission for this age (Matt. 28:20; cf. Acts 11:21). He is building his church, and the enemy will not be able to thwart his purposes (Matt. 16:18). Paul assures us that nothing can stand successfully against us, for God is always working out his purposes in and through us, and his love insulates us from harm (Rom. 8:28–39).

2. *When the Lord's chosen leaders succumb to self-focused ambition, they can fall prey to jealousy and fear and thus oppose the Lord's purposes.* The narrator also focuses on Saul's opposition to David and paints a tragic picture of one who is consumed by jealousy, overcome by fear, and obsessed with destroying God's chosen leader. Saul may be viewed as paradigmatic of those who oppose God's program, including those who seek to destroy the greater David, the messianic king Jesus, and those who today seek to destroy his followers. However, Saul is a member of the Lord's covenant community, Israel, and even occupies a leadership position within that community. For this reason he is best seen as paradigmatic of those within the church who allow jealousy and self-interest to so consume them that they become enemies of God. The New Testament denounces such individuals and warns them that God's discipline will be severe (1 Cor. 4:18–21; 2 Cor. 12:20; Gal. 5:19–21; Titus 3:10–11; James 3:14–16; 3 John 9–10).

Illustrating the Text

God protects his people as he grants them success in the mission to which they are called.

Church History: Martin Luther. On October 31, 1517, Luther (1483–1546) changed the course of human history when he nailed his Ninety-Five Theses to the church door at Wittenberg, accusing the Roman Catholic Church of multiple heresies. Pope Leo X then pronounced him a heretic. Refusing to recant his views before the Diet of Worms, he stated the following famous words: "Unless I am convinced by proofs from Scriptures or by plain and clear reasons and arguments, I can and will not retract, for it is neither safe nor wise to do anything against conscience. *Here I stand. I can do no other. God help me. Amen.*" On May 25, 1521, at the Diet of Worms, the

Martin Luther's study in Wartburg Castle, where he translated the Bible into German

emperor condemned Luther as an outlaw and thus endangered his life. Snatched from the Diet by powerful friends, he was hidden away at Wartburg Castle for about a year, from which he ventured out in disguise to speak. Meanwhile he continued his work of translation, putting the Bible into the language of the people. Martin Luther was the first person to translate and publish the Bible in the commonly spoken dialect of the German people. The Luther German New Testament translation was published in September 1522. The translation of the Old Testament followed, resulting in an entire German-language Bible in 1534.

Selfish ambition and jealousy are destructive and divisive within the covenant community.

Bible: Genesis 29–50. In this story we see the dramatic consequences of Joseph's brothers' jealousy of him because he is beloved by his father, a jealousy that causes them to try to destroy him.

Film: *Amadeus.* In this memorable treatment of Mozart's troubled life (1984), jealousy is a prominent theme, the jealousy of the composer and musician Salieri toward the great Mozart. Salieri bargains with God: "If I am a good man, will you allow me to become an extraordinary composer?" Upon meeting Mozart, Salieri realizes that Mozart is indeed a superior musician, a fact that enrages him since he considers himself to be a person of greater character. His anger at

David's Growing Ambition

Why does David finally accept Saul's offer to marry his daughter? When David rejects Saul's offer of Merab by appealing to his lowly social status, one senses David is using this as an excuse due to his suspicions about Saul's intentions. Having to dodge a spear will do that to a person! Why would he change his mind when Michal is offered? Perhaps David is succumbing to Saul's strategy to some degree and becoming enamored with the royal court and the possibilities it presents. We know that David is interested in material gain (17:26). When he describes himself as "a poor man and little known" (18:23), he may be hinting that he cannot afford to accept such an offer. In other words, his reply in response to the offer of Michal may really be David's way of saying, "I'll accept if the price is right." After all, once Saul makes the bride affordable, David seems to jump at the opportunity. Is success, fueled by the assurance that he has supporters in the royal court, starting to go to David's head?

The first time we are made privy to David's thoughts by the all-knowing narrator, we are told that David is pleased to enter the royal court (18:26). When one correlates David's initial recorded words (17:26) with his initial recorded thoughts, a theme emerges, as Steussy explains: "David is keenly aware of political position and possibilities for his own advancement."[a]

[a] Steussy, *David: Biblical Portraits*, 54. See as well McKenzie, *King David*, 87. Berlin makes a convincing case that David never loves Michal and uses her strictly to further his political ambitions (*Poetics and Interpretation*, 24–25); likewise says Lawton, "1 Samuel 18," 425.

God sours his spirit, and he grows destructive toward Mozart. He speaks viciously about Mozart whenever he can, humiliating him and his wife, and even ruins his reputation with significant people. Salieri's jealousy is not unlike what often infiltrates the church: musicians jealous of other musicians, pastors threatened by their elders or others gifted in leadership or preaching, and laypeople jealous of others' good fortune.

The "Nine Lives" of David

Big Idea *Whether by divine providence or direct intervention, God is capable of protecting his chosen servants from those who seek to destroy them.*

Understanding the Text

The Text in Context

In chapter 18 Saul used different methods to try to kill David on three separate occasions (18:10–11, 17, 25). The pattern continues in chapter 19: (1) Saul orders Jonathan to kill David (19:1), (2) he again throws a spear at David (19:10; cf. 18:10–11), (3) he orders his henchmen to arrest David and bring him to the royal palace for execution (19:11–15), (4) he sends three separate companies of soldiers to Ramah to capture David (19:20–21), and (5) he himself goes to Ramah to arrest David (19:22–24). Saul's efforts to kill David continue in chapter 20, forcing David to flee for his life.

In this chapter (as well as chap. 20) the narrator continues to mount his case that David is God's chosen king. The Lord continues to protect David and to foil Saul's attempts to murder him, whether by Jonathan's intercession, David's agility in dodging Saul's spear, Michal's cunning in helping David escape, or the Spirit's supernatural intervention.

The narrator emphasizes David's innocence, primarily through the verbal testimony of Jonathan, who protests his father's

attempt to kill David (19:4–5; cf. 20:32). Jonathan depicts David as a humble servant of Saul (19:4), a claim that is subsequently supported by David's submission to Jonathan's authority (cf. 20:7–8, 41).

Historical and Cultural Background

As part of her scheme to help David escape from her father, Michal puts an idol in David's bed to make Saul's servants think that he is ill and sleeping. The fact that an idol is in Michal's home, or at least readily accessible to her, is alarming. This particular kind of idol (*terapim*) is referred to in a handful of other contexts (Gen. 31:19, 34–35; Judg. 17:5; 18:14, 17–18, 20; 1 Sam. 15:23; 2 Kings 23:24; Ezek. 21:21; Hosea 3:4; Zech. 10:2). *Terapim* are used in divination (Ezek. 21:21; Zech. 10:2). They may be "ancestor figurines used in necromancy" (communication with the dead).[1] The image is probably not an object of worship, but rather a means of acquiring information.

In these chapters Saul prophesies three times. In two instances he seems to exhibit ecstatic behavior. In 10:6 Samuel informs Saul that he will be "changed into a different person" as he prophesies; according to 19:24, Saul "stripped off his garments" while prophesying and "lay naked" on the ground all night and day. Prophetic activity in the Old Testament world was sometimes accompanied by such ecstatic behavior, which served as a sign that the person prophesying had been gripped by an outside spiritual power. Extrabiblical examples of such behavior abound. The Egyptian official Wen-Amon described the following incident that occurred on his visit to the Phoenician city of Byblos (in about 1100 BC): "Now while he was offering to his gods, the god took hold of a young man of his young men and put him in a trance. . . . Now it was while the entranced one was entranced that night that I found a ship headed for Egypt" (COS, 1:90). Some prophets engaged in trance behavior that was often violent and uncontrolled. In a text from Ugarit a man complains: "My brothers bathe in their own blood like ecstatics" (cf. 1 Kings 18:28–29).[2] According to the Mesopotamian creation myth *Enuma Elish* (4.88), the goddess Tiamat was "beside herself" like an ecstatic and "turned into a maniac" (COS, 1:398).

Interpretive Insights

19:1 *to kill David.* Five times in this chapter reference is made to Saul's intending to kill David (vv. 1, 2, 5, 11, 15). Initially his command to kill David appears in an indirect quotation (v. 1). Then his intention to kill is described by his son (vv. 2, 5) and the narrator (v. 11). But in the end we hear Saul himself state his intention in no uncertain terms (v. 15).

Jonathan had taken a great liking to David. This same expression is used in 18:22 in Saul's message to David, sent via

his servants. Of course, in that case Saul is lying and attempting to deceive David into seeking marriage to Michal, at the peril of his life (vv. 21, 23–25). In contrast to Saul's deceptive claim, the narrator here affirms Jonathan's genuine fondness for David.[3] The contrast contributes to the narrator's presentation of Jonathan as a literary foil to his father. Jonathan fully supports David, while Saul tries to murder him.[4] Jonathan's loyalty to David also supports the narrator's presentation of David as one who is not seeking to usurp Saul's throne, for Jonathan would not favor a traitor.

19:4 *Let not the king do wrong to his servant David.* Jonathan's words testify to David's innocence and Saul's guilt; as such they contribute powerfully to the narrator's agenda of exonerating David and indicting Saul.

what he has done has benefited you greatly. In this context more than simple beneficial action is in view. Jonathan counts David as Saul's "servant" and stresses that he has done no wrong against Saul. Consequently David's good deeds can be viewed as loyal actions on Saul's behalf.[5]

19:5 *The* LORD *won a great victory for all Israel, and you saw it and were glad.* Jonathan's view of the battle as ultimately the Lord's victory is consistent with David's interpretation of it (17:47) and with his interpretation of his own heroic action on an earlier occasion (14:6, 10, 12). By reminding his father of this theological reality, Jonathan casts David in the role of the Lord's instrument of victory, which Saul readily accepted on that occasion. Why now does Saul want to kill one who has served the king and the Lord so effectively?

There is irony here. The heroic acts of both Jonathan and David have been the catalyst for the Lord's intervention, which has resulted in a military victory for Israel. But after both occasions, Saul tries to kill the hero (14:44; 18:11; etc.). Following his victory over the Ammonites, Saul refused to execute his detractors, even though some of his supporters urged him to do so (11:12–13). His reason for showing mercy was that the Lord had "rescued Israel" (or "won a victory in Israel," the same expression used by Jonathan in 19:5). As in Saul's case, the Lord has won a victory for Israel through David. The proper response, as earlier, is celebration, not murder.

19:6 *As surely as the Lord lives.* This is not the first time Saul makes an oath that he does not keep (14:44). Saul swears that David will not die but then seeks to kill him on several occasions, only to be foiled in his efforts. The narrator depicts Saul as one who foolishly seeks to keep a misguided oath and as one who breaks a proper one. An oath should be indicative of one's highest priorities, but Saul's are misplaced.

19:9 *But an evil spirit from the Lord came on Saul.* In 16:14 the evil spirit began to torment Saul in conjunction with the departure of the Lord's Spirit. In 18:10 it came upon him with force in conjunction with his anger and jealousy (see vv. 8–9). Here it takes him over after he has promised

not to harm David (19:6). But there is also a reference to David's continued success (v. 8), which apparently is the catalyst for renewed jealousy and fear on Saul's part, though this is not stated. What is shocking is that the spirit undermines a proper action by Saul. It seems as if the Lord, through this spirit that is sent by him, refuses to let Saul do right, for the Lord regards Saul as his enemy (cf. 28:16–18). (For more on this issue, see "Theological Insights" below.)

First Samuel 19 records the second time that Saul has tried to kill David with his spear. Shown here is a warrior holding a spear on an eighth-century relief from Arslan Tash, Syria.

19:10 *Saul tried to pin him to the wall.* The use of the verb "pin" (*nakah*) sets up a vivid contrast between Saul and David that facilitates the narrator's pro-David agenda. In verses 5 and 8 this same verb is used to describe how David strikes down the Philistine champion and armies. While David is striking down the enemies of Israel, Saul is trying to strike down the Lord's chosen servant.

19:17 *Why did you . . . send my enemy away?* Saul casts David in the role of his enemy. This is ironic since on two earlier occasions Saul refers to the Philistines as his "enemies" (14:24; 18:25). In his warped perspective, David is no different than they are.

19:24 *He stripped off his garments, and he too prophesied in Samuel's presence.* Saul's prophesying is tragically ironic. On an earlier occasion the Lord's Spirit caused him to prophesy, prompting observers to ask: "Is Saul also among the prophets?" (10:10–13). The prophesying was a sign to Saul that he had been chosen by God to be king (cf. 10:1–8). The Lord energized Saul with his Spirit so that he might attack Israel's enemy, the Philistines (see the comment on 10:7). But now Saul's prophesying has a different purpose: it thwarts his murderous plan and incapacitates him, preventing him from attacking David, so that God's new chosen one can escape (20:1). There is also a contrast with the second episode of Saul's prophesying, recorded in 18:10–11. On that occasion an evil spirit prompts Saul to try to murder David. But in this most recent episode, God's Spirit reduces Saul to a harmless ecstatic to *prevent* violent action against David.

Theological Insights

This account is a reminder of what can happen to those like Saul, whom God rejects as a result of blatant disobedience. The prospects are indeed frightening. In response to Jonathan's convincing defense of David's loyalty, Saul agrees to make peace with David (19:6). But then, as David experiences even more success, the evil spirit from the Lord overcomes Saul and prompts him to try to kill David (19:9–10), igniting another series of attempts on David's life. This leaves Saul so obsessed with destroying David that he is ready to kill anyone he perceives to be David's ally, even his own son and heir apparent (see 20:33). The Lord's treatment of Saul is reminiscent of how he hardened Pharaoh's heart as a judgment upon Pharaoh, who time after time refused Moses's ultimatum that he release God's enslaved people. In the end the divine hardening even caused Pharaoh to reverse his decision once he had responded properly (Exod. 8:8–15; 9:27–10:1; 10:16–20, 24–29; 14:4, 8). Surely the divine hardening brought Pharaoh's deep-seated motives and desires to the surface (cf. Exod. 9:30).[6] Perhaps that is the case with Saul as well. Before he came under the influence of the evil spirit, he blatantly disobeyed the Lord and displayed pride and jealousy (15:12; 18:8–9). Furthermore, following the initial spear-throwing incident (18:10–11), Saul's murderous and deceptive actions are attributed to his fear, not the evil spirit (18:12, 15, 29). To the exiles, Saul's experience is a warning of the consequences of disobedience and divine rejection. Disobedient servants of God can end up being the enemies of God.

Teaching the Text

God does not insulate his chosen servants from trouble and danger, but he does protect them. In these chapters the narrator continues to develop an important theme from chapter 18: God's protection of his chosen servants. This surely presupposes that they need protection. Indeed, God's chosen servants inevitably face danger in a hostile world. One need only read the psalms to be convinced of this. The lament psalms in particular often speak of enemies and implore God for his protection and deliverance (see, among others, Pss. 3; 5; 7; 9; 11; 13; 22; 25). In Psalm 23 David expresses his confidence in God as his provider and protector. He recognizes that sometimes God must lead his people through a dark ravine, where predators may lurk. But God's presence assures his people and vindicates them in the presence of their enemies. In Isaiah 43:1–2 the Lord, speaking to the exiles, assures them that he is their Creator and Redeemer and promises them that he will protect them from even the most dangerous threats, symbolized by water and fire. Jesus warns his followers that they will have trouble in this

world (John 16:33). Recognizing that the world will hate them, he asks the Father to protect them from the evil one (17:14–15) and eventually to take them to heaven to live with him (17:24). Though God's people may suffer persecution and martyrdom, in the end nothing, even physical death, can separate them from God's enduring love (Rom. 8:28–39).

Illustrating the Text

God's people are not insulated from danger.

Christian Autobiography: *Living Sacrifice,* **by Helen Roseveare.** Dr. Helen Roseveare (b. 1925) was an English missionary to the Congo from 1953 to 1973, where she practiced medicine and taught the nationals how to do medical work. She remained in the Congo even as the political situation was becoming very threatening in the 1960s. Taken prisoner by hostile forces, she remained in their

David wrote many lament psalms where he bemoans the oppression by his enemies and pleads with God to provide protection and deliverance. This ivory book cover depicts David dictating the Psalms (tenth to eleventh century AD).

custody for a number of months, during which she was subject to cruel beatings and raped repeatedly. After being released from prison, she returned to England for a short time but then went back to the Congo to found a medical school and hospital facility. Her legacy of aiding the peoples of many different countries who needed not only basic provisions but also medical care has been recorded in her books and in articles.

About her multiple hardships on the mission field, including the treatment by rebels, she recounts,

> Beaten, flung on the ground, kicked—teeth broken, mouth and nose gashed, ribs bruised—driven at gunpoint back to my home, jeered at, insulted, threatened, I knew that if the rebel lieutenant did not pull the trigger of his revolver and end the situation, worse pain, and humiliation lay ahead. It was a very dark night. I felt unutterably alone. For a brief moment, I thought God had failed me. . . . And in desperation, I almost cried out against Him: "It is too much to pay."[7]

God protects his people.

Christian Autobiography: *Living Sacrifice,* **by Helen Roseveare.** Continuing the story told above, Roseveare gives ringing affirmation of God's sovereignty and protection:

> In the darkness and loneliness, He met with me. He was right there, a great, won-

derful, almighty God. His love enveloped me. Suddenly the 'Why' dropped away from me, and an unbelievable peace flowed in, even in the midst of the wickedness. And He breathed a word into my troubled mind: the word *privilege.* "These are not your sufferings; they are not beating you. These are My sufferings."[8]

Hymn: "If Thou but Suffer God to Guide Thee," by Georg Neumark.

Here are some sample lines from this hymn (1641) of confidence in God:

> If thou but suffer God to guide thee,
> And hope in Him through all thy
> ways,
> He'll give thee strength, whate'er
> betide thee,
> And bear thee through the evil days.
> Who trusts in God's unchanging
> love
> Builds on the rock that naught can
> move.
>
> Be patient and await His leisure
> In cheerful hope, with heart
> content,
> To take whate'er Thy Father's
> pleasure
> And His discerning love hath sent,
> Nor doubt our inmost wants are
> known
> To Him who chose us for his own.[9]

God's Protection Takes the Form of a Faithful Friend

Big Idea *Sometimes God protects his chosen servants through other faithful servants who are willing to put God's agenda above self-interest.*

Understanding the Text

The Text in Context

Saul persisted in his efforts to kill David, but Jonathan saved David again, risking his own life in the process. David was finally forced to run away, setting the stage for the next part of the story: David needs to wander from place to place to escape Saul's hostility.

As in the previous chapters, the narrator presents contrasting responses to God's chosen king. Saul becomes obsessed with killing David, while Jonathan continues to do everything in his power to protect David, even though, from the human perspective, it does not seem to be in his best interests (cf. 20:31, 33). Though Jonathan is technically David's superior, he recognizes David's destiny and treats him accordingly (20:14–17).

Interpretive Insights

20:1 *What have I done?* David's protest reiterates Jonathan's earlier argument (19:4–6) and provides further evidence of his innocence and Saul's guilt.

20:2 *Never!* Jonathan, who obviously agrees with David, apparently has not seen or yet heard about the latest attempts on David's life (19:9–24). These take place after Saul has vowed to Jonathan that David will not be killed and has reinstated David within the royal court (19:6–7).

20:4 *Whatever you want me to do, I'll do for you.* This statement does not necessarily indicate that Jonathan views David as his superior and himself as subservient. Similar statements are made elsewhere by those who are in a socially inferior (Num. 23:26; Ruth 3:5) or superior (Num. 22:17; Ruth 3:11) position. But in either case the statement does indicate the speaker's willingness to carry out the wishes of the addressee and play the role, as it were, of a servant, at least in the specific situation in which they find themselves.

20:8 *show kindness to your servant.* David views himself as Saul's servant (17:32, 34, 36), a fact that Jonathan appeals to in his defense of David (19:4). Since Jonathan is the king's son and heir apparent (20:31), David calls himself "your servant" when speaking to Jonathan (vv. 7–8). Apparently the terms of the covenant between David and Jonathan make provision for protection (18:3). The narrator's portrait of David as a self-professed servant of Jonathan contributes to his pro-David agenda by demonstrating that David is loyal to Saul and his house and does not plot to overthrow the king.

20:14 *show me unfailing kindness.* Realizing that the Lord will fulfill his prayer of blessing for David (v. 13) and cut off his enemies (v. 15), Jonathan asks David to show covenantal loyalty (*hesed*) to him and his descendants. Typically a king, when establishing a new dynasty, will wipe out the offspring of the former king to solidify his rule and prevent any attempt to reclaim the throne. In Jonathan's case, he expects to be the new king's second-in-command (see 23:17).[1]

20:15 *when the LORD has cut off every one of David's enemies.* David is not a would-be usurper or traitor. On the contrary, the Lord's enabling presence and intervention will elevate David to the throne (see 23:17).

20:16 *Jonathan made a covenant with the house of David.* Jonathan makes another covenant (cf. 18:3), this time with "the house of David." This suggests that the provisions of the covenant will extend to their descendants (cf. vv. 14–15, 42). It also implies that the Lord will establish a dynasty for David (v. 15).

20:17 *And Jonathan had David reaffirm his oath.* According to the Hebrew

Key Themes of 1 Samuel 20

- The Lord protects David through loyal Jonathan.
- Jonathan's commitment to God's chosen servant necessitates self-denial and places him in harm's way.

text, Jonathan makes David swear an oath again. This reading is problematic for at least two reasons: (1) There is no prior Davidic oath recorded in the immediate context, except for the one in verse 3, where the oath simply emphasizes David's belief that his life is in grave danger. If we retain the Hebrew text, the prior oath must be one made in conjunction with the original covenant Jonathan made with David,

Jonathan plans to send a message to David about whether to stay or flee by shooting arrows toward a target in the field and instructing his servant how to find them. Shown here is an archer with bow and arrow from Tell Halaf, Syria (1200–900 BC).

recorded in 18:3. (2) The relationship of 20:17b to the statement is unclear. How would Jonathan's intense loyalty to David (already affirmed in 18:1, 3) motivate him to make David swear an oath promising to protect him and his descendants? For these reasons it seems more likely that the Septuagint preserves the original reading: "And Jonathan again made an oath [of loyalty] to David." In this case, the prior oath could be one made in conjunction with the original covenant (18:3), but more likely it is the vow and self-imprecation recorded in verses 12–13, in which Jonathan expresses his loyalty to David. Understood in this way, verse 17b makes good sense: Jonathan again swears allegiance to David because of his deep commitment/loyalty ("love") for him.[2]

20:27 *the son of Jesse.* Three times in this scene Saul refers to David as "the son of

Jesse" and refuses to call him by name (see also vv. 30–31).[3] But in his response to his father, Jonathan uses David's name to refer to his friend (v. 28). Earlier Saul has called David by name several times (cf. 18:8, 11, 22, 25; 19:22), but the change here indicates his growing hostility as he distances himself emotionally from his son-in-law.

20:30 *Saul's anger flared up.* See the comment above at 18:8. Saul expressed righteous anger when he heard of the Ammonite threat against Jabesh Gilead (11:6), but his anger became self-centered and misdirected when he heard the women suggest that David was worthy of greater honor than he was (18:8). His anger against Jonathan is also misdirected, prompted by his belief that his son is siding with David against him.

20:31 *neither you nor your kingdom will be established.* Contrary to Samuel's

prophecy (13:13–14), Saul desires to establish a royal dynasty, and he views Jonathan as the heir apparent. But Jonathan is not harboring such delusions (20:15–17; 23:17).

20:33 *Saul hurled his spear at him to kill him.* For the second time in the story, Saul tries to kill his own son (cf. 14:44). He tries to murder Jonathan with his spear, just as he tried to kill David on two occasions (18:11; 19:10). This is a turning point in Saul's obsessive quest to kill David; from this time onward, he will demonstrate hostility toward those who support David. The incident foreshadows his slaughter of the priests and their families at Nob (chap. 22). The verb translated "kill" is *nakah*, "strike." It is used earlier of Jonathan's striking down Israel's enemies (13:3; 14:14). The contrast is stark: like David, Jonathan struck down the enemies of God, and now Saul tries to strike down his own son. The

irony is heightened even more when one considers that the verb was used earlier to describe how Saul struck down the enemies of Israel (14:48; 15:7). Now he is treating his own son as if he were an enemy.

20:41 *bowed down before Jonathan.* The expression used here indicates an attitude of submission; the subordinate party is always the one who falls before a superior in this manner (Josh. 5:14; Ruth 2:10; 1 Sam. 25:23; 2 Sam. 1:2; 9:6; 14:4, 22; 2 Kings 4:37; 2 Chron. 20:18; Job 1:20).

Theological Insights

This account also expresses the primary theme of the preceding chapters: in the face of danger, the Lord protects his chosen servants (see 1 Sam. 18 and 19 above, under "Teaching the Text"). In this chapter the Lord protects David through the loyalty of

When David bows three times before Jonathan it is a sign of submission and respect. Here the remaining residents of a recently defeated Elamite town honor their new ruler (far left) by bowing before him (Assyrian palace relief, Nineveh, 660–650 BC).

faithful Jonathan, illustrating the point that the Lord often accomplishes his redemptive work in the world through human instruments who are committed to his purposes, even when it may not seem to be in their best interests. Jonathan is an example to exilic readers of the importance of supporting God's program and chosen leader.

Teaching the Text

1. *Sometimes God protects his chosen servants through other faithful servants, who are committed to God's program.* As noted above, Jonathan serves as a literary foil for Saul in this story. Saul opposes God's revealed will and chosen servant, but Jonathan accepts God's plan and embraces his chosen servant (see the comments under "Teaching the Text" for chapter 18). Jonathan knows God has chosen David to be king and does everything in his power to protect David.

2. *Commitment to God's plan and to his chosen servant necessitates self-denial and sometimes places one in harm's way.* Jonathan is a paradigm of obedience and submission. Even though he is the heir apparent to Saul's throne, he refuses to follow the path of personal ambition or yield to his father's sinful wishes (20:31). Indeed, he sincerely pledges his loyalty to the chosen king and prays for his success (20:13–17), even though his decision makes him the object of his father's wrath and jeopardizes his life (20:30–33). Like Jonathan we must support God's program, even when it involves self-denial and puts us in harm's way. Jonathan's absolute loyalty to David should inspire us to demonstrate the same allegiance to David's greater Son and

God's chosen Servant, the Lord Jesus Christ (Matt. 10:37–39; Luke 12:8–9).

Though the friendship of David and Jonathan is inspiring, this is not fundamentally a story about friendship. In the larger literary context of 1 Samuel, this account is not designed to teach the reader lessons about friendship. Certainly one can use their friendship for illustrative purposes, *if* one's primary text for a lesson or sermon is dealing with that theme (see, e.g., Prov. 17:17; 18:24). But if one is teaching or preaching through 1 Samuel, the real point of the story lies elsewhere. Throughout this section of the book, the narrator is validating David's claim to the throne of Israel and demonstrating that God has rejected Saul. As noted above, Saul disobeys God and resists his plan, while Jonathan submits to God and embraces his chosen servant. The point of the story—and of Jonathan's friendship with David, when contrasted with his father's hostility toward him—is this: one must fully support God's plan and his will rather than allowing pride and personal ambition to stand in the way of and impede what God is trying to accomplish.

Illustrating the Text

God protects his chosen servants in the midst of grave danger.

Christian Biography: *Tortured for Christ,* **by Richard Wurmbrand.** A Romanian evangelical minister and one of Romania's most widely known Jewish believers, also a leader and author, Wurmbrand spent fourteen years in Communist imprisonment, often undergoing torture. When the Communists seized Romania, Wurmbrand immediately began an underground ministry to his people and to the invading Russian soldiers. He was eventually arrested in 1948 and spent three years in solitary confinement, seeing only his captors, while his wife, Sabina, served as a slave laborer. Because of his growing international fame, diplomats from various foreign embassies asked for his release. Eventually his release was negotiated, and he testified in Washington before the Senate's Internal Security Subcommittee, at this point stripping to the waist and showing eighteen deep torture wounds on his body. His testimony has gone worldwide.

Believers are called to self-denying commitment to God even in the face of potential harm and danger.

Christian Biography: John and Betty Stam. The story of the Stams, both graduates of Moody Bible Institute and missionaries to China in the 1930s, is compelling both for the poignancy of their martyrdom and the acceptance and trust they showed in the face of their deaths. After marrying and having a baby daughter while working in Tsinan, they were asked by their mission to relocate to Tsingteh and work under what seemed like safe conditions. John was cautious, but the couple concluded that their move would be fine. Then they were taken captive by a group of two thousand Communists. Betty's great concern all along was for her baby, whose life was spared numerous times by miraculous means. Finally Betty and John were to be led to their execution. Betty laid her baby down for the last time; turning to follow the soldiers, she committed baby Helen to the protection of God, remembering a vow she had made long before: "All the people whom I love are to take a second place in my heart. . . . Work out Thy whole will in my life, at any cost, now and forever. To me to live is Christ. Amen." Following this prayer, she was forced to watch the execution of her husband; witnesses say she faltered, then became strong and knelt for her own beheading.[4] The baby was rescued and lived to be an adult. A poem by missionary E. H. Hamilton was written to commemorate the martyrdom of the Stams, his fellow missionaries. The theme of it is "Afraid? Of What?"[5]

David on the Run

Big Idea *Even when faith wavers, the Lord confronts his chosen servants with their divinely appointed destiny.*

Understanding the Text

The Text in Context

As David left Jonathan, he knew that Saul was now fully committed to murdering him. The king tried to kill him in a variety of ways, but each time David escaped (chaps. 18–19), once through the Lord's direct intervention (19:23–24). Apparently unaware of Saul's latest attempts to kill David (19:9–24), Jonathan was confident that his father would not harm David (cf. 19:6–7). But when Saul rejected Jonathan's latest attempt to defend his friend, and Jonathan had to dodge one of his father's spears (20:30–33), Jonathan realized the truth and warned David. The situation looked bleak for David, but he still had a devoted friend and protector in Jonathan. The narrator keeps David's destiny before us through the words of Jonathan, who prayed for David's well-being (20:13, 16), expressed his confidence that the Lord would subdue David's enemies (20:15–16), and renewed his allegiance to the future king (20:17). Though David is still on the run, he has every reason to be confident: after all, David has escaped once again, the king's son has recognized David's destiny

and is fully behind him, and the Lord has demonstrated his ability to protect David. But human emotions can be fickle, and in this next episode David's faith wavers.

Yet the Lord reminds David of his destiny and his past success, ironically using the lips of the Philistines to do so (21:11). David leaves the land of Judah, but to his credit, his humiliating experience in Gath reminds him to wait on God's guidance (22:3). Through a prophetic message from Gad, God calls him back to his own land to face up to his destiny (22:5). David has found a "stronghold" (*metsudah*) in Moab (22:4–5), where he feels secure, but it is time for him to realize that the Lord is his true stronghold and source of protection. Through the coming years, David indeed learns this lesson. Later, as he reflects on how God has delivered him from all his enemies (2 Sam. 22:1), he declares that the Lord is his stronghold (see 22:2, where the word *metsudah* is translated "fortress").

Historical and Cultural Background

First Samuel 22:2 states that "all those who were in distress or in debt or discontented" (ca. four hundred men) gather to David at Adullam. Later they hire out their services (25:4–8, 15–16; 27:6–11). Such mercenary groups appear elsewhere in Israel's early history (cf. Judg. 11:3–11; 1 Kings 11:23–25). These groups resemble the *habiru*, mercenaries mentioned in the Amarna letters who disturbed Canaan in the early fourteenth century BC. The *habiru* were organized into small groups, probably consisting of fifty to one hundred men.[1] For further discussion, see *ZIBBCOT*, 288–89.

Interpretive Insights

21:1 *Ahimelek trembled*. Nob is located just two miles southeast of Gibeah, Saul's home, and it is likely that news of Saul's attempts on David's life have reached the priest. The reference to Ahimelek's fear sets the mood for this chapter, in which David himself will be overcome by fear (v. 12) and, for the first time in the story, is depicted as being in a panic.

Why are you alone? Why is no one with you? By quoting the priest, the narrator highlights David's vulnerability and introduces even more tension into the developing plot. How will David now respond, given that he is a wanted man?

21:2 *As for my men*. David makes up a story, claiming the king has sent him on a secret mission and that his soldiers are waiting for him in another location. But it is not until he reaches the cave of Adullam that any companions join him (22:1–2).[2]

21:4 *consecrated bread*. According to priestly ritual, this "bread of the Presence" (v. 6) has been placed before the

Lord, but it is then replaced with fresh bread on the Sabbath (Exod. 25:30; 35:13; Lev. 24:5–9; 1 Chron. 9:32). Once the bread is removed from the Lord's presence, the Aaronic priests are to eat it in a holy place. Since David is in a desperate situation, Ahimelek is willing to bend the rules, provided David and his "men" have kept themselves consecrated for battle by refraining from sexual contact with women (cf. Deut. 23:9–14; Josh. 3:5; 2 Sam. 11:11–12).

21:7 *one of Saul's servants was there*. By pointing out the priest's fear (v. 2) and now informing us that one of Saul's servants is present, the narrator goes out of his way to heighten the drama of the story. We (and David) suspect that this mercenary will inform the king of what has happened. In chapter 22 our worst fears are realized (cf. 22:8–9, 18–19, 22). Doeg's Edomite identity marks him as an especially dangerous character to the exilic readers of the history, for by this time the Edomites are viewed as archenemies of Israel (see Isa. 34:5–17; 63:1–6; Obad. 1–21).

Model of the table of the bread of the Presence, from the tabernacle replica at Timna, Israel

21:8 *I haven't brought my sword.* David's explanation is illogical. He obviously needs a weapon (or else he would not ask for one), yet he claims that the king's business is so urgent that he had to leave without one. It is unlikely that a seasoned soldier like David would leave on a mission without being properly equipped for the task. Later David will show this same propensity to panic and speak illogically when under extreme stress (see 2 Sam. 11:14–15).

21:9 *There is none like it; give it to me.* David gladly takes Goliath's sword (last seen in David's tent following his victory over the Philistine champion; 1 Sam. 17:54). In his desperation David's attitude toward this pagan warrior's weapon has certainly changed (cf. 1 Sam. 17:45). In David's defense, perhaps it symbolizes for him the Lord's ability to protect him and give him victory against powerful enemies (cf. 1 Sam. 17:46, 51), but one wonders. David seems to view it as his source of defense, not simply as a trophy.[3] The irony continues in the next verse as David flees to Goliath's hometown to seek asylum.

21:12 *was very much afraid.* In a radically desperate move, David flees to enemy territory, seeking asylum with Achish, the Philistine king of Gath, located about twenty-five miles southwest of Nob. However, when he hears the Philistines referring to him as a king and recalling his military exploits against their armies, he gets cold feet. For the first time in the story, the narrator actually describes David as being afraid, and he emphasizes the point by adding "very much." This is painfully ironic, for in chapter 17, just before David courageously met the Philistine champion's challenge, Saul and the Israelites were paralyzed by great fear (vv. 11, 24). Now David, ironically armed only with Goliath's sword and seeking asylum in Goliath's hometown, is reduced to fear in the presence of a Philistine ruler because the once-fearful Saul is chasing him! Furthermore, he now is in the very position Saul has hoped he would be—in the power of the Philistines (cf. v. 13, "in their hands," with 18:17, 21, 25).[4]

21:13 *pretended to be insane.* In his great fear, David pretends to be insane, spitting on the doorposts.[5] This description of David's behavior contributes to the theme of this episode. Overcome by desperation, David is acting out of character, not just when pretending to be insane, but also throughout this episode. There may even be an ironic parallel to Saul's behavior. When Saul threatened David, God's Spirit protected David by turning Saul into a prophet for a day and causing him to act in a bizarre manner (1 Sam. 19:23–24). Now David, having seemingly run from the Lord's care, must act in a bizarre manner to ensure his own safety. But David's attempts at self-preservation—which involve lying to a priest, trusting in a defeated enemy's weapon, and seeking a position in the army of a Philistine ruler—have backfired. He cannot escape his past or his destiny; ironically, the Philistines remind him of both when they call him "the king of the land" and recall his fame as a warrior (v. 11).

22:2 *he became their commander.* From Gath, David goes to the cave of Adullam, located about twelve miles east of Gath on the edge of Judah's territory. David, who has once served as a commander (*sar*) in Saul's army (18:13), is now the commander (*sar*) of a ragtag group of social outcasts. His prestige has slipped.

22:3 *David went to Mizpah in Moab.*
Perhaps the king of Moab feels allegiance
to David due to David's ancestry (on his
father's side he is descended from the
Moabite Ruth).

22:5 *Go into the land of Judah.* David
has found security in the "stronghold" (*metsudah*) of Moab,[6] and his wavering faith is
recovering as he waits to see what God will
do for him (v. 3). We are not told why the
prophet tells him to return to Judah, but it is
likely that the Lord views David's departure
as contrary to his divinely ordained destiny.

Theological Insights

The exilic readers of the history can undoubtedly relate to David's circumstances
and fears. They too are living outside the
land of promise and feel vulnerable in a
hostile world. They are tempted to focus
on what they can see, but they need to
focus on God and his promise. They have
a divinely appointed destiny and need to
look both backward and forward. In Isaiah
40 God reminds them of his sovereignty
over the world, his commitment to them,
and his intention of fulfilling his purposes
through them. David's experience is a reminder to them not to panic or rely on their
own meager devices to protect themselves.
They must wait on God and trust him for
prophetic guidance and supernatural enablement (see 40:31).

Teaching the Text

1. *God sometimes puts his people in a place
where they must face up to their destiny
and trust him, but danger can cause faith
to waver.* God does not promise to keep

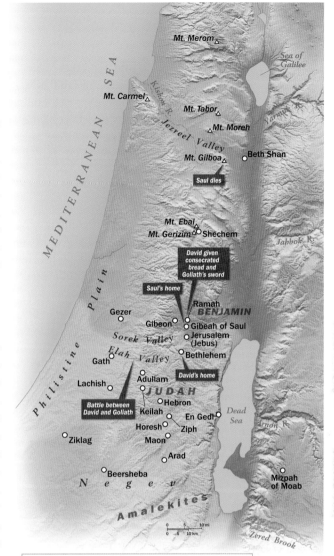

Significant places and events in the interaction
between David and Saul

his chosen servants from danger. On the
contrary, in his providence he sometimes
puts his people in a place where they must
face up to their destiny and trust him. But
danger can cause faith to waver, and God's
chosen servants do not always maintain
their confidence and perspective in the face
of challenges. When faith wavers, one can
lose focus on God and act in ways that contradict one's creed and experience.

David's experience illustrates this. When he faced Goliath, he remembered how God had delivered him in the past (1 Sam. 17:37), and he courageously challenged the Philistine, announcing that God does not deliver by "sword or spear" (v. 47). But in this episode David, overcome by panic and fear, asks for a "spear or sword" (21:8). He jumps at the opportunity to take Goliath's sword, declaring it to be an incomparable weapon (v. 9), and then goes to Gath to seek security from his enemies (v. 10). It is as if David is becoming Goliath, armed with his sword and going to his hometown. David is obviously walking by sight, not faith, and trusting in his own wits. When viewed from a strictly human perspective, his actions are perhaps understandable. After all, desperate times call for desperate measures, or so they say. But walking by sight eventually fails, and David, who has earlier lied to Ahimelek, is forced to live out a lie by pretending to be a madman. This denial of his real identity is the culmination of a series of actions that deny God's mighty work in his past and his divinely appointed destiny.

2. *Even when his chosen servants falter, the Lord confronts them with their destiny.* As David runs for his life, he acts in desperation, but the Lord does not turn his back on his chosen servant. When David denies his own theological creed by asking Ahimelek for a spear or sword (cf. 1 Sam. 17:47), the priest informs him that only the sword of Goliath is available (21:9). But Ahimelek, almost as a rebuke, describes the Philistine as the one "whom you killed in the Valley of Elah." Whether the priest intends this as a subtle reminder or not, his words confront David with his past success and creed. Why would David want to use the sword of a warrior whom the sword did not protect?[7] But even when he is reminded of his mighty victory in this way, David is so overcome by panic that he can focus only on the sword's dimensions, as if it can provide deliverance.

When David arrives in Gath (armed with the weapon of the late Gittite champion!), the Lord uses the Philistines, albeit inadvertently, to confront David with his destiny and remind him of his past success. They call David "the king of the land," as if they are aware of his private anointing

Aerial view of Tell es-Safi, biblical Gath, one of the five cities that made up the Philistine pentapolis

by Samuel. They also recall the song of the Israelite women, who celebrated his victory over Goliath of Gath with the words, "Saul has slain his thousands, and David his tens of thousands" (v. 11). But again, David misses the message and instead focuses on the danger that their recognition of him entails. His nearly fatal mistake in Gath apparently brings him to his senses, however. He is ready to wait on God, albeit in a stronghold in a foreign land (22:4–5). At that point, the Lord directly intervenes through his prophet Gad and tells David to go home to Judah. David's experience is a reminder that the Lord pursues his chosen servants when they try to run away, whether due to fear or other reasons (cf. 1 Kings 19; Jon. 1).

Illustrating the Text

When believers allow their faith to waver, they ignore what God has done in their lives and deny their relation to God.

Literature: *The Lion, the Witch and the Wardrobe*, by C. S. Lewis. After Lucy has been to Narnia and comes back to tell the story, all her siblings doubt her and make fun of her. The professor stops this exchange by asking Lucy's siblings if they have always found her truthful, to which they reply that they have. The professor then says, "a charge of lying against someone whom you have always found truthful is a very serious thing; a very serious thing indeed."[8] In the same way, if we have found God to be truthful in the past, our doubt is a serious thing indeed.

Poetry: "In All My Fear," by Thomas More. This Catholic saint (1478–1535) was imprisoned in the Tower of London in 1534 for his refusal to take the oath required by the First Succession Act, thereby disparaging the power of the pope and King Henry's marriage to Catherine of Aragon. In 1535 he was tried for treason and beheaded. This prayer is a touching request of God for grace to overcome fear in the name of the Savior who experienced fear and agony himself.

God will go to some lengths to get the attention of his people when they disobey.

Bible: The story of Jonah.

Quote: "The Returning Backslider," by John Bunyan.

> A returning backslider is a great blessing (I mean intended to be so) to two sorts of men. . . . The uncalled are made to hear him and consider; the called are made to hear him, and are afraid of falling. . . . O brethren, saith the backslider that is returned, did you see how I left my God? did you see how I turned again to those vanities from which some time before I fled? Oh! I was deluded; I was bewitched; I was deceived: for I found all things from which I fled at first, still worse by far when I went to them the second time. . . . Ay, but this man is come again, wherefore there is news in his mouth; sad news, dreadful news, and news that is to make the standing saint to take heed lest he fall. . . . I would not tempt him that stands to fall; but the good that a returning backslider has received at God's hands, and at the hand of Christ, is a double good; he has been converted twice; fetched from the world and from the devil, and from himself twice (oh grace!), and has been made to know the stability of God's covenant, the unchangeableness of God's mind, the sure and lasting truth of his promise in Christ, and of the sufficiency of the merits of Christ, over and over.[9]

Saul on the Rampage

Big Idea *God regards as enemies those who oppose his chosen servants.*

Understanding the Text

The Text in Context

In this next episode the focus briefly shifts from David to Saul, and we see the tragic aftermath of David's visit to Ahimelek (21:1–9). Saul accuses the priests of being traitors and murders them and their families. Only one, Abiathar, escapes. He goes to David, who welcomes him and promises him protection.

The contrast between Saul and David cannot be sharper. While Saul is murdering the Lord's priests, David is seeking their protection. Saul's hostility has reached new depths. This heightens the tension of the story, for if Saul kills the Lord's priests, then no one is safe, certainly not David. This paves the way for the episodes to follow in which Saul relentlessly pursues David.

Interpretive Insights

22:6 *spear in hand.* This seemingly incidental detail is ominous, because on earlier occasions Saul has used his spear to try to kill David (18:10–11; 19:9–10) and David's loyal friend Jonathan (20:33).

22:7 *men of Benjamin!* Saul appeals to his officials on the basis of tribal allegiance. By focusing on his tribal identity, Saul is threatening Israel's unity, as the Benjamites of Gibeah have done once before (see Judg. 19–21). This foreshadows tribal tensions to come in the story (see 2 Sam. 2).

fields and vineyards. Saul reminds them that

As Saul meets with his officials he implies that it is he, not David, who will be able to supply them with fields, vineyards, and groves. If Saul is planning to reward loyalty by providing land, he is acting like the other kings in the ancient Near East. This tablet records the granting of land by Babylonian king Nabu-apla-iddina (right), to his high official (875–850 BC).

they have an economic advantage with a fellow Benjamite on the throne. Saul's language shows that he is now viewing himself and operating as the typical oppressive king that Samuel warned about. Samuel told them that such a king would appoint their sons as military officers (8:12), as well as take their "fields and vineyards" and give them to his officials (8:14). It is obvious that Saul, though still officially the king of Israel, has departed from the kingship ideal of the Deuteronomic law (cf. Deut. 17:20) and is no different from the kings of the nations.

22:9 *the son of Jesse.* Doeg mimics Saul's derogatory description of David (see the comment on 20:27) and thus makes it clear that he has allied himself with the king's perspective and agenda.

22:14 *Ahimelek answered the king.* In contrast to Saul's derogatory reference to David as the "son of Jesse" (v. 13), Ahimelek, like Jonathan, calls David by name (cf. 20:27–28). The inclusion of Ahimelek's defense is important to the narrator's strategy, for he, like Jonathan, testifies to David's loyalty to Saul (cf. 19:4–5).

22:17 *kill the priests of the* Lord. Once again the narrator depicts Saul as bent on murder. In addition to his attempts on David's life (see esp. 18:11; 19:1–2, 10–11, 15), twice Saul has tried to kill his own son (14:44; 20:33), the second time because of his loyalty to David. As noted above, that attempt on Jonathan's life foreshadows Saul's slaughter of the priests of Nob, for in both cases Saul directs his anger at one whom he perceives to be David's ally.[1] Saul's own words condemn him, for he acknowledges that these are "priests of the Lord." By commanding that they be executed, he

Key Themes of 1 Samuel 22:6–23

- Saul's obsession with retaining his kingship prompts him to murder those whom he perceives as traitors.
- By opposing God's chosen servant, Saul ends up actively opposing God himself.

takes an adversarial stance against the Lord himself. Twice more in the following verses the narrator uses the phrase "priests of the Lord" to emphasize the enormity of Saul's crime (vv. 17, 21).[2] In both cases it reflects the perspective of the characters; we see this if we highlight the phrase: in verse 17 Saul's servants refuse to carry out the king's orders, realizing it would be an atrocity to kill the Lord's priests. In verse 21 Abiathar reports to David that Saul had the audacity to kill "the priests of the Lord."

were unwilling to raise a hand. The scene is reminiscent of an earlier incident when Saul's men refused to allow Saul to kill Jonathan (14:45). In both cases Saul's servants risk the king's anger because they know he is intending to kill the innocent. By including their reactions in the story, the narrator enhances his portrait of Saul as one who is unfit to rule.

22:18 *Doeg the Edomite turned and struck them down.* The fact that Saul uses an Edomite to murder the priests should be appalling to the exilic readers of the history, for by this time the Edomites are viewed as archenemies of Israel (see Isa. 34:5–17; 63:1–6; Obad. 1–21). The narrator presents Saul in a sinister light, as one allied with Edom in an effort to wipe out the Lord's priests. Surely such an individual is totally unfit to rule over God's people.

22:19 *He also put to the sword.* Earlier this expression is used in war contexts. In most cases it describes Israel's divinely authorized killing of the Canaanite-Amorite nations at the time of the conquest (Num. 21:24; Josh. 8:24; 10:28, 30, 32, 35, 37, 39; 11:10–12, 14; Judg. 1:8, 25).[3] It depicts Saul as one who launches a genocidal holy war against the Lord's priests and consequently as one who is an archenemy of God himself.

men and women, its children and infants. The language eerily echoes the Lord's earlier command to Saul to wipe out the Amalekites (15:3).[4] On that occasion Saul failed to completely carry out the Lord's command to kill an archenemy of Israel, prompting the Lord to reject Saul as king. But now, filled with hatred for the Lord's chosen king, Saul slaughters the Lord's priests with an efficiency that should have been reserved for God's enemies.[5]

22:21 *Saul had killed the priests of the* LORD. Doeg has actually done the killing, but the priest rightly attributes the crime to Saul, for he gave the order to commit the atrocity (vv. 18–19). The priest's words undoubtedly reflect the Lord's perspective. Later the prophet Nathan will accuse David of murdering Uriah, even though it is technically the Ammonites who have killed him (2 Sam. 12:9).

22:22 *I am responsible for the death of your whole family.* Was David's self-incrimination really deserved? It depends on how soon he knew Doeg was present, but the narrative is unclear in this regard (21:7–8). Nonetheless, his confession

"So Doeg the Edomite turned and struck [the priests] down" (1 Sam. 22:18). This relief shows an Assyrian soldier striking down an enemy (palace at Nimrud, 865–860 BC).

does suggest the possibility that he anticipated Doeg's actions and could have somehow shielded Ahimelek. If so, this suggests that David, when under stress, is willing to forfeit the well-being and even the lives of others to save his own skin. Even if this is not the case and Ahimelek is simply the victim of being in the wrong place at the wrong time, the incident has a foreshadowing function: an innocent man, loyal to David, dies as a result of a scheme designed to save David's skin. In this case the story sets us up for a startling contrast. If David's self-incrimination is unjustified, false guilt, it nevertheless shows a sensitive spirit and genuine concern for others, characteristics that will be sorely lacking in the account of his murder of Uriah.

22:23 *don't be afraid.* David was afraid in the presence of Achish (21:12), but now that he is again relying on the Lord's prophetic guidance (22:3, 5), he can give reassurance to others.

You will be safe with me. David's concern for the priest shows he is an ally of the Lord, while Saul has become the Lord's enemy.

Theological Insights

This episode shows how Saul's disobedience culminates in his actively opposing the will of God. Thus the story is a vivid reminder to the exilic readers of what can happen to people who alienate themselves from God. Indeed, their ancestors have traveled down this path, following in the footsteps of the northern kingdom (see 2 Kings 17:1–23; 21:1–15, 19–22; 24:3–4, 19–20). Their rebellion prompted divine judgment, which culminated in the exile. Saul's tragic descent and decline should motivate the exiles, and all who read his story, to avoid the path in which he has chosen to walk. (See further under "Teaching the Text" below.)

Most regard the slaughter of the priests, who are descendants of Eli through Ahimelek, Ahitub, and Phinehas (1 Sam. 14:3; 22:9–11), as a fulfillment of the judgment pronounced on the house of Eli in 1 Samuel 2:33. This is clearly the case if, following the Qumran text and the Septuagint, one understands "a man" in 2:33 as referring to Abiathar and reads the last clause of the verse, "will fall by the swords of men." However, it is possible that these ancient witnesses have harmonized the text to 1 Samuel 22 and do not preserve the original reading.

If one retains the Hebrew text of 2:33, it is difficult to know exactly what the text is saying, but possibly it is speaking more

Abiathar's Role in the Story to Come

Abiathar is a faithful companion to David and subsequently serves along with Zadok (1 Sam. 23:6, 9; 30:7; 2 Sam. 8:17; 15:24, 27, 29, 35–36; 17:15; 19:11; 20:25). However, when it comes time for David's successor to be crowned, Abiathar sides with Adonijah (1 Kings 1:7, 19, 25, 42; 2:22) rather than Solomon. Solomon expels him from service, fulfilling the prophecy given to Eli, but Solomon does not kill him, because he has been loyal to David (1 Kings 2:26–27).

generally of the premature death of each of Eli's successors (cf. vv. 31–32) and predicting that they will experience hardship, even though the Lord will not remove them from office immediately. In this case, it is not certain that 1 Samuel 22 is a fulfillment of the prophecy against Eli. After all, the narrator does not specifically state that the slaughter at Nob fulfills the prophecy, as he does regarding Abiathar's demotion in 1 Kings 2:27. It is possible that the prophecy speaks in general terms initially (1 Sam. 2:31–33), before focusing specifically on the premature deaths of Hophni and Phinehas (v. 34) and the demotion of Abiathar (v. 36). If so, then Saul's murderous attempt to wipe out the priestly line of Eli should not be viewed as fulfilling the prophecy. Though it does result in the premature death of several of Eli's descendants, it runs counter to God's stated intention to preserve Eli's line, albeit in a weakened condition.

If the slaughter at Nob does fulfill the prophecy of 2:33 (though that seems unlikely), then we face a difficult theological dilemma, but not one that is insurmountable. The narrator clearly presents Saul's actions as criminal, yet ironically in this scenario he is also an instrument in bringing God's prophecy of judgment to pass. This does not mean that God endorses Saul's actions. Eli's sin has deprived his line of God's special favor and protection, and God in his providence is bringing about the fall of Eli's house through wrongly motivated, sinful human actions. There are possible analogies to this (Isa. 5:26–30; 10:5–34).

Teaching the Text

1. *Obsession with power can skew reality and cause one to see enemies where they do not exist.* Despite the Lord's decrees (13:13–14; 15:26–29), Saul has become obsessed with power and prestige. He is prepared to do whatever is necessary to retain his position as Israel's king, even if it means murdering those whom he perceives as his enemies. Time and again those around Saul remind him of David's innocence and loyalty to him, but he has decided that David is an enemy and misinterprets any defense of David as proof that the one protesting is an ally of his perceived enemy and a traitor to the crown (see 20:32–33; 22:13–17). In his warped thinking, this justifies their execution. Ironically, David himself will eventually fall into the trap of preserving one's position and power at all costs, even the life of a loyal servant (2 Sam. 11).

2. *Disobedient servants of God can end up actively opposing God's purposes.* It is difficult to believe that the Spirit-empowered, magnanimous, victorious warrior king described in 1 Samuel 11 could become the irrational, paranoia-stricken mass murderer of 1 Samuel 22. Yet one can easily trace the downward spiral: Saul's disobedience to God's clear commands led to his rejection as king over Israel. But rather than resigning himself to God's unalterable decision, Saul stubbornly refuses to accept it and insists on preserving his rule and his dynasty. As his

inflated view of himself grows (see 15:12), he tightly grasps his royal position, with no intention of letting go (18:6–9). Tormented by an evil spirit sent from God and overcome by jealousy and fear, he actively opposes and even tries to kill David, whom he views as the greatest threat to his throne and undoubtedly suspects is the successor the Lord has characterized as "better" than he is (15:28). Saul's hostility toward David reached a new low when he tried to kill his own son Jonathan for defending David's honor and loyalty (20:32–33). But it reaches an even deeper level when he slaughters the Lord's priests and an entire town, including women, children, and livestock. By opposing David, the Lord's chosen servant, Saul is opposing God and actively assuming the role of God's enemy. This adversarial stance rises to the surface in this episode, for Saul himself acknowledges they are "the priests of the LORD" (22:17) and uses an Edomite, of all people, to carry out his murderous deed. Saul's descent from God's servant to God's enemy is a sobering reminder of the self-destructive consequences of blatant disobedience.

Illustrating the Text

Power corrupts, generates jealousy and fear, and produces a paranoia that casts allies in the role of enemies.

Literature: *Lord of the Flies,* by William Golding. Few fictional works illustrate so vividly the terrible fate that befalls Saul in this passage as this well-known work of fiction (1954) by this Nobel Prize–winning British author (1911–93), which was also made into two films (1963, 1990). *Lord of the Flies* tells the story of a group of English schoolboys (showing the indiscriminate power that sin can exercise by corrupting the youth) marooned on a tropical island after their plane is shot down during a war, probably nuclear. Separated from civilization and its order and rules, the boys on the island gradually descend into violence and chaos. As the boys break into cliques, some behave peacefully and work together to create the order needed for effective survival, while others become greedy and power hungry, lawless and dangerous, eventually savage, engaging in the murder of the gentlest among them. What becomes evident is the impulse to suspicion and brute power of some of the boys, the working out of which becomes so devastating, a power full of paranoia.

History: One could pick any of a number of world leaders who have decimated countries, committed genocide, or repressed and silenced their people. Stalin, Mussolini, Franco, and Hitler are obvious choices; others have been Fidel Castro, Idi Amin, and Saddam Hussein.

When those who once served God turn and rebel against him, they become his enemies.

Philosophy: Friedrich Wilhelm Nietzsche. Nietzsche (1844–1900) was one of the most influential philosophers in modern history and is often even referred to as the greatest German philosopher since Kant and Hegel. Born into a family of Lutheran pastors, he was called "the little minister," and people thought he would become a pastor himself. His faith was still strong at nineteen, but then he abandoned that faith as a student at the University of Bonn. About the same time he also contracted syphilis, which would eventually lead to the dementia of which he died.[6]

Friedrich Wilhelm Nietzsche (1844–1900)

Nietzsche developed great hostility toward Christianity and proceeded to attack it with great vitriol, seeing Jesus as weak. He envisioned a race of supermen who would renounce any kind of compassion and gentleness, an ideology that later appealed to the Nazis and the followers of Mussolini. Some of his most well-known works are *The Birth of Tragedy* and *Thus Spake Zarathustra*. He once wrote, "I condemn Christianity. I raise against the Christian church the most terrible of all accusations ever uttered. It is to me the highest of all conceivable corruptions. . . . A man of spiritual depth needs friends, unless he still has God as a friend. But I have neither God nor friends."[7]

The Lord Guides, Encourages, and Protects David

Big Idea *The Lord guides, encourages, and protects his chosen servants in their darkest hours.*

Understanding the Text

The Text in Context

Saul's intention to destroy David was never clearer than in chapter 22, which tells how Saul murdered the priests of Nob simply because he believed they had conspired with David against him. As the story continues, the tension is high because God told David to return to Judah (22:5), placing him in harm's way. But chapter 23 shows that the God who places his servant in harm's way also guides and protects; this theme of divine guidance and protection dominates the story in the coming chapters. It contributes to the author's agenda of contrasting David with Saul. As we see in chapter 23, Saul claims divine assistance (see v. 7), but it is clear that God is really helping David. The Lord gives the Philistines into David's hand, but he also uses the Philistines to divert Saul and to protect David.

First Samuel 22:20–23 describes Abiathar's arrival at David's camp, while 23:6 informs us that David is at Keilah when Abiathar arrives. Since 23:5 states that David and his men go to Keilah (from the forest of

Hereth? [22:5]), Abiathar's arrival takes place after or during the deliverance of Keilah. This means that the events of 1 Samuel 22:6–23:6 are not in strict chronological order. Saul's slaughter of the priests at Nob is roughly contemporaneous with David's victory over the Philistines at Keilah, while Abiathar's two arrival scenes correspond (1 Sam. 22:20–23; 2 Sam. 23:6). One may think of a chronological flashback occurring at 23:1:

Saul's slaughter of priests (22:6–19) / Abiathar's arrival (22:20–23)

FLASHBACK: David's victory at Keilah (23:1–5) / Abiathar's arrival (23:6)

The contrast between David and Saul is sharp. While Saul is murdering the Lord's priests, David is accomplishing what Saul should be doing: delivering people from the Philistines (see 9:16). David then protects the one remaining priest from the murderous Saul.

Interpretive Insights

23:2 *he inquired of the Lord.* David's action marks a significant turning point.

Earlier he was wavering in his faith, but now he actively seeks the Lord's will as he sees a need in Israel.

Go, attack. These words echo the Lord's earlier commission to Saul (15:3, concerning the Amalekites), suggesting that David now occupies the role once assigned to Saul.

and save Keilah. The Lord (v. 3) and the narrator (v. 5) cast David in the role of savior. This places David in a long line of saviors, including Othniel (Judg. 3:9), Ehud (Judg. 3:15), Shamgar (Judg. 3:31), Gideon (Judg. 6:14), Tola (Judg. 10:1), Samson (Judg. 13:5), and yes, even Saul (1 Sam. 9:16). Ironically, David is now carrying out God's original wishes for Saul, demonstrating that David has supplanted Saul as the Lord's chosen leader.

23:3 *Here in Judah we are afraid*. The inclusion of "in Judah" reminds us that the Lord, speaking through his prophet, told David to "go into the land of Judah" (22:5). Demanding that David confront his destiny, the Lord has placed him in harm's way. But this reference to the fear of David's men also reminds us of the situation before David's victory over the Philistine champion. The men of Israel were paralyzed with fear

(17:11, 24), but David courageously stepped forward in faith and defeated the Philistines through God's enablement (17:46–47). History is about to repeat itself (23:4–5).

23:4 *and the LORD answered him*. On an earlier occasion Saul asked the Lord if he should attack the Philistines (14:37), but the Lord did not respond. Here David asks twice if he should attack the Philistines, and both times the Lord responds to him with a clear, affirmative answer (cf. vv. 11–12).

I am going to give the Philistines into your hand. The language echoes David's confident statement to the Philistine champion (17:47) and contrasts with the silence Saul received when he asked if the Lord would give the Philistines into his hand (14:37).

23:5 *He inflicted heavy losses*. Once again the narrator emphasizes that David's panic and fear have ended; now he is

The Lord instructed David to attack the Philistines who were stealing the processed grain from the threshing floors of the town of Keilah. Threshing floors were large and open flat spaces, usually on a hilltop like the one shown here, and were therefore difficult to protect.

acting like the David who has defeated the Philistines in the past.

23:6 *brought the ephod down with him.* This parenthetical note explains how David inquires of the Lord while in Keilah (see vv. 9–12). In Exodus 28:4–6 and several other texts, an ephod appears to be a priestly or cultic garment, which in some cases is used to obtain a divine oracle (1 Sam. 23:9–10; 30:7–8).

23:7 *God has delivered him into my hands.* Saul believes that divine providence is working to his advantage, rather than to help David. He bases this on the wrong assumption that David has acted unwisely in taking refuge in a walled town.

23:8 *Saul called up all his forces.* This form of the verb "called up" (Piel of *shama'*) is used only here and in 15:4, where it describes how Saul, in response to the Lord's command (v. 3), "summoned" his army to attack the Amalekites (v. 2). Now, ironically, Saul is again summoning an army, but for the purpose of besieging Keilah and capturing David. (For a similar ironic echo of the account in chap. 15, see 22:19 and the comment there.)

23:12 *They will.* David should be learning an important lesson here. Earlier he sought refuge with human beings (Achish of Philistia and the king of Moab), but humans are unreliable and will do what is expedient even when they should be grateful for past favors. The Lord alone is a dependable refuge.

23:13 *David had escaped.* This is the fifth time the narrator has reported that David "escaped" (*malat*; see 19:10, 12, 18; 22:1). The repetition highlights a theme: even though he faces almost constant danger, David always escapes. Here the verb

counters Saul's statement in verse 7. Divine providence is clearly on David's side, not Saul's. Whether he is the target of a spear, seemingly trapped in his own house, at the mercy of Achish in Gath, or hemmed in within the walls of Keilah, divine providence opens a door of escape.

23:14 *God did not give David into his hands.* There is irony here that contributes to the contrast between David and Saul: the Lord has given the Philistines into David's hand (23:4), and later he will give Saul into David's hand (24:10; 26:23). But God will not give David into Saul's hand.

23:16 *helped him find strength in God.* Once more, using the witness of Saul's own son and heir apparent, the narrator emphasizes the Lord's choice of David and his rejection of Saul.

23:18 *The two of them made a covenant.* This is the third covenantal transaction involving David and Jonathan. On the first occasion, Jonathan took the initiative to make the agreement (20:8). He pledged his loyalty to David and promised to protect him (18:3; 20:8–9). On the second occasion, Jonathan affirmed his loyalty to David's "house," and David pledged his loyalty to both Jonathan and his descendants (20:16–17, 42). The terms of this third covenant (23:18) are not given, but we can safely assume that it reaffirms earlier commitments. Perhaps it pertains to Jonathan's declaration that he will be David's second-in-command (v. 17). This would entail David's assuring Jonathan that he will indeed be given this position in the royal court, as well as Jonathan's reaffirming his loyalty to David.

23:21 *The LORD bless you.* Saul has deluded himself into thinking that the Lord is on his side (v. 7), so he thinks nothing of pronouncing a blessing on the Ziphites, who have conspired with him to kill David. This is only the third time in the Former Prophets that an individual has called upon the Lord to bless someone else. On both of the prior occasions the blessing was tainted (Judg. 17:2; 1 Sam. 15:13). Pious-sounding blessings do not necessarily mean that the heart where they originate is morally pure.

for your concern for me. This account illustrates the point that "concern" (or compassion), in and of itself, is not necessarily a proper emotional response. In fact, on an earlier occasion the Lord told Saul not to spare the Amalekites (15:3), yet he and his army did so (15:9, 15), prompting divine judgment. (The Hebrew word translated "spare/spared" in the NIV has the primary meaning "show compassion.") Here Saul attributes "concern," or "compassion" (KJV), to the Ziphites, but their compassion, if it even exists, is misguided.

Theological Insights

In the midst of grave danger, David experiences God's guidance, encouragement, and protection. While God grants David direct revelation, he also intervenes providentially, using Jona-

than to encourage David and the Philistine raiding parties to divert Saul's attention away from David so that he might escape. Indeed, God's use of the Philistines illustrates his sovereign providence at work. At the beginning of the chapter the Lord gives the Philistines into David's hand; David defeats the Philistines and saves the city of Keilah (vv. 4–5). At the end of the chapter the Philistines invade the land, forcing Saul to return from his pursuit of David just when it appears that he has trapped him (vv. 26–28). This account should encourage the exilic readers of the history. They too are in a precarious position, but David's story is a reminder that God does not abandon his chosen servants even when he places them in harm's way.

Teaching the Text

1. *The Lord may place his chosen servants in harm's way, but he guides, encourages, and protects amid danger.* David is seemingly safe in Moab, but the Lord tells him to return to Judah and face up to his destiny (22:5). In giving David this command, the

The ancient site of Keilah, modern Khirbet Quila, a border town between the Shephelah and the Judean hill country

Lord is placing him in harm's way. Saul apparently has an effective intelligence network that is able to track David's movements (23:7, 13, 19, 25). From the human perspective, David's situation appears dire, so much so that Saul becomes convinced divine providence is on his side, not David's (v. 7), and the Ziphites assume that Saul will prevail and agree to give him aid in his relentless quest to capture David (vv. 21–23).

But the Lord takes care of David amid danger, proving that when he leads his people into harm's way, he does not abandon them. The Lord warns David that Keilah is not a safe place to stay, ironically through the ephod brought by Abiathar. When Saul killed the priests of Nob, he effectively cut off communication with God. Abiathar escaped, bringing with him the ephod that David uses to gain vital information that allows him to escape (vv. 9–12). By the Lord's providence, right after David hears that Saul has indeed come out to take his life (v. 15), Saul's son and heir apparent Jonathan shows up and encourages David by reminding him of his destiny (vv. 16–18). David surely is tempted to walk by sight, not faith, but Jonathan helps David to see beyond circumstances. Finally, the Lord even uses the Philistines to divert Saul so that David can escape (vv. 26–28). Believers today cannot expect direct revelation from God, but they can find assurance in the realization that God providentially guides his people (Ps. 23:3–4).

2. *Sin has such a blinding effect that God's enemies can delude themselves into thinking that God is actually on their side.* In chapter 22 we see Saul's obsession with power as skewing his perception of reality to the point that he begins to see enemies where none exist. As one comes to chapter 23, it is somewhat shocking to find that Saul, despite his attack on the Lord's priests, believes God is actually on his side (v. 7a) and even asks the Lord to bless the Ziphites for collaborating with him in his efforts to kill David (v. 21). But when one looks at Saul's reasoning, his misguided assumption makes more sense. In typical fashion, Saul bases his beliefs and actions on sight. Because David has put himself in a precarious position (v. 7b), Saul assumes that God has engineered the circumstances in his favor. His limited focus, based strictly on what his eyes see at a specific time, stands in sharp contrast to his son Jonathan's perspective, which is based on the prophetic word of God (cf. 15:28–29), as well as the obvious fact that the Lord is with David (18:12, 14, 28). Saul's actions remind us that people, even when they oppose God's purposes and violate his moral and ethical standards, can delude themselves into thinking that God is on their side. When this happens, they can easily misinterpret circumstances in such as way as to validate their delusions. At the foundation of Saul's delusion is a fundamental character flaw: he consistently walks by sight, not by faith.

Illustrating the Text

God guides, encourages, and protects his chosen servants amid danger.

Bible: Daniel 6:1–18. The story of Daniel in the lions' den.

Film: *Soul Surfer.* This film (2011) is based on Bethany Hamilton's book, *Soul Surfer: A True Story of Faith, Family, and Fighting to Get Back on the Board* (2004). The film recounts the dramatic story of Bethany, who was born and raised on the island of Kauai, Hawaii. Naturally gifted, she was a talented surfer, winning competitions and obtaining endorsements even when she was a preteen. At the age of thirteen, in 2003, her promising future seemed over when a fifteen-foot tiger shark bit off her left arm below the shoulder in an attack soon picked up by the press nationwide. Amazingly, Bethany survived even though she lost 60 percent of her blood, her life saved only by an act of God. More startling, less than one month later she returned to her board to surf again. Her testimony to the grace of God in performing this miracle, and the way she has thrived since the tragic accident, forms a remarkable story—a good illustration of God's protection and encouragement in the life of his children.

Sin blinds the enemies of God into thinking they are objects of his favor.

Literature: *The Deputy,* by Rolf Hochhuth. Just fourteen when Hitler died, Hochhuth (b. 1931), a German author and playwright, wrote this play as a statement of moral outrage against what he considered Pope Pius XII's sympathies for Hitler's atrocities against the Jews. Much revered, this pope was/is considered a great pope, but Hochhuth savaged him for what he perceived to be his indifference toward, even abetting of, the genocide of the Jews for the sake of the political power of the church. The truth of Hochhuth's virulent criticism has been brought into question by many, and very articulately by Trappist monk and literary critic Thomas Merton. However, Hochhuth's central question remains—"When the Church is faced with a critical choice between the most basic of all its moral laws, the law of love for God and for man, and the practical, immediate options of power politics, is she now so accustomed to choosing the latter that she is no longer able to see the former?"[1]

History: In the name of religion, even the name of God, many abuses have been perpetrated. Members and leaders of Catholic and Protestant churches, as well as the Mormon Church, have molested young women and men, often using religious language and, in some cases, their belief system, to abet their crime. Court cases have been fought and are pending in many denominations and faith persuasions in which the perpetrator appears unrepentant and even defends his or her own behavior. Stories abound on the web. There are local fundamentalist groups and individuals who believe God has spoken to them and who abuse power in their families, their churches, or the institutions they lead in the name of what they perceive to be those divine communications. Much like Saul, they become obsessed with power, and the power distorts their thinking.

David Spares Saul's Life

Big Idea *The Lord vindicates his chosen servants when they look to him for justice.*

Understanding the Text

The Text in Context

Chapter 23 ends with David's escaping from Saul, yet one suspects that this is but a respite in the unfolding conflict. Indeed, once he has dealt with the Philistine problem, Saul resumes his pursuit of David. This time divine providence hands David an opportunity to kill Saul, yet he refuses to do so. Instead, he confronts Saul, protests his innocence, and appeals to God for justice. Throughout this section of 1 Samuel, the narrator's purpose is to demonstrate beyond the shadow of a doubt that David, not Saul or one of his descendants, is the rightful king of Israel. The speech by Saul becomes Exhibit A in the narrator's defense. The heir apparent to Saul's throne, Jonathan, has already acknowledged David's destiny; now Saul himself confesses the truth. He admits that David is in the right and that he (Saul) has acted sinfully. Saul blesses David, asking the Lord to repay him for his good deed. He also admits that David will become king, and he even asks David to promise that he will not wipe out his family line. David's oath to Saul, by which he promises to spare Saul's descendants, is also important in the following story, for David's commitment to keep it (2 Sam. 9) demonstrates his faithfulness to both Jonathan and Saul, proving that he is not a usurper who masterminds their demise.

Historical and Cultural Background

David's respect for Saul as the Lord's anointed ruler is consistent with God's choice of Saul and with the ancient Near Eastern concept of kingship as being divinely ordained (e.g., see *ZIBBCOT*, 367–68). David also recognizes Saul as his "father" (v. 11). Saul is David's father-in-law, but the term may indicate more than a literal sense in this context. David may be addressing Saul as his benefactor and protector (cf. the use of the term "father" in Job 29:16; 31:18; Isa. 9:6; 22:21; 1 Cor. 4:15) to remind him of his dependence on him. In a ninth-century BC Phoenician inscription from Samal, Kulamuwa speaks of his concern for his people: "But I was to some a father; and to some I was a mother; and to some I was a brother" (*COS*, 2:148). In another Phoenician inscription, dating to around 700 BC, Azatiwada claims, "Ba'al made me a father and a mother to the Danunians" (*COS*, 2:149).

Interpretive Insights

24:4 *I will give your enemy into your hands.* The prophecy cited by the men is not recorded elsewhere in the history, though we have no reason to doubt their recollection.[1] However, the prophecy does not state that David should or will kill his enemy. It simply says that he will gain the upper hand over his enemy, and it seemingly gives him permission to do as he sees fit or desires.

[He] cut off a corner of Saul's robe. David cuts off an edge of Saul's robe so he can offer it as proof that he had the opportunity to kill the king but spared his life (see v. 11). Attempts to see symbolism in this action are speculative.

24:5 *David was conscience-stricken.* The verbs in verses 4–5 are used elsewhere of David's killing Goliath (see "cut" [*karat*] in 1 Sam. 17:51 and "strike" [*nakah*] in 17:46, 49–50). But here the terms are used of David's harmless removal of a strip of Saul's robe and of his own conscience's striking his soul with guilt. This use of the verbs highlights the irony of the scene. David can view Saul as an enemy and strike him dead. But he refuses to do so, because he

Key Themes of 1 Samuel 24

- Though David can kill Saul, he refuses to do so, proving that he is loyal to Saul and is willing to wait for the Lord to give him the throne of Israel.
- David appeals to the Lord for justice and is vindicated when Saul exonerates and blesses him.

does not consider Saul to be an enemy. As far as David is concerned, Saul is still his "master" and "the LORD's anointed" (v. 6). His loyalty and innocence have never been so clearly revealed in the story as at this point.

24:6 *the anointed of the LORD.* Israel's king has been referred to as "anointed" earlier (2:10, 35; 12:3, 5; 16:6), but the precise phrase "anointed of the LORD" appears for the first time here. David uses this title of Saul three times in this passage (twice in this verse and again in v. 10) and six times later (1 Sam. 26:9, 11, 16, 23; 2 Sam. 1:14, 16).[2] It may play off the phrase "priests of the LORD" in 1 Samuel 22:17, 21—the only other place in this context where a title is used with the divine name to refer to a human who serves the Lord in some capacity. David refuses to raise his hand

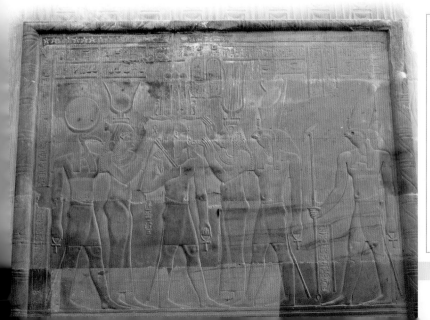

David honors Saul as king because Saul was anointed by Samuel as God's choice for Israel. Other nations in the ancient Near East also believed that the authority to govern was given by the deity to the king. For example, on this relief depicting his coronation, Ptolemy XII is surrounded by Egyptian gods. From left to right stand Toth, Nut, Ptolemy VII, Isis, Horus, and Ra-Hokharty (temple of Kom Ombo, Egypt, first century BC).

1 Samuel 24

against the Lord's servant (in this case, the anointed ruler), but Saul has not hesitated to kill the Lord's servants (the priests).

24:7 *to attack Saul.* "Attack" translates the same Hebrew phrase ("rise up against") as does "rebelled against" in 22:13. Saul accused Ahimelek of aiding and abetting David, whom he charged with "rising up against" him. But here in chapter 24 Saul's accusation is exposed as false. David is not rising up against the king; on the contrary, he does not even allow his men to do so.

24:8 *My lord the king!* With this form of address David acknowledges Saul's position and his own submission to the king's authority.[3] Yet the last time someone addressed Saul with the words "my lord," that person ended up dead despite making a powerful case for his innocence (see 22:12), so at this point there is tension in the plot.

24:10 *the LORD delivered you into my hands.* There is irony here when one contrasts David's words with the narrator's statement in 23:14, "God did not give David into his hands."

I will not lay my hand. The Hebrew expression "lay/raise a hand" was last used in the story in 1 Samuel 22:17, which says that Saul's servants refused to "raise a hand"

(*shalah yad*) against the Lord's priests. Their restraint, like David's, stands in stark contrast to Saul's murderous aggression against the priests and against David.

24:11 *my father.* David goes out of his way to express Saul's authority over him. He addresses him as "my lord/master" three times (vv. 6, 8, 10), "king" once (v. 8), "king of Israel" once (v. 14), and "LORD's anointed" three times (vv. 6, 10). Here he uses yet another title, "my father," which suggests his dependence upon the king.

24:12 *May the LORD judge.* David's determination to leave vengeance in God's hands (v. 12) stands in contrast to the earlier portrait of Saul, who was obsessed with getting revenge on his enemies (14:24; 18:25).

24:16 *David my son.* Earlier in the story Saul called David by name several times (18:8, 11, 22, 25; 19:22), but then he began calling him simply "the son of Jesse" (20:27, 30–31; 22:7–8, 13 [22:17 is an exception]). But here Saul uses his proper name, followed by "my son." The latter is a positive response to David's cry, "my father" (v. 11).

And he wept aloud. This expression elsewhere describes a response of extreme sorrow (Gen. 21:16; 27:38; Judg. 2:4; 21:2; Ruth 1:9, 14; 1 Sam. 11:4; 2 Sam. 3:32; 13:36; Job

David's encounter with Saul occurs somewhere in the region of En Gedi, where he has been hiding. En Gedi is a large oasis, with the Dead Sea to the east and Judean wilderness to the west. Its abundant caves, rugged landscape, and water supply (pictured here) made it an ideal hideout.

2:12).[4] On at least one occasion feelings of guilt appear to be present (Judg. 2:4), but by itself the expression need not imply this. Usually there is a sense of loss or regret that prompts this emotional response.

24:17 *You are more righteous than I.* This statement and the one made in 26:21 compose the most important evidence of David's innocence in the entire story. Together they form a foundation for the narrator's defense of David. Saul has accused David of betraying him and plotting against him, but these two confessions undercut those false charges.

24:19 *May the* LORD *reward you.* This blessing, like David's appeal for justice, sets the framework for the rest of the story. David's success can be interpreted as the outworking and fulfillment of this well-deserved blessing.

24:20 *I know that you will surely be king.* Jonathan has told David that his father knows David will be king (23:17). Now for the first time Saul publicly acknowledges that David is destined to rule Israel, and he even states this conviction emphatically (the infinitive absolute appears in the MT before the finite form of the verb).

the kingdom of Israel will be established in your hands. Saul finally acknowledges that the Lord's pronouncement regarding his kingdom (13:14) will be realized.[5]

24:22 *So David gave his oath to Saul.* David's positive response to Saul's plea (v. 21), like his covenant with Jonathan (20:42), demonstrates his honesty in this matter. If he had designs on overthrowing Saul and seizing his throne, he would not agree to this. Usurpers typically kill the offspring of the former king to solidify their power.

David and Saul's Sons

According to 1 Samuel 14:49, Saul has three sons: Jonathan, Ishvi, and Malki-Shua. In 1 Samuel 31:2 two of these sons are mentioned (Jonathan and Malki-Shua), but a third is named Abinadab, not Ishvi (see 1 Chron. 10:2). The lists in 1 Chronicles 8:33 and 9:39 include Jonathan, Malki-Shua, Abinadab, and Esh-Baal (= Ish-bosheth; see 2 Sam. 4:1). It is uncertain if Ishvi should be viewed as an alternative name for Malki-shua or Ish-bosheth. In the providence of God, three of Saul's sons, including Jonathan, die with him in battle (1 Sam. 31:2), while a fourth, Ish-bosheth (Esh-Baal), is murdered (2 Sam. 4). David has nothing to do with their deaths and therefore does not violate his oath to Saul. Though he is unable to prevent their deaths, he commends those who retrieve the corpses of Saul and his three sons from Beth Shan, where they were publicly exposed (1 Sam. 31:12), and he carries out swift justice against Ish-bosheth's assassins (2 Sam. 2:4–7; 4:12). In 2 Samuel 21 we discover that Saul had other sons, as well as grandsons. In this instance, David turns two of Saul's sons and five of his grandsons over to the Gibeonites to be executed, though he spares Jonathan's son, Mephibosheth.[a] The Gibeonites demand the lives of seven descendants of Saul as retribution for crimes Saul committed against them. This incident might appear to violate David's oath to Saul, but in actuality it does not, because of the legal ramifications involved. For further discussion, see the comments on 2 Samuel 21:1–14 below.

[a] This Mephibosheth is to be distinguished from Mephibosheth, the son of *Saul,* mentioned in 2 Sam. 21:8.

Theological Insights

Saul has forfeited his leadership status (cf. 13:13–14; 15:28–29), and God has chosen David as his successor (16:12–13), but God has not yet actually removed Saul from the throne and replaced him with David. Confronted with an apparent golden opportunity to make God's declared purpose a reality and avenge the wrongs Saul has committed against him, David refuses to kill Saul and instead appeals to God as judge. God vindicates him, for Saul acknowledges David's innocence and even blesses him.

David's appeal and Saul's blessing are particularly important to the developing story line and to the narrator's strategy: they provide a legal framework in which to interpret subsequent events. From this time forward, David's ultimate and complete vindication is inevitable. His eventual success and Saul's demise can be viewed as the outworking of God's justice in response to David's appeal and ironically as the fulfillment of Saul's prayer of blessing (24:19b). The justice-vindication theme links this episode with the story of Hannah's vindication. Like Hannah, David faces persecution and appeals to God. As in Hannah's case, the Lord vindicates him by intervening on his behalf. Like that first episode in 1 Samuel, this episode encourages the exilic readers of the story, for it is another reminder that God does indeed vindicate his oppressed people when they turn to him for justice.

Teaching the Text

1. *When the fulfillment of God's promise is delayed, God's chosen servants must resist the temptation to force the issue, and they must instead do what is right and wait for God's timing.* In this episode David's behavior is a model of how God's chosen servants should respond amid oppression. Resisting his men's interpreta-

tion of circumstances and refusing to impose his own spin on God's promise (v. 4), David chooses to respect Saul and to wait for the promise to materialize in God's own good time. He does not know when God will give him the throne, but he does know that it is wrong for him to lift his hand against the Lord's anointed and that he can trust God's just character. This is a relevant episode for all those who possess a promise from God but find themselves in a precarious position where the promise is delayed and may even seem to be in jeopardy. It encourages the oppressed people of God to wait on him and to take refuge in his justice, rather than trying to force the issue through their own efforts.

2. *When enduring oppression as one waits for God's promise to materialize, one must look to God for vindication.* In the face of injustice and persecution, David refuses to take vengeance into his own hands and appeals to God as the righteous Judge (v. 12). Though God does not yet give David the throne, he does vindicate him. Saul acknowledges David's innocence, pronounces a blessing upon him, and even assures him that his destiny will be realized. David's decision to look to God as his vindicator, rather than to follow the advice of his men,

David had a chance to take Saul's life in the cave at En Gedi, but he refused to kill Saul. Pictured here are several caves at En Gedi.

is a reminder that vengeance belongs to the Lord (Deut. 32:35; Rom. 12:17–21).

Illustrating the Text

It is crucial that believers maintain their integrity and wait for God's timing.

Church History: François de Salignac de La Mothe Fénelon. Fénelon (1651–1715) was the archbishop of Cambrai, France, during the seventeenth and early eighteenth centuries. While holding office, he had the opportunity of becoming the spiritual adviser to a small number of devout people at the Court of Louis XIV. Under Fénelon's wise direction, these believers decided to live a spiritual life amid an immoral court. Fénelon wrote a number of spiritual letters to guide those under his tutelage. What follows is a portion of letter 8 in modern paraphrase:

> We can listen to endless sermons about Christian growth, and become perfectly familiar with the language, and yet be as far from its attainment as ever. Our great aim should be to be deaf to self, to listen quietly to God, to renounce every bit of pride and devote ourselves to living. Let's learn to talk less and do more without caring whether anyone sees us or not.[6]

Quote: St. Teresa of Avila. This renowned Spanish nun (1515–82) once wrote, "Let nothing disturb thee; let nothing dismay thee. All things pass; God never changes: Patience attains all that it strives for. He who has God finds he lacks nothing: God alone suffices."[7]

The believer must leave vengeance and the vindication of evil in God's hands.

Film: *The Straight Story.* Directed by David Lynch, this much-acclaimed film (1999) chronicles a trip made by 73-year-old Alvin Straight (played by Richard Farnsworth) from Laurens, Iowa, to another town in Iowa, Mount Zion, to mend the relationship with his 75-year-old brother Lyle, from whom he has been bitterly estranged. Alvin's legs and eyes are too compromised for him to obtain a driver's license, so he hitches a trailer to his recently purchased, used John Deere 110 tractor and sets off on the 240-mile journey. During Alvin's six-week journey across rural America, he meets people he helps and who help him. The encounters are moving, inspiring, and poignant. The movie has been called a modern odyssey of a man dealing with his own mortality, past mistakes, and the lasting bonds of family. This film creatively demonstrates how one can change, the power produced by abandoning the need for vindictiveness, and the value of persevering in forgiveness—a powerful call to let go of one's rigid ideas of fairness.

David Listens to the Voice of Wisdom

Big Idea *The Lord's chosen servants should embrace the wisdom that he provides.*

Understanding the Text

The Text in Context

Chapter 24 ends with David's being vindicated as Saul acknowledged David's innocence, pronounced a blessing upon him, and assured him that he would someday be the king of Israel. However, he did not invite David to return to the royal court; Saul and David went their separate ways (v. 22). As we move to chapter 25, Saul remains backstage for a brief time as the narrator focuses on David's dealings with the wealthy but foolish Nabal, and his wise wife, Abigail. In chapter 24 David refused to take vengeance into his own hands; instead, he appealed to God for vindication. In chapter 25 this theme of vengeance emerges again. Nabal insults David, prompting David to seek vengeance against him. But wise Abigail intervenes and very diplomatically warns David that such a deed would be unworthy of Israel's future king. David recognizes her as God's messenger and praises the Lord for keeping him from doing something unwise. David instead waits on the Lord and is vindicated when the Lord mortally strikes down Nabal. David's restraint and reliance on God's intervention are fitting for one who will rule Israel. Once more David stands in contrast to Saul, who is obsessed with getting revenge on his enemies (14:24; 18:25), has been on a mission to take an innocent life (David's; cf. 1 Sam. 19:5), and has already killed the innocent priests of Nob and their families (1 Sam. 22). The voice of wisdom, embodied in Abigail (25:3, 33), reiterates what Saul himself has confessed (24:16–21): David is destined to be king. Only a fool (like Nabal—and Saul?) would resist God's purposes.[1]

Historical and Cultural Background

See the comments above under "Historical and Cultural Background" for 21:1–22:5.

Interpretive Insights

25:1 *Now Samuel died.* Samuel anointed both Saul and David as king and announced the Lord's rejection of Saul and choice of David. The death of God's spokesman appears to seal Samuel's prophetic word and the destiny of Saul and David.[2] Indeed, the death of Samuel, the first major character to appear in the book, does not bode well for the second major character to appear in the book: if literary order is preserved, it is now Saul's turn to die and leave the stage. Yet from the Davidic perspective, Samuel's death adds tension to the story, because David has lost his greatest supporter and is on his own, as it were.[3]

25:3 *She was an intelligent and beautiful woman.* The term translated "intelligent" (*sekel*) describes a moral quality, not just mental aptitude (cf. Ps. 111:10; Prov. 3:4; 12:8; 13:15; 16:22; 19:11; 23:9). Those who possess this characteristic are contrasted with perverse and faithless fools. In this chapter Abigail embodies wisdom and, in the providence of God, is sent to David as the voice of wisdom (see vv. 32–33).

25:8 *Please give your servants and your son David whatever you can find for them.* Typical outlaws might have pounced on Nabal's men and robbed him of his sheep, but David's men show restraint and actually protect Nabal's workers (see vv. 15–16) from wandering outlaw groups and foreign raiders. How should we interpret David's motives and actions? David may be op-

Key Themes of 1 Samuel 25

- David embraces the wise advice that the Lord provides through Abigail.
- The Lord judges Nabal because of his foolish disdain for the Lord's chosen servant.

erating in accordance with the practices of his time. He and his men need to stay alive. To do so, they must creatively scrounge for provisions. To his credit, David refuses to become a bandit who robs and pillages. Instead, he offers his services, as it were, expecting to be rewarded for providing "protection," when he has the power to simply take what he wants. In other words, as outlaws go, David is the more civilized type. From his perspective his actions are deserving of favor, and Nabal's response is deserving of death (cf. vv. 21–22). Here he probably simply reflects the code of the day.

25:10 *Who is this son of Jesse?* Nabal calls David "this son of Jesse," echoing the derogatory manner in which Saul and Doeg have referred to him (1 Sam. 20:27, 30–31; 22:7–9, 13).[4]

Many servants are breaking away from their masters. Abigail knows a great deal

about David, including his past victories and Saul's hostility (vv. 28–31). So we can assume that Nabal also knows who David is. Consequently his comment about servants' breaking away from their masters reveals his perspective. His attitude stands in stark contrast to that of his wise wife, who is well aware of David's destiny.[5] Her words suggest that Nabal should have responded positively to David because of who David is: the Lord's chosen king and the protector of Israel.

25:17 *disaster is hanging over our master.* In verse 3 Nabal is characterized as "mean" (or "evil," *ra'*) in his dealings. Here Nabal's servants recognize that "disaster" (*ra'ah*) is imminent because of Nabal's insulting response to David. The similarity in sound suggests that the disastrous consequences of Nabal's behavior mirror his evil character and are appropriate.

wicked man. The phrase used here to characterize Nabal also describes Eli's sons (2:12) and the individuals who despised Saul after he was presented to Israel as their king (10:27). The narrator (v. 3), Nabal's servant (v. 17), and Nabal's wife (v. 25) all depict him as a wicked man.

25:21 *He has paid me back evil for good.* Again the word *ra'ah*, "evil," echoes the description of Nabal as evil

(note *ra'* in v. 3; see the comment on v. 17 above). His actions are consistent with his character.

25:22 *May God deal with David.* The Hebrew text reads, "May God deal with the *enemies* of David." The Septuagint, which reads simply, "May God deal with *David*," likely preserves the original reading here. As stated in the Hebrew text, the vow appears to be an attempt to avoid the implication that David has placed himself under a serious self-imprecation when he fails to fulfill the vow.[6] However, since this is an inappropriate and rash vow (vv. 32–34), God will not and does not hold David accountable for failing to keep it. Obedience is better than adhering to ritual (cf. 15:22), so David would only compound matters by fulfilling it. His decision not to carry it out is wise and commendable.[7]

25:23 *bowed down before David with her face to the ground.* Abigail's humble response to David mirrors David's earlier response to Saul (24:8). David has shown the king of Israel, the Lord's anointed, the proper respect by calling him "my master/lord" (*'adon*, 24:6, 8, 10). Abigail shows the

In 1 Samuel 24:8, David prostrates himself to show honor to Saul, and in 25:23 Abigail does the same to show honor to David. In this Egyptian painting, foreigners prostrate themselves before Akhenaten to show their respect (Karnak, fourteenth century BC).

same kind of respect to David, addressing him as "my lord/master" (*'adon*) fifteen times (vv. 24–31, 41) and referring to herself as his "servant/maidservant" (*'amah*) six times (vv. 24–25, 28, 31, 41). By way of contrast, Nabal rudely dismisses David's servants and suggests that David is merely a rebellious servant of Saul (25:10).

25:25 *He is just like his name.* There is a Hebrew word *nabal*, "fool," but surely Nabal's name did not have this meaning. It was probably derived from a homonym meaning "noble" or "adept" (see *HALOT*, 663–64). But Abigail, playing off the homonym "fool," suggests that his name matches his character, for he displays "folly" (*nebalah*, related to *nabal*, "fool").

25:28 *lasting dynasty.* Abigail's statement anticipates the Lord's dynastic promise, in which he declares his intention to build an enduring "house" (royal dynasty) for David (2 Sam. 7:16).

wrongdoing. Abigail prays that no "wrongdoing" (*ra'ah*) will be found in David. Such behavior is characteristic of Nabal (vv. 3, 21) but is inappropriate for the future king of Israel. The implication seems to be that Nabal's offensive response, while certainly wrong, is not worthy of death. The shedding of his blood would be unwarranted and equally wrong. David seems to concur with this (vv. 32–34).

25:30 *has appointed him ruler over Israel.* Abigail's words echo both the Lord's original announcement to Samuel that he has chosen a Benjamite to lead Israel (9:16; cf. 10:1) and his later decree that he has rejected Saul and chosen someone else to lead Israel (13:14). Her use of this term to refer to David confirms the decree and signals the change about to take place (see 2 Sam.

5:2; 6:21; 7:8), but it is also a reminder that David will serve under the Lord's authority.

25:31 *needless bloodshed.* Jonathan warned Saul not to kill David, for he had no reason to do so (19:5). But Saul has nevertheless persisted in his attempts to murder David. Here Abigail politely warns David that killing Nabal would constitute needless (*hinnam*, the same word used by Jonathan in 19:5) bloodshed. In contrast to Saul, David takes heed to this wise warning (v. 32).

25:33 *good judgment.* The relatively rare Hebrew word (*ta'am*) refers to discernment, in this case in the moral and ethical realm. Such discernment is a characteristic of the wise (Ps. 119:66; Prov. 26:16). According to Proverbs 11:22, a beautiful woman's attractiveness is negated if this quality is absent. But Abigail is both wise and beautiful (see v. 3).

25:39 *who has upheld my cause.* The language used here of God's judgment upon Nabal echoes the description of the demise of Abimelek (Judg. 9:56–57), another evildoer who acted as if he were a king (cf. 9:56).

asking her to become his wife. David's marriage to Abigail, while not pleasing to our monogamous sensibilities, may have a positive function literarily, for it depicts him as embracing the voice of wisdom and as receiving an obvious blessing that a fool like Nabal never deserved. Abigail's lone son (Kileab = Daniel; 2 Sam. 3:3; 1 Chron. 3:1) is not presented in a negative light as a contender for the throne later in the story.

Theological Insights

Nabal the fool and wise Abigail represent two contrasting responses to David—

rejection (25:10–11) and submission (vv. 23–25, 42)—as well as two different destinies based on their responses. Nabal ends up dead, while Abigail ends up joining the royal court (vv. 38, 42). As such, they are, on the one hand, a reminder of how the covenant community should respond to God's chosen king, David, and, on the other hand, a warning of what will happen to those who reject his king. Obviously this reminder and warning will be of the utmost importance in the time of David, as he tries to solidify his reign. Yet the message is also significant to the exiles as they consider the future of the covenant community and the role of the ancient Davidic dynasty in that community.

The theme of divine justice continues to be prominent in the account of David and Nabal. As in the case of Saul (see 24:15), David decides to leave his vindication in God's hands rather than seeking his own justice. Because David listens to Abigail's wise advice and waits for God to resolve his grievances against Nabal, the Lord does indeed vindicate him when he judges Nabal (25:39) and then gives Nabal's wife to David. Like the incident recorded in chapter 24, this episode encourages the exilic readers of the story, for it is another reminder that God does indeed vindicate his oppressed people when they turn to him for justice.

Teaching the Text

1. *God's chosen servants should embrace the wise advice that he provides.* As Solomon acknowledges, God's chosen servants need divine wisdom (1 Kings 3), especially, as in the case of David, when their honor is

Seeking to appease David's anger, Abigail humbly offers him gifts of food from her household supply and asks for forgiveness for her husband's offense. In the ancient world, gifts were typically given or exchanged to build social or political relationships, as shown in this Egyptian painting. Here people from Africa are bringing goods from their home countries to the King of Egypt (tomb-chapel of Sebekhotep at Thebes, 1400 BC).

offended and they are tempted to vindicate themselves. But attempts at self-vindication, even when one has a seemingly just cause, can compromise one's integrity and prove to be the antithesis of faith in God. Abigail reminds David that bloodshed will be unbecoming for the king of Israel and that his destiny is safe and secure within the Lord's promise (vv. 26–31). As the embodiment of wisdom (vv. 3, 33), she has been sent by the Lord to David (vv. 32, 39). To his credit, he listens to the voice of wisdom, correctly perceives her as God's messenger, and decides to trust in God's promise and timing, rather than in his sword. Violent retaliation for perceived wrongs is rarely, if ever, a wise response, for the wisdom that comes from God promotes peace, not strife (James 3:13–18; cf. Prov. 14:29).

2. *The Lord vindicates his chosen servants against those who oppose them.* The theme of divine vindication recurs in 1 Samuel (see 1:1–2:11; chap. 24). The timing of such vindication is in God's hands. In this case, David does not need to wait long. The morning after Abigail returns home from her meeting with David, she informs Nabal of his narrow escape from David's wrath. Nabal has a stroke, and ten days later the Lord strikes him dead (vv. 37–38). We cannot assume that vindication will always come so quickly; it may not. Yet God is just and will hold evildoers accountable for their misdeeds, bringing their "wrongdoing down on [their] own head" (v. 39; see Judg. 9:56–57; 1 Kings 2:32–33, 44; Joel 3:4; Obad. 15; Ps. 7:16). But we must patiently wait for God's timing (Rom. 12:19; 2 Thess. 1:5–10).

Illustrating the Text

The believer must embrace divine wisdom, particularly when tempted to pursue self-vindication.

Christian Autobiography: *Prison Letters,* **by Corrie ten Boom.** The story of Corrie ten Boom (1892–1983) during World War II is well known. Corrie had suffered with a tremendous need for vengeance. After Corrie was released from prison following the war, she felt the need to write a letter to the man who had revealed her family's rescue operations to the Germans. She writes about that: "I was free, and knew then as I know now it was my chance to take to the world God's message of the victory of Jesus Christ in the midst of the deepest evil of man." Written on June 19, 1945, part of the letter to her betrayer reads:

Today I heard that most probably you are the one who betrayed me. I went through 10 months of concentration camp. My father died after 9 days of imprisonment. My sister died in prison, too.

The harm you planned was turned into good for me by God. I came nearer to Him. . . . I have forgiven you everything. God will also forgive you everything, if you ask Him. He loves you and He Himself sent His Son to earth to reconcile your sins, which meant to suffer the punishment for you and me. You, on your part, have to give an answer to this. . . . Never doubt the Lord Jesus' love. He is standing with His arms spread out to receive you. I hope that the path which you will now take may work for your eternal salvation.[8]

Divine justice will be delivered to those who treat God's people with disdain and hostility.

Quote: Martin Luther. The reformer Luther (1483–1546) confidently wrote,

Our God will fulfill the promise of his word. He is on our side. No matter how the wicked strangle, imprison, and persecute, I am the more certain that God is my protection. Our doctrine must prevail: their doctrine must perish. God is our defense; he will see us through whether here or elsewhere. God is our refuge, to him we flee for safety.[9]

Film: *The Ten Commandments,* **by Cecil B. DeMille.** Though the film (1956) is very old, it is still regularly shown on television every year. The film clip of the Israelites' walking through the Red Sea on dry land, after which the same sea drowns the Egyptians in their chariots, is a dramatic illustration of the force of God's justice.

David Spares Saul's Life—Again

Big Idea *The Lord vindicates his chosen servants when they look to him for justice.*

Understanding the Text

The Text in Context

For a second time in the story, the Ziphites report David's whereabouts to Saul (cf. 1 Sam. 23:19). Earlier Saul confessed David's innocence and even asked the Lord to bless David (1 Sam. 24:16–21), but now again the king is ready to hunt David down and kill him. David decides once more to demonstrate his loyalty to Saul. Though the Lord again seemingly delivers Saul into his hands, David refuses to strike the Lord's anointed. When Saul realizes that David has again spared his life, he confesses his sin and promises not to harm David in the future. David appeals to the Lord for vindication, and Saul blesses him and assures him of future success.

The similarity of this episode to the one recorded in 1 Samuel 24 is striking. The events are clearly distinct, as the many differences in incidental details indicate. However, at their thematic core the accounts are parallel. By recording both of these incidents, the narrator establishes beyond all doubt David's innocence and Saul's guilt. If Saul's confession in 24:17 is Exhibit A in the narrator's defense of

David, then the corresponding confession in 26:21 becomes Exhibit B.

Interpretive Insights

26:5 *Then David set out and went to the place where Saul had camped.* On the earlier occasion, David did not seek an encounter with Saul. But in this second incident, David is the aggressor and actively seeks a confrontation with Saul so that he can reaffirm his innocence and once again challenge the king's unjust treatment of him.

26:7 *with his spear stuck in the ground near his head.* This bit of detail heightens the tension of the plot, because the proximity of Saul's spear highlights the temptation David faces to rid himself of his enemy with one quick stroke. Saul's spear has been mentioned before: on two occasions he tried to kill David with it (18:10–11; 19:9–10), and once he threw it at David's best friend, his own son Jonathan, for supporting David (20:33). In 22:6 it is mentioned again just before Saul launches his campaign against David and murders the priests at Nob for allegedly siding with David. Saul's spear symbolizes the king's hostility toward David and the mortal danger that Saul represents for him. But now David could rid himself

Key Themes of 1 Samuel 26

- Though David again has the opportunity to kill Saul, he refuses to do so, proving that he is loyal to Saul and is willing to wait for the Lord to give him the throne of Israel.
- David again appeals to the Lord for justice and is vindicated when Saul exonerates and blesses him.

of this threat to his life by grabbing his enemy's spear and transferring its location from the ground to Saul's head.

26:9 *the LORD's anointed*. See the comment on 24:6 above.

26:10 *the LORD himself will strike him*. The verb translated "strike" (*nagap*) is the same one used in 25:38 to describe how the Lord "struck" Nabal dead. David has seen the Lord's vindication in Nabal's case, and he is confident that the Lord will take Saul's life in his own good time, whether by natural causes or in battle. David's words ominously foreshadow Saul's death (see chap. 31).

26:12 *the LORD had put them into a deep sleep*. As in earlier incidents, the Lord's intervention on David's behalf is apparent (see 23:14, 27–28; 25:32, 38–39).

26:17 *David my son*. See the comment on 24:16 above. Once again Saul's form of address is a spontaneous admission of David's loyalty.

my lord the king. As before, David goes out of his way to express his allegiance and submission to Saul (see the comment on 24:8

above).[1] He addresses Saul as "my lord" three times (vv. 17–19), calls him "king" six times (vv. 15–17, 19–20, 22), refers to him as the Lord's "anointed" twice in Saul's hearing (vv. 16, 23), and describes himself as Saul's "servant" twice (vv. 18–19).

26:19 *If the LORD has incited you against me*. David reasons that Saul's obsession with killing him is the result of either divine or human deception. David has good reason to suspect the Lord of deceiving Saul.[2] After all, because of Saul's blatant disobedience, the Lord has decreed the demise of the king and his family (1 Sam. 13:13–14; 15:26–29). Shortly after this the Lord dispatched an evil spirit to torment Saul (16:14–16, 23; 18:10; 19:9). David was hired to bring relief to Saul whenever this spirit tormented him (16:23). On two occasions the spirit incited Saul to try to kill David (18:10–11; 19:9–10). In light of these experiences, one can easily conclude that Saul's unrelenting attempt to kill David is a sign of the Lord's disfavor with Saul. In other words, as an act of divine judgment, the Lord is prompting Saul

Abishai, David's Nephew

Abishai is one of three sons of David's sister Zeruiah; the others are Joab and Asahel (2 Sam. 2:18; 1 Chron. 2:16). Abishai is a bold warrior (2 Sam. 21:16–17) and ready to kill at the drop of a hat (2 Sam. 3:30; 16:9–10; 19:21; 20:10). He and his brothers become a tremendous burden to David (2 Sam. 3:39; 16:10; 19:22).

to do this evil thing, as proof to everyone that the king is unfit to rule. If this is the case, David argues, then Saul should present an offering to God in an attempt to appease God's anger (cf. 3:14).[3]

The other option, from David's perspective, is that evil men are behind this, advising Saul to kill David (cf. 24:9). If this is the case, David prays that the Lord will judge these men, for the king's pursuit, prompted by their advice, is putting pressure on David to leave Judah. This is equivalent to depriving him of his rightful inheritance in the Lord's covenant community. Worse yet, they are essentially encouraging him to run away to another land and worship other gods, in direct violation of God's covenant (Deut. 11:16; 13:6–18; 17:2–7; Josh. 23:16). But David remains a loyal servant of the Lord, as his appeal makes clear (1 Sam. 26:20). If he must die, he wishes that it would be close to the Lord's presence. This confession of loyalty to the Lord is important, for David has already sought asylum in Philistine territory (21:9–15) and is about to do so again (27:1–12). By including this quotation, the narrator makes it clear that David has not renounced his God.

26:21 *I have sinned.* This statement and the one made in 24:17 (see the comment there) compose the most important evidence of David's innocence in the entire story. Together they form a foundation for the narrator's defense of David. Saul has accused David of betraying him and plotting against him, but these two confessions undercut those false charges. For the third time in the story the words "I have sinned" come from Saul's lips. When confronted by Samuel after his failure to wipe out the Amalekites, he twice acknowledged that he had sinned (15:24, 30). His son Jonathan warned him that taking David's life would be sin (19:4–5), and now Saul admits the truth of this. The verbal linking of this confession of guilt with the earlier one is a powerful literary device: by it the narrator characterizes Saul as a sinner. His sin in the Amalekite affair has prompted God to formally reject him as king and to withdraw his Spirit. Most of his energy after that incident has been directed toward David's demise, but by his own admission, his efforts have been sinful.

Come back, David my son. This invitation contributes to the narrator's depiction of David as innocent, for it shows that David, by Saul's own admission, is not a threat to him.

I have acted like a fool. This confession echoes Samuel's rebuke of Saul, following his decision to offer the sacrifice at Gilgal before Samuel's arrival (13:13). The verbal link between this verse and 13:13 (the only other passage in which this verb occurs in 1 Samuel) contributes to the narrator's characterization of Saul. Samuel's assessment of him on that earlier occasion is still true, by Saul's own admission.

26:24 *so may the LORD value my life and deliver me from all trouble.* David's words echo his confident affirmation before his victory over Goliath (see 17:37, where the verb translated "deliver" in 26:24 occurs twice). The verbal link characterizes David

Once again, David refuses to kill Saul, even though he stands right next to the sleeping king, a stabbing weapon within easy reach. This Assyrian relief shows Tiglath-Pileser III with upraised spear standing over a captured enemy (palace at Nimrud, 728 BC).

as one who trusts in the Lord's protective power in both the past and the present, in contrast to Saul, who is depicted as a foolish sinner in both the past and the present (see v. 21).

26:25 *So David went on his way.* Apparently David's rejection of Saul's offer and promise (v. 21) is a wise decision, because 27:4 implies that Saul gives up his quest only when David flees to Gath.

Theological Insights

Like the episode recorded in chapter 24, this account highlights David's refusal to promote his own interests, and his faith in God's justice and timing. Once more David refuses to kill Saul and instead appeals to God as judge. God vindicates him, for Saul acknowledges David's innocence and even blesses him. It is especially significant that these are the last words Saul ever speaks to David. Again David's appeal and Saul's blessing are significant to the narrator's strategy: they remind us that later events must be understood within a legal framework. David's complete vindication is inevitable. His eventual success and Saul's demise can be viewed as the outworking of God's justice in response to David's appeal and, ironically, as the fulfillment of Saul's prayer. For the exilic readers of the story, this account reiterates the important theme that God does indeed vindicate his oppressed people when they turn to him for justice.

While there is thematic continuity between the two accounts, the episode in chapter 26 does exhibit at least two additional and distinctive elements. First, the verbal linking noted above highlights the narrator's characterization of Saul as a foolish sinner (cf. 26:21 with 13:13; 15:24, 30) and his depiction of David as one who trusts in God's power to deliver (cf. 26:24 with 17:37). Second, David's warning to Saul raises the possibility that God himself is deceiving Saul (26:19). We are reminded that, in addition to rejecting Saul and removing his enabling Spirit, God sent an "evil spirit" to oppress and oppose Saul. In this way observers will know that Saul no longer enjoys God's favor. God opposes his enemies in different ways. He sometimes allows sinners to pursue evil actions, which in turn prompt God's judgment (Rom. 1:18–32). He may even harden or deceive his enemies (Rom. 9:18; 2 Thess. 2:11–12).[4] The sobering words of Hebrews 10:31 remind us that it is "a dreadful thing to fall into the hands of the living God."

Teaching the Text

The two primary themes in this episode are the same as those in chapter 24:

1. *When the fulfillment of God's promise is delayed, God's chosen servants must resist the temptation to force the issue and must instead do what is right and wait for God's timing.* As in the earlier episode, David's behavior is a model of how God's chosen servants should respond amid oppression. As we stated earlier, David's restraint is an example for all those who possess a promise from God but find themselves in a precarious position where the promise is delayed

and may even seem to be in jeopardy. It encourages the oppressed people of God to wait on God and to take refuge in his justice, rather than trying to force the issue through their own efforts.

2. *When enduring oppression as one waits for God's promise to materialize, one must look to God for vindication.* As we noted with regard to the earlier incident, David refuses to take vengeance into his own hands and appeals to God to reward him for his restraint by protecting him (vv. 23–24). As before, Saul acknowledges David's innocence, pronounces a blessing upon him, and even assures him of future success. David's decision to look to God as his vindicator, rather than following the advice of his men, is a reminder that vengeance belongs to the Lord (Deut. 32:35; Rom. 12:17–21).

Illustrating the Text

The believer must wait on God's timing, maintaining integrity during the wait.

Poetry: St. Patrick. This prayer by St. Patrick (387–493), who was born in Scotland and traveled throughout Ireland while preaching the simple gospel of Jesus Christ, has been called one of the most powerful Christian poems written. It is a declaration of faith in which Patrick asks to be protected in the hour of need, and it was written in the first year of his missionary life. It echoes David's dependence on God as he refuses to take vengeance. One version of the prayer is as follows:

> I bind myself today,
> To the power of God to guide me,
> The might of God to uphold me,
> The wisdom of God to teach me,
> The eyes of God to watch over me,

The ear of God to hear me,
The Word of God to speak for me,
The hand of God to protect me,
The way of God to lie before me,
The shield of God to shelter me,
The host of God to defend me,
Christ with me, Christ before me,
Christ beneath me, Christ above me,
Christ at my right, Christ at my left,
Christ in breadth, Christ in length,
   Christ in height,
Christ in the heart of every man
   who thinks of me,
Christ in the mouth of every man
   who speaks to me,
Christ in the eye of every man that
   sees me,
Christ in the ear of every man who
   hears me.
Salvation is the Lord's
Salvation is the Lord's
Salvation is the Lord's
Let thy salvation, O Lord, be ever
   with us.[5]

The believer must leave vengeance and vindication in God's hands.

Film: *Death Sentence.* Prudence is a virtue seldom discussed and not to be confused with goodness. C. S. Lewis said that prudence is taking the time and effort to think about what you are doing and what might come of it. Prudence contains discernment and acts wisely. *Death Sentence* (2007), a movie based on the novel by Brian Garfield, demonstrates the consequences of ignoring prudence, of taking vindication into one's own hands, the opposite of what is taught in 1 Samuel 26. It is a violent and disturbing film that tells the story of Nick Hume (played by Kevin Bacon), initially a mild-mannered executive with a perfect family and life. One horrifying night when his car breaks down in a dangerous area, he witnesses the brutal death of his son at the hands of a sociopathic gang. This event changes Hume forever. Embittered by grief, he eventually comes to a disturbing conclusion that he must go to any length to avenge his son's death. After the desire for vengeance has infected him, Hume gradually becomes like the evil characters who first victimized his son. The movie teaches the evil of such self-proclaimed vigilante justice.

David Flees to Gath—Again

Big Idea *When faith wavers, the Lord's chosen servants sometimes compromise their identity and resort to desperate measures that place them in a precarious position.*

Understanding the Text

The Text in Context

Convinced that Saul will never really abandon his quest to kill him, David, for the second time in the story, seeks asylum with Achish, the Philistine king of Gath (cf. 1 Sam. 21:9–15). On the first occasion David was alone, got cold feet, and left in fear. But on this second occasion, he has his own private army with him. He offers his services to Achish as a mercenary and border guard. Achish assigns him to Ziklag, located about twenty-five miles south-southwest of Gath.

On his first visit to Gath, David deceived Achish into thinking he was insane. On this second occasion, David again deceives Achish. After convincing Achish to assign him to a relatively distant outpost, where he can operate free of the king's scrutiny, David raids the nearby non-Israelite peoples to acquire food and provisions for his men and their families. However, David reports to Achish that he is raiding Judah and its allies (the Kenites), so that the king will think he has transferred his loyalties from his homeland to Achish. To ensure that Achish does not discover what he is really

up to, David leaves no survivors among his victims. This account supports the narrator's defense of David by showing that he does not really become a traitor to Israel. Though he moves to Philistine territory and even claims to kill Judahites and Kenites, he is really killing the enemies of Israel.[1]

However, the story does not end with this subterfuge. Unfortunately for David, his deceit threatens to backfire against him. Convinced of David's loyalty, Achish summons David and his men to join his forces for his upcoming battle with Israel. David swears his allegiance, and Achish promotes him to bodyguard. But then the story is suspended and the focus returns to Saul. The reader must wait to find out what happens to David. Will he really march out to do battle against his own countrymen?

David's return to Gath brings the story of his exile full circle. Earlier, after Jonathan told him of Saul's desire to kill him, he fled in desperation to Nob and then to Gath (chap. 21). But then the Lord told him to return to Judah and protected him from Saul's repeated attempts to capture him. This culminated with Saul's acknowledging David's innocence and even inviting him to return to the royal court. The Lord has protected and seemingly vindicated him, but David decides to flee to Gath again.

A closer look at the parallelism within these chapters reveals a pattern, which may be outlined as follows:

A   David's faith wavers; he runs away and lives in exile (21:1–22:5).
B   Saul rejects the Lord by killing his priests (22:6–23).
C   The Lord guides David and gives him victory over Israel's enemy (23:1–5).
D   The Lord protects David and reminds him of his destiny (23:6–18).
E   The Ziphites report David's whereabouts, and Saul seeks him (23:19–29).
F   David spares Saul, and Saul acknowledges David's innocence (chap. 24).
D′ The Lord protects David and reminds him of his destiny (chap. 25).
E′ The Ziphites report David's whereabouts, and Saul seeks him (26:1–3).
F′ David spares Saul, and Saul acknowledges David's innocence (26:4–25).
A′ David's faith wavers; he runs away and lives in exile (27:1–28:2; 29:1–11).

Key Themes of 1 Samuel 27:1–28:2

- When faith wavers in the face of persecution, the Lord's chosen servants sometimes compromise their identity.
- When faith wavers, the Lord's chosen servants sometimes resort to desperate measures that place them in a precarious position.

The corresponding B′ and C′ elements in the outline seem to be missing, but they actually appear in chapters 28 and 30 and complete the parallelism:

B′ The Lord rejects Saul and announces his death (28:3–25).
C′ The Lord guides David and gives him victory over Israel's enemy (chap. 30).

The structure may be viewed as follows: A B C D E F // D′ E′ F′ A′ B′ C′. The thematic cluster A B C / A′ B′ C′ forms bookends for the section.

Tell Sera, the mound shown here, is one of the possible sites for biblical Ziklag.

Interpretive Insights

27:1 *I will be destroyed by the hand of Saul.* Just before this, David has assured Abishai that the Lord will eliminate Saul, whether by natural causes or in battle (26:10). In mentioning the second possibility, he speaks of Saul's perishing (*sapah*). But now, in an abrupt shift, he convinces himself that he will be "destroyed" (*sapah*) by the hand of Saul. Despite assurances from Jonathan, Saul, and Abigail that he will indeed prosper (23:17; 24:20; 25:30–31; 26:25), David's faith in God's promise wavers.[2]

The best thing I can do is to escape. Twice in this verse, David speaks of escaping (both "escape" and "slip" translate *malat*). Five times before this, the narrator has reported that David "escaped" (*malat*; see 19:10, 12, 18; 22:1; 23:13). God's providence protected David from Saul's spear, Saul's officers who came to arrest him in his own home, the Philistine king Achish, and the fickle residents of Keilah. But now he decides to take matters into his own hands, bring about his own escape, and again leave the land where his destiny is to be realized. The first time he did this he encountered even greater danger and ended up being humiliated, before being told by the Lord to return home (21:9–22:5). This second excursion to Gath will prove to be no different.

27:5 *your servant.* The irony continues. David has used this phrase when speaking to both the Lord (23:10–11; cf. 25:39) and his anointed king Saul (17:32, 34, 36; cf. 26:18–19), but now he refers to himself as the servant of Achish, as if his allegiance has shifted (see also 28:2).

27:8 *raided the Geshurites, the Girzites and the Amalekites.* Three people groups

The location of Ziklag is not known with certainty. Tell Sera (Tell esh-Sharia), Tell Halif (Tell Khuweilifeh), and Tell Beersheba (Tell es-Seba) have been suggested as possibilities and are shown on this map. Any of these locations would have allowed David to carry out raids on Israel's enemies. The map also shows the location of the Geshurites and the Amalekites. The Girzites' territory is unknown.

are listed as David's victims. The Geshurites (not to be confused with a people by the same name who live east of the Jordan River; 2 Sam. 3:3; 13:37–38) are included in a list of peoples the Israelites were to conquer (Josh. 13:2), so they are legitimate candidates for the genocidal policy described here.[3] The Girzites are mentioned only here in the Old Testament; the marginal reading in the Hebrew text emends the form to Gezerites, but Gezer is located too far north (north of Gath) to be within the range of David's military operations.[4] The Amalekites are hated archenemies that God intends to annihilate (cf. 1 Sam. 15:1–3). Ironically, David, out of expedience, is fulfilling the Lord's wishes more efficiently than Saul has done (cf. 15:7–9).[5]

27:12 *He has become so obnoxious to his people, the Israelites, that he will be my servant for life.* Though David's loyalties remain with Israel and his ruse is successful, he has compromised his identity.

28:2 *I will make you my bodyguard for life*. Confident of David's loyalty, Achish promises to appoint him as his bodyguard (Hebrew, "a guard for my head"). At this point Achish's words are dripping with irony. David, who once cut off the head of the hero of Gath and hauled it away as a trophy of war (17:51, 54), will now be responsible for guarding the head of the ruler of Gath![6] From one perspective, this highlights the naïveté of Achish and the providential protection of David. When viewed from another angle, the situation is disturbing because of its incongruity. The one who defeated Israel's archenemy, the Philistine hero from Gath, is now protecting the ruler of Gath. Such things can happen when an Israelite king pursues God's chosen servant into exile, and when God's chosen servant loses focus on his destiny.

Theological Insights

How are we to assess David's behavior in this chapter? Against the background of the story's macroplot, David's actions are probably to be understood in a negative light. One could certainly blame Saul for what happens (cf. 26:19), but the Lord has protected David and reminds him of his destiny time and time again (cf. 1 Sam. 23–26). Yet his faith wavers, and he leaves the land he is destined to rule. He resorts to deceit, as he has done before (cf. 1 Sam. 21–22), rather than seeking the Lord's will (as he did in 1 Sam. 23). While he cleverly avoids needing to attack his own people and (unwittingly?) fights the Lord's battles against Israel's ancient foes, his deceit eventually puts him in a compromising and dangerous position, from which only God's providence can rescue him (cf. 1 Sam. 29).

A noteworthy literary feature of this account is the absence of God's name (see 21:10–15 as well). David, at least temporarily, has all but turned his back on his destiny and compromises his identity as the Lord's servant. How appropriate that the Lord seems to be absent from the scene! This chapter illustrates what can happen when God's people in desperation seek their own security at the expense of their identity and integrity. Certainly this is an important lesson for the exilic readers of the history, who are in a precarious position in a foreign land.

Yet in this story is a silver lining of sorts. Just as when the ark went to Philistine territory (1 Sam. 4–6), God will not be thwarted by the failures of his people. In his providence he gives David the opportunity to kill the enemies of Israel while stationed in a Philistine outpost and under the authority of a Philistine king. Furthermore, providence even places David in the position of the king's bodyguard, where the unsuspecting Philistine ruler is vulnerable.

Teaching the Text

1. *When faith wavers in the face of persecution, the Lord's chosen servants sometimes compromise their identity.* Saul has persisted in his attempts to kill David, even after the king has confessed his wrongdoing and pronounced a blessing upon his eventual successor (cf. 24:16–20). Though Saul has again confessed his own guilt and David's innocence, promised to no longer harm David, and even invited David back to the royal court (26:21), the stress of persecution has brought David to the edge of his emotional cliff. The Lord has

consistently encouraged him by reminding him of his destiny (23:17; 24:20; 25:30–31; 26:25), and in his stronger moments David himself speaks with assurance of his vindication (26:10) and appeals to God's justice (24:12; 26:23–24). But finally David breaks emotionally and decides to turn his back on his destiny, at least temporarily. Moving to Philistine territory does bring relief from the immediate threat (Saul, 27:4), but it also forces David to compromise his identity. Though the narrator makes it clear that David never really turns traitor and attacks his own people, David does claim and pretend to be Israel's enemy and Achish's loyal servant. One wonders if he feels any pangs of conscience when the words "your servant" come from his mouth as he stands before Achish (27:5; 28:2). Does he remember that this is the phrase he used to describe his relationship both to the Lord and to Israel's king?

2. *When faith wavers, the Lord's chosen servants sometimes resort to desperate measures that place them in a precarious position.* Not only does David compromise his identity; his exile to Philistine territory also forces him to resort to desperate measures. While his slaughter of Israel's enemies is probably to be understood in a positive light from the narrator's perspective, his deceit, while necessary for his survival, is disturbing at best. It foreshadows the duplicity he displays in the attempted cover-up of his adulterous affair with Bathsheba and murder of Uriah. Indeed, moral flaws sometimes develop from behavioral choices in seemingly gray areas. After all, in the end David's self-preservation scheme and deception of Achish work, and he escapes unscathed. Could this success, in a situa-

tion where some might not fault him for using deceit, be convincing him that such schemes are necessary when one faces a crisis, even of one's own making?

David's wavering faith, which prompts his seeking asylum with Achish, also puts him in a precarious position. His deception, which works just fine for a time, actually works too well. Achish enlists him in his army, and in due time David will be caught between a rock and a hard place, for Achish expects him to fight against Israel (see chap. 29). Only the Lord's providential intervention saves him from the desperate situation in which he finds himself (cf. 29:4–11).

Illustrating the Text

Wavering faith can cause God's servants to compromise their identity.

Bible: Luke 22:47–62. In this passage, Judas betrays Christ, and Peter, afraid for his welfare, denies Christ three times. Judas recognizes his failures as a true disciple of Christ and commits suicide. Peter weeps bitterly after his denial.

Quote: *All the Days,* by Vance Havner. Havner (1901–86) was a preacher at twelve and ordained at sixteen; he spent decades as a much-in-demand speaker. He wrote the following in this collection of daily devotionals:

But all who have companioned with trouble and walked the dark valley find a kinship not only with . . . David and Jeremiah and Paul and many another who at times hung their harps on the willows. For the believing soul, December should indeed be as pleasant as May, but there are times when even May can be dreary. Faith goes ahead anyway, not doubting the sun because the clouds obscure it, believing God anyway, assured . . . we shall yet praise Him who is the health of our countenance and our God.[7]

Wavering faith can cause God's servants to place themselves in precarious situations.

Bible: Luke 22:51–62. In the account noted above, Peter compromises his identity as a disciple of Christ temporarily because his faith has wavered, and he is afraid.

A steadfast faith relies on the character of God and his historic provision for his children.

Prayer: "The Serenity Prayer." One of the most well-known prayers of our time, a portion of which was picked up and made famous by Alcoholics Anonymous in the 1950s, this prayer is thought to have been written originally by Reinhold Niebuhr (1892–1971) as part of a sermon.

This prayer speaks eloquently of the powerful effects of a serene spirit that trusts steadfastly in God for each day, accepting what is given as from his hand, peaceful in the knowledge of his divine oversight and in the promise of eternity.

History: In *The Attentive Life* (2008), Leighton Ford, head of Leighton Ford Ministries and former member of the Billy Graham Evangelistic Association, tells the following story:

> When the bombs were falling on Europe during World War II, thousands of orphaned children were placed in refugee camps. There they were safe and fed. But since many of them had almost starved, they could not go to sleep at night: they feared that when they woke up they would have nothing to eat. At last someone came up with the idea of giving each child at bedtime a small portion of bread. They went to sleep holding it and thinking, *Tonight I had something to eat, and tomorrow I will eat again.*[8]

Faith is the bread in our hands, given by a trustworthy giver, the promise that His provision will be there in the morning.

Séance in Endor: Bad News from Beyond the Grave

Big Idea *Those rejected by God forfeit his guidance and must face the inevitability of judgment.*

Understanding the Text

The Text in Context

The narrator briefly suspends the story of David's escapades while based in Philistine territory and turns his attention back to Saul. In chapters 29–30 he resumes David's story before again focusing on Saul in chapter 31. The switch back and forth between the two principal characters reflects their geographic separation, yet also foreshadows their contrasting destinies. David and Saul are now moving on different paths: David will move closer to assuming the throne of Israel, while Saul's place of residence will soon become the grave (cf. 28:19).

In chapter 28 we find the culmination of Saul's self-destruction. When he disobeyed God by failing to wipe out the Amalekites (chap. 15), he sealed his fate and became God's enemy (28:16–19). From that time forward until 28:6, there is no record of Saul's consulting the Lord; he never even had another audience with Samuel during the prophet's lifetime (15:35). Neither did he receive divine revelation, except for the occasion when God overwhelmed him with his Spirit and turned him into a prophet for a day in order to protect David (19:23–24). Saul eventually killed the Lord's priests at Nob, apparently with no concern that he was cutting himself off from the divine revelation they could provide (cf. 22:10, 13, 15). Indeed, the one priest who did escape, Abiathar, later used an ephod to mediate divine revelation on David's behalf (23:9–12; 30:7–8). When fearful Saul finally does inquire of the Lord, it is quite appropriate that the Lord refuses to answer (28:6). The contrast in the story between God's silence and his willingness to respond to David's inquiries (23:1–4, 9–12; 30:7–8) highlights a fact that became apparent as far back as chapters 15–16: God has rejected Saul but chosen David. In chapter 28 the repetition of Samuel's prophecy and his specific identification of David as the one mentioned in more vague terms on that earlier occasion (cf. 28:17 with 15:28) simply confirms what we have known to be true from the time of David's anointing (16:12). The announcement of Saul's impending defeat (28:19) functions as the sentence of death that prepares us for the tragic account recorded in chapter 31.

Historical and Cultural Background

In the introduction to this episode, the narrator informs us that Saul, in fulfillment of the Mosaic law (Deut. 18:9–13), has "expelled the mediums and spiritists from the land" (v. 3; cf. v. 9). In its most basic sense, the Hebrew word translated "medium" (*'ob*) appears to refer to a pit used by a medium to conjure up the spirits of the dead.[1] By extension the word can refer to the spirit that is conjured up by use of the pit (cf. Lev. 20:27; Isa. 29:4). However, in several other texts the term refers to the person who is a medium (agent), especially when it is plural and paired with "spiritists" (see Lev. 19:31; 20:6; Deut. 18:11; 1 Sam. 28:3, 9; 2 Kings 21:6 = 2 Chron. 33:6; 2 Kings 23:24; Isa. 8:19; 19:3). In 1 Chronicles 10:13 (referring to Saul's visit to the medium) the word seems to refer to the medium herself. As we see in 1 Samuel 28, these mediums try to conjure up the spirits of the dead (cf. Isa. 8:19). The spirit would speak in a low voice from the pit (Isa. 29:4), perhaps even through the vocal apparatus of the conjurer (Lev. 20:27 may imply this). The

word translated "spiritist/s" (or "knowing one/s") never appears in isolation: it is always paired with "medium," suggesting that the phrase refers to a single person, a medium/spiritist that is "in the know," as it were. Special knowledge about the future through contact with the dead is in view.[2]

When called up from Sheol, the underworld residence of the dead, Samuel seems perturbed and asks Saul why he has "disturbed" him (v. 15). This same verb appears in Isaiah 14:9, where it describes how the arrival of the dethroned king of Babylon causes Sheol to be "all astir." Sheol in turn "rouses" the deceased kings who sleep there. The word also appears in a fifth-century BC Phoenician tomb inscription, which warns the reader not to "disturb" the one lying in the coffin (Tabnit, a former king of Sidon; see *COS*, 2:181–82). Does Samuel really appear to the medium and speak to Saul? A straightforward reading of the text indicates that he does. He delivers

Saul was fearful because a coalition of Philistine forces had gathered at Aphek and marched to make camp at Shunem. Shunem is nestled into the southwest side of the Hill of Moreh and lies across the Harod Valley from the Gilboa range. Saul would have had this view as he looked across the valley toward Shunem.

a legitimate prophecy that honors God and is later fulfilled.

According to verse 6, the Lord does not respond to Saul's attempts to discover the divine will. Dreams, Urim, and prophets are legitimate means of divine revelation in ancient Israel, in contrast to mediums/spiritists. The Urim and Thummim may have been marked lots or objects that would provide a simple "yes" or "no" answer. One thinks that this device would easily yield an answer, so it is puzzling why Saul receives none. But based on a parallel from ancient Assyria, it may be that one needs to receive the same answer multiple times in succession for an answer to be legitimate. This would more readily explain why Saul can receive no answer.[3]

Interpretive Insights

28:3 *Now Samuel was dead.* The note is foreboding; it casts the pall of death over the story that follows. The first major character to appear in the book is dead and gone; now it is Saul's turn to die and leave the stage.

mourned for him and buried him. The next time the terms "mourned" and "bur-

ied" occur in the story, they are used of Saul (1 Sam. 31:13; 2 Sam. 1:12; 2:4–5).

Saul had expelled the mediums and spiritists from the land. Since this is in accordance with the Mosaic law, Saul's expulsion of the mediums is commendable. However, the narrator does not include this observation here to cast Saul in a positive light. On the contrary, this observation only reinforces the narrator's indictment of Saul: it shows that when the king consults the medium at Endor, he is committing an act he knows to be in violation of God's law.

28:4 *set up camp.* The only other time the Hebrew text states that both the Philistines and Israelites "set up camp" in preparation for war is in 1 Samuel 4:1, just before Israel's defeat and Eli's death. The parallel is ominous, for on that occasion Israel suffered a humiliating defeat, just as they will in the upcoming battle (see 28:19).

28:5 *terror filled his heart.* This is particularly foreboding. The only other time in 1–2 Samuel this expression is used is in the case of Eli, whose heart trembled over the fate of the ark of God, just before the news of its capture prompted his fatal accident (see 4:13).

Even though Saul had "expelled the mediums and spiritists from the land" (1 Sam. 28:3), there was still one at Endor. Its exact location is uncertain. One possibility is Khirbet es-Safsafeh (Tell Zafzafot). All that remains of the site is the small mound covered by one tree and some bushes shown here in the foreground. Mount Tabor is in the distance.

28:6 *He inquired of the* LORD, *but the* LORD *did not answer him.* The only other time this verb (*sha'al*, "ask") is used of Saul's inquiring of God is in 14:37; as here, that text informs us that the Lord did not answer him. By way of contrast, when David inquired of the Lord, he received a quick reply (23:1–4).

28:8 *Consult a spirit for me.* Saul's use of the verb "consult" (*qasam*) eerily echoes Samuel's words to him on the occasion of his rejection as king: "rebellion is like the sin of divination [*qesem*]" (15:23). In the Lord's sight, Saul's disobedience is tantamount to divination, a forbidden practice in which, ironically, he is now engaging.

28:14 *wearing a robe.* The reference to Samuel's prophetic robe (*me'il*) is ironic and foreboding, for it recalls how Saul tore Samuel's robe (15:27), an incident that occasioned part two of Samuel's decree of judgment against Saul (15:28), a message that he will soon repeat to the king (28:17).[4]

28:17 *to David.* In detailing the fulfillment of his prediction, Samuel uses past-tense verb forms for a rhetorical purpose. Though the transfer of the kingdom has not actually transpired yet, it is as good as done, for Saul will die the next day (v. 19).

28:19 *The* LORD *will deliver both Israel and you into the hands of the Philistines.* There is an ironic contrast between this statement and the Lord's assuring words to David in 23:4. We also see poetic justice here: Saul has tried to kill David by the hand of the Philistines (18:17, 21, 25), but now the Lord will deliver Saul into the hands of the Philistines.[5]

you and your sons. The inclusion of Saul's sons in the judgment announcement signals the end of his dynasty (13:13–14)

and echoes the earlier judgment upon Eli and his sons (2:34).[6]

28:22 *let me give you some food.* There may be a contrast between this scene, which follows Saul's final meeting with Samuel, and his first meeting with the prophet.[7] On that first occasion, Samuel invited Saul to share a meal with him in preparation for his anointing as king (9:19–10:1). But on this second occasion, it is a medium who invites Saul to eat right after Samuel has announced his impending death.

Theological Insights

God's decree of judgment against Saul is seemingly delayed, but finally it arrives. As Saul's demise approaches, he first experiences God's silence, an appropriate punishment for one who has failed to carry out God's orders and who later kills the Lord's priestly mediators. As Saul disobeys the Lord one last time by consulting an outlawed medium, the Lord finally speaks, at Saul's request, through the prophet Samuel. If Saul somehow thinks he will receive guidance or consolation from Samuel, he is mistaken. Samuel reminds Saul of his sin and of God's decree of judgment, which will be fulfilled on the next day. Saul's experience is a sober reminder that God's word is reliable. His unconditional decree of judgment (15:27–29) is certain of fulfillment. This story should resonate with the exiles, for they too have experienced the consequences of sin and the outworking of God's decree of judgment. But the Lord is about to open the door of restoration, and they need to make sure they do not repeat the mistakes of the past.

Teaching the Text

1. *Disobedience can cut off the communication lines with God.* This principle is related to one that has already appeared in 1 Samuel, in the story of Eli and his sons (2:12–36), who forfeited their special priestly position and dynasty because of disobedience, and in chapters 13 and 15, where Saul forfeited his dynasty and kingship due to disobedience. In those instances disobedience deprived Eli and Saul of special privileged positions granted by God. Being called to a special position, like Eli and Saul were, did not insulate them from divine discipline. We find a corollary of this in chapter 28, where Saul is cut off from communication with God. When he seeks divine guidance in a crisis, God remains silent (v. 6). This is appropriate, for Saul has disobeyed the Lord, opposed the Lord's chosen servant, and even killed the priests at Nob, whose job in part is to serve as mediators between the leaders of Israel and God (cf. 22:10). One finds this same principle in Amos 8:11–12, where the Lord announces that he will no longer reveal his will to those who have rejected his prophetic word (cf.

Amos 2:12; 7:12). Much like Saul, they will desperately seek some word from God but receive none.

First Samuel 28:6 and Amos 8:11–12 focus primarily on God's refusal to speak. But communication is a two-way street. If God's silence is one side of the coin, then his refusal to hear prayer is the other. The Bible also makes it clear that sin can hinder one's prayers (Ps. 66:18). According to Peter, failure to honor one's wife can hinder a husband's prayers (1 Pet. 3:7). God typically does not respond to the prayers of his enemies (2 Sam. 22:42) and those who rebel against him (1 Sam. 8:18; Prov. 28:9; Mic. 3:4). Those experiencing divine discipline must first offer a prayer of repentance before they can expect God to restore his blessing (2 Chron. 7:13–14).

2. *When God announces judgment unconditionally, the fulfillment of the decree is certain.* This theme has also appeared earlier in the story (see chaps. 4 and 15). As illustrated in the account of the fall of Eli and his sons, God's unconditional decree of judgment cannot be averted. Though much time has passed and the fulfillment of the decree seems to be delayed, Saul too meets his demise. Both Eli's and Saul's stories demonstrate that God's word is reliable and must be taken seriously.

Illustrating the Text

Disobedience creates a communication barrier between God and the sinner.

Quote: *How to Pray,* by R. A. Torrey. In this wise and ever-fresh classic (1900), scholar and preacher Torrey (1856–1928) addresses how sin can hinder prayer.

Sin hinders prayer. Many a man prays and prays and prays and gets absolutely no answer to his prayer. Perhaps he is tempted to think that it is not the will of God to answer, or he may think that the days when God answered prayer, if He ever did, are over. So the Israelites seem to have thought . . . that the Lord's hand was shortened that it could not save, and that His ear had become heavy that it could no longer hear. . . . Many and many a man is crying to God in vain, simply because of sin in his life. It may be some sin in the past that has been unconfessed and unjudged, it may be some sin in the present that is cherished, very likely is not even looked upon as sin; but there the sin is, hidden away somewhere in the heart or in the life, and God "will not hear."[8]

God's unconditional decrees are reliable.
See also the "Illustrating the Text" sections of 1 Samuel 4 and 15.

Literature: *The Pilgrim's Progress,* by John Bunyan. More than once in this work and in particular in one of the scenes in the Interpreter's House, Bunyan stresses that "judgment" is not a bad word; it means that what we do matters to God, who is not benign and indifferent. God loves us enough to let our failures catch up with us. He lets us suffer the consequences of our bad choices so that our characters are refined and we come to understand our failings. Thus God's unconditional decrees work for accountability.

History: A central trait in the make-up of tyrants and power-abusers, one that has consistently marked individuals throughout history, is that they completely miscalculate the consequences of their actions. Columnist Arnold Beichman once pointed out in a commentary in the *Washington Times* that Hitler misjudged Winston Churchill and British courage. Hirohito and his admirals confidently thought they could defeat the United States by surprise attack at Pearl Harbor. And Saddam Hussein miscalculated and ignored the intelligence that said President George W. Bush would go to war. Hussein apparently felt that all this was a gigantic bluff. Certainly some of these tyrants, particularly Hussein, got away with years and even decades of evil.[9] Just as these tyrants miscalculated the inevitable result of their arrogance, just as they underestimated informed judgments, so too those who spit in the face of God's unconditional decrees underestimate their final reliability.

Escaping a Tangled Web

Big Idea *When his chosen servants find themselves in a precarious position, the Lord is able to deliver them by his providence and renew their faith through his guidance and protection.*

Understanding the Text

The Text in Context

In 1 Samuel 29 the focus shifts back to David as the story continues where chapter 27 left off. A chronological flashback comes in chapter 29. According to 28:4, the Philistine army was encamped at Shunem when Saul visited the medium in Endor. The next day the Philistines and the Israelites fight on Mount Gilboa (31:1; cf. 28:19). But 29:1 has the Philistines assembling at Aphek, on the coastal plain about forty miles southwest of Shunem, before marching northeast "up to Jezreel" (29:2, 11). So the events of chapter 29 must have occurred *before* Saul's visit to Endor, located two miles from Shunem. By delaying the report of David's expulsion from the Philistine army until after the account of Saul's visit to Endor, the narrator heightens the tension of the story's plot. As we hear Samuel announce Saul's impending death (28:19), we wonder if David and his men will need to face Saul in battle or, worse yet, somehow be responsible for Saul's death.[1]

Chapter 29 relieves this tension by showing how David escapes the tangled web that his deception has woven. David's critics

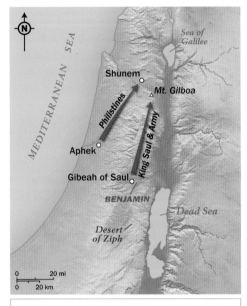

The Philistine coalition, which included David and his men, assembled at Aphek, but they marched to Shunem only after sending David away. In response to this Philistine threat, Saul assembled his army on Mount Gilboa. This map shows the movements of troops.

may have accused him of being a traitor and of fighting against Israel. After all, David claimed to have killed Judahites (27:10), and he actually marches with the Philistine army (29:1). But in reality he has fought the enemies of Israel while under Achish's authority (27:8) and is released from service because the Philistine commanders are not convinced of his loyalty (29:4–5). Following his dismissal from the Philistine ranks, David travels back to Ziklag, tracks down the Amalekites who have kidnapped the families of his group, and defeats them, probably on the very day the Philistines fight against Saul at Gilboa (30:1–17).[2] So, rather than fighting against his own people and king, David is far from Gilboa, fighting against the enemies of God, the Amalekites. Though the narrator is critical of David's wavering faith and does not veil its negative consequences, he makes it clear that David is not a traitor to his people. Ironically, while Saul is dying as a result of his failure to wipe out the Amalekites on an earlier occasion (28:18–19), David is killing these ancient enemies of Israel.

As noted earlier (see chap. 27, "The Text in Context"), the sequence of events in chapters 27–30 reflects the pattern in 21:1–23:5.

A David's faith wavers; he runs away and lives in exile (21:1–22:5).
B Saul rejects the Lord by killing his priests (22:6–23).
C The Lord guides David and gives him victory over Israel's enemy (23:1–5).
A′ David's faith wavers; he runs away and lives in exile (27:1–28:2; 29:1–11).
B′ The Lord rejects Saul and announces his death (28:3–25).
C′ The Lord guides David and gives him victory over Israel's enemy (chap. 30).

The A′ and C′ elements mirror A and C, but the relationship between the B and B′ elements is more subtle. Saul's rejection of the Lord (by killing the Lord's servants) is

Key Themes of 1 Samuel 29–30

- In the face of a difficult dilemma, the Lord providentially delivers David.
- In the face of an escalating crisis, David renews his faith in the Lord and experiences the Lord's guidance and protection.

appropriately reversed in B′, as the Lord reaffirms his rejection of Saul through the message of his servant Samuel.

Interpretive Insights

29:1 *The Philistines gathered all their forces at Aphek.* Following Samuel's announcement of Saul's impending death (28:19), this reference to Philistine troops congregating at Aphek is particularly ominous.[3] The only other time in 1–2 Samuel that Philistine troops are seen at Aphek is in 1 Samuel 4:1, just before Israel's tragic defeat and the capture of the ark. In that battle and its aftermath, the rejected priest Eli and his sons died; in the upcoming battle, described in chapter 31, the rejected king Saul and three of his sons will die.

29:6 *As surely as the LORD lives.* This is the first time the Lord's name is used in the account of David's exile to Philistine territory (27:1–12; cf. 21:10–15), and, ironically, it occurs on the lips of a Philistine. Like the words of the Philistine servants on an earlier occasion (see 21:11), the mentioning of David's God is a providential reminder to him of who he really is and where his allegiance should be.

29:8 *But what have I done?* At this point the story takes a curious turn as David protests his innocence. On three previous occasions David protested his innocence with the question "What have I done?" (17:29; 20:1; 26:18). Each time he was truly innocent of the charges brought against him. But this time the question is just another plank in his deception.[4] Perhaps David assumes from Achish's initial explanation (vv. 6–7) that there is little if any chance that he will be allowed to fight, so he protests to make it look like he really is loyal. After all, if he agrees too readily with the Philistine leaders' assessment, it might look as though they are right. David may also be concerned that the Philistine leaders might have heard about his deceptive actions in the Ziklag region. (In v. 6, Achish gives little detail; he simply says that the leaders consider David unreliable.) If so, by asking Achish for evidence of disloyalty, he may hope that the king will give more detail about the leaders' suspicions. If there is any hint that David's deceit has been uncovered, he and his men can flee for safety while the Philistines are engaged in battle with Israel.

It is possible, however, that David really does hope to persuade Achish to let him go into battle. Ever the opportunist, David might decide to

turn on the Philistines during the battle, just as the Philistine leaders suspect. David's reference to "my lord the king" is tantalizingly ambiguous.[5] Who exactly is "my lord"? Surely Achish thinks he is the referent, but earlier David uses the words "my lord the king" three times when speaking to Saul (1 Sam. 24:8; 26:17, 19). Three other times he calls Saul "my lord" (1 Sam. 24:6, 10; 26:18). On the lips of deceitful David, these words may very well refer to Saul, whom the Philistine commanders recognize as David's lord (29:4). Even Achish, perhaps subconsciously, refers to David as Saul's servant (29:3) and to Saul as David's lord (29:10)![6]

30:7 *Bring me the ephod.* The contrast with Saul is obvious: the Lord no longer communicates with Saul, the murderer of the priests of Nob, through legitimate means (1 Sam. 28:6), but he does speak to David, the protector of the lone survivor of the massacre at Nob.[7] Through the spirit of Samuel, the Lord announces that Saul will die and Israel will experience defeat, but he assures David of victory.[8]

30:11 *They found an Egyptian.* Divine providence is once again evident in the story.[9] Saul has experienced this type of providential control of circumstances on the occasion of his initial encounter with Samuel (9:11; 10:2–3),

David tried to kill all the Amalekites. However, 1 Samuel 30:17 records that four hundred young men on camels escaped. This Assyrian relief shows Arab soldiers fleeing a battle on camelback (palace at Nineveh, 645–635 BC).

but now divine providence is working on behalf of David.

30:17 *David fought them.* In contrast to Saul, who failed to carry out the Lord's command to destroy all the Amalekites (chap. 15), David does his best to kill them all.[10] Both before and after Samuel's reminder to Saul of his failure to destroy the Amalekites (28:18), the narrator depicts David as doing everything in his power to kill them (cf. 27:8).

30:23 *delivered into our hands.* God's intervention on behalf of David and his men stands in stark contrast to his abandonment of Saul and the Israelite army, whom he handed over to the Philistines (28:19).

30:25 *David made this a statute and ordinance for Israel.* Though not yet king, David is already exercising an authoritative leadership role, foreshadowing his accession to the throne.[11]

Theological Insights

The Lord's name is not mentioned in chapter 27 and appears only once in chapter 29, ironically on the lips of Achish as he emphasizes his confidence in David (v. 6). Yet we must not assume that God is absent from the scene. As in the book of Esther, his presence may not be immediately evident, but his unseen providential oversight is apparent. David has painted himself into a corner, but the Lord, working through the suspicion of some cautious Philistine officers, delivers him from the dilemma he faces and prevents him from needing to march against his own people and the king to whom he has pledged his allegiance. This protection becomes a key theme in chapter 30 (v. 23), where David once again actively looks to the Lord for strength amid

a severe crisis (v. 6) and seeks the Lord's guidance (vv. 7–8). The Lord assures him of success and enables him to defeat his enemies (v. 23). The story is a reminder to its exilic readers not only of the negative consequences of wavering faith, but also of God's providential protection. It also reminds them of the importance of seeking divine guidance and expressing gratitude to God for his intervention.

Teaching the Text

1. *When the faith of his chosen servants wavers and they find themselves in a precarious position of their own making, the Lord is able to providentially deliver them from danger.* The story of David's second visit to Achish of Gath, like the episode recorded in 21:10–15, illustrates the negative consequences of wavering faith. David's deception works for a time, but it works too well. Convinced of his loyalty, Achish insists that David join his forces in the upcoming battle against Israel and is ready to elevate David to the position of his bodyguard (28:1–2). David has to continue to carry out his ruse to almost ludicrous proportions. Even if he marches into battle with the Philistines and then turns on them, opponents of David could call his character into question. He has indeed woven a tangled web of deception, from which there appears to be no easy way out. But God's providence works through the Philistine officers, who are suspicious of David because of his past military success against their armies (29:5). Ironically, though David has officially, albeit deceptively, allied himself with the enemy, divine providence will not allow him to carry out the deception any longer. He

brings to the Philistines' remembrance David's true status, yet enables David to slip away unharmed.[12] Yet one should not assume from this story that God always extracts his servants so easily when their faith wavers. Sometimes he does so; at other times he allows them to experience the pain of negative consequences. In either case, his mercy is apparent.

2. *In times of crisis the Lord's chosen servants should look to him for security.* As in chapters 21–23, we see the stark contrast between the desperate David, who seeks refuge with Achish, and the exemplary David, who seeks the Lord's guidance and protection. Before Achish, David is a pretender who resorts to extreme deceit to stay alive. On both occasions God, speaking through the Philistines, confronts David with who he really is and then providentially causes the Philistines to expel him. Once freed from his efforts at self-preservation, David does what he should have been doing in the first place. He seeks the Lord's guidance through the ephod the Lord has provided (23:1–6, 9–12; 30:7–8) and sees firsthand the Lord's enabling and protective hand. Believers today cannot expect nor should they seek direct revelation from God such as David receives through the use of the

Not only was the Lord able to deliver David from danger, but he used David to deliver the residents of Ziklag from the hands of their captors, the Amalekites. This relief shows women, a child, and livestock taken captive by an invading Assyrian army (palace at Nimrud, 865–860 BC).

priestly ephod. But they can find assurance in the realization that God providentially guides his people, and they can consciously and actively look to him for security.

Illustrating the Text

In his providence, God sometimes delivers his chosen servants from the consequences of wavering faith.

Christian Biography: *The Shorter Life of D. L. Moody,* **by A. P. Fitt.** Moody's (1892) voyage with his son from Southampton, England, on board the North German

Lloyd steamship *Spree*, was unforgettable. Three days into the crossing, the propeller shaft on the ship broke, and it looked like the vessel was sinking. "That was an awful night," Moody wrote, "the darkest in all our lives! [Everyone was] waiting for the doom that was settling upon us! No one dared sleep. . . . I was passing through a new experience." Moody continues, "I had thought myself superior to the fear of death. I had often preached on the subject and urged Christians to realize this victory of faith. During the Civil War I had been under fire without fear. I was in Chicago during the great Cholera epidemic, and went around with the doctors visiting the sick and dying. . . . But on the sinking ship it was different." Moody then relates that the problem was not his own soul: the problem was his realization that "perhaps the next hour would separate me forever from all these, so far as this world was concerned. . . . It was the darkest hour of my life! I could not endure it." Though he finally came to a place of peace through prayer, he never forgot the darkness of those hours.[13]

Renewed faith experiences the protection of God.

Christian Biography: *The Shorter Life of D. L. Moody,* **by A. P. Fitt.** This theme

could be illustrated by continuing the story above. After continuous prayer, Moody experienced renewed faith, and he slept more soundly than he could remember ever having slept before. He declared, "I can no more doubt that God gave answer to my prayer for relief than I can doubt my own existence." At about 3:00 a.m., his son awakened him and told him to come on deck. There they saw deliverance as the steamer *Lake Huron* approached; its lookout had seen this ship's signals of distress. "Oh, the joy of that moment," Moody later wrote, "when those . . . passengers beheld the approaching ship! Who can ever forget it?" Moody then wonders if the rescue ship could tow their helpless boat one thousand miles to Queenstown. He writes, however, that now he "had no fear." No storms came to them, watertight compartments kept the ship afloat, the cables held, and they made it. Yet some passengers went through terrible psychological distress: one even leaped overboard and drowned. Some Christians whose faith faltered called themselves Jonahs. Still Moody's faith had miraculously been renewed.[14]

Tell It Not in Gath!

Big Idea *Rebellion against the Lord culminates in humiliating defeat, but the demise of the Lord's rebellious servants is to be lamented, not celebrated.*

Understanding the Text

The Text in Context

Chapter 31 returns the focus of the story to Saul and picks up where chapter 28 left off. Samuel's prophecy of Saul's impending death and of Israel's defeat (28:19) is fulfilled. In 2 Samuel 1 the focus returns to David. There is a flashback at the beginning of the chapter: verse 1 informs us that this episode takes place on the third day after Saul's death, while 1 Samuel 31 ends at least a week after Saul's death.

This account of Saul's death and David's response to it, like the other episodes recorded earlier, is designed to prove David's right to the throne and to vindicate him from charges of wrongdoing.[1] Saul's divinely ordained defeat and death (1 Sam. 28; 31) contrast with David's God-ordained victory (1 Sam. 30). But David's motives can be questioned, and his role in Saul's death may be unclear to many. After all, David is officially working for Achish the Philistine at the time of the battle and has even been seen marching with the Philistines as they prepare to engage Saul's troops in battle. Furthermore, David somehow ends up with Saul's royal insignia in his posses-

sion (2 Sam. 1:10). Does David aid and abet Israel's enemies? Is he somehow responsible for Saul's death? The story makes it clear that he is not at Gilboa; in fact, during the battle he is way down south, killing Amalekites, Israel's archenemies, and distributing loot from the victory to the people of Judah. The royal insignia come to him by accident, though one may surmise that this is by God's providential design. For the perceptive observer, this acquisition is a reminder that David is God's chosen successor to the throne and a foreshadowing of his reign over Israel. Nevertheless, David does not interpret the incident in that manner. The death of Saul and his sons clears the pathway to the throne for David, but he does not celebrate. When he finds out about Saul's death, he executes the man who claims to have killed the king. He also composes a lament for Saul and Jonathan as a somber testimony of his loyalty. As his first act after being enthroned in Hebron, he will later reward the men of Jabesh Gilead for their loyalty to Saul (1 Sam. 31:11–13; 2 Sam. 2:1–7). The narrator absolves David of any involvement in Saul's death and demonstrates David's continuing loyalty to Saul as he prepares to fulfill his God-ordained destiny.

Historical and Cultural Background

In David's lament he remarks that Jonathan's "love" for him was "more wonderful than that of women." This certainly does not suggest or imply that David and Jonathan had a homosexual relationship, as some have suggested.[2] David uses "love" here in the sense of loyalty or allegiance within a covenantal context, an idiom that one finds in ancient Near Eastern literature.[3] David's point may be that Jonathan's allegiance to him was even stronger and more enduring than the romantic love between a man and woman. Another option is that Jonathan's loyalty meant more to him than even the romantic love he experiences from women.

Interpretive Insights

31:1 *Now the Philistines fought against Israel; the Israelites fled before them.* The description of Israel's defeat echoes 1 Samuel 4:10, the only other passage in 1 Samuel where the Philistines "fight" and Israel "flees." On that earlier occasion, the ark was captured and the priest Eli and his sons died. On this occasion, Israel's king and three of his sons are killed. In both cases dynasties (one priestly, the other royal) experience divine judgment in

fulfillment of the Lord's prophetic decree through his prophet Samuel.

31:2 *they killed.* This is only the second time in 1 Samuel that the narrator uses this verb (*nakah*, "smite, kill") to describe the Philistines' killing Israelites. The other occasion was when the ark was captured (4:2). The picture of the Philistines' smiting Israel is tragically ironic since the verb has been used several times of Israel, Jonathan, Saul, or David's killing Philistines (7:11; 13:3–4; 14:31; 17:26, 49–50, 57; 18:6, 27; 19:5, 8; 21:9; 23:2, 5).

31:4 *Saul said to his armor-bearer.* This incident is reminiscent of the account of Abimelek's death (cf. Judg. 9:54).[4] Both Abimelek and Saul, knowing death is inevitable, command their armor-bearer to kill them, using the words "Draw your sword." Like Abimelek, Saul is guilty of mass murder (Judg. 9:5; 1 Sam. 22:18) and deserves his fate. In contrast to Abimelek, Saul is the chosen servant of God, but in the end he falls so far from God's ideal for

The Israelites may have planned to have the battle in the valley between the two army camps. Instead the Philistines forced Israel to retreat and pursued them back up the slopes of Gilboa. This is the view the Philistines would have had as they moved across the valley toward Mount Gilboa.

him that he dies like one of the most evil characters on the pages of the Former Prophets.

31:6 *So Saul and his three sons and his armor-bearer and all his men died.* This report is particularly tragic when one recalls the story of Jonathan and his armor-bearer, recorded in 1 Samuel 14. On that occasion Jonathan and his courageous armor-bearer ignite a victory for Saul's army, but now Saul, Jonathan, and a terrified armor-bearer all die in defeat.

31:9 *They cut off his head.* Ironically, Saul is now in the role of Goliath, and the Philistines are in the role of David (1 Sam. 17:51).

to proclaim the news. For the second time in 1 Samuel, reference is made to a message being sent (*basar*). When the ark was captured, a messenger announced to Eli the news of Israel's defeat at the hands of the Philistines (4:17), and here the Philistines proclaim the news of their victory over Israel. Once again the narrator links the two events.

31:11 *the people of Jabesh Gilead.* The men of Jabesh undoubtedly perform this courageous act out of loyalty and devotion to Saul (cf. 2 Sam. 2:4b–7), who earlier rescued them from the cruel Ammonite conqueror Nahash (cf. 1 Sam. 11). This brief account adds to the tragic dimension of this episode: it reminds us of Saul's finest hour in the aftermath of his darkest one. The conqueror of Nahash is reduced to ashes and bones.

31:12 *they burned them.* If Saul's sin and confession with respect to the Amalekite spoil echoed Achan's sin and confes-

The Philistines cut off Saul's head and hung his body on the walls of Beth Shan. The Balawat gate bands show a similar gruesome scene with a body impaled on a pole outside the city, as well as severed heads displayed on the city walls (palace of Shalmaneser III, 858–824 BC).

sion (see the comment above on 15:24), then it is possible that the burning of his and his sons' corpses echoes Achan's death (Josh. 7:25).[5]

31:13 *tamarisk tree.* This is the second reference to a tamarisk tree in 1 Samuel (the only other mention of the tamarisk in the entire OT is in Gen. 21:33). On the first occasion, Saul was sitting under a tamarisk tree holding his spear just before slaughtering the priests of Nob (22:6). Now the murderer of God's priests is reduced to bones and buried under a tamarisk tree.[6]

1:1 *After the death of Saul, David returned from striking down the Amalekites.* As the focus shifts back to David, the narrator contrasts dead Saul with victorious David. Furthermore, David has defeated the Amalekites, whom Saul has refused to annihilate, thus bringing about his eventual demise (28:18–19).

1:10 *I stood beside him and killed him.* Some are troubled by the contradictions between the account of Saul's death in 1 Samuel 31:3–4 and the Amalekite's version of what happened in 2 Samuel 1:6–10. But the narrator's account must be given preference.[7] It is likely that the Amalekite fabricates his story in an effort to please David and gain his favor.[8]

1:12 *They mourned and wept and fasted.* The narrator goes out of his way to emphasize the depth of David's grief by heaping up verbs that indicate lamentation. This is the only place in the Old Testament where all three of these verbs are used together.

the nation of Israel. The Hebrew text has "house of Israel," an expression that is used in the Former Prophets in only two passages before this. In Joshua 21:45 the narrator remarks that God fulfilled his promises to Israel by giving them the land, while in 1 Samuel 7:2–3 he tells how the "house of Israel" lamented their sin and Samuel then assured the "house of Israel" that genuine repentance would result in deliverance from the Philistines. Here the phrase once more shows up in a context of lamentation, but this time the "house of Israel" has met defeat at the hands of the Philistines in a tragic reversal of past victories.

1:15 *strike him down!* This verb (*paga'*) is used in this sense in only one other passage in 1–2 Samuel (in 1 Sam. 10:5 it has the sense of "meet," with no violent connotation). In 1 Samuel 22:17–18 it is used of striking down the priests at Nob; in verse 18 Saul commands Doeg to "strike down" priests who are innocent of wrongdoing. Here David commands one of his men to "strike down" an Amalekite who, as far as David can tell, is guilty of murdering God's anointed king. Saul's unjust crime stands in sharp contrast to David's just retribution. Furthermore, Saul orders the death of the priests because he perceives them to be loyal to David. But David's command of execution is an expression of his loyalty to Saul, further demonstrating the injustice of Saul's action against the priests.

So he struck him down, and he died. When divine providence delivered Saul into his hands, David, the rightful king in waiting, resisted the temptation to exploit the situation, for he did not dare to attack God's anointed (cf. 1 Sam. 24:4–7; 26:7–11, 23–24). Why then should he allow an Amalekite to get away with dishonoring the Lord's anointed one?

1:17 *David took up this lament.* David's lament is the third poem to appear in 1–2 Samuel. The first, Hannah's thanksgiving song (1 Sam. 2:1–10), anticipates the victory of the Lord's anointed king (v. 10). The second, the women's victory song (1 Sam. 18:7), celebrates the military success of Saul and David. But this third poem marks a tragic reversal: David mourns the death of the Lord's anointed.

1:19 *How the mighty have fallen!* These words appear three times in the lament and express its primary theme (see vv. 25, 27). The appearance of the verb "fall" in a militaristic sense recalls the earlier disaster when Israel fell before the Philistines, the ark was taken, and Eli fell over and broke his neck when he heard the horrible news (1 Sam. 4:10, 18). But there is also tragic irony here, for on three earlier occasions the verb "fall" was used for humiliating Philistine defeats (5:3–4; 14:13; 17:49, 52).

Theological Insights

We have pointed out the parallels between the account of Saul's death and the story of the ark's capture (1 Sam. 4; see the comments above on 31:1, 2, 9–10). With Israel's defeat at Gilboa, the tragic defeat at Aphek/Ebenezer has been repeated. Saul's death clears the path for David to ascend the throne, but that theme is not the emphasis of these chapters. The defeat at Gilboa is not cause for celebration. The mood is one of loss and humiliation, as David's lament expresses. Surely this tone of sadness and embarrassment resonates with exilic readers of the story, for they are experiencing loss and humiliation as well. They know all too well that rebellion against God brings judgment, and judgment in turn brings death and lamentation (see Lam. 1–5).

Teaching the Text

1. *Rebellion against God culminates in humiliating divine discipline.* Saul rebelled against God and forfeited his dynasty and royal position. Abandoned by God's Spirit, he became fearful of David and persisted in his efforts to kill him. His most heinous act was the murder of the Lord's priests at Nob for allegedly committing treason against him. God stopped communicating with Saul and regarded him as an enemy (1 Sam. 28:16). In his final message to Saul, the Lord announced that he would hand Saul and his army over to the Philistines, and that Saul and his sons would die (28:19). This prophecy is realized at Mount Gilboa. God's disciplinary judgment is severe, as the horrible details recounted in chapter 31 testify. The gruesome description of how the Philistines treat the bodies of Saul and his sons is especially sobering. The account illustrates the truth of Hebrews 10:31—"It is a dreadful thing to fall into the hands of the living God"—and of Galatians 6:7: "Do not be deceived: God cannot be mocked. A man reaps what he sows."

2. *The demise of God's rebellious servants is to be lamented, not celebrated.* Even though Saul's death is the result of divine discipline and clears the way for David to take the throne, David does not celebrate. David has expected the Lord to deal decisively with Saul (26:10) and has even appealed to God for vindication (24:15), but when Saul's death finally arrives, David does not gloat or express any kind of vindictive satisfaction. Instead, he eulogizes Saul and mourns his death. For David, Israel's loss outweighs any personal gain he might derive from Saul's death. His reaction is a reminder that the demise of God's rebellious servants is to be lamented, not celebrated. After all, the Lord chose and anointed Saul, and Saul won victories for Israel and delivered the nation from its enemies on several occasions. His demise is tragic and antithetical to God's ideal for Saul (13:13). But lamentation is appropriate for other reasons. Saul's demise has broader consequences. Three of his sons die as well, including Jonathan, David's faithful friend and covenant partner. In fact, divine discipline humiliates the entire community (2 Sam. 1:19), and the reality of Israel's loss and humiliation grips David at a deep emotional level (1:12). In the end, the demise of God's rebellious servants is to be lamented, because it shatters God's ideal for the individual, often causes innocent people to suffer as well, and brings shame to the entire covenant community.

Illustrating the Text

To rebel against God is to suffer humiliating consequences.

Literature: *Paradise Lost*, by John Milton. Few works describe rebellion against God and its consequences as well as Milton's (1608–74) famous work. These are lines from the opening book that describe Satan's mutiny and its results:

> . . . his Pride
> Had cast him out from Heav'n, with all his Host
> Of Rebel Angels, by whose aid aspiring
> To set himself in Glory above his Peers,
> He trusted to have equal'd the most High,
> If he oppos'd; and with ambitious aim
> Against the Throne and Monarchy of God
> Rais'd impious War in Heav'n and Battel proud
> With vain attempt. Him the Almighty Power
> Hurld headlong flaming from th' Ethereal Skie
> With hideous ruine and combustion down
> To bottomless perdition, there to dwell
> In Adamantine Chains and penal Fire,
> Who durst defie th' Omnipotent to Arms. . . .
> Such place Eternal Justice had prepar'd
> For those rebellious, here thir Prison ordain'd
> In utter darkness, and thir portion set
> As far remov'd from God and light of Heav'n
> As from the Center thrice to th' utmost Pole.[9]

The proper response to the divine discipline of failed leaders is grief.

Quote: "Meditation XVII," by John Donne.

> No man is an island, entire of itself; every man is a piece of the continent, a part of the main; if a clod be washed away by the sea, Europe is the less, as well as if a promontory were, as well as if a manor of thy friend's or of thine own were; any man's death diminishes me, because I am involved in mankind, and therefore never send to know for whom the bell tolls; it tolls for thee.[10]

In these famous words, Donne (1572–1631) shows how deeply we are diminished by the tragedies of others.

Christian Nonfiction: *Leap over a Wall*, by Eugene Peterson. In these reflections on 1 and 2 Samuel (1997), Peterson (b. 1932) writes of David's lament:

> David lamented because he cared. [Here] we have access to an aspect of experience that's absolutely essential if we're going to live God-responsively, live God-abundantly.
> . . . [Today] there's no lament because truth isn't taken seriously, love isn't taken seriously. Human life doesn't matter as *life*-God-given.
> . . . David not only lamented with this lamentation, he ordered the people to learn it: memorize it and inhabit it as *their* experience. . . . A failure to lament is a failure to connect.[11]

The Road to the Throne Is Covered with Blood

Big Idea *The Lord fulfills his promises to his chosen servants as his people depend on his providence and align their desires with his purposes.*

Understanding the Text

The Text in Context

With Saul's death, David's path was open to the throne of Israel. This next part of the unfolding story (2:1–5:5) tells how David fulfills his destiny and ascends the throne. This is a distinct literary unit, marked out by an inclusio. It begins with David's being anointed in Hebron by the men of Judah (2:1–4) and ends with all Israel coming to Hebron and anointing him king over the entire nation (5:1–5). In between, the narrator tells how Benjamite opposition is eliminated, but not by any wrongdoing on David's part.

After Saul's death, David does not try to seize the throne. He first asks the Lord if he should even return to Judah, and when he does, in response to the Lord's positive reply, the men of Judah come to him and anoint him king. Saulide opposition to David is in time removed, but the narrator is quick to absolve David of any wrongdoing. David commends the men of Jabesh Gilead for their loyalty to Saul, and

he tries to maintain a nonaggression policy against the house of Saul. Abner eventually transfers his loyalty to David and recognizes David's divine calling (3:17–18), only to be murdered by Joab. Benjamite assassins murder Ish-bosheth, whose death David swiftly avenges (4:11–12). David does not endorse the murders of Abner and Ish-bosheth, and the narrator absolves him of complicity in their deaths (cf. 3:28, 37; 4:9–11).

The narrator's overall portrayal of David is definitely positive, especially when he is contrasted with Saul, who desperately tried to hold on to his royal power and treated David as an enemy. However, along the way the seeds of trouble are planted: David's harem grows, and he fails to bring Joab to justice for his murderous attack on Abner. His growing attention to women will escalate (cf. 5:13) and culminate in his devastating affair with Bathsheba, and his lack of attention to justice within his own royal court and family will contribute to Absalom's rebellion, with its attendant chaos and pain.

Historical and Cultural Background

When the Israelites make David king, they recall an oracle in which the Lord says that David will "shepherd" his people (5:2). The metaphor of the king as a divinely appointed shepherd is common throughout the ancient Near East. Examples abound from Egypt, Sumer, Babylon, and Assyria.[1] For example, a Sumerian text describes the god Enlil's choice of King Shulgi as follows: "Enlil chose Shulgi in (his) pure heart, he entrusted the people to him. The lead-rope and the staff he hung on his arm—he is (henceforth) the shepherd of all the lands" (COS, 1:553).

Interpretive Insights

2:1 *David inquired of the* LORD. David has learned through experience that he must consult the Lord for direction (1 Sam. 23:1–4; 30:8).[2]

2:6 *I too will show you the same favor because you have done this.* David's message to Jabesh Gilead is important for several reasons. Saul is dead, but not due to David's actions in any way. David, the loyal follower of Saul, is Saul's rightful successor, and he welcomes the allegiance of Saul's loyal subjects.

3:9 *what the* LORD *promised him on oath.* Abner's confession is another piece of crucial evidence in the narrator's apology for David. Even Saul's loyal general (v. 8) acknowledges David's right to the throne.[3]

The metaphor of king as shepherd is visualized when Egyptian pharaohs are depicted holding the crook and flail. The crook, a shepherd's tool, is symbolic of his shepherding role. The flail is thought to be an agricultural tool. (Funerary figurine from King Tutankhamen's tomb, fourteenth century BC)

3:18 *For the* LORD *promised David.* The promise as quoted by Abner does not appear earlier in the story. Ironically it resembles God's promise to Saul (see 1 Sam. 9:16; 10:1 [LXX]). In Abner's mind, David has replaced Saul as God's chosen deliverer of Israel. Abner joins the other characters in the story that have acknowledged

David's Wives

Following Saul's death, David's power steadily grows (2 Sam. 3:1). However, before continuing the story of David's rise to the throne of Israel (2 Sam. 3:6–5:5), the narrator stops and informs us that David fathers six sons from six different wives while he is ruling in Hebron (2 Sam. 3:2–5). His royal court is growing with the help of his ever-expanding harem. Before this, we were told that David had only two wives (Ahinoam and Abigail; 1 Sam. 25:43; 30:5; 2 Sam. 2:2), excluding Michal, whom Saul gave to a man named Paltiel (1 Sam. 25:44). But now we read of four additional wives. One might conclude that this list is, as Anderson suggests, "an indication of divine blessing and approval."[a] Yet the report of David's expanding royal court is disturbing in light of Deuteronomy 17:17, which stipulates that the king of Israel must not multiply wives. As the story continues, tensions will develop within this crowded royal court, especially between the half brothers Amnon (son of Ahinoam) and Absalom (son of Maacah). David's growing harem suggests that he is becoming enamored with the trappings of kingship and is modeling his kingship after the cultural pattern of other nations.

[a] Anderson, *2 Samuel*, 50. Bergen also puts a positive spin on these verses: "Through the use of a genealogical table, the writer demonstrated David's obedience to the Torah mandate to 'be fruitful and multiply' (cf. Gen. 1:28)." He adds: "The Torah implicitly permitted kings to possess more than one wife, though they were not to have 'many wives' (cf. Deut. 17:17). Since David was not explicitly condemned for this number of wives, the writer may have considered David to be in compliance with the letter of the Torah in this matter" (*1, 2 Samuel*, 305). However, the narrator does not need to explicitly condemn David since the king's actions are clearly in violation of the law. See also Cartledge, *1 and 2 Samuel*, 384.

David's royal destiny, including Jonathan (1 Sam. 23:17), Saul (24:20), and Abigail (25:28–30).

3:21 *my lord the king.* David addressed Saul in this way (24:8; 26:17), and he referred to Saul as Abner's lord and king (1 Sam. 26:15). But now that Saul has passed from the scene, Abner has switched his allegiance, and David accepts his loyalty. Before this, David has been referred to as "(a) king" (1 Sam. 16:1; 2 Sam. 2:4, 7, 11; 3:17) or even as "king of the land" (by the Philistines; 1 Sam. 21:11). But Abner's use of the article ("the king") marks a turning point in the description of David. Eight more times in this chapter he will be called "the king," seven times by the narrator (vv. 24, 31–33, 36–38; in v. 23 he is called "the king" in a quotation).

3:28 *I and my kingdom are forever innocent before the* LORD *concerning the blood of Abner.* The text goes out of its way to exonerate David. It tells us that David did not know about Joab's message or the murder until after the fact. When he does find out, he protests his innocence, calls a curse down on Joab and Abishai, orders and leads a state-sponsored funeral procession, and calls another curse down upon Joab for good measure.

4:2 *from the tribe of Benjamin.* It is important to the narrator's defense of David to identify the assassins as Benjamites. Two of Ish-bosheth's own tribal kinsmen kill him, not David's supporters.

4:8 *Saul, your enemy.* The Benjamite assassins cast Saul in the role of David's "enemy." Others have done the same,

Joab killed Abner in one of the side chambers of the city gate at Hebron. Shown here are the remains of six side chambers of a city gate (Solomonic gate at Hazor, tenth century BC).

including the narrator (1 Sam. 18:29), David's men (24:4), Saul (24:19), and Abishai (26:8), but David did not use this designation for Saul, and his response here shows that he does not view Saul in this manner.

the LORD has avenged my lord the king. Earlier David appealed to the Lord for justice and prayed that the Lord would avenge Saul's offenses against him, but he refused to lift a hand against Saul (1 Sam. 24:12). Having consistently taken this stance toward Saul, he is not about to tolerate this crime against Saul's innocent son (cf. v. 11).

4:11 *when wicked men have killed an innocent man.* David has them executed on the spot for murdering an innocent man. He characterizes them as "wicked men" (*resha'im*). Earlier David quoted a proverb that used this same term: "From evildoers [*resha'im*] come evil deeds" (1 Sam. 24:13a). David refused to lift a hand against Saul, because he realized that to do so would be an evil deed, characteristic of evildoers, and he wanted to demonstrate to all that his intentions toward Saul were not evil. Having refused to do evil himself, he is not going to tolerate such a deed being done on his behalf.

5:1 *All the tribes of Israel came to David.* The inclusion of "all" depicts national unity and emphasizes the complete support that David receives (cf. Josh. 24:1; 1 Sam. 10:20). The tribes of Israel initiate this covenant with David; he does not solicit their support (cf. 2:4).

We are your own flesh and blood. They identify themselves as David's "own flesh and blood" ("your bone and your flesh" [AT]), emphasizing their common ancestry as descendants of Jacob. The expression is used elsewhere of flesh-and-blood kin-

David and Michal

How should we assess David's demand to have Michal returned to him (3:14)?[a] On the one hand, one could argue that David's demand is only fair; after all, he has risked his life to marry Michal, and Saul has no right to take his wife away from him. Ish-bosheth even complies with the demand, apparently agreeing with the legality and fairness of it. On the other hand, the move seems motivated by political ambition. By reclaiming Michal, David reminds everyone that he is Saul's son-in-law and has a legitimate place in Saul's royal court. With Michal as one of his wives, David will be in a better position to negotiate with the Benjamites. The incident may even have a darker, more sinister dimension to it that foreshadows David's crime against Bathsheba and Uriah.[b]

[a] David's demand does not violate Deut. 24:1–4. This law envisions a situation where a man divorces a woman, who then marries a second husband. If the second husband then divorces her or dies, the first husband may not remarry the woman. The law does not apply in David's case, because David apparently never agreed to a divorce from Michal; Saul simply took her from him while he was a fugitive and gave her to another man. On the legal background of this passage, see McCarter, *II Samuel*, 115; and Cartledge, *1 and 2 Samuel*, 390.
[b] Kessler, "Sexuality and Politics," 416–22.

ship relations (Gen. 29:14; Judg. 9:2; 2 Sam. 19:12–13).

5:2 *You will shepherd my people Israel, and you will become their ruler.* There is no earlier reference to the oracle quoted, but it appears to allude to Samuel's statement to Saul regarding the one who would succeed him (1 Sam. 13:14) and is similar to Abigail's assuring word to David (25:30).[4] The people do not grant unbridled authority to David, however. The divine oracle speaks of him as a shepherd who will care for the LORD's people, and here they refer to him as "ruler" (*nagid*), not "king" (see the comments above on 1 Sam. 9:16; 10:1; 13:14; and 25:30).

Theological Insights

Saul's death brought humiliation to Israel. Even the new king in waiting, David, responded with sorrow and lamentation.

However, as in the case of Eli's death and the capture of the ark, the darkness of judgment was not permanent (cf. Ps. 30:5). God's decree of judgment against Saul proved to be reliable, but so is his promise to place David on the throne of Israel. David seeks the Lord's guidance and waits on divine providence. The Lord in turn brings to realization the promise he has stated in conjunction with his rejection of Saul (1 Sam. 13:14; 15:28) and has reiterated on several occasions through various voices (20:15; 21:11; 23:17; 24:20; 25:28; 26:25; 28:17). For the exiles, suffering the humiliation of defeat, this is encouraging. The Lord has promised that he will eventually restore his people by raising up a new David, who will lead them into a new era of divine blessing (see esp. Isa. 9:6–7; 11:1–16; Jer. 23:5–6; 30:8–9; 33:15–26; Ezek. 34:23–24; 37:24–25; Hosea 3:5; Amos 9:11–12; Zech. 12:7–14).

Teaching the Text

1. *Though the fulfillment of God's promises may seem to be delayed and even jeopardized, God is faithful to bring them to realization.* As David ran from Saul and then, following Saul's death, reigns over the region of Judah for seven and a half years, he must be wondering when God will fulfill his promise to place him on the throne of Israel. Despite apparent delays and opposition, God's promise is fulfilled.

God's people today wait and pray for his promise of a kingdom of peace to be realized in conjunction with the second coming of the new, ideal Davidic king, Jesus the Messiah (Matt. 6:10). Though it may seem to be delayed, causing some to scoff and doubt, it will arrive in God's own good time (Matt. 24:36; 2 Pet. 3:3–11).

2. *The Lord's chosen servants trust in his timing and do not resort to wrongdoing while waiting for the fulfillment of the divine promise.* On several occasions, David came close to death and wavered in his faith. But to his credit, he did not force the issue by killing Saul or by trying to seize the throne following Saul's death. He is not involved in any way in the murder of Abner or Ishbosheth. David knows that the Lord is his protector (4:9), and he waits on the Lord to fulfill his promise.

3. *God's people do well to recognize his purposes and act accordingly.* As noted above (see "Theological Insights"), God has made known his intention to replace Saul on the throne of Israel; many, including Saul and those closest to David, recognize David as God's choice to be Saul's successor. When Saul has been killed and David has returned, Judah and then in due time Israel align themselves with God's purpose. Through David's military exploits under Saul, the Lord has previewed his future king for Israel; finally the people, recognizing David's gifts and calling, willingly anoint

David reigned over the region of Judah from the city of Hebron for seven and a half years before he became king over all of Israel. Shown here is the area around Hebron.

him as their king in recognition of God's purposes for him and Israel.

Illustrating the Text

God's seemingly delayed promises are nevertheless reliable.

Letters: *Letters and Papers from Prison*, by Dietrich Bonhoeffer. Bonhoeffer (1906–45), a German pastor, theologian, and martyr, understood the pain of delay as he became a part of a movement to overthrow Hitler. Arrested in 1943, he was hanged a few weeks before the Allied liberation. Letters found after his death show his anguish over separation from his family and fiancée, reflecting the full range of his feelings while imprisoned. Yet, while being honest, Bonhoeffer affirms trust in God's promises and faithfulness in spite of circumstances: "Who stands fast?" he writes. "Only the man whose final standard is not his reason, his principles, his conscience, his freedom, or his virtue, but who is ready to sacrifice all this when he is called to obedient and responsible action in faith and to exclusive allegiance to God—the responsible man who tries to make his whole life an answer to the question and call of God."[5]

God may use secondary causes, including human decisions, to accomplish his purposes.

Quote: *Leap over a Wall*, by Eugene Peterson.

So many people quit reading the Bible or repudiate it: "I can't read the Bible, especially the Old Testament—too much fighting, too much brutality." That's exactly why Christians *do* read it: we find God's

David and Joab

By cursing Joab, David places the matter in God's hands. But, as king of Judah, does not David have the authority to be God's instrument of justice? Indeed, on his deathbed he instructs his royal successor Solomon to bring Joab to justice—a command that Solomon obeys (1 Kings 2:5–6, 28–34). Furthermore, David is fully capable of implementing swift justice when he so desires, as the accounts in 2 Samuel 1 and 4 illustrate.

Though David disapproves of Joab's deeds, perhaps he decides, maybe even subconsciously, that it is convenient to have him around.[a] At any rate, David's paralysis reflects a character flaw that will emerge later in the story. David is sometimes unable to deal justly with those closest to him (cf. 2 Sam. 13:21; 1 Kings 1:6). Some suggest that David does not bring Joab to justice because Joab is operating within the boundaries of the ancient rules of blood vengeance, which the Old Testament allows but regulates (cf. Num. 35:9–34). However, if this is the case, then are not David's curses unjustified? Furthermore, David calls Joab's deed "evil" (2 Sam. 3:39). Perhaps, some may argue, Joab's deed can be justified as an act of war, but David rules this option out in his deathbed speech to Solomon when he accuses Joab of killing Abner in a time of peace (1 Kings 2:5). Solomon executes Joab as an act of justice, explaining that Joab is guilty of murdering Abner and Amasa (1 Kings 2:31–33).

[a] Cartledge, *1 and 2 Samuel*, 394; Steussy, *David: Biblical Portraits*, 58.

purposes being worked out in the precise moral and political, social and cultural conditions that we wake up to each morning, a world of shabby morality and opportunist companions, religious violence, religious propaganda—the many, many sons of Zeruiah that are too hard for us.[6]

God's people must align themselves with his revealed purposes.

Letters: *Letters and Papers from Prison*, by Dietrich Bonhoeffer. "God is not a 'god of gaps.' . . . We are to find God in what we know, not in what we don't know," Bonhoeffer says. "It is his will to be recognized in life, and not only when death comes; in health and vigour, and not only in suffering."[7]

David the Conqueror

Big Idea *The Lord accomplishes his purposes through those who promote his kingdom agenda and act in accordance with his reliable promises.*

Understanding the Text

The Text in Context

Israel has been humiliated by the Philistines and torn by civil strife, but finally the tribes have united and made David king in accordance with God's purposes. David immediately takes the ancient site of Jerusalem as a prelude to establishing a central sanctuary there. He also seeks the Lord's guidance and experiences his supernatural intervention in battle as he defeats the Philistines. Though Saul is dead and gone, the narrator continues to make his case for David's legitimacy. Saul led Israel to a humiliating defeat, but David reverses that disaster and turns the tables on the Philistines through the guidance and empowerment of the Lord, something that has been denied to Saul (1 Sam. 28:6). David obeys the Lord's command (2 Sam. 5:25), in contrast to disobedient Saul (1 Sam. 13:13–14).

Historical and Cultural Background

This chapter records two prebattle oracles of victory (vv. 19, 23–24), both of which are fulfilled (vv. 20, 25). Such oracles, delivered by a deity to a king, are common in the ancient Near East. For example, the goddess Ishtar assures the Assyrian king Esarhaddon: "Fear not, O King! Because I have spoken to you (in an oracle), I will not abandon you. Because I have encouraged you, I shall not let you come to shame. I will help you cross the river safely. . . . With my own hands, your foes I shall annihilate. . . . O Esarhaddon, in Arbela, I am your good shield" (*ANET*, 605). King Zakkur of Hamath, when besieged by enemies, appeals to his god Ba'alshamayn, who replies through "seers and diviners": "Do not be afraid! Since I have made [you king, I will stand] beside you. I will save you from all [these kings who] have besieged you." He reports that his god "answered" him (*COS*, 2:155). The Egyptian king Ramesses III, following a victory, praises his god: "I have returned in valor, my arms (laden) with captives, . . . through the decree which issued from thy mouth. That which thou hast promised has come to pass."[1]

In verse 24 the Lord instructs David to wait until the Lord marches ahead of him into battle. The concept of a deity marching ahead of his appointed leader also appears in the Tel Dan Inscription (A5), where the author states that his god Hadad went before him into battle (*COS*, 2:161; for Assyrian parallels to this motif, see *COS*, 2:161n5).

Interpretive Insights

5:6 *marched to Jerusalem to attack the Jebusites*. In the initial conquest of the land, the men of Judah defeated and burned Jerusalem (Judg. 1:8), but neither the Judahites nor the Benjamites were able to establish complete control over the city (Josh. 15:63; Judg. 1:21). The Jebusites, a Canaanite people whom Israel should have destroyed (Deut. 7:1–2; 20:17), remained entrenched in the city, confident that no one could conquer their well-fortified position, located on what is the southeast corner of later Jerusalem. In obedience to God's ancient command to Israel, David now defeats the Jebusites.[2] David emerges as a leader who intends to finish what Joshua and Judah started.

5:8 *Anyone who conquers the Jebusites will have to use the water shaft to reach those "lame and blind" who are David's enemies*. The Hebrew text reads, "Whoever strikes the Jebusites, and he will touch the *tsinnor*, and the lame and the blind hate the soul of David [or, "the ones hated by the soul of David," reads the MT mg.]." The passage poses several interpretive

challenges: (1) The meaning of the word *tsinnor* is uncertain. Many assume that it means "water shaft." In this case the text may refer to the way in which David's men invade the fortress. Some identify this water shaft with Warren's shaft, a fifty-foot vertical shaft discovered in 1867. However, the lexical basis for this interpretation is shaky, and some contend that this shaft was not accessible in David's day (for helpful discussion, see *ZIBBCOT*, 2:433–35). Interpreters have offered several other alternatives for the meaning of the word and the statement.[3] (2) If one follows the reading of the Hebrew text, then the lame and blind are described as hating David. The terms "lame" and "blind" are figurative, playing on the boastful claim of the Jebusites that even the blind and lame can defend the city (v. 6). If one follows the marginal reading, then the lame and blind are the objects of David's disdain. But this does not

David may have conquered the city of Jerusalem by entering through the "water shaft" (2 Sam. 5:8). Recent archaeological evidence seems to indicate that the water system of Jerusalem constructed by the Canaanites was elaborate and sophisticated. Shown here is the entrance to the tunnel that would have led the residents to a safely guarded water supply.

mean that David dislikes those with handicaps (cf. his kind treatment of Mephibosheth); it refers instead to his attitude toward the Jebusites, who use the imagery in their taunt. In either case, the final statement in the verse apparently refers to any surviving Jebusites being banned from the royal palace (Hebrew, "the house").

5:9 *David then took up residence in the fortress.* Designating Jerusalem as his capital makes good sense politically since the city is situated near the border of the north and south (Judah).[4] The city also symbolizes David's military prowess and intention to carry out the Lord's ancient command to defeat Israel's enemies. After all, he has uprooted a people that remained entrenched in the city and defied Israel since the time of the original conquest of the land.

5:10 *because the LORD God Almighty was with him.* This divine title (a variation on the traditional "LORD of Hosts") highlights the Lord's sovereignty and military might, envisioning him as one who sits enthroned over his heavenly council (see the comment at 1 Sam. 1:11). He sits enthroned above the cherubim of the ark of the covenant, the earthly symbol of his heavenly throne (1 Sam. 4:4; 2 Sam. 6:2). Perhaps the use of the title here anticipates the account of the ark in the next chapter.

5:12 *David knew that the LORD had established him as king over Israel.* Hiram, king of Tyre (located north of Israel in Phoenicia), recognizes David's royal status

Hiram, the king of Tyre, sent cedar logs to David (2 Sam. 5:11). Cedar from the forests of Lebanon was highly prized for building large structures like palaces. This Assyrian relief from the palace of Sargon II may show cedars from Lebanon being transported by river (716–713 BC).

and supplies the materials and expertise for the building of David's royal palace. To David, this recognition by a foreign neighbor confirms the fact that the Lord has established him as king.

for the sake of his people Israel. In accord with the Lord's royal ideal (Deut. 17:14–20) and the Lord's oracles to David (2 Sam. 3:18; 5:2), David realizes that the Lord has raised him up for the sake of his people, Israel.

5:21 *The Philistines abandoned their idols.* Following Saul's death, the Philistines "proclaim the news in the temple of their idols" (1 Sam. 31:9). But now, ironically, the Philistines abandon those same idols as they flee from David. David has reversed Israel's fortunes and brings humiliation to their enemy by carrying off their so-called gods. There is also an echo of an earlier humiliating defeat, when the Philistines carried off the ark as a trophy of war (1 Sam. 4:11).[5]

5:24 *the sound of marching.* This is an echo of Judges 5:4, where Deborah and Barak, in celebrating the Lord's victory over the Canaanites, describe him as marching from Edom to do battle. (To this point in the Former Prophets, the root *tsaʿad* [march] is used in only these two texts.) It is as if the Lord is renewing his mighty deeds through David.

the LORD *has gone out in front of you.* This may echo Deborah's words to Barak (Judg. 4:14).

5:25 *David did as the* LORD *commanded him.* The narrator depicts David as an obedient servant, who carries out the Lord's commandment. As such, he is a model of how God's covenant people should act (see Deut. 5:32). The contrast with disobedient Saul is undoubtedly intentional (cf. 1 Sam. 13:13–14).

Theological Insights

Through his obedient servant David, the Lord reverses Israel's humiliation and begins to establish David's kingdom for the benefit of his covenant people. In the process he renews his mighty deeds as he intervenes for Israel in battle and again demonstrates his ability to overwhelm Israel's enemies. Surely all of this resonates with the exiles. The Lord has promised to

David's Expanding Harem

The narrator informs us that David continues to expand his harem, adding concubines and wives, who give him at least eleven more sons (vv. 13–16).[a] The pattern is the same as in 3:1–5, where a comment about David's growing strength is followed by a harem report. In light of the positive assessment of David in 5:10 and 12, one is tempted to say that this note about an expanding harem is included to impress the reader with David's growing status and to picture him as one whom God blesses with numerous offspring, who in turn make his royal house stronger.[b] After all, verse 10 does say that the Lord is with David.

But throughout David's story the narrator includes negative aspects of David's career, often without comment. As in 2 Samuel 3:2–5, we must look beyond the surface and not allow the positive aspects of David's career to color our interpretation of every detail. Deuteronomy 17:17 prohibits Israel's king from multiplying wives. While David's harem, composed mostly of "local girls," does not turn his heart from the Lord, his acquisition of more and more wives suggests that he has bought into the thinking of the surrounding culture to some degree, and it sets a bad precedent that proves detrimental to Solomon. As for the reference to God's being with David (v. 10), this hardly implies that all of David's actions must be interpreted in a positive light. Judges 1:19 observes that the Lord is with the men of Judah, but then informs us that they are not able to defeat the Canaanites. Here the reference to the Lord's presence contributes to the tragic irony of the report. The same may be true in 2 Samuel 5. Despite God's enabling presence (v. 10), which David himself recognizes (v. 12), David continues to operate according to the wider cultural pattern, in violation of the Deuteronomic ideal.[c]

[a] The first four of these, whose names appear in v. 14, are sons of Bathsheba (cf. 1 Chron. 3:5), so the narrative is proleptic at this point; 1 Chron. 3:6–9 adds two names (Eliphelet and Nogah, thus totaling nine sons) and tells us that other sons were born to the concubines.

[b] Bergen, *1, 2 Samuel*, 323–24; Cartledge, *1 and 2 Samuel*, 416, 420. Steussy is not so confident and detects "ambivalence," arguing that David's growing number of wives and children may indicate "divine favor" or "abused royal privilege" (*David: Biblical Portraits*, 59). See as well Arnold, *1 and 2 Samuel*, 455–56.

[c] One potential objection must be addressed. In 1 Kings 11:1–8, where Solomon is denounced for marrying foreign wives and worshiping their gods, Solomon's disloyalty is contrasted with David's loyalty (vv. 4, 6). This may seem odd if indeed David's harem building foreshadows Solomon's sin, as we are suggesting. However, the contrast in Kings is between Solomon's idolatry and David's loyalty in cultic matters. Yet this hardly exonerates David for his harem. The point is not that David's harem building involves idolatry (it does not), only that it violates the letter of the law, reflects an assimilation to cultural concepts of kingship, and sets a bad precedent for Solomon.

give them a new Davidic ruler, who will lead them to unprecedented heights and establish a secure kingdom (Isa. 9:1–7; 11:10–16; Amos 9:11–15).

The reliability of the divine word is an important theme in this chapter. In the face of the Philistine threat, we see David at his best, seeking the Lord's guidance and winning victories through the Lord's power. In the past, whenever he sought the Lord's will, the Lord answered him with an assuring word that was a precursor to success (1 Sam. 23:1–5; 30:7–8; 2 Sam. 2:1) or with a word of warning that enabled David to escape danger (1 Sam. 23:9–12). In his song of thanks, written after the Lord delivers him from all his enemies, David affirms that the Lord's word is "flawless" (or "purified," like metal that is refined and free of impurities) and that "he shields all who take refuge in him" (2 Sam. 22:31). This affirmation appears in a context where David celebrates that the Lord trained and energized him for battle. The "word" of the Lord to which he refers is the prebattle oracle that assures him of success and enables him to charge fearlessly against his enemies.

Teaching the Text

1. *The Lord accomplishes his purposes through those who promote his kingdom agenda.* David's first act as king over a united Israel is to take care of some unfinished business. When they conquered the land, Israel failed to take the Jebusite stronghold in Jerusalem, but now David conquers it and builds a palace there, thus declaring, "This city now belongs to Israel." His desire to obey the Lord's ancient command regarding the conquest of the land is exemplary. The Lord honors David with his enabling presence and secures his reign, for David's actions are consistent with God's goal of establishing his kingdom on earth. Surely today God's chosen servants do not promote God's kingdom by fighting wars and killing Philistines! But God promises his enabling presence to those who carry out his commission as a prelude to the consummation of his kingdom (Matt. 28:18–20; Acts 28:31).

2. *The Lord accomplishes his purposes through those who act in accordance with his reliable promises and trust in his power.* In carrying out God's purposes, David confronts opposition from the Philistines, but he seeks the Lord's guidance, follows the Lord's instructions, and experiences the Lord's supernatural intervention. God's word proves to be completely reliable. Today God's chosen servants do not "inquire" of the Lord the way David did, receive specific customized orders, or hear

"David then took up residence in the fortress and called it the City of David. He built up the area around it, from the terraces inward" (2 Sam. 5:9). This excavated area has uncovered what is known as the "stepped-stone structure" (shown here). Thought to have originally been part of the Jebusite city and then enlarged by David, it may have supported a large civic structure like a fortress.

God's army marching in the trees above them. But God has communicated his purpose for this age and made promises that his people can trust.

Illustrating the Text

God accomplishes his purposes through those who promote his kingdom agenda.

Christian Biography: *A Passion for Souls,* **by Lyle Dorsett.** This is a biography (1997) of D. L. Moody, businessman, national and international evangelist, and cofounder of the famed Moody Bible Institute in Chicago. Arguably one of the most important American figures of the nineteenth century, Moody was born and raised in poverty, had little education, and seemed an unlikely figure to accomplish significant things for God. However, introduced to Christ through the influence of a lay Sunday school teacher, Moody was consumed with doing God's work. He was "always on the alert for souls," Dorsett writes. "Through [his] determination to focus on God and not on himself, lives were transformed. Even the *New York Times* had to admit that 'the work accomplished . . . by Moody will live. The drunken have become sober, the vicious virtuous, the worldly and self-seeking, unselfish, the ignoble noble, the impure pure.'" Moody's response to praise was always the same, that if the Holy Spirit was working through God's servants, great results would follow.[6]

Film: *Braveheart.* In this film (1995), starring Mel Gibson as William Wallace, a thirteenth-century Scottish knight gains recognition when he comes to the forefront of the First War of Scottish Independence by opposing King Edward I of England. The film won five Academy Awards and was nominated for an additional five. Gibson's speech in the film about freedom, about warring against cruelty, has the ethos of David in the Old Testament. He says, "I am William Wallace. I seek a whole army of countrymen to defeat tyranny. What will you do without freedom? We will fight, and we may die. You may fight and live for a while. They can take our lives but not our freedom." While William Wallace is not precisely fighting God's battle, his spirit of courage and determination in the face of evil parallels the way in which God's people must promote his kingdom agenda.

God accomplishes his purposes as Christians trust his reliable promises.

Missionary Autobiography: *They Called Me Mama,* **by Margaret Nicholl Laird.** Laird (1897–1983) spent fifty years in missionary work in the Central African Republic and has been honored by various organizations for her groundbreaking work. Among other seemingly dangerous and impossible tasks, she was asked to work among the cannibals in Ippy when she had three very young children. Over and over, we are told, "her big heart and enormous physical stamina helped her envelop the Africans in her love as she taught them to love and trust Christ."[7] After the death of her husband, she pursued her vision for a hospital at Ippy to meet desperate needs. The mission told her it was impossible. She persevered, asking for just five minutes to speak of the need in this church and that. One by one, every part of the vision fell into place. The hospital was built. The book contains many incidents that serve as riveting examples of this principle.

The Ark Finds a Resting Place

Big Idea *The Lord's willingness to dwell among his people is cause to celebrate, but he expects his people to respect his holiness.*

Understanding the Text

The Text in Context

When Samuel was young and Eli was old, the Philistines captured the ark of the covenant (1 Sam. 4). The ark wreaked havoc in Philistine territory: the image of Dagon in the Ashdod temple ended up decapitated, and the Philistines' cities were devastated by a plague (1 Sam. 5). The Philistines sent the ark back to Israelite territory, but when it arrived in Beth Shemesh, several curiosity seekers were struck dead when they failed to show it proper respect (1 Sam. 6). Finally the men of Kiriath Jearim took the ark to their town, where it remained for many years (1 Sam. 7:1–2).[1] After David has conquered Jerusalem and built his palace there, he decides to make the city the religious center of Israel. For this to happen, the ark, symbolizing God's presence among his people, must be brought to the city. It is appropriate that the Lord reside in a central sanctuary in the city, for he is the one who possesses ultimate authority over Israel and has chosen David as his vice-regent (2 Sam. 6:2, 21). The arrival of the ark is the prelude to David's decision to build the temple (2 Sam. 7).

Interpretive Insights

6:3 *They set the ark of God on a new cart.* The fact that they use a new cart suggests sincerity on their part and recognition that the ark is deserving of special treatment. One might think that this is a legitimate way to transport the ark, since the Philistines used a new cart to send it back to Israel, without any apparent negative consequences (1 Sam. 6:7–14). However, by loading the ark onto a cart, David violates the instructions of God's law (Exod. 25:12–14; Num. 4:5–6, 15). The ark is supposed to be carried with poles by certain Levites. Furthermore, David's men are not Levites, nor are Abinadab's sons (see 1 Chron. 15:13, 15).

6:7 *The LORD's anger burned against Uzzah.* This is one of only two instances in 1–2 Samuel where the Lord's anger is said to burn against someone (cf. 2 Sam. 24:1). Elsewhere in the Former Prophets, his anger burns against Israel (Josh. 7:1; 23:16; Judg. 2:14, 20; 3:8; 10:7; 2 Sam. 24:1; 2 Kings 13:3); this reference to an individual's being the object of his anger is unique. In other cases it is the collective rebellion of the covenant community that prompts

God's anger, but in this case it is an individual action, suggesting its particularly grave nature.

God struck him down. The Lord tolerates the people's disobedience to a point (see the comment on 6:3 above), but when Uzzah touches the ark, it is "the straw that breaks the camel's back." However innocent his intentions may be, his action betrays a certain lack of reverence for the ark.[2] God has to remind his people that his holiness must not be violated.

6:8 *because the LORD's wrath had broken out against Uzzah.* The language used here is ironic; this is the same verb (*parats*) used in 5:20 to describe how the Lord broke out against the Philistines, prompting David to name the place accordingly (the name Baal Perazim means "lord of the outburst[s]").[3] But here the Lord breaks out against one of his own people, casting Uzzah in the role of God's enemy. The place of his death is appropriately named Perez Uzzah, "outburst against Uzzah."

Key Themes of 2 Samuel 6

- David sincerely celebrates when the ark, the symbol of the Lord's presence, arrives in Jerusalem.
- David's good intentions are not enough to prevent the Lord from angrily punishing the one who violates his holiness.

6:9 *David was afraid of the LORD.* This is one of just two instances in 1–2 Samuel where David is said to be afraid (cf. 1 Sam. 21:12, where he fears Achish). His response is certainly warranted. According to the regulations of kingship outlined in Deuteronomy 17:14–20, the king is to read God's law so that he might fear the Lord (vv. 18–19). David's unfamiliarity with the law regulating transporting the ark has prompted God's anger and elicited an appropriate response from David. He now has a healthy respect for the Lord's holiness.

6:13 *When those who were carrying the ark.* David transports the ark properly this time, a fact verified in the parallel account in 1 Chronicles 15:1–15 (cf. Exod. 25:14; 37:5).

he sacrificed a bull and a fattened calf. The only other context in the Old Testament where anyone sacrifices (*zabah*) a bull (*shor*) and a fattened calf (*meri'*) is in 1 Kings 1:19, 25, where Adonijah sacrifices bulls and calves as

Bringing the ark to Jerusalem was a joyous occasion accompanied by music, singing, and dancing. The celebrating turned to fear, however, because God's instructions for transporting the ark were not obeyed. Shown here are musicians and a dancer on a tenth- to eighth-century BC Neo-Hittite relief from Carchemish, Turkey.

part of his premature coronation ceremony. Perhaps David views the entry of the ark into Jerusalem as a coronation ceremony of sorts for the Lord, represented by his ark. (See the comment on v. 15 below.)

6:14 *Wearing a linen ephod.* A linen ephod is mentioned only two other times in 1–2 Samuel. In both cases, it is worn by those serving in a priestly capacity (1 Sam. 2:18; 22:18; then 1 Chron. 15:27 is parallel to 2 Sam. 6:14). Apparently David is functioning here as a royal priest of sorts (cf. Ps. 110:4). According to the parallel passage in 1 Chronicles 15, the Levitical priests who are carrying the ark also wear linen robes for the occasion (v. 27). David's exercising of a legitimate royal priestly function in conjunction with the Levites contrasts with Saul, who disobeyed Samuel's order and overstepped his boundaries by usurping Samuel's role (see 1 Sam. 13:12).

6:15 *with shouts and the sound of trumpets.* The reference to the sound of the trumpet (*qol shopar*) is reminiscent of the scene at Sinai (Exod. 19:16, 18; 20:18), while the association of shouting with a trumpet blast recalls the march of the ark around Jericho (Josh. 6:5, 20). A trumpet blast is also part of a royal coronation (2 Sam. 15:10; 1 Kings 1:41), so it is possible that the procession of the ark

As the ark enters the city of Jerusalem, King David is "leaping and dancing before the Lord" (2 Sam. 6:16). This plaque known as the "Dancer of Dan" shows a figure dancing and playing a lute (fourteenth to thirteenth century BC, Dan, Israel).

is viewed as an enthronement of the Lord (see the comment on v. 13 above). Psalm 47:5 may recall this event.

6:16 *she despised him.* This is only the fourth time the verb "despised" (*bazah*) has been used in 1–2 Samuel. The Lord rebuked Eli and his sons for despising him (1 Sam. 2:30; cf. 2 Sam. 12:9–10). Twice the Lord's anointed was the object of another's inappropriate disdain (1 Sam. 10:27; 17:42). Since Michal is the third party in the story to despise the Lord's anointed, we should probably interpret her action in a negative light (see further discussion below on v. 23).

6:20 *How the king of Israel has distinguished himself.* We are not told Michal's underlying motives for criticizing David. She may resent the fact that he has supplanted her father as king, and she is probably bitter about how she has been treated. David has married other wives but then insists that she be taken from (her current husband) Paltiel and added to David's harem. Though one might be tempted to sympathize with her, her attack on David on this occasion is unjustified. Her accusation is petty and unfair, while David's response reveals his heart for God (v. 21). The spirit of Saul lives on in his daughter: he falsely accused David, so does she.

6:23 *had no children to the day of her death.* Coming on the heels of Michal's argument with David, this report appears to be the narrator's way of saying she is in the wrong and gets what she deserves. Her childless condition also means that Saul's family line will have no part in the Davidic royal dynasty. It is possible that a child born to David and Michal would have first claim to the throne because Michal is David's first wife. But Michal's failure to have children eliminates that possibility.[4]

Theological Insights

The sovereign and omnipresent God of the universe cannot be confined to an earthly dwelling place (1 Kings 8:27). He rules over his creation from his heavenly throne (Deut. 26:15; Ps. 33:13–14). Nevertheless, he condescends to live among his covenant people, Israel, whom he has delivered from Egypt in order that he might be their God and dwell in their midst (Exod. 29:45–46; cf. Lev. 26:11). Moses anticipated that God would choose a special place in the land to serve as a national worship center (Deut. 12:5, 11; 14:23; 16:2, 6, 11; 26:2). Shiloh became the first such center (Josh. 18:1) but was destroyed when the Philistines captured the ark in the days of Eli (1 Sam. 4; cf. Ps. 78:60–61 and Jer. 7:12). After its return to Israel, the ark has remained in exile until David brings it to Jerusalem.

Several psalms, especially the songs of Zion (Pss. 46; 48; 76; 84; 87; 122), exalt Jerusalem as the Lord's dwelling place. Because God lives and rules from the city, it enjoys his protection and blessing. These psalms express an ideal, a portrait of what Jerusalem should and could be if its leaders and people remain loyal to the God who lives among them. However, as the prophetic books make clear, the people's disobedience causes God to abandon his city (Ezek. 10–11), leaving it wide open to enemy invaders who shatter once and for all the false, theologically incorrect optimism of the city's sinful people and deluded false prophets (cf. Jer. 7:4; 8:19; 21:13). The Zion ideal is not an unconditional guarantee of continual divine protection and blessing; it will be realized only as long as the people are loyal to God.

For the exiles, living in the aftermath of the shattered ideal of Zion theology, the account of David's bringing the ark to Jerusalem is cause for both sorrow and renewed hope. The joy that accompanies the ark's arrival in Jerusalem stands in stark contrast to the reality that God has abandoned the city. But the story also brings renewed hope: the prophets, who have announced the city's downfall, have also promised that God will eventually restore Zion. They anticipate a day when the Lord will return to Jerusalem and again take up residence within it, restoring the joy of his people (among other texts, see Isa. 1:21–28; 2:2–4; 4:5–6; 14:32; 25:1–5; 27:2–6; 33:5; 54:11–17; 60:4–22; 61:4–6; 62:1–2; 65:17–18; Jer. 30:17–20; 31:38–40; Ezek. 43:1–5; Joel 3:17; Zech. 8:3). Yet the story also challenges them, for it is a reminder that the God who desires to dwell among his people also expects them to treat him with the respect that his royal authority deserves.

Teaching the Text

1. *The Lord's willingness to dwell among his people is cause to celebrate.* The Zion ideal of God's residing among his people

stirred the imagination of the early church. The New Testament expands the ideal to include realities beyond the literal restoration of Jerusalem. The author of Hebrews uses Zion in a figurative sense to refer to the heavenly city, populated by God, the angels, and the "church of the firstborn" (12:22–23; cf. 13:14 and Gal. 4:26). The apostle John envisions a new Jerusalem descending from heaven following the final judgment (Rev. 21:1–22:6). This city, called "the bride, the wife of the Lamb" (21:9), will be inhabited by the people of God from all ages (cf. 21:12–14, the symbolism of which alludes to both the tribes of Israel and the church). This extension of the Zion ideal beyond its Old Testament limits illustrates how the full potential of biblical motifs is sometimes realized in the progress of revelation: imagery and motifs are utilized as analogies and symbols.

2. *The Lord expects his people to respect his holiness.*

David and the people of Israel are excited about bringing the ark to Jerusalem and are worshiping the Lord with all kinds of musical instruments (2 Sam. 6:5). But God strikes the well-meaning Uzzah dead for touching the ark. This account demonstrates that seemingly good intentions, even when accompanied by sincere and robust expressions of worship, do not negate disobedience. The ark is to be transported in a specified way: it is not some common object that anyone may touch. The Lord desires to have a personal relationship with his people and to dwell among them. But his willingness to live amid his people does not mean he can be treated as something common. His holiness must be respected, as the men of Beth Shemesh (1 Sam. 6:20) and Uzzah discover (see comments on 1 Sam. 6, under "Teaching the Text"). In the end, obedience is fundamental, and genuine worship takes place only when obedient people respect God's holiness as they celebrate his presence among them.

The punishment of Uzzah seems harsh, but sometimes human beings make bad decisions and place themselves in situations where no good choices are left. We cannot assume that God will deliver us from the consequences

Since the loss of the temple and the ark of the covenant, observant Jews have treated the Torah, part of the Jewish Scriptures, with the same honor and respect with which the ark was treated in the Old Testament. In the synagogue, the Torah is carefully and reverently stored in an ornamental cabinet known as the Torah Ark. It is behind an inner curtain that imitates the veil of the Holy of Holies. Carvings or mosaics of these receptacles have been found in the archaeological remains of early synagogues. In Capernaum, a lintel from the fourth-century AD synagogue shows a Torah Ark being transported on a cart.

of those initial bad choices. Uzzah and his companions, for whatever reason, make a bad choice to transport the ark improperly, so when it begins to tip, there are no good choices left, only negative consequences.

Illustrating the Text

Genuine worship is the celebration of God's presence among his people.

Quote: *A Royal "Waste" of Time,* by **Marva J. Dawn.** Dawn (b. 1948) is a theologian, teacher, speaker, and author. She has written a great deal of intelligent and thoughtful material on worship in the church and among Christians because of worship's controversial status for many years. She cuts a path between traditional and contemporary worship—but what she argues for is God as "infinite center":

> I think our churches need to do much deeper thinking about what it means to worship God, what it means to nurture and to live the life of faith. . . . We have to stop asking which style of music to use and ask instead what will help us keep God at the center.
>
> The truth leads to many questions that we who plan worship and the worship space must ask. Does the order of worship clearly reflect that God is the Subject? Is there too much focus on the pastor or musicians that would detract from participants' awareness that God is the inviter? Does the worship space reveal God's special presence? . . . God is . . . also the Object of our worship, so indeed we do properly ask "For whom is worship?" too.[5]

Respecting God's holiness is an inseparable part of genuine worship.

Quote: *The Knowledge of the Holy,* by **A. W. Tozer.**

> Neither the writer nor the reader of these words is qualified to appreciate the holiness of God. Quite literally a new channel must be cut through the desert of our minds to allow the sweet waters of truth that will heal our great sickness to flow in. We cannot grasp the true meaning of the divine holiness by thinking of someone or something very pure and then raising the concept to the highest degree we are capable of. God's holiness is not simply the best we know infinitely bettered. We know nothing like the divine holiness. It stands apart, unique, unapproachable, incomprehensible and unattainable. . . . Holy is the way God is. To be holy He does not conform to a standard. He is that standard.[6]

Hymn: "Holy, Holy, Holy," by **Reginald Heber.**

> Holy, holy, holy! Though the darkness hide thee,
> though the eye of sinful man thy glory may not see,
> only thou art holy; there is none beside thee,
> perfect in power, in love and purity.
>
> Holy, holy, holy! Lord God Almighty!
> All thy works shall praise thy name, in earth and sky and sea.
> Holy, holy, holy! Merciful and mighty,
> God in three persons, blessed Trinity.

The Lord Decides to Build David a House

Big Idea *The Lord's irrevocable promise to David is reliable and guarantees the realization of his purposes for his covenant community.*

Understanding the Text

The Text in Context

David has transported the ark, the symbol of God's presence, to Jerusalem (2 Sam. 5). Knowing that the Lord is the true King of Israel (2 Sam. 6:2), who has defeated his enemies (5:17–25; 7:1), David naturally desires to build a "house" (a temple, or palace) for this victorious King.[1] The Lord will eventually allow a temple to be built (1 Kings 5–6), but the time is not yet right, nor is David the one whom he has chosen for this task (2 Sam. 7:13). The Lord turns the tables on David and promises that he will build *him* a "house," or dynasty. From this point onward, this theme dominates the story. In the aftermath of David's great sin, the situation in the royal court becomes chaotic, but the Lord sustains David and, in fulfillment of his promise, establishes one of David's sons, Solomon, as the king of Israel.

Historical and Cultural Background

Some have compared God's covenantal promise to David with royal grants attested in the ancient Near East. In such grants a king rewards a subject's faithfulness with a gift, which can take the form of a dynasty

Hittite treaty of Tudhaliya IV with Kurunta (thirteenth century BC)

and/or land. Weinfeld proposes that the Davidic promise follows the pattern of the promissory grants, which, though typically conditional, can be unconditional in special cases.[2] But Knoppers argues that the Davidic covenant differs from the grants in structure, form, and content.[3] While the grants are, for the most part, conditional, Knoppers does acknowledge that parallels exist between the formulation of the Davidic covenant in 2 Samuel 7 (and Ps. 89) and the Hittite treaty of Tudhaliya IV with Ulmi-Teshup. In both cases, a continuing dynasty is assured, even if a son is disobedient and must be severely disciplined.[4] Likewise, in Tudhaliya's treaty with Kurunta (COS, 2:103–4), he assures Kurunta that "he will not throw out his son," even if the son "commits treason" and is subjected to severe discipline. (In the case of the Ulmi-Teshup treaty, provision is even made for the disobedient son to be executed.) The disobedient son will not lose his "house" (dynasty) or land; it must be given to his direct descendant.

This is similar to the Davidic promise, in which the Lord makes it quite clear that disobedience will bring divine discipline and cause the king to forfeit present benefits, but the promise itself, sustained by God's loyal love (*hesed*), will not be nullified (2 Sam. 7:14–16). The Lord anticipates the possibility of rebellion but asserts that human failure will *not* invalidate his promise to David. In fact, the divine discipline administered by God through human instruments is viewed as an expression of his love for the Davidic king, as the language of verse 14 makes clear (see comments below).

Contrary to many of the grants, in David's case there is no indication that God's

Key Themes of 2 Samuel 7

- The Lord makes an irrevocable promise to David that is designed for the benefit of his people Israel.
- David responds to the Lord's promise with humble gratitude and praise.

promise is given as a reward for David's loyalty.[5] It is merely an extension of God's original sovereign choice of David to rule over Israel (vv. 9–10, 21). This choice is made on the basis of what God sees in David's character (or "heart"; cf. 1 Sam. 13:14; 16:7), prior to any actions David performs after his anointing.

Interpretive Insights

7:1 *the LORD had given him rest from all his enemies around him.* The following chapters describe David's wars against the surrounding nations. In the Lord's response to David (2 Sam. 7:11), he promises to give David rest from all his enemies, as if this has not yet been achieved. Thus 2 Samuel 7:1 (cf. v. 9 as well) probably refers to a time during David's reign when there is peace—a brief interlude between the Jebusite/Philistine wars (2 Sam. 5) and the campaigns described in 2 Samuel 8–12. The language reflects Moses's promise to Israel (Deut 12:10; 25:19) and is reminiscent of the description of Joshua's conquest (Josh. 21:44; 23:1), the only other passages where such language is used before 2 Samuel 7. The narrator views David as the instrument of the Lord in fulfilling the Mosaic promise and renewing the success of Joshua. In Deuteronomy 12:10–11 Moses instructs the people to worship the Lord at a central sanctuary once they experience rest from their enemies. It is understandable that David, once the Lord has given him rest from his enemies, seeks to establish a central sanctuary where such worship can occur.[6]

7:3 *for the* LORD *is with you.* This is the eighth time in the story that reference has been made to the Lord's being with David. The narrator (1 Sam. 18:12, 14, 28; 2 Sam. 5:10), Saul's servant (1 Sam. 16:18), and Nathan recognized this fact, while both Saul and Jonathan prayed that the Lord would be with David (1 Sam. 17:37; 20:13). In verse 9 the Lord states that he has indeed been with David in all of his endeavors. The constant reminders of the Lord's presence with David contrast with his abandonment of Saul (1 Sam. 16:14; 28:15–16).

7:5 *my servant David.* This is the second time the words "my servant" have been used by the Lord to describe David (cf. 2 Sam. 3:18). Before this, the Lord has used these words of only three other characters: Abraham (Gen. 26:24), Moses (Num. 12:7–8; Josh. 1:2, 7), and Caleb (Num. 14:24). In the case of Abraham and Caleb, the Lord uses this phrase in conjunction with his covenantal promises, just as he does here with David (v. 8). While the use of this phrase highlights David's important position, it also is a reminder that ultimate authority belongs to the Lord, the one whom David serves.

Are you the one to build me a house to dwell in? This is not a rejection of David's proposal, for later in this speech the Lord consents to the building of a temple, though he makes it clear that David's son will build it (vv. 12–13). The Lord wants to make sure that everyone understands that the Lord cannot be confined to a temple. He

The Lord promised a lasting dynasty for David. The Davidic dynasty was still recognized some 130 years after David's death. In this 840 BC inscription found at Tel Dan, the conquering king uses the phrase "House of David" to describe the kingdom of Judah.

will allow his "Name" to dwell in a temple (v. 13) and reveal his presence there, but he actually lives far beyond the heavens above (see 1 Kings 8:27).

7:8 *ruler over my people Israel.* As in 5:2, the Lord refers to Israel as "my people" and to David as "ruler" (*nagid*), not "king" (see the comments above on 1 Sam. 9:16; 10:1; 13:14; 25:30; 2 Sam. 5:2).

7:10 *I will provide a place for my people Israel and will plant them.* The Lord's primary purpose in elevating David is to make his covenant people secure. The wording of this promise may seem odd here, since the Lord planted his people in the land hundreds of years before this. However, the following statement (vv. 10b–11) makes it clear that the nation's security, not mere possession of the land, is in view. Throughout the period of the judges, oppressive invaders subjugated

Israel, but the Lord will enable David to establish a secure nation.

7:13 *I will establish the throne of his kingdom forever.* Saul forfeited a perpetual dynasty (1 Sam. 13:13), but the Lord promises that he will establish a lasting dynasty for David (see v. 16 as well). Though the word "covenant" is not used here, Psalm 89 views the Lord's promise as covenantal in nature (vv. 3, 28; cf. 2 Sam. 23:5) and speaks of it as being an oath sworn by the Lord (vv. 3, 35, 49).[7]

7:14 *I will be his father, and he will be my son.* The Lord declares that the Davidic king will enjoy a special relationship with him, comparable to that of a father and son. According to the royal psalms, the king's status as "son" comes with an inheritance: worldwide dominion (Pss. 2:7–9; 89:25–27). Psalm 2 speaks of this aspect of the Lord's promise as a formal statute or decree (v. 7).[8]

When he does wrong. The verb used here (*'awah*) does not refer to a simple oversight or minor transgression. It is used elsewhere of serious sins and acts of rebellion (1 Sam. 20:30; 2 Sam. 19:19; 24:17; 1 Kings 8:47 = 2 Chron. 6:37; Esther 1:16; Job 33:27; Ps. 106:6; Prov. 12:8; Jer. 3:21; 9:5; Dan. 9:5).

I will punish him. The verb used here (*yakah*) refers to corrective discipline. According to Proverbs 3:12: "The LORD disciplines [*yakah*] those he loves, as a father the son he delights in." The use of this same verb in 2 Samuel 7:14 is consistent with the preceding declaration that the Lord will regard the Davidic king as his son.

a rod wielded by men. Several proverbs mention the "rod" (*shebet*) as an implement used by a father to discipline a son (Prov. 13:24; 22:15; 23:13–14; 29:15). Such discipline is motivated by parental love (13:24).

7:15 *But my love will never be taken away from him, as I took it away from Saul.* This declaration ensures that the promise is irrevocable. The term translated "love" (*hesed*) refers to loyalty, often in a covenantal context. But the term does not necessarily carry an inherent meaning of unconditional, enduring loyalty. The Lord committed himself to Saul, but Saul forfeited his relationship with the Lord by his rebellion. But here the Lord announces that he will never withdraw from his relationship with the Davidic dynasty, as he did with Saul. (For further discussion, see "Additional Insights: The Davidic Covenant" below.) Psalm 89 highlights the Lord's loyal love in relationship with the Lord's promise to the Davidic dynasty (vv. 1–2, 14, 24, 28, 33, 49).

7:20 *you know your servant.* David uses the verb "know" here in its covenantal sense of "recognize in a special way, give special recognition to" (see Amos 3:2).[9] Ten times in this prayer David refers to himself as the Lord's servant, emphasizing his submission to the Lord's authority (vv. 19–21, 25–29).

7:23 *And who is like your people Israel?* David recognizes that the Lord's promise to establish his dynasty is a corollary of his choice of Israel to be his people. Ultimately the Lord's choice of David is for the benefit of his covenant people.

7:25 *keep forever the promise you have made.* David's prayer that the Lord will indeed keep his promise may seem inappropriate, since the Lord has affirmed his intention of establishing David's dynasty and never cutting him off from his loyal love (vv. 13–16). But rather than being evidence of lack of trust in God's faithfulness, this prayer is probably a polite way of seconding

giving the exiles reason to be encouraged and optimistic about their future.

Teaching the Text

1. *The Lord's irrevocable promise to David secures the future blessing of his covenant people.* This is one of the most important passages in the Old Testament because here God affirms his commitment to David and his dynasty. God's covenant with David and its attendant promises guarantee a glorious future for God's covenant people (see vv. 10, 23–24). Certainly the line of David failed in history, Israel went into exile, and David's dynasty appeared to come to an end. But the promise, which is rooted in the Lord's faithful character and sovereign choice of David, remained intact as the prophets looked forward to its fulfillment through an ideal Davidic king. In the course of time Jesus emerges as this king (Luke 1:32, 69; Rev. 22:16), and the promise to David finds its complete realization in and through him.

2. *The beneficiaries of the Lord's faithful promise to David should respond in humble gratitude and praise.* As the Lord's new covenant community and the beneficiaries of his promises to David, the people of God should respond with humble gratitude and praise. The Lord's promise to David is part of his redemptive work on behalf of his people, which enhances God's reputation and demonstrates his incomparability (vv. 22–23; cf. 1 Sam. 2:1–2; 2 Sam. 22:31–32).

the divine decree. It expresses David's willingness to be the Lord's chosen servant and to carry out the great responsibilities that being the recipient of the promise entails.[10]

Theological Insights

The Davidic promise, viewed subsequently as a covenant confirmed by an oath, is irrevocable (2 Sam. 7:11–16; Pss. 89:20–37; 110:4; Jer. 33:14–26). If the Davidic king does wrong, the Lord will discipline him, as a father does a son, but he will not revoke his promise.[11] The promise has important implications for Israel; it assures the nation of a glorious future (2 Sam. 7:10, 24). This hope persists into the exilic and postexilic periods (see "Additional Insights" at the end of this unit),

Illustrating the Text

The Lord's promises are realized even when they appear to have failed.

Bible: Habakkuk 3:17–19.

The believer must respond to God's promises with humble gratitude.

Hymn: "Now Thank We All Our God," by **Martin Rinckart.** German pastor Rinckart (1586–1649) served in the walled town of Eilenburg during the Thirty Years' War of 1618–48. Eilenburg was an overcrowded refuge for the surrounding area, where fugitives suffered from epidemic and famine. Four pastors served in Eilenburg at the time of the Great Plague. One abandoned his post, and Pastor Rinckart officiated at the funerals of the other two. As the only pastor left, Rinckart conducted many funeral services each day, totaling finally in the thousands, among them his wife. Still, Pastor Rinckart wrote the following prayer (1663) for his children to offer to the Lord:

> Now thank we all our God
> With hearts and hands and voices;
> Who wondrous things hath done,
> In whom this world rejoices.
> Who, from our mother's arms,
> Hath led us on our way,
>   With countless gifts of love,
>   And still is ours today.

Nikolaikirche in Eilenburg, Germany, where Martin Rinkart served as archdeacon

The Davidic Covenant

Standing in tension with the unconditional promise of a lasting Davidic dynasty are passages where the continuation of the dynasty appears to be conditional (cf. 1 Kings 2:1–4; 6:11–13; 8:23–26; 9:3–9; 1 Chron. 28:9; Ps. 132:11–12; Jer. 17:24–25; 22:1–9). In Psalm 89:39a the psalmist even laments that the Lord has "renounced" the Davidic covenant. The verb appears to be synonymous with "rejected" and "spurned" (v. 38).

Perhaps the best way to resolve this tension between texts is to conclude that the promise in its essence is irrevocable and certain of fulfillment, while the conditional statements refer to experiencing the benefits of the covenant at any given point in time. The promise remains secure because it is grounded in the Lord's sovereign choice of David prior to his becoming king (2 Sam. 7:8) and establishes a father-son relationship (v. 14). One sees this as well in Psalm 89, where the covenantal promise and God's initial choice of David to be king are linked (vv. 19–25). As in 2 Samuel 7, the Lord specifically states that disobedience by the Davidic king cannot invalidate the promise itself (Ps. 89:30–37), for their relationship is that of a father to a son (vv. 26–29). As for the lament that follows in verses 38–51, the language, especially in verses 38–39, may be viewed as hyperbolic and dynamic—a feature of the lament genre. Furthermore, though the psalmist uses strong language, it need not imply that the rejection is permanent (see Lam. 3:31;

cf. Pss. 44:23; 77:7). One might conclude that the promise of 2 Samuel 7:12–15 pertains only to Solomon (cf. 1 Kings 2:12, 24), but Psalm 89:29–30 indicates that the promise is extended to Solomon's offspring as well (note esp. "sons").

To summarize, the Davidic promise is dependent on divine faithfulness for its ultimate realization, not on the performance of David or his successors. But, much like the irrevocable Abrahamic covenantal promise (cf. Gen. 18:19), obedience by David's successors is essential for realization of the promise at any given time. Their failure might make it appear that the promise has failed, but this "failure," if we can call it that, is strictly temporary. The texts that view the covenant as irrevocable use different language than those that speak of conditions. In 2 Samuel 7 the Lord speaks of "establishing" (*kun*) David's kingdom, throne, and house (vv. 12–13, 16, 26; cf. Ps. 89:4, 37; 1 Kings 2:12). But the texts that present conditions do not use this verb when speaking of the Lord's fulfilling his promise or establishing (1 Kings 9:5 uses *qum*) the king's throne. Several of them say that David's "successor" will "never fail" to be "on the throne of Israel" (the Hebrew speaks of a successor not being "cut off" from the throne or the Lord's presence; 1 Kings 2:4; 8:25; 9:5; cf. Ps. 132:11–12).

The tension between the covenant's unconditional and conditional dimensions is resolved through Jesus, the ideal Davidic king, who is fully obedient and will bring about the complete and lasting realization of the promise. In the end, God's sovereign choice of David and his faithful commitment to his promise override the sins of imperfect Davidic rulers, whose failures delay realization of the promise but do not invalidate it.

This proposed resolution to the problem is consistent with the way the Davidic dynasty is viewed in the exilic and postexilic periods. The Former Prophets end with a reminder that the flame of the Davidic dynasty is still flickering, albeit in exile (2 Kings 25:27–30). For this historian there is still hope for a revival of the Davidic kingdom. Haggai (2:20–23) attaches great hope to David's descendant Zerubbabel, while Zechariah views him as fulfilling Jeremiah's prophecies concerning David's "branch" (Zech. 3:8; 6:12–13; cf. Jer. 23:5; 33:15). It appears that this exilic–postexilic hope is based on the assumption that the Davidic promise is indeed irrevocable. The absence of a Davidic king on the throne does not nullify the promise. Historical developments after the exile show that the promise of a permanent dynasty does not mean that the dynasty will necessarily enjoy an uninterrupted reign. Uninterrupted rule may have been the Lord's intention and ideal, but human disobedience has compromised the ideal without invalidating the promise.

Some assume that in Isaiah 55:3–5 the Davidic covenant is democratized and transferred to the entire nation. It does seem that the Davidic promises are extended to the nation here, but this does not mean that the nation replaces the Davidic dynasty as the recipient of those promises. Isaiah 55:3–5 relates the new covenant to the fulfillment of the Davidic promises and emphasizes that the nation will be a primary beneficiary of the latter.[1] The passage anticipates the national blessings that will result when the Davidic ideal is realized. Eaton, responding to the view that the Davidic promises are here transferred to the nation, states:

> But there is nothing in the text to express such a drastic change; it seems that these scholars are making it fit their own misreading of royal elements in earlier chapters. For it is entirely natural that the text should mention blessings accruing to the nation from the Davidic covenant, without thereby implying a break with the central point of the covenant, a covenant expressly described here as eternal. God's work with the king always had implications for the people. . . . The nation is to be blessed within the radius of the Davidic covenant, but the destiny of the royal house remains. . . . It would be a poor sort of eternity that the covenant would have, if its heart were taken out.[2]

Blenkinsopp observes that the democratization view of Isaiah 55:3–5 "goes some way beyond what the author says." He adds, "Furthermore, it is difficult to understand why this analogy [nation to David] would be used if the author was not persuaded of the permanence of Yahveh's commitment to David and the dynasty."[3]

Fighting Wars and Keeping a Promise: David Establishes an Ideal of Kingship

Big Idea *The Lord blesses his chosen servants when they rely on his protection and seek to reflect his character in their dealings with others.*

Understanding the Text

The Text in Context

The narrator's positive portrayal of King David continues in these chapters. Once David became king over all Israel, he conquered the Jebusite stronghold of Jerusalem and then turned the tables on the Philistines. He brought the ark to Jerusalem and intended to build a house (temple) for it. But then the Lord surprised David by announcing that he intended to build a house (dynasty) for David. He promised to establish David's throne and assured him that, even if his descendants are disobedient, this will not nullify the promise. Armed with the Lord's assuring promise to make the nation secure (2 Sam. 7:10–12), David now embarks on more military campaigns, and the Lord demonstrates his commitment to David by giving him still more victories. David in turn demonstrates his loyalty to the Lord by adhering to some Deutero-

nomic regulations pertaining to kingship, ruling in a just manner over Israel, and acting with goodwill toward Jonathan's son Mephibosheth and Nahash's son Hanun. Still more military successes follow, but the conflict with Ammon sets the stage for a shocking turn of events in chapter 11.

Historical and Cultural Background

The Ammonite king Hanun's treatment of David's servants (10:4) is particularly humiliating in a culture where beards are a source of male identity and public nudity is considered shameful (Isa. 20:4). But what makes the action particularly insulting is the fact that messengers represent the one who sends them and are to be treated with the same respect as their master. This is why the angel of the Lord at times speaks as God (Gen. 31:11–13; Judg. 2:1–3), while humans who encounter the angel sometimes react as if they have seen God himself (Gen.

16:13; Judg. 6:22; 13:22). In the Ugaritic Baal myth, the god Yamm's messengers enter the divine assembly, refuse to bow before El, and report their lord's words. The god El addresses them as Yamm and speaks to them as if he is talking directly to Yamm (*COS*, 1:246). When Hanun humiliates David's messengers, he insults David himself and the nation he rules. This explains why David regards the insult as an act of aggression and responds militarily.

Interpretive Insights

8:1 *David defeated the Philistines and subdued them.* The appearance of both the verbs "defeat" (*nakah*) and "subdue" (*kana'*) is significant. The only other passage in 1–2 Samuel in which they both appear is 1 Samuel 7:11, 13, where they describe Samuel's victory over the Philistines. Several times Israel is said to "defeat" the Philistines (1 Sam. 14:31; 18:27; 19:8; 23:5; 2 Sam. 5:20, 24–25), but the addition of "subdue" suggests that this is a victory that exceeds others and casts David in the role of one who duplicates the great accomplishment of Samuel.

8:3 *when he went to restore his monument at the Euphrates River.* The Hebrew text regarding Hadadezer (of Zobah, north of Damascus) reads, "when he went to return his hand along the

Key Themes of 2 Samuel 8–10

- As the Lord gives David military success, David demonstrates his trust in the Lord in accordance with the regulations of kingship.
- David promotes justice and demonstrates faithfulness.

River." A traditional marginal reading has "the Euphrates River" (cf. 1 Chron. 18:3). It is not certain what the expression "return his hand" would mean in this context, though it might carry the sense "restore his power." To further complicate matters, 1 Chronicles 18:3 reads, "when he went *to set up* his hand," reading the verb *natsab*, "set up," rather than *shub*, "return." In this case "hand" would refer to a monument (see 1 Sam. 15:12, where the same expression occurs). As the text stands, it is not clear who is the subject of the verb "went" (or "set up"), David or Hadadezer. One option is that David invades Hadadezer's territory while Hadadezer is conducting a campaign to Mesopotamia.[1] Another option is that David, while conducting a campaign to the Euphrates, defeats Hadadezer along the way.[2] In this case it is preferable to read the verb as "set up," for, as far as we know, David has not established his authority in Mesopotamia, so it cannot be said that he is restoring it.[3] If indeed David

The Moabites brought tribute to David. This was a common practice in the ancient Near East. Defeated nations were required to supply the conquering kings with goods and services. In this relief from the Black Obelisk, tribute of silver, gold, tin, ivory tusks, and ebony is being brought to the Assyrian king, Shalmaneser III, from the defeated king, Qarparunda, from the area of south Turkey.

conducts a campaign to the Euphrates, then he is seeking to extend Israel's authority to the ideal limits of the promised land (Gen. 15:18; Deut. 1:7; 11:24; Josh. 1:4).[4]

8:4 *He hamstrung all but a hundred of the chariot horses.* David's action is reminiscent of what Joshua did to the Canaanites' chariot horses (Josh. 11:6, 9).[5] Once more David is depicted as a new Joshua and as one who intends to finish what Joshua started (see comments on 2 Sam. 5:6 and 7:1 above). It is obvious that David does not appropriate Hadadezer's chariot force. On the contrary, he is obedient to the Deuteronomic law that prohibits Israel's king from accumulating horses, presumably for purposes of building a chariot force (Deut. 17:16).

8:6 *The L*ORD *gave David victory wherever he went.* The focus of the first five verses has been on David and his victories. But now the narrator informs us that it is the Lord who is responsible for David's success. To make sure the point is clear, he repeats this statement in verse 14. Since the account of David's ascension to the throne of Israel, the narrator has emphasized the Lord's enablement and protection of David (5:10, 19, 24; 7:1, 3, 9, 11).

8:11 *King David dedicated these articles to the L*ORD*, as he had done with the silver and gold from all the nations he had sub-*

dued. In accordance with the regulations of kingship (cf. Deut. 17:17), David does not keep the silver and gold he captures. Instead, he dedicates the plunder to the Lord.[6]

8:13 *David became famous.* David's fame is a fulfillment of the Lord's promise: "Now I will make your name great" (2 Sam. 7:9).[7]

8:15 *David reigned over all Israel.* Jonathan's prediction regarding David's destiny has come true (1 Sam. 23:17).

doing what was just and right for all his people. David has followed Moses's exhortation to the judges and officials of Israel (Deut. 16:18–19).

9:1 *to whom I can show kindness.* Years before, David promised his comrade Jonathan that he would protect his children (1 Sam. 20:15–16, 42). He also promised Saul that he would not destroy his descendants (24:21–22). Circumstances beyond David's control have decimated Saul's and Jonathan's offspring, but David hopes there is someone left to whom he might show favor. The word translated "kindness" (*hesed*) refers to faithfulness, often in a covenantal context. David used this word when he appealed to Jonathan for protection (20:8), and Jonathan also used it when he blessed David and asked him to show favor to him and his descendants (20:14–15).

9:3 *to whom I can show God's kindness.* The wording is identical to verse 1, except that now David refers to "God's kindness" (*hesed*).

David dedicated to the Lord all the plunder he took after his victories. This Assyrian relief shows scribes making a record of the plunder being gathered by the soldiers (palace at Nineveh, 640–620 BC).

Perhaps recalling Jonathan's appeal, he desires to mirror God's faithful character in his treatment of Jonathan's descendants (cf. 1 Sam. 20:14).[8]

9:7 *Don't be afraid.* David's assuring word to Mephibosheth is ironic, for years before, when David was running from Saul, Jonathan encouraged David with these same words as he assured him that he would indeed someday rule over Israel (1 Sam. 23:17). Now David takes the opportunity to repay that favor by encouraging Jonathan's son.

I will surely show you kindness. The expression "show kindness" (*'asah hesed*) is used over forty times in the Old Testament, but only here is it stated emphatically by adding the infinitive absolute of the verb. David wants Mephibosheth to know that he is serious about fulfilling his promise to Jonathan.

10:2 *I will show kindness to Hanun son of Nahash, just as his father showed kindness to me.* The word "kindness" (*hesed* again) in this context probably refers to loyalty within the context of a treaty relationship between the two kings. Once again the narrator portrays David as one who is committed to faithfulness in his relationships. David values this characteristic in others (2 Sam. 2:5–6) and seeks to demonstrate it in his dealings with others.

10:3 *Hasn't David sent them to you only to explore the city and spy it out and overthrow it?* This is not the first time that David has been falsely accused of having deceptive motives (cf. 1 Sam. 22:13; 24:9; 25:10). In the past the Lord vindicated him and will do so again by giving David and his army victory over the Ammonites and their Aramaean allies.[9]

David's Treatment of the Moabites

David's treatment of the Moabites is harsh and cruel, but it makes sense in the rough-and-tumble world in which he lives. He cannot let the Moabites return home en masse to fight again another day. But neither can he wipe them out completely, for the absence of an adult male population in Moab would weaken his eastern border and make it impossible for the Moabites to provide tribute. So David acts in a pragmatic manner. He kills two-thirds of the Moabite soldiers, eliminating the possibility of a renewal of hostility anytime soon, and allows one-third to return home, ensuring that Moab will be able to produce and send tribute on a regular basis.

10:13 *they fled.* The narrator emphasizes the magnitude of Israel's victory. Four times he describes the enemy as fleeing (*nus*; vv. 13–14, 18), and twice he speaks of them being routed/defeated (*nagap*; vv. 15, 19).

10:15 *routed by Israel.* There may be an echo of Samuel's great victory over the Philistines (1 Sam. 7:10). The expression "routed by Israel" occurs in 1–2 Samuel in only these two passages (cf. also 10:19). See the comment on 8:1.

Theological Insights

David is at his best in these chapters: winning victories through the Lord's enablement, acting in accordance with Deuteronomic regulations of kingship, promoting justice, and seeking to act faithfully in his dealings with others. Unfortunately, David's story takes a tragic turn for the worse, but the prophets look forward to the coming of a new David, who will establish justice, restore the covenant community from exile, reunite the people, defeat Israel's traditional enemies, and provide security for the nation (Isa. 9:7; 11:1–16; Jer. 23:5; Ezek. 34:23–24; 37:24–25; Mic. 5:2–6). The account of David's successes, when correlated with the voice of the prophets,

David trusted in the Lord for victory rather than amassing large numbers of horses and chariots like those shown in this Assyrian battle scene (palace at Nimrud, 865–860 BC).

encourages the exiles, for it gives them a glimpse of what the future will be like when the Lord's promises to David are fulfilled.

Teaching the Text

1. *The Lord blesses his chosen servants when they rely on his power to protect them.* When David defeats Hadadezer's forces, he does not add the enemy's chariots and horses to his army but hamstrings the horses, as Joshua did when he defeated the Canaanites. He accepts tribute of gold and silver from the king of Hamath but dedicates it to the Lord. His actions are in accordance with the Deuteronomic regulations of kingship (Deut. 17:16–17) that prohibit the king from accumulating horses (for chariots) and wealth. In the surrounding cultural model of kingship, both of these provide security, but the Lord wants his king to trust in him alone for security.[10] David's faith in the Lord's power to deliver proves to be well founded (8:6, 14).

The Lord's superiority to human armies, symbolized by the chariot horse, is a major theme in the Old Testament. The horse, though stronger and faster than men (Jer. 12:5), is made of flesh, susceptible to physical weakness (1 Kings 18:5), and unable to resist the Lord's power (Isa. 31:3). One might prepare the horse for battle, but success comes from the Lord (Prov. 21:31). Men of faith trust in the Lord, not horses, for their security (Ps. 20:7; Hosea 14:3) because they realize that he bestows his favor on the obedient and faithful, not on the strong (Pss. 33:17–19; 147:10–11).

This faith in the Lord is wisely placed, for time and again he demonstrates his superiority to horses and chariots on the battlefield (Exod. 15:1, 19, 21 [cf. Deut. 11:4; Isa. 43:17]; Josh. 11:4–11; Judg. 4:3, 15; 5:4–5, 19–22). With a mere battle cry, he disposes of horses and chariots (Ps. 76:6) and then invites the scavengers to devour the flesh of the dead horses (Ezek. 39:20). Haggai and Zechariah picture a culminating battle as being highlighted by the Lord's victory over horses and chariots (Hag. 2:22; Zech. 10:5; 12:4; 14:15).[11]

2. *The Lord blesses his chosen servants when they seek to reflect his just and faithful character in their relationships.* David is committed to reflecting the Lord's just and faithful character in his reign. He does what is "just and right for all his people" (8:15), seeks to exhibit godlike faithfulness to Jonathan's offspring in fulfillment of an old promise (9:3), and tries to show good-

will to the son of a faithful ally (10:2). In this way he establishes an ideal that will be fully realized in the messianic king (Isa. 9:7; 32:1, 16–17; Jer. 23:5; 33:15). Living in a just and righteous manner is the Lord's ultimate goal for his covenant community (Gen. 18:19). The qualities of justice and righteousness are the essence of genuine religion (Prov. 21:3) and are the foundation of Israelite law (Deut. 16:18–20).

Illustrating the Text

God blesses those who forsake the world's strength and rely on his power instead.

Missions: Share an example from the life of a missionary the congregation supports or a group from the church that went on a short-term mission trip. Highlight the way in which forsaking and stepping beyond the comfort and security of home allowed God's power and provision to shine through.

Bible: Briefly reference the life of the apostle Paul and his extraordinary missionary impact. Then share Philippians 3:1–11, in which Paul testifies about forsaking his human credentials in order to know and proclaim the surpassing power of the gospel.

Bible: Reference the story of David and Goliath in 1 Samuel 17:38–47, pointing out that David had learned this lesson as a young man, choosing to set aside the armor Saul gave him for protection and stand before Goliath armed only with a shepherd's sling and the protection of his God.

Application: Challenge listeners to consider if God might be calling them to explore this idea by fasting in the upcoming week. Regardless of the provision from which they temporarily abstain (food, technology, affections, entertainment, spending, etc.), the effect of fasting is the same: it is a chance to cease relying on self-provision and worldly supplies and focus on finding satisfaction in God's strength shown in weakness. You may even suggest that those wishing to go deeper consult resources like John Piper's *A Hunger for God*, or Richard J. Foster's sections on fasting in his classic work *Celebration of Discipline*. Including a short quote from one of these works could also enhance your illustration.

God blesses those who emulate his just and faithful character in relationship with others.

Testimony: Consider inviting a business owner, teacher, or community leader in the congregation to humbly share the ways in which God has been faithful to offer opportunities for influence and responsibility when he or she has sought to bring Christian ethics and character to the table.

Family Life / Parenting: Draw a connection to a common family experience: catching a child reflecting a parent's habits and character when interacting with others. The key to the illustration is not whether the behavior or habit observed made the parent proud or embarrassed; rather, the key is in describing the experience of seeing values from the home inevitably being reflected in a child's relationship to others.

Human Experience: In almost every other religion, *humans* create and raise up *gods* to call on in worship who will reflect *their* personal and cultural values: fertility, prowess in battle, wealth, intelligence, vengefulness, and so on. The biblical view inverts this idolatry as *God* creates and raises up *humans* and calls them to worship by reflecting *his* values in their persons and cultures.

"Oh, What a Tangled Web We Weave": Power Poisons the Conscience

Big Idea *The Lord's chosen servants cannot hide their sins from him.*

Understanding the Text

The Text in Context

Empowered by the Lord, David has experienced great success militarily and made Israel more secure than it has ever been. He obeyed the Deuteronomic regulations pertaining to the accumulation of chariot horses and wealth, promoted justice for all, and tried to model God's faithfulness in his relationships. But suddenly the story takes a shocking downward turn as David's blatant violation of God's law brings chaos into his life, the royal court, and the nation. Earlier David was portrayed as a new Joshua/Caleb who fearlessly defeats Israel's intimidating enemies (see "Theological Insights" for 1 Sam. 17). But now he turns into a new Samson: he sees an attractive woman and allows lust to enslave him (see comments on v. 2 below). This is especially alarming because the narrator earlier depicted Saul in Samson-like terms (see comments on 1 Sam. 10:7; 11:6; 14:24), and now David looks very Saul-like (see comments on vv. 1 and 14 below). These echoes of Samson and Saul create tension in the plot. Will David's

lust be fatal, as it was for Samson? Will the Lord reject David, as he rejected Saul? As the story unfolds, we discover that the answer is "no" in both cases. God preserves David and retains him as king in accordance with his promise (2 Sam. 7:14). Yet David pays dearly for his sin, and the chaos of the judges' period is revisited when the king spurns God's law and does what is right in his own eyes.

Actually, David's fall has been foreshadowed. David has followed the Deuteronomic regulations with regard to horses and wealth, but not in another area. Twice earlier the narrator spoke specifically of David's expanding power. But in both cases, the narrator then included a harem report, drawing attention to the fact that David is pursuing, at least in this regard, a model of kingship in the wider culture, contrary to the Deuteronomic ideal. David grew in prominence, but these reminders that he is violating the regulation concerning royal harems (Deut. 17:17) are disturbing and cast a cloud over his successes. The pattern is as follows:

David grows stronger while the house of Saul grows weaker (2 Sam. 3:1).

Harem report (2 Sam. 3:2–5).

David's power grows as God strengthens him (2 Sam. 5:10, 12).

Harem report (2 Sam. 5:13–16).

So when we read of David's great success in empire building in 2 Samuel 8 and 10, we almost expect to read about further additions to the harem. Our expectation is realized as we read of Bathsheba's entry into the harem. David's abuse of power in taking Uriah's wife and life is consistent with the pattern. David's royal position has clearly gone to his head. He acts accordingly and brings his kingdom crashing down around his still intact (by the mercy and covenant faithfulness of God) throne.

Interpretive Insights

11:1 *But David remained in Jerusalem.* The clause structure in the Hebrew text (subject placed before the verb) draws attention to this statement. Following the account of David's great military exploits in 2 Samuel 10:17–18, he appears to be in the wrong place at the wrong time. Sometimes that can prove to be disastrous.

11:2 *he saw a woman bathing.* The only other time the statement "he saw a woman" appears in the Former Prophets is in the story of Samson (Judg. 14:1; 16:1). The story of Samson's death begins ominously with his visit to a Philistine prosti-

tute (16:1). Now 2 Samuel 11 records how David, the new Joshua/Caleb who fearlessly defeated a giant in the name of the Lord, is transformed into a new Samson, whose lust emasculates his military strength.

The woman was very beautiful. The structure of the Hebrew clause (subject first) draws attention to this observation. The description of Bathsheba's physical beauty echoes the description of David when he first appeared in the story (cf. 1 Sam. 16:12). David's gaze falls on one who is every bit his physical equal; he apparently has met his match. Will he succumb to the temptation of using his power to take what he desires?

11:3 *the wife of Uriah.* The servant's identification of the woman as "the wife of Uriah" should stop David in his tracks, for she belongs not only to another man, but to a man who is one of David's very best soldiers (2 Sam. 23:39).

11:4 *David sent messengers to get her.* The Hebrew reads, "sent messengers and took." The verb "took" (*laqah*) was

From the rooftop of his palace David saw a woman bathing. This bath with interior seat may have been used for ritual immersion and purification. It was found near the water libation installation at Tel Dan, Israel (ninth century BC).

also used earlier when David added women to his harem (1 Sam. 25:39–40, 43; 2 Sam. 3:15; 5:13). David's taking Bathsheba is the culmination of a disturbing trend (see comments on 1 Sam. 25:39; see the first two sidebars in the unit on 2 Sam. 2:1–5:5 and the sidebar in the unit on 2 Sam. 5:6–25).

The use of this verb to describe David's greed also links this text with several earlier passages where characters greedily take something: 1 Samuel 2:14 (Eli's sons take meat from the people); 8:3 (Samuel's sons take bribes), 11–16 (the king will take sons, daughters, crops, servants, and livestock); 15:21 (the people take the items devoted to destruction); 2 Samuel 4:7 (the assassins take Ish-bosheth's head in order to impress David). David has suddenly joined a club of miscreants and resembles the hypothetical foreign-looking king described by Samuel.[1]

Now she was purifying herself from her monthly uncleanness. The grammatical structure (subject followed by predicate) indicates that this statement is parenthetical or circumstantial, not part of the main narrative sequence. It informs us of Bathsheba's ritual condition at the time she has relations with David. She is ritually cleansing herself, now that her seven-day period of menstrual impurity has ended. As McCarter explains, this information is significant, for it informs the reader that she is ripe for conception and means that anyone close to the scene will know that Uriah, who is away fighting in Ammon, cannot be responsible for Bathsheba's pregnancy.[2]

11:5 *The woman conceived and sent word.* Prior to this in the chapter, David has "sent" three times (vv. 1, 3–4). This reflects his royal authority: he gives an order, and others carry out his wishes. But David abuses his authority in sending for Bathsheba, and his actions will boomerang. Bathsheba "sent" a message informing David that she is pregnant. This sets in motion a series of devious actions that lead to the murder of Uriah. The deed in turn prompts the Lord to send the prophet Nathan to confront David with his sin (12:1).

11:9 *But Uriah slept at the entrance to the palace.* Uriah refuses to "sleep" (*shakab*) with his own wife (v. 11) while the army is engaged in battle. Instead, for two consecutive nights he sleeps (*shakab*) in the palace among David's servants (vv. 9, 13). The same verb used to describe David's adulterous act with Bathsheba (cf. v. 4, "he slept with her") here epitomizes Uriah's loyalty to his king. David sees the naked Bathsheba "one evening" (v. 2), falls prey to his lust, and commits adultery with her; drunken Uriah resists the temptation to sleep with his wife and sleeps with the servants "in the evening" (v. 13).

11:11 *As surely as you live, I will not do such a thing!* Uriah's words are ironic in two respects and, from the reader's perspective, serve to condemn David: (1) Uriah disobeys the king's command (vv. 8–9), but his defense is a reminder that loyalty to the Lord and his cause (v. 11a) supersedes even royal authority. (2) While Uriah considers it wrong to sleep with his own wife while the army is engaged in Ammon, David has no such qualms. In fact, he even sleeps with *another man's* wife!

11:14 *David wrote a letter to Joab and sent it with Uriah.* David's sending a letter with murderous intent (v. 14) is ironic: years earlier Saul abused his royal authority and sent messengers out with the intent of arresting and killing David (1 Sam. 19:11, 14–15, 20–21). Now David is no longer the victim but has occupied the role of Saul.

11:15 *Then withdraw from him so he will be struck down and die.* David's plan for Uriah's death is absurd, for it will involve telling all the soldiers but Uriah to withdraw at a specified time so he will stand isolated before the enemy. Even if such a plot can be concocted, Uriah will probably retreat when he sees the others turn back. Ironically, in plotting to kill Uriah by putting him in harm's way, David is following in the footsteps of Saul, who tried to kill David by sending him on a difficult mission against the Philistines (1 Sam. 18:25). Earlier David used the verbs "strike down" (*nakah*) and "die/kill" (*mut*) together to describe how he killed predators who threatened his sheep (17:35), and the narrator used them to describe how David struck down Goliath (17:50) and Shobak, the Aramaean general (2 Sam. 10:18). But now David uses them in his order to Joab as he tries to kill, not an enemy, but one of his own loyal soldiers. Rather than being another heroic act on David's part, his murderous action now re-

sembles the deeds of Joab, who "stabbed" (*nakah*) innocent Abner so that he "died" (*mut*; 2 Sam. 3:27), and of the assassins who "stabbed" (*nakah*) and "killed" (*mut*) innocent Ish-bosheth (2 Sam. 4:7).

11:16 *he put Uriah at a place where he knew the strongest defenders were.* Joab recognizes the folly of David's plan, but this loyal general also realizes he must carry out the spirit of his master's command.[3] There is no way Uriah can "safely" die without sacrificing some others as well.

11:25 *Don't let this upset you; the sword devours one as well as another.* Ironically David's proverbial statement will prove to be true in his own family (see 2 Sam. 12:9–10).

11:27 *David had her brought to his house.* Bringing Bathsheba into the palace after the period of mourning might seem to be an act of kindness, but David is seeking to cover his tracks. With Uriah dead and gone, many might assume that sometime during his visit to Jerusalem, he had relations with his wife and fathered a child. But there are several servants who know better. By marrying Bathsheba, the king can silence all doubt and safely claim the child as his own.[4]

But the thing David had done displeased the Lord. David seems to be safe, but then we are reminded that David cannot hide his crimes from the watchful eye of the Lord. David tells Joab, "Don't let this upset you" (Hebrew, "Let this thing not be evil in your eyes"). But the Lord will not be pacified as easily as Joab. Using David's words, the narrator informs us that David's deeds "displeased" the Lord (Hebrew, "The thing that David had done was evil in the eyes of the Lord").

Theological Insights

David violates the seventh (adultery) and tenth (coveting another man's wife) commandments and then, in his attempt to cover his tracks, breaks the sixth (murder) and eighth (theft) as well (Exod. 20:13–15, 17; Deut. 5:17–19, 21).[5] His actions create a theological tension in the developing story line. He clearly violates the law of Moses and is guilty of capital offenses (Lev. 20:10; Num. 35:30–31; Deut. 22:22), yet the Lord has made an irrevocable promise to him, albeit with a stern warning regarding infractions (2 Sam. 7:11–16). So the reader wonders how this tension will be resolved. As the story continues, we see both God's mercy and his discipline revealed as David's reign and dynasty are spared, while at the same time he is punished severely and fairly for his crimes (for further remarks, see chap. 12, under "Theological Insights").

This account reminds us of two important theological truths that permeate Scripture: (1) Fallen human nature is fundamentally flawed and capable of the most heinous crimes. After assuming the throne of Israel, David has been, for the most part, a model of a godly king. But eventually David's power gets the best of him. In the end both his successes and his failures leave us yearning for a godly leader. Surely the exilic readers experience this desire, especially as they reflect on the prophets' visions of an ideal Davidic king to come. (2) The account also reminds us that the omniscient God sees all that human beings do and assesses all that he sees from a moral perspective. He often allows evil actions, but he does not approve of them and holds evildoers accountable for their behavior, as David quickly finds out.

Teaching the Text

1. *Power can be a breeding ground for sin, and sin, once conceived, can consume those who try to cover it up.* This account of David's crimes provides an anatomy of how sin can invade and consume one's soul. David has experienced success and established a model of what a king should be. He seeks God's will, values and celebrates God's presence among his people, responds humbly to God's gracious promise, trusts in God for security, promotes justice, and seeks to mirror God's faithful character in his relationships with others. Yet the potential for self-promotion is present from the beginning of his story (see the second sidebars in the units on 1 Sam. 16, 17, and 18), and David's steady harem building gives the reader reason for pause (see the first two sidebars in the unit on 2 Sam. 2:1–5:5 and the sidebar in the unit on 2 Sam. 5:6–25). In reality, David, like all of us, is always one step away from disaster. Sometimes possessing power becomes the catalyst for taking that disastrous step. When David sees what he wants, he takes what he wants because he has the power to do so. Realizing that his royal position is in jeopardy because of his sinful act, he then becomes obsessed with retaining his power and image at all costs, much like Saul before him. One crime leads to another as his sin snowballs. As we will see in chapter 12, he even becomes calloused to his sin, though he remains quite capable of self-righteously denouncing sin in others. In short, David's tragic collapse illustrates vividly the truth of James 1:14–15: temptation prompts desire, which gives birth to sin, which produces death. As we will see with David, only the mercy of God can spare one from the ultimate deadly consequence of sin.

2. *We cannot hide our sin from God.* In an effort to retain his power, David desperately scrambles to cover up his crimes. Just when it looks as if he has succeeded (aided by the cooperation of Joab and the silence of Bathsheba), the narrator introduces the Lord into the story, who has been strangely absent throughout this chapter. If David somehow thinks that the ark's presence with the army in Ammon (v. 11) means that the Lord himself is out of town, he is in for a rude awakening. As David points out in one of his psalms, no one can escape God's notice, even by fleeing to the ends of the earth or hiding in the darkness (Ps. 139:7–12). As David declares in another of his poetic compositions, the Lord looks down from his heavenly throne and sees all that happens on the earth (Ps. 11:4). He assesses people's actions in light of his moral standards and gives both the righteous and the wicked what they deserve (vv. 5–7).

David orchestrated Uriah's death as a cover-up for his sin with Bathsheba. While the Israelite army was besieging the city of Rabbah (modern Amman, Jordan), Uriah was killed as the battle drew close to the city wall. Archaeological excavations show that Rabbah-Amman has been continuously occupied since the tenth millennium BC. The most visible remains are from the Roman, Byzantine, and Arabic occupations. Shown here are Roman walls at the Amman Citadel, which in some sections have been built above Iron Age and Middle Bronze Age structures.

Illustrating the Text

Power can breed sin, and sin can consume the sinner.

Christian Autobiography: *Born Again*, by Chuck Colson. In 1974 Colson pleaded guilty to Watergate-related offenses and, after a volatile investigation, served seven months in prison. In the wake of his search for meaning and purpose, Colson wrote the book *Born Again* (1976). In it he discusses the political scandal and its effects, including the resignation of President Richard M. Nixon on August 9, 1974. The event is an example of the corrupting nature of power.

We must remember that God's omniscience extends to everything we do, even in secret.

Bible: "Omniscient" is a word that means "knowing everything." Scripture declares that God's eyes see everywhere (Job 24:23; Pss. 33:13–15; 139:13–16; Prov. 15:3; Jer. 16:17; Heb. 4:13). He searches all hearts and observes everyone's ways (1 Sam. 16:7; 1 Kings 8:39; 1 Chron. 28:9; Ps. 139:1–6, 23; Jer. 17:10; Luke 16:15; Rom. 8:27; Rev. 2:23). In other words, he knows everything about everything and everybody all the time.[6]

"Your Sin Will Find You Out":
The Lord Confronts His Sinful Servant

Big Idea *The Lord disciplines his sinful servants but also extends forgiveness and mercy.*

Understanding the Text

The Text in Context

Thanks to the help of Joab and the silence of Bathsheba, David appeared to get away with the murder of Uriah and even ended up adding Uriah's beautiful wife to his harem. But the last words of chapter 11 suggest that the story will take a turn for the worse for David. Chapter 12 tells how the Lord confronts David with his sin. The Lord announces that he will severely punish David, and the rest of the story focuses on the tragic consequences of David's sin and records how David pays his own self-imposed fourfold penalty in full (12:6). Yet there is also a silver lining: the Lord tempers his punishment of David with mercy, and the rest of the story shows how the Lord preserves both David's life and his dynasty. The Davidic covenant promises are not cancelled by David's disobedience. In this respect, this chapter and those that follow contribute, oddly enough, to the narrator's apology for David. Yes, David disobeys the Lord and is severely punished for his crimes, but in contrast to the Lord's treatment of Saul, the Lord does not reject his dynasty or remove him from the throne. Indeed, the fact that David's throne remains secure, in spite of his heinous sin and its consequences, is proof of God's commitment to him.

Historical and Cultural Background

When David's baby dies, he laments, "I will go to him, but he will not return to me" (v. 23). This is a statement not of hope, but of finality. David understands that no one returns from the land of the dead. Passage between the realms of the living and the dead is strictly one direction. In ancient Mesopotamian texts, the subterranean world of the dead is called "the land of no return." Seven gates close behind the one who enters this land, preventing a return to the land of the living (cf. Pss. 9:13; 107:18; Jon. 2:6; see "The Descent of Ishtar to the Underworld," *COS*, 1:381–84).

Interpretive Insights

12:1 *The Lord sent Nathan to David.* In chapter 11 David twice "sent" for Bathsheba—the first time to sin with her (v. 3), the second time to cover up his sin (v. 27). He "sent" for Uriah in an effort to cover his sinful tracks (v. 6) and then "sent" him back to Joab, carrying his own death warrant (v. 14). His sending reflects his royal authority: he just speaks a word, and others respond to carry out his wishes. But there is one who has authority even over the king. Displeased with David's actions (11:27), the Lord "sent" his prophet Nathan to confront David.[1]

12:3 *and even slept in his arms.* The description of the little lamb is dripping with irony and double meaning. The man would let the lamb sleep in his arms. Nathan uses the word *shakab*, "sleep, lie down," the same verb used to describe how David "slept" with Bathsheba (11:4). The poor man's lamb was "like a daughter to him." The word *bat*, "daughter," echoes Bathsheba's name (*bat-sheba'*).

12:4 *he took the ewe lamb that belonged to the poor man.* Again Nathan uses irony and double meaning. The verb "took" (*laqah*) is the same one used to describe how David took Bathsheba and slept with her (cf. 11:4). Nathan uses a story about abuse of power rather than one about adultery and murder, because such abuse is at the core of David's crimes.

12:5 *the man who did this must die!* The Hebrew text calls the perpetrator

"a son of death." This phrase is used in only two other passages (1 Sam. 20:31; 26:16). In 1 Samuel 20:31 Saul calls David a "son of death" (AT), one doomed to die by royal decree. Now, ironically, David unwittingly characterizes himself in this same way. David did not deserve death on that earlier occasion, but now he does (cf. Num. 35:30–31).

12:6 *He must pay for that lamb four times over.* Uriah unknowingly carried his own death warrant back to Joab; now David unwittingly pronounces his own sentence, confirming it by prefacing to it an especially emphatic oath formula.[2] The legal background for David's decision is found in Exodus 22:1, which states that one who steals a sheep must repay the owner's loss fourfold. The fulfillment of the sentence comes in the following chapters, as David loses four sons: the anonymous child to whom Bathsheba gives birth, Amnon, Absalom, and Adonijah.[3] All die prematurely, the last three by violence/ murder. Absalom, David's

One of the characters in the story Nathan tells to point out David's sin is a poor man who owns only one little ewe lamb. This Sumerian statue shows a person holding a small sheep (second millennium BC).

favorite, is killed, like Uriah, through the instrumentality of the cruelly devoted Joab (2 Sam. 18:14).

12:7 *This is what the* LORD, *the God of Israel, says.* Nathan's use of this introductory formula is ironic. The last time David heard such a formula from Nathan was when the prophet announced to him the Lord's promise of an enduring dynasty (2 Sam. 7:5, 8), which includes provisions for how rebellion will be handled. Now the time has come for those provisions to be implemented. On that earlier occasion, the Lord's announcement included a rehearsal of all that the Lord had done on David's behalf (7:8–9), just as this announcement does (12:7–8).

12:9 *Why did you despise the word of the* LORD . . . ? The Lord accuses David of despising his word, which is the same as despising his very person (v. 10). The verb used here (*bazah*) also appears in 1 Samuel 2:30 in the Lord's denunciation of Eli. The association with Eli and his sons does not bode well for David.

by doing what is evil in his eyes. David has despised the Lord's word by committing murder and theft. The expression, "do what is evil in the eyes of" the Lord, occurs on one other occasion in 1–2 Samuel. Samuel accused Saul of doing "evil in the eyes of the LORD" when he failed to wipe out the Amalekites (1 Sam. 15:19). Moving further back in the Former Prophets, we see that the expression appears frequently in Judges to characterize sinful Israel (2:11; 3:7, 12; 4:1; 6:1; 10:6; 13:1). The intertextual linking with Saul and with idolatrous Israel of the judges' period does not bode well for David.

Because David orchestrated Uriah's death, he was held just as responsible as the Ammonites who actually killed him. According to 2 Samuel 11:24, Uriah was killed as the army drew close to the city and became targets for archers on the city walls. This Assyrian relief shows a city under siege with archers on the walls (palace at Nimrud, 728 BC).

You struck down Uriah the Hittite with the sword. The only time the expression "strike down with the sword" occurs prior to this in 1–2 Samuel is in 1 Samuel 22:19, where Doeg, acting on Saul's orders (v. 18), slaughtered the inhabitants of Nob. The intertextual linking with Doeg/Saul does not bode well for David.

and took his wife to be your own. From the Lord's perspective, David's marriage to Bathsheba is an act of theft because only the murder of Uriah makes it possible. Once again the verb "took" (*laqah*) is used of David (see also v. 10), linking him with others who are described as greedily taking something (see the comment above on 11:4).

with the sword of the Ammonites. From the Lord's perspective the Ammonite warriors who cut Uriah down were a mere instrument in David's hands.

12:10 *the sword will never depart from your house.* Poetic justice characterizes the Lord's punishment of David. David (not the Ammonites or even Joab) has killed Uriah, and now the sword will devastate David's house. Three of David's sons later die violent deaths (2 Sam. 13:28–29; 18:14; 1 Kings 2:24–25): Absalom kills his rival Amnon, and Solomon kills his rival Adonijah, both doing so through the instrumentality of another. Joab, who arranged the death of Uriah, later kills Absalom.

12:11 *I will take your wives and give them to one who is close to you.* This is fulfilled when Absalom rebels against his father and violates the royal harem (2 Sam. 16:22). David slept with Uriah's wife (v. 12), so one who is close to him (his own son!) will "lie" (*shakab* again; cf. 11:4) with his wives. David's sin was in secret, but this humiliating punishment will occur in broad daylight for all Israel to see. The Lord's use of the word "take" (*laqah*) echoes David's crime (cf. 12:9–10) and contributes to the theme of poetic justice.

12:13 *I have sinned against the LORD.* On the one hand, David's confession of his guilt places him in bad company. In the Former Prophets to this point, the only individuals to say the words "I have sinned" are Saul (1 Sam. 15:24, 30; 26:21) and Achan (Josh. 7:20). On an earlier occasion David was able to say to Saul, "I have not sinned" (1 Sam. 24:11), but he cannot claim innocence now. On the other hand, his confession of his guilt, without any attempt to deny wrongdoing or to justify his actions, sets him apart from his predecessor (1 Sam. 13:11–12; 15:13–25).

The LORD has taken away your sin. In this case, divine forgiveness does not entail a dismissal of charges or an elimination of all consequences. It simply means a reduced sentence: David's life will be preserved. But there will still be severe consequences. In addition to those already outlined (vv. 10–12), the baby born to David and Bathsheba will die (v. 14).

12:14 *you have shown utter contempt for the LORD.* There is an echo of the narrator's description of Eli's sons, who treated the Lord's offering with contempt (1 Sam. 2:17). The charge of treating the Lord with contempt is serious, for elsewhere those who do so are evil and enemies of God (Pss. 10:3, 13; 74:10, 18; Isa. 1:4) and receive severe punishment (Num. 14:23; 16:30).

12:15 *the LORD struck the child.* The Lord struck (*nagap*) Nabal (1 Sam. 25:38), and David anticipated that he would strike Saul (1 Sam. 26:10). But now, ironically, the verb is used with David's child as the object. Actions directed toward David's enemies in the past are now directed toward David.

12:16 *David pleaded with God for the child.* As David later explains (v. 22), he is not sure if the pronouncement in verse 14 is implicitly conditional. His earlier oath in verse 5 unconditionally condemns four sons ("lambs"), but he still hopes that this child will not need to be one of the casualties.

spent the nights lying in sackcloth on the ground. There may be an echo here of David's sin. He had "slept" (*shakab*) with Bathsheba (11:4); now he is "lying" (*shakab*) on the ground before the Lord, confronted with the harsh consequences of his sin.[4]

12:25 *he sent word through Nathan.* Earlier the Lord "sent" Nathan to confront

David and pronounce his penalty, but now he sends word to David to name this next son Jedidiah, "loved by the Lord" (NIV mg.). This act of sending counterbalances the earlier one (see the comments on v. 1 above) and tempers divine discipline with mercy.[5]

12:29 *David mustered the entire army and went to Rabbah, and attacked and captured it.* We have heard this language used to describe David's victory before (cf. 1 Sam. 17:32; 23:5; 2 Sam. 5:7; 8:4). David is again doing what he does best: fighting the wars of the Lord.

Theological Insights

The Lord's response to David's sins reveals much about his justice and mercy: (1) The Lord confronts his servants when they rebel against him (Heb. 12:8). (2) The Lord's discipline is just and can be very severe. (3) The Lord is willing to forgive his repentant servants, yet forgiveness does not necessarily mean that all consequences are eliminated. (4) The Lord ultimately assures his repentant servants of his continuing love. For the exiles, the first two principles are all too clear in their experience.

The Lord has confronted their fathers through his prophets and has disciplined his covenant people by sending them into exile. Those who have confessed their sin and sought reconciliation with the Lord are very much aware that forgiveness does not erase all consequences. But the Lord's naming of Jedidiah (Solomon) encourages them, for it is a reminder of the Lord's enduring love for both David and Israel (cf. 2 Sam. 7:22–24).

Teaching the Text

1. *The Lord disciplines his sinful servants, sometimes severely, because he is a just God and must punish wrongdoing appropriately.* David treated the Lord with contempt by blatantly violating four of the Ten Commandments. The Lord is not about to let him go unpunished. The Lord's disciplinary judgment is appropriate and fair, mirroring David's sin in several respects. David's sons will perpetuate his crimes of sex and violence. As the patriarch Jacob learned many years before David, what goes around comes around in God's moral supervision of his world: those who sow discord will eventually reap it (Prov. 22:8; Hosea 10:13; Gal. 6:7–8).

2. *The Lord is willing to extend his forgiveness and mercy to his repentant servants because he is a faithful God whose love for his covenant people is enduring.* To David's credit, he confesses his sin when Nathan confronts him. (Psalm 51 expresses

David conquered Rabbah and took the king's crown. This Iron Age II basalt figure wearing an Egyptian-style headdress may be an Ammonite king or god (eighth to seventh century BC).

the emotions he feels on that occasion.) The Lord extends forgiveness to David, yet forgiveness does not erase all the consequences of his sin. Nevertheless it does release David from the punishment his capital crime deserves, and it preserves his life, as well as his royal position. (Psalm 32 may express the sense of relief that he experienced at this time.) Furthermore, the Lord softens the pain of his discipline by giving David and Bathsheba another son shortly after the death of their infant son. The Lord even makes this child the special object of his love, assuring David of his enduring love and his commitment to David's dynasty.

On what basis does the Lord forgive David? Though Nathan does not say in this passage, it seems, based on 2 Samuel 7, that his covenantal commitment to David, rooted in his sovereign choice of David, prompts the Lord to extend forgiveness to one so unworthy of his mercy. The Old Testament affirms that by his very nature the Lord is a forgiving God (Exod. 34:6–7; Num. 14:19; Mic. 7:18–19). His forgiveness arises out of his compassion, grace, patience, and faithful love (cf. Neh. 9:17; Pss. 86:15; 103:8–10; 145:8; Joel 2:13; Jon. 4:2). Although God's very nature predisposes him to forgive his sinful people when they repent (cf. Ezek. 33:11), his covenant promises and his concern for his reputation also motivate him in this direction. When interceding for future sinful generations, Solomon reminds the Lord that Israel is his people and his inheritance, whom he has taken for himself from Egypt (1 Kings 8:51). Micah 7:18–20 relates God's merciful, loving forgiveness with his unconditional promises to the fathers.

Illustrating the Text

Divine discipline is severe even when forgiveness is extended.

Literature: *King Lear,* by William Shakespeare. This play (1608), viewed by many as full of biblical allusions, is a study in the consequences of King Lear's fatal pride and his humiliation. When the play opens, the eighty-year-old king is blinded by power and selfishly requires tangible expressions of love and devotion from his three daughters. Two of them, Goneril and Regan, accommodate to what he wants; Cordelia, in her genuine love, refuses sentimentality. Lear is too self-absorbed to appreciate true goodness and banishes Cordelia. Then his life unravels. Through a series of dark circumstances, Lear is humbled and turns to God in prayer. However, though he is changed by divine forgiveness, the consequences of his selfish life are tragic: at the end, Cordelia dies. Lear cries out, "Howl, howl, howl, howl! O, you are men of stones: / Had I your tongues and eyes, I'd use them so / That heaven's vault should crack" (act 5, scene 3).

The Lord's predisposition is to forgive because he is faithful to his covenant promises.

Contemporary Song Lyrics: "*You Take Me Back,*" by Jeremy Camp.

Prayer: *The Prayers of Peter Marshall,* by Peter Marshall. Marshall (1902–49) was a prominent preacher and for a time was chaplain of the US Senate. In one prayer, Marshall prays to God the Father as a prodigal child, acknowledging his sin and asking for God's love.[6]

You Reap What You Sow

Big Idea *The Lord ensures that justice is satisfied, sometimes by allowing one's children to repeat the parent's sins.*

Understanding the Text

The Text in Context

The Lord confronted David with his sin and announced that he would severely punish him. Through Nathan's entrapment technique, he even maneuvered David into imposing his own penalty. David must pay fourfold for his theft of Uriah's wife (2 Sam. 12:6). The first installment of this payment came almost immediately, as the first baby born to Bathsheba and David died. Now in chapter 13 David makes the second installment as his children follow in his footsteps. The third and fourth installments are made in later episodes of the unfolding history.

Interpretive Insights

13:1 *Amnon son of David fell in love with Tamar, the beautiful sister of Absalom son of David.* The text goes out of its way to emphasize that Amnon and Tamar are siblings (actually, half siblings). Both the narrator (v. 2) and Amnon (vv. 6, 11; cf. v. 5 as well) refer to Tamar as Amnon's "sister." David (v. 7), the narrator (vv. 8, 10), Tamar (v. 12), and Absalom (v. 20) all refer to Amnon as Tamar's "brother." At the very

least, this highlights the fact that Amnon violates a member of his own family.

13:4 *Why do you, the king's son, look so haggard?* Jonadab's question hints at the privileges that Amnon enjoys as the king's son, yet Amnon has become obsessed with the one thing that he seemingly cannot have, his half sister Tamar. We have seen the pattern before. David has several wives and concubines to satisfy his physical desires (5:13; 12:8), but he greedily grabs a woman who is off-limits to him. Amnon will repeat his father's sin.

13:7 *David sent word.* This is another echo of David's crimes that reverberates throughout the chapter. David, who sent (*shalah*) for Bathsheba (11:4) and then sent her husband to his death (11:14–15), plays a role, albeit unwittingly, in both of his sons' crimes. He sends a message instructing Tamar to go to Amnon's house, where she is raped, and then later sends Amnon to his demise (v. 27). In chapter 11 the narrator portrayed David as possessing absolute sovereignty: he sent people where he willed (vv. 1, 3–4, 12, 27) and by a mere message accomplished his desires (vv. 6, 14). But he used his power to satisfy his lust and cover up his crime. In chapter 13 he continues to exercise his authority over others, but now it backfires against him as the Lord providentially oversees the fulfillment of David's self-imposed penalty.

13:11 *Come to bed with me, my sister.* This is another echo of David's sin. The verb "lie down, sleep" (*shakab*), used of David's intercourse with Bathsheba (11:4), appears five times in verses 5–14, twice with a sexual connotation (vv. 11, 14).

13:12 *No, my brother!* Among several parallels between the account of the rape of the Levite's concubine (Judg. 19–21) and this account of the rape of Tamar, the most striking are these:[1]

1. Both acts are called an "outrageous/wicked thing" (*nebalah*; Judg. 19:23–24).
2. Israel's horrified response to the concubine's murder (Judg. 19:30) sounds much like Tamar's appeal to Amnon: "Such a thing should not be done in Israel!"
3. Both passages use the same Hebrew verb (*'innah*, "abuse, humiliate") to describe the crime (cf. Judg. 19:24; 20:5 with 2 Sam. 13:12, 14, 22, 32).
4. The Ephraimite's appeal to the men of Gibeah (Judg. 19:23) is structurally identical to Tamar's words to

Key Themes of 2 Samuel 13

- David's sons repeat their father's sins, and a new period of moral chaos begins to engulf Israel due to David's refusal to punish their crimes.
- David pays the second installment of the self-imposed penalty for his crimes.

Amnon (2 Sam. 13:12). This expression ("No, my brother[s]!" plus a prohibition) occurs nowhere else in the Old Testament but in these two texts.

5. Both Amnon and the men of Gibeah reject the warning given to them (Judg. 19:25; 2 Sam. 13:14, 16).
6. After raping Tamar, Amnon callously tells her, "Get up and get out!" (2 Sam. 13:15). His words (*qum* and *halak*) echo the Levite's statement to his concubine the morning after her horrible experience: "Get up; let's go!" (Judg. 19:28).

The narrator seems to subtitle Amnon's rape of Tamar as "Gibeah Revisited" (which itself was Sodom revisited).

13:13 *You would be like one of the wicked fools in Israel.* The term translated "wicked fools" is *nabal*, which echoes the name of Nabal, who foolishly opposed David (1 Sam. 25:25). Ironically, such folly now characterizes the royal house. Adding to the irony is the fact that Amnon is following the "wise" advice of Jonadab, whom the narrator sarcastically calls "a very shrewd [or, "wise"] man" (v. 3). The royal house has become a place where wisdom is perverted, along with morality.[2]

13:15 *hated her with intense hatred.* Just as Amnon, instigated by his shrewd friend Jonadab, perverts genuine wisdom (see comment on v. 13 above), so he perverts genuine love. The love he feels toward Tamar (v. 1) is mere physical lust, as implied in verse 1 by the reference to Tamar's beauty and as demonstrated by his later actions. Once he has satisfied his lust, he is ready to cast her off. She now has no identity in his eyes; as a mere object of his satisfied lust, she is simply "this woman" (v. 17).[3]

13:21 *he was furious.* David should reprimand his son in some tangible way. But David responds passively: he simply becomes angry.[4] The original text (preserved in the LXX) specifically states that he does not reprimand Amnon because, as his firstborn son, he is loved by David.[5] His passivity in dealing with Amnon will come back to haunt him when Absalom takes matters into his own hands. By refusing to punish Amnon, David refuses to defend the rights of his daughter Tamar.[6] Nevertheless, Tamar is eventually vindicated, at least to some degree (see v. 31).

13:27 *so he sent with him Amnon.* There is an echo of David's crime (11:4; see the comment on v. 7 above), as well as an echo of Amnon's. David unwittingly sends the unsuspecting Tamar to her demise at Amnon's request (v. 7); now he unwittingly sends the unsuspecting Amnon to his demise at the urging of Tamar's brother, Absalom.

13:28 *"Strike Amnon down," then kill him.* This is another echo of David's crime,

Absalom invited the sons of David to a sheepshearing celebration at Baal Hazor, where he killed Amnon. This is an aerial view of the area around Baal Hazor.

driving home the point that Amnon's death is part of the penalty for his sin. David told Joab to draw back from Uriah so he would be "struck down and die" (11:15). These same verbs (*nakah* and *mut*) appear in Absalom's instructions to his men.

Be strong. Absalom's exhortation to his men, which follows his command to murder Amnon, echoes David's calloused command to Joab following the murder of Uriah (11:25; the verb *hazaq* is used in both texts).[7] This reverberation of David's crime suggests that the son is repeating his father's crime and contributes to the theme of poetic justice.

13:31 *tore his clothes.* Tamar's vindication begins. In the aftermath of her rape, she tears her robe, the symbol of her virginity, to express her outrage and grief (vv. 18–19). Now David, who has not defended her honor, tears his garments in sorrow over the news of Amnon's death.

and lay down on the ground. Earlier David assumed this posture as he begged the Lord to spare the infant's life (12:16); now he assumes it again as he mourns the death of Amnon. The verbal repetition links the deaths of the infant and of Amnon, reminding us that they are the first two installments paid by David for his crimes.

13:32 *Jonadab son of Shimeah.* David's nephew Jonadab (see v. 3) is a literary foil for David in this chapter. In chapter 11 David was the instigator of the plot against Uriah and utilized his power to carry out his deceptive plan. But here in chapter 13 he is on the outside and looking in. He allows his royal authority to be exploited to deceptive ends but is not aware of his sons' plots until it is too late. By way of contrast,

The Legal Background of Tamar's Request

According to the Mosaic law, a man is forbidden from having sexual relations with his sister, whether a half sister (daughter of one's father only) or a full sister (daughter of both parents). Violation of this law is a serious, perhaps even capital, offense (Lev. 18:9, 11; 20:17; Deut. 27:22 [cf. Ezek. 22:11]).[a] Rape of a virgin is a crime but not a capital offense. The violator must pay a monetary fine and marry the victim (Deut. 22:28–29).

In light of these laws, how are we to interpret Tamar's arguments (2 Sam. 13:13, 16)? If we take them at face value, it seems that (1) Amnon could have asked David for her hand in marriage and (2) Amnon could have married her after the rape without further repercussions. In fact, her argument in verse 16 may reflect the law pertaining to the rape of a virgin (Deut. 22:28–29). Her initial reaction to Amnon's aggression is shock. She knows the law and is outraged that he would even think of committing an incestuous act with her (v. 12). However, frightened by the prospect of being raped, perhaps she attempts to deflect Amnon's aggression by suggesting that he could ask the king for her hand in marriage. The king would probably refuse to do so, but does Amnon realize that? Amnon obviously has little, if any, regard for the law; perhaps he would fail to see the flaw in her proposal, and she could escape. Following the rape, her first inclination is to protect her honor and her future. She knows a sibling marriage is out of the question legally, but her emotions overpower her reason as she demands that Amnon marry her and not cast her out to a life of shame and unfulfilled womanhood.

---

[a] The penalty for persons who violate this law is to "be cut off from their people" (Lev. 18:29), to "be publicly removed from their people" (20:17). According to Deut. 27:22, such an individual is "cursed." However, it is uncertain what specific form this penalty is to take. Options include capital punishment (though Lev. 20:2–5 seems to distinguish between being "cut off" by God and being "put to death" by the community), excommunication from the community, and direct punishment by God in the form of premature death. Wenham (*The Book of Leviticus*, 285–86) prefers the third option. Another possibility is that the guilty party's "line is terminated," a punishment carried out by God. See Milgrom, *Leviticus*, 66.

the crafty Jonadab is on the inside. He helps Amnon instigate his deception and is aware of Absalom's intentions to avenge his sister. As a foil, his awareness serves to highlight David's ignorance and helplessness before the inexorable providence of God. Others know of Absalom's intentions but do not communicate this important fact to the king.

13:36 *wept very bitterly*. This is another link with the death of David's infant son. On that earlier occasion he "wept" (12:21–22) as he begged the Lord to spare the child; now he weeps again over Amnon's death (cf. v. 31).

13:39 *longed to go to Absalom*. Being a pardoned capital offender himself, David finds it impossible to execute justice against another capital offender who also happens to be a family member.

Theological Insights

As noted earlier (see the comment above on 11:2), the narrator casts David in the role of a second Samson. David's Samson-like sin brings into the royal house the kind of chaos typical of the judges' period. Soon after that, chaos spreads to the whole nation when Absalom starts a civil war (cf. Judg. 20–21).

The Lord's justice is clearly at work in this chapter. Installment two of David's self-imposed fourfold penalty is paid (cf. 12:6): Absalom murders Amnon for raping his sister Tamar. There are echoes of David's crimes in both the rape of Tamar and the murder of Amnon, driving home the point that divine justice is indeed being satisfied. Divine justice is also apparent when the pain of Tamar, whose just cause David ignores, is repeated in David's experience (13:31; see comment above). Divine providence is also an important theme here. Though some are aware of Absalom's murderous intentions, David is kept in the dark until it is too late to prevent the crime.

The story is certainly relevant to its exilic readers, for they too are experiencing the consequences of sin—both their own and their fathers'. The account is a sobering reminder of the warning in Exodus 20:5 (cf. Deut. 5:9): those who oppose God experience divine punishment throughout their lifetime (that is, to the third and fourth generations) and witness the consequences of their rebellion among their children.

Teaching the Text

1. *Divine justice is satisfied, even when human justice fails*. David pays installment two of his self-imposed penalty. In the process Nathan's prophecy that the sword will not depart from David's house proves true (cf. 12:10).[8] David's crimes of sexual sin and murder are repeated as Amnon's unbridled lust leads him to violate Tamar, prompting Absalom's deceptive murder of his brother. David fails to bring either of his sons to justice; yet this breakdown of human justice does not impede divine justice, which is being inexorably satisfied by divine providence. Ironically and tragically, David's failure to hold Amnon accountable for his crime actually facilitates the outworking of divine justice. His paralysis prompts Absalom to seek vengeance against Amnon and then eventually to challenge the royal authority of his father, whom he views as a dismal failure in carrying out his royal responsibility to establish justice in the land (see 15:3–4).

In all of this one surely must not overlook the fact that human sin typically brings with it collateral damage: innocent people suffer due to the evil actions of others. In David's case, the life of his daughter Tamar is ruined. Yet even here divine justice is evident as her intense pain (13:19) becomes a reality in David's life in the aftermath of Amnon's murder (vv. 31, 36) and, later, after the death of Absalom (18:33–19:4).

2. *Sometimes the most painful aspect of divine discipline is when the Lord allows the children to repeat the sins of the parents.* As noted above, one sees the outworking of divine justice and divine providence in the death of Amnon. But one should not view this in an overly deterministic manner. The Lord often works out his purposes in the world through human instruments. In some cases he simply allows them to act in accordance with their nature, without violating their freedom in any way. The Lord does not make Amnon or Absalom act contrary to their sinful nature. Children are predisposed to follow the example of their parents, whether for good or evil. David, by sinning in the way he did, planted the seeds for what subsequently happens within his family. The unbridled lust and abuse of power that he exhibited in the Bathsheba affair surfaces in his son Amnon, and the deceit and capacity to murder that he exhibited in the Uriah matter surfaces in his son Absalom. In both cases, the acorn does not fall far from the tree.

Illustrating the Text

Divine justice is satisfied even when human justice fails.

Church History: As in the case of David long ago, we know that Christians are not exempt from hurting others, from cheating and deceiving their public. In the last two decades we have heard the stories of Jim and Tammy Bakker, Jimmy Swaggart, other televangelists, and contemporary musicians who took enormous donations while lining their pockets and living lavishly, some of them even committing serious moral indiscretions. The Catholic Church presently struggles with its priests who have abused children and teenagers. Divine justice is being served: the reputation of some of those who have committed such violations are ruined. God, in reality, is not mocked.

Quote: *Creation in Christ*, by George Mac-Donald. MacDonald (1824–1905) asserts,

> Justice demands your punishment, because justice demands, and will have the destruction of sin. . . . God, being the God of justice, that is of fair-play, and having made us what we are, apt to fall and capable of being raised again, is in Himself bound to punish in order to deliver us—else is His relation to us poor beside that of an earthly father.[9]

It is a horror to parents to see their children repeat their own sins.

Lyrics: "Cat's in the Cradle," by Harry Chapin. In this, his most famous song (1974), Chapin (1942–81) writes the story of a father who has been too busy to attend to his son, to talk to him, or to spend time with him. He keeps promising the boy that they will get together and have some good times. In the refrain, the child, from the time he is small, responds that he wants to be like his father. As his son grows up, the dad finally wants to spend time with him, but as predicted, that child has become just like dad and is more interested in his own life. The father's recognition is seen in the poignant final lines.

A Prodigal Son Comes Home in Body, but Not in Spirit

Big Idea *One's failure to do what is just can have serious personal repercussions.*

Understanding the Text

The Text in Context

After the murder of Amnon, Absalom found asylum with his maternal grandfather, the king of Geshur (13:37–38; cf. 3:3). After three years, David calmed down and no longer desired to take hostile action against Absalom (13:39). Sensing an opening, Joab now works hard to persuade David to let Absalom come home. David agrees, but he does not reinstate Absalom to the royal court right away. Eventually, however, he accepts Absalom fully, again at the instigation of Joab. This sets the stage for Absalom's rebellion, which forces David to flee the city and brings about the death of Absalom, the third installment of David's self-imposed penalty. The close literary linking of Joab and Absalom prompts one to look back in the story, for both are murderers whom David treats leniently. Yet the literary link also has a foreshadowing function, for Joab will eventually kill the rebel Absalom.

Historical and Cultural Background

Absalom accuses his father of failing to fulfill his royal responsibility of promoting justice in the land and presents himself as a champion of justice (15:3–6). In the ancient Near Eastern world, one of a king's primary responsibilities is to promote and execute justice in his realm.[1] If a king fails to do so, he is considered unfit to rule. A good illustration of this can be seen in the Ugaritic Kirta Epic, which tells how King Kirta's son Yatsubu accuses his ill father of neglecting justice and declares his intention

Absalom accuses David of neglecting his responsibility to administer justice in Israel. This was an important role for a king in the ancient Near East. This relief from the top of the Hammurabi Law Stele shows Hammurabi giving an account of his acts of justice to the god Shamash.

to take the throne: "You let your hands fall slack; you do not judge the widow's case, you do not make a decision regarding the oppressed, and you do not cast out those who prey upon the poor. Before you, you do not feed the orphan, behind your back the widow. . . . So descend from your kingship, I will reign" (COS, 1:342).

Interpretive Insights

14:1 *Joab . . . knew.* We are not told Joab's motives. We do know that throughout the story Joab has acted in a way that he perceives is in David's (and his own) best interests. A careful examination of the Tekoan woman's speech suggests that Joab is concerned that the death of Amnon, followed by the banishing of Absalom, has jeopardized the dynasty in some way (v. 7). David has other sons who are close to Absalom in age (3:2–5), but perhaps Joab regards them as less-worthy candidates to succeed their father (see comments on v. 25 below).

14:2 *Joab . . . had a wise woman brought from there.* In the preceding chapter, Amnon followed the advice of the "wise man" Jonadab to trick his father (13:3–5). Now Joab uses a "wise woman" in his attempt to trick the king. David's royal court is depicted as a place where wisdom is perverted and used for deceptive purposes. Yet David himself has set this pattern of deceit in his handling of Uriah. Once again, so-called wisdom is turned on its head: David accepts advice that is anything but wise (see 14:13–14).

14:17 *like an angel of God in discerning good and evil.* Such discernment is viewed as a fundamental characteristic of wisdom (see v. 20; cf. Gen. 3:5–6) and as something possessed by divine beings (cf. Gen. 3:5,

Key Themes of 2 Samuel 14:1–15:12

- Joab is responsible for Absalom's return to Jerusalem and his reinstatement within the royal court.
- Exploiting his father's weakness, Absalom promotes himself as king.

22; Prov. 30:3). Ironically, David's decision to restore the murderer Absalom, like his earlier one regarding the murderer Joab, proves that he does not possess such discernment. (For fuller discussion, see under "Theological Insights" below.)

14:20 *he knows everything that happens in the land.* Again the woman's (really Joab's) claim is ironic, for the narrator depicts David as one who is ignorant of what is going on around him and who discovers the truth only once it is too late.

14:25 *In all Israel there was not a man so highly praised for his handsome appearance as Absalom.* At this point the narrator stops and comments on Absalom's physical appearance, his abundant hair, and his children. These details may seem irrelevant to the story line, but they do have a foreshadowing function. Absalom's physical appeal makes him a prime candidate for king, given the human tendency to judge on the basis of outward appearances (see 1 Sam. 16:7). He already has three sons (14:27), demonstrating his capacity to establish a royal dynasty.[2] He also has a beautiful daughter named Tamar, apparently the namesake of her unfortunate aunt. This seemingly incidental detail forces us to recall what happened to Absalom's sister and reminds us of how Absalom, from his perspective, took justice into his own hands due to his father's paralysis. Soon Absalom will present himself as the true champion of justice (see 2 Sam. 15:1–6).

14:30 *Go and set it on fire.* The incident depicts Absalom (once again!) as one who is not afraid to resort to destructive and risky measures to get his own way.[3] His behavior here and in the following account may contain echoes of less-than-admirable characters that have appeared in the pages of the Former Prophets. Like Absalom, Abimelek committed fratricide (Judg. 9:1–6), promoted himself as king, and set fire to the property of others (v. 49). Like long-haired Absalom (cf. 2 Sam. 14:26), long-haired Samson set fire to a grainfield when he felt he had been treated with disrespect (Judg. 15:3–5). If these are indeed echoes, the intertextual linking does not bode well for Absalom, for the rash behavior of Abimelek and that of Samson both prove to be self-destructive.

14:32 *if I am guilty of anything, let him put me to death.* This can be interpreted in one of two ways: (1) Absalom regards himself as innocent of any wrongdoing in the matter of Amnon, or (2) he is convinced that his weak-willed, indulgent father will never punish him. In either case, he desires his innocence to be established legally.

14:33 *And the king kissed Absalom.* Not knowing the extent of Absalom's bitterness and ambition, David unwittingly opens the door to a rebellion. Worse yet, by reinstating Absalom, he overlooks Absalom's guilt and by default, like it or not, condones Absalom's murder of Amnon. In his intercession on behalf of Absalom, Joab has not even gone this far. In the story he gives the woman to tell, Absalom's guilt is obvious,

To get Joab's attention, Absalom orders his servants to set Joab's barley fields on fire. Shown here is a barley field in Israel.

as the clan's reaction makes clear (14:7a). The reason for sparing the murderer is purely pragmatic: to ensure the continuation of the father's name (v. 7b).

15:1 *Absalom provided himself with a chariot and horses.* According to the standards of the culture, Absalom's acquisition of a chariot and horses gives him a royal aura (see 1 Sam. 8:11; 1 Kings 1:5).

15:3 *but there is no representative of the king to hear you.* David's paralysis undoubtedly colors Absalom's view of his father's ability to reign. He apparently views David as a dismal failure in carrying out his royal responsibility to promote justice in the land. Absalom may be exaggerating or even misrepresenting the real situation (cf. 2 Sam. 8:15). After all, the woman of Tekoa has received a hearing with the king and a favorable response that shows sensitivity to her plight.[4]

15:6 *so he stole the hearts of the people.* By demonstrating sympathy for the people's needs, Absalom wins their loyalty ("stole their heart," a Hebrew phrase that occurs elsewhere only in Gen. 31:20, 26, where, as here, it refers to deceitful behavior).

15:8 *If the LORD takes me back to Jerusalem.* Absalom may be fabricating this story to justify a visit to Hebron, where he plans to declare himself king. But it may also reflect his belief that (1) the Lord is the one who engineers his return to Jerusalem, and (2) his divinely authorized return to the city is a sign of divine favor and of his royal destiny.

15:10 *Absalom is king in Hebron.* Absalom's choice of a place of enthronement is ironic: this is where David was first publicly proclaimed king over Israel (5:1–5). In David's case the tribes of Israel came to Hebron and offered him the kingship in accordance with the Lord's promise. By way of contrast, Absalom initiates matters with the tribes of Israel, encouraging them to proclaim him king. Unlike the account of his father's rise to the throne, this account contains no reference to his being anointed (cf. 5:3).[5] His rise to kingship, rather than being based on a divine promise, is called a "conspiracy" (v. 12).

Theological Insights

In this account one detects the tension between justice and mercy. Through the woman of Tekoa, Joab appeals to David to show leniency to the murderer Absalom (as David showed to the murderer Joab!). He utilizes a theological argument (v. 14). Death is inevitable for all (as the death of Amnon illustrates), but God is not in the business of taking away life. On the contrary, Joab claims, God devises ways to reconcile to himself those who have been banished. One cannot help but think of David's experience. Despite his capital crimes, God forgave his sin and allowed him to retain his position as king. There surely is truth in what Joab claims. The Lord is predisposed to save, not destroy (cf. Ezek. 33:11).

But the issue is not this simple. God does not automatically restore the banished: he restores those who repent and turn from their wicked ways. Divine leniency was extended to David in part because he confessed his sin (2 Sam. 12:13) and did so, unlike Saul, without trying to first deny or justify his behavior (cf. 1 Sam. 13:11–12; 15:13–25). Furthermore, David's later behavior, while plagued by naïveté and weakness at times, is consistent with his confession of sin and demonstrates genuine humility before God (see 2 Sam. 15:25, 31; 16:11–12; 19:23). But in the case of Joab and Absalom, there is no remorse, only an escalation of their self-serving, murderous behavior. As the Teacher says, there is "a time to kill and a time to heal" (Eccles. 3:3), and it takes wisdom to know which is appropriate in any given case. Despite the woman's description of David (14:17, 20), David will make the wrong choice with Absalom, just as he had with Joab, and will live to regret it.

Teaching the Text

One overriding principle emerges from this account: *The perversion of justice in the form of leniency to unrepentant wrongdo-* *ers can be potentially disastrous.* David's failure to bring unrepentant wrongdoers to justice comes back to haunt him. Joab, who was reprimanded but not punished for his murder of Abner (2 Sam. 3:22–39), remains in an influential position and is instrumental in bringing Absalom back into David's good graces, a decision that proves to be nearly disastrous for David. David's failure to bring Amnon to justice following his rape of Tamar prompts Absalom, in the name of justice, to commit murder and convinces Absalom that his father is unjust. This view of his father as an unfit ruler, when combined with Absalom's hubris, leads to civil war. Joab believes leniency is the best policy because it mirrors God's predisposition to restore the out-

One example of Absalom's hubris was to acquire a chariot and horses and fifty men to run ahead of him. This Assyrian relief shows only two soldiers ahead of King Tiglath-Pileser III's chariot (palace at Nimrud, 730–727 BC).

casts (14:13–14), but as explained above, this is simplistic. It takes great wisdom to know when mercy, rather than justice, is the proper course of action. Within the church, restoration is always the ultimate goal in dealing with wrongdoing, but there are times when strict disciplinary action is needed for that to be accomplished (see 2 Cor. 2:5–11 [cf. 1 Cor. 5:11–13]; 7:8–11; 2 Thess. 3:6–15).

Illustrating the Text

The perversion of justice in the form of leniency to unrepentant wrongdoers can be potentially disastrous.

Christian Autobiography: *Surprised by Joy,* **by C. S. Lewis.** One of the most quoted lines from Lewis's (1898–1963) account of his conversion is "The hardness of God is kinder than the softness of men, and His compulsion is our liberation."[6]

Graduation Speech: **Jacob Neusner.** Neusner (b. 1932) is a well-known but controversial Judaic scholar. In the spring of 1981, while a professor at Brown University, Neusner wrote a mock graduation address for the student newspaper. It appeared in Brown's *Daily Herald* on June 12, 1983.[7] Students and faculty alike were offended, but it also won him some approval and then great acclaim when picked up as a national news story. Often called mean-spirited, it nevertheless underlines the principle above: encouraging leniency when rigor is appropriate actually encourages laziness in the spirit and attitude of students.

In the powerful speech, Neusner contends that the faculty has no reason to "take pride" in the graduating class because they did not prepare the students for the real world. Failing to be rigorous, the faculty did not tell the truth about the students' shoddy, "boring," and inadequate work. Furthermore, they put up with late papers and petty arguments, gave easy B's, and did not "distinguish the excellent from the ordinary." As a result, the students have grown lazy, become quitters, and see themselves as more interesting and gifted than they really are. "We have prepared you for a world that does not exist," says Neusner. "Outside, quitters are not heroes." They will be "ill-advised" if they continue to do that in the outside world. There they had "best not defend errors but learn from them."

David Runs for His Life—Again

Big Idea *In the midst of a crisis, submission to the Lord's will and wise action go hand in hand.*

Understanding the Text

The Text in Context

The tension in the plot heightens in this episode of the story. When the news of Absalom's revolt and widespread support reaches Jerusalem, David decides to flee the city immediately. Apparently he feels that the city is indefensible, and he does not want Absalom to slaughter the city's people (v. 14). Yet all is not lost: the foundation is laid for a favorable resolution to the plot as David places his destiny in the Lord's hands (v. 26) and then takes actions that will prove to be of utmost importance. He sets up a spy network that will prove valuable (cf. 15:28, 35–36 with 17:15–22) and enlists Hushai to counteract Ahithophel's influence in the royal court (cf. 15:34 with 17:7–14).

Interpretive Insights

15:13 *The hearts of the people of Israel are with Absalom.* The language recalls the Shechemites' response to evil Abimelek (Judg. 9:3). If the echo is intentional, Absalom's misguided, rebellious allies are likened to Abimelek's misguided, rebellious followers, creating another literary link between two figures who are guilty of fratricide (see 13:29–30). We know how Abimelek's rebellion ended (Judg. 9:52–57), so this does not bode well for Absalom, even though he appears to have the upper hand at this point.

15:16 *but he left ten concubines to take care of the palace.* This apparent sidenote should grab the attention of the careful reader, for it brings to mind one of the elements in Nathan's prophecy (12:11–12; cf. 16:21–22). Amid this crisis we are reminded once more that everything transpiring is rooted in David's crimes.

15:21 *there will your servant be.* For whatever reason, David refers to Absalom as "the king" (v. 19 AT) and advises Ittai the Gittite to enlist in Absalom's service (v. 20). But Ittai will have none of it. Calling David "my lord the king," he vows his allegiance even if it means death. Loyal Ittai is a literary foil for deceitful Absalom and his band of rebels.[1]

15:25 *Take the ark of God back into the city.* David refuses to use the ark as if it were a magical charm or palladium by which one could manipulate or compel God (cf. 1 Sam. 4) or an object designed to ensure his personal protection. It belongs in the place David has designated as its dwelling place.[2] He does not assume that it will, by its very presence in the city, bring blessing to Absalom.

If I find favor in the LORD's eyes. David realizes that his destiny is in the Lord's hands, and he submits himself to the divine will.

15:31 *LORD, turn Ahithophel's counsel into foolishness.* Sometimes the Lord answers prayers through human instruments. In this case the answer to David's prayer immediately appears in the person of Hushai (v. 32).[3] David's suggestion that Hushai frustrate Ahithophel's advice (v. 34), when compared with his prayer that the Lord would make Ahithophel's advice foolish (v. 31), shows that David understands the providential working of the Lord quite well.[4]

Theological Insights

David's response amid this crisis reflects a balance between reliance on God and pragmatism. On the one hand, he resigns himself to God's sovereign decisions and refuses to try to manipulate or compel God. On the other hand, he also prays specifically that God will thwart his enemies, he sets up a spy network in Jerusalem, and he instructs loyal Hushai to use deception and counter Absalom's advisers. His reaction is reminiscent of Jacob: when

Key Themes of 2 Samuel 15:13–37

- David submits himself to the Lord's sovereign will and looks to the Lord for protection.
- David also makes shrewd decisions and uses his loyal supporters to the best possible advantage.

confronted with the frightening prospect of meeting Esau, he responds by praying fervently for God's blessing (Gen. 32:9–12) while at the same time implementing some very pragmatic measures to protect himself and his family (32:3–8, 13–23). Trust in God and wise actions are complementary, not antithetical—an important lesson for God's people in all ages to remember. The book of Ruth also holds trust in divine sovereignty and human responsibility in balance. It shows us that God is concerned about needy people, yet it also reminds us that God often meets their needs through people who are willing to do what is right and to sacrifice for the good of others.

Shown here is the Kidron Valley and the slopes of the Mount of Olives, the route David took as he left the city of Jerusalem.

Teaching the Text

One overriding principle emerges from this account: *In times of crisis it makes sense to entrust one's destiny to the Lord while at the same time praying for divine aid and making wise plans.* As noted above, David submits his destiny to the Lord's sovereign will, recognizing that apart from the Lord's favor, he will not be delivered and vindicated (vv. 25–26). To his credit, he refuses to try to manipulate God. But this does not mean that he adopts a fatalistic, do-nothing attitude. On the contrary, he prays specifically that the Lord will thwart the advice of Ahithophel, who has shifted his allegiance to Absalom (v. 31). Furthermore, he does everything in his power to set up a system of spies and counteragents who will promote his best interests and keep him informed of Absalom's intentions. The Lord's people must avoid the extreme of fatalism ("Let go and let God"), which stresses the role of divine sovereignty but downplays the importance of petitionary prayer and human responsibility; they must also avoid the other extreme of self-reliance ("God helps those who help themselves"), which stresses the role of human responsibility but downplays divine sovereignty. Our sovereign God typically works out his purposes in response to prayer and through human agency. One sees this in David's case, where the Lord providentially begins to answer his prayer regarding Ahithophel immediately through loyal Hushai, who just happens to meet David at the top of the hill after David has prayed while ascending it (vv. 30–32).

Blind poet and author John Milton dictates *Paradise Lost* to his daughter, in a painting by Eugène Delacroix, 1826.

Illustrating the Text

Submitting to divine sovereignty also includes the necessity of prayer and of taking wise action as appropriate.

Literature: "Sonnet 19," or "When I Consider How My Light Is Spent," by John Milton. In February 1652, the English poet Milton (1608–74) completely lost his eyesight. Unbelievably, this occurred before he wrote his best works, including the immortal epic poem *Paradise Lost.* Milton had written a few of his great poems before 1652, but he had not yet achieved fame. What makes this sonnet (1652–55) so pertinent to the principle above is that as he writes it, he is concerned about how he can serve God in such a condition. As he works through his dilemma, he compares the situation to the parable of the talents. He wonders if God demands "day-labour, light denied." He hears the answer that though God doesn't need our gifts, we must bear his yoke and serve him. Milton then concludes that, at that moment, it must mean standing and waiting, submitting to God's sovereignty. Nevertheless he begins to take the action necessary to use his gift greatly in the years that follow.

> When I consider how my light is
>   spent,
> Ere half my days, in this dark world
>   and wide,
> And that one Talent which is death
>   to hide
> Lodged with me useless, though my
>   Soul more bent
> To serve therewith my Maker, and
>   present
> My true account, lest he returning
>   chide;
> "Doth God exact day-labour, light
>   denied?"
> I fondly ask. But patience, to
>   prevent
> That murmur, soon replies, "God
>   doth not need
> Either man's work or his own gifts;
>   who best
> Bear his mild yoke, they serve him
>   best. His state
> Is Kingly. Thousands at his bidding
>   speed
> And post o'er Land and Ocean
>   without rest:
> They also serve who only stand and
>   wait.

Quote: *This Day We Fight!*, by Francis Frangipane.

The Lord is not pleased with the spiritual passivity and indifference so prevalent among His people. We are aware daily that terrorists could attack with massive destruction, or we watch the advance of perversion in our cultures, yet many Christians remain prayerless and inactive. This is in spite of the Lord's promise that if we will come before Him, humbling ourselves in earnest prayer, He will empower us to pursue our enemies and defeat them. But instead of seeking God's face on behalf of the lost, too many of us are immobilized by the grip of a passive spirit. I am not talking about the level of energy in our bodies, but the level of fire in our obedience.[5]

Literature: *Hamlet*, by William Shakespeare.

This enduring work (1599–1601) is Shakespeare's (1564–1616) longest play and one of the most influential and most discussed English tragedies. The play shows the consequences of not taking action thoughtfully and wisely. While the play is variously interpreted, it seems clear that Hamlet, terribly disturbed by the murder of his father and his mother's quick marriage to the murderer, his uncle, does not make decisions or act thoughtfully, as he needs to. In his most famous soliloquy (act 3, scene 1) he contemplates suicide:

> To be or not to be . . .
> . . . the dread of something after
>   death,
> The undiscovered country from
>   whose bourn
> No traveler returns, puzzles the will.

He recognizes that there is a supernatural force, and he declares, "Conscience does make cowards of us all." However, he then proceeds to act rashly, and by the end of the play everyone but the narrator is dead.

The Lord Thwarts a Curse

Big Idea *The Lord vindicates his repentant servants when they humbly submit to his discipline.*

Understanding the Text

The Text in Context

Absalom has gained widespread support and declared himself king. Even David's counselor, Ahithophel, has switched his allegiance. Knowing that Absalom would soon march with his army to Jerusalem, David has hastily left the city and was forced once more to run for his life. In this crisis David has submitted to God's sovereign will, but he also has prayed and wisely enlisted the support of those who remained loyal to him. In this next section we see his reliance on the Lord vindicated. As Abigail

earlier did (1 Sam. 25:18), now Ziba brings provisions for David, and, in the face of hostile opposition from Shimei, a relative of Saul, David again places his destiny in the Lord's hands and refuses to take vengeance against a member of Saul's family (2 Sam. 16:5–13). In fact, as he has done on one occasion with Saul, he prohibits Abishai from killing his perceived enemy (16:9–10; cf. 1 Sam. 26:8–11). These literary links with 1 Samuel 25–26 bode well

David, his family, and his loyal supporters left Jerusalem and headed into the Judean wilderness. Shown here is a view of the Judean wilderness looking back toward the Mount of Olives.

for David: the Lord delivered him earlier, and he will do so again.

David's eventual vindication in the face of Shimei's curse also contributes to the narrator's apology for David, a theme that has not been as prominent in the story since the account of David's sin, but one that nevertheless remains present, if at times beneath the surface, throughout the unfolding narrative. Shimei's curse is not realized (the Lord does not hand the kingdom over to Absalom) because his accusation that David has murdered members of Saul's household is false (2 Sam. 16:7–8).

Interpretive Insights

16:1 *He had a string of donkeys saddled and loaded.* One cannot help but be reminded of Abigail's gift to David and his men. The lists of provisions are identical in some respects and similar in others:

Abigail's Gift (1 Sam. 25:18)	Ziba's Gift (2 Sam. 16:1)
200 loaves of bread	200 loaves of bread
2 skins of wine	1 skin of wine
5 sheep	—
5 seahs of roasted grain	—
100 cakes of raisins	100 cakes of raisins
200 cakes of pressed figs	100 cakes of summer fruit (i.e., figs)

Just as the Lord providentially provided for the fugitive David on that earlier occasion, so he is providing for the fugitive David now.

16:3 *Today the Israelites will restore to me my grandfather's kingdom.* Taking Ziba's report at face value, David decrees that (supposedly) disloyal Mephibosheth's

Key Themes of 2 Samuel 16:1–14

- The Lord provides for the physical needs of David and his supporters.
- David trusts the Lord to vindicate his innocence in the face of Shimei's false accusation.

property be given to (supposedly) loyal Ziba (v. 4).

16:5 *he cursed.* The only other individual to curse David in 1–2 Samuel is Goliath (1 Sam. 17:43). The intertextual link does not cast Shimei in a very positive light.

16:8 *for all the blood you shed in the household of Saul.* It is likely that Shimei and other Benjamites believe that David is responsible for the deaths of Saul and Jonathan (after all, David was employed by the Philistines at the time of Saul's death), Abner (after all, it was David's nephew and right-hand man, Joab, who murdered Abner), and Ish-bosheth (after all, Ish-bosheth's murderers took their victim's head to David). It is also possible that Shimei is referring, at least in part, to the incident recorded in 2 Samuel 21:1–9, which tells how David hands seven descendants of Saul over to the Gibeonites for execution.[1] But the narrator absolves David of guilt in all of these instances. Shimei's accusation is unfounded and based on superficial, circumstantial evidence.

16:9 *Let me go over and cut off his head.* David's response to Shimei's false accusations and hostility is a reminder of his own innocence. Once before Abishai volunteered to kill a perceived enemy (Saul himself!), and David ordered him not to do so (1 Sam. 26:7–12). That incident was proof of his loyalty to Saul; the episode is replayed here, as it were, as a reminder that David has never taken or endorsed any hostile actions against Saul or his royal house.

16:10 *Curse David.* From his past experience with Saul, David realizes that opposition and the suffering it entails are part of God's sovereign design (see the comment above on 1 Sam. 26:19).

16:11 *for the* Lord *has told him to.* David's words to Abishai express his reliance on the Lord. David undoubtedly realizes that he is being punished for his earlier crimes. His very own son is seeking his life, and David suspects that the Lord himself has prompted Shimei to utter his curse. Actually, if the curse fails to materialize, David's innocence with respect to the house of Saul will be proved, so David is willing to suffer this indignity in the meantime.

16:12 *and restore to me his covenant blessing.* David's use of the verb "restore" (*heshib*) counterbalances Shimei's use of the term (cf. "repaid" in v. 8).[2] David submits to the justice of God: if Shimei's charge that the Lord is repaying David for crimes against Saul's house is wrong, perhaps the Lord will demonstrate the false nature of the accusation by repaying him with good.

The political ambitions of Absalom caused David to flee for his life. Other kings in the ancient Near East had similar challenges for their throne. Sennacherib, shown here with one of his advisers, was killed by his sons because of their desire for kingship.

Theological Insights

David accepts what Shimei is dishing out as part of God's discipline. This does not mean that David agrees with Shimei's accusation, but he is willing to accept such unjust treatment as coming from the hand of God. David realizes that God is merciful, even in the midst of dishing out punishment. After all, following the death of David's infant son as punishment for his crimes, the Lord has given him a child and named him Jedidiah, as a sign of his favor (see 12:24–25). David hopes that the Lord will take notice of his suffering and grant him favor in the face of Shimei's curse.[3]

Teaching the Text

When undergoing divine discipline, it is wise to submit to the will of God. In the face of Shimei's physical violence, insults, and false accusations, David does not strike back in anger or vengeance, but submits to the Lord's discipline. In the aftermath of his crimes and Nathan's prophecy, he recognizes that he is subject to divine discipline, and he understands that God sometimes sends unjust suffering for disciplinary reasons. He is content to place his destiny in the Lord's hands, knowing that the Lord is capable of vindicating and delivering him (16:12). David articulates this same notion in Psalm 38, where he acknowledges that his suffering is due to his sin (vv. 1–4). Surrounded by enemies who hate him without cause (vv. 16–20), he begs for the Lord to vindicate him before them and deliver him from his self-imposed suffering (vv. 5–15, 21–22). David is broken in the face of Shimei's cursing. We no longer see the manipulative David exploiting his power with no regard for the lives of others (cf. 2 Sam. 11), but a lamenting David who is submissive to the sovereign plan of God. Though David's

Ziba's Deception

As the story unfolds, we are in for a surprise. When David returns to the city after Absalom's death, Mephibosheth greets the king, declares his loyalty, and claims that Ziba has lied (19:24–30). David is not certain who is telling the truth, so he reverses his earlier decree to Ziba and divides Mephibosheth's property evenly between Ziba and Mephibosheth. Mephibosheth declines the offer, claiming that his only concern is the king's safety. Does the text give us any clue to resolve the dilemma? In 19:24 the narrator tells us that Mephibosheth has been mourning since the day David left the city. This is a peculiar way for him to act if he expects to be made king (cf. 16:3). In retrospect, the explanation given by Ziba for Mephibosheth's absence seems unlikely. Apparently Ziba has been lying. Through this deception he is able to rob his master of at least half his wealth.

Yet as we read 16:1–4, we do not yet know all of this. All we see at this point is that the Lord has provided for David. But once we read the story a second time, knowing all the facts, this episode takes on an additional dimension. The incidents involving Ziba and Mephibosheth illustrate the point that many who live under David's rule are really just self-serving. Just as Ziba turns on his master Mephibosheth and expresses loyalty to David only for the sake of personal gain, so many Israelites, including David's trusted adviser Ahithophel, have turned to a new master, Absalom, because they think it is to their advantage to do so. In this way the narrator reminds us just how precarious David's situation is, at least from a human perspective. (We saw this much earlier with the people of Keilah [1 Sam. 23:1–13].) But despite David's apparent vulnerability, the Lord uses Ziba's improperly motivated gift to care for David and delivers him from all the self-serving, deceptive individuals that are potentially a threat to his throne.

suffering is disciplinary, the Lord does not abandon him.

Illustrating the Text

It is crucial that believers submit to divine discipline rather than trying to vindicate themselves.

Quote: *Reaching for the Invisible God,* by **Philip Yancey.** Yancey (b. 1949) is a best-selling author of many books.

David and Shimei

When the coup is over and David returns to Jerusalem, Shimei meets him and begs for mercy (2 Sam. 19:18–23). Abishai again asks for permission to kill Shimei, but David again refuses. He has been vindicated and delivered from Shimei's curse, but he refuses to seek vengeance, announcing that he will not stain this day of deliverance with blood. Unfortunately, the desire for vengeance finally does win out in David's soul. On his deathbed he urges his son Solomon to kill Shimei violently as retribution for how he has treated David (1 Kings 2:8–9).

Anyone who has lived through the sordid affairs of Watergate and Monica-gate has a sense for what David *could* have done. The Republican Richard Nixon lied and authorized hush money to cover up his crimes; a tape-recording, not a confession, brought him down. The Democrat Bill Clinton solemnly looked into a camera and deceived an entire nation; a stained dress, not a confession, led to his impeachment. Nixon could barely force himself to mutter, "Mistakes were made"; Clinton admitted only what had been proven and broadcast to the world.

The contrast of David's first words could not be greater: "I have sinned against Thee, Lord." . . . As his poetry makes clear, he led a God-saturated life.[4]

Quote: "Before the Next Sex Scandal." This editorial ran in *Christianity Today* (April 2006). Applying this principle of discipline to the fall of our leaders, which the editorial reports is only too frequent, the writer stresses the pronounced difference between the results of submission to discipline as exercised by the church and the lack of accountability often present in the church. The only way we can guard pastors, churches, and "the vulnerable for the sake of the Gospel" is for the pastor to "repent and submit." Pastors who will not may have to be isolated so that outsiders see that the church is seri-ous about holiness. Tragically, repentance is not guaranteed, and this, of course, affects restoration.[5]

Literature: *The Scarlet Letter,* by Nathaniel Hawthorne. This well-known novel (1850) is about the consequences of an adulterous relationship between Hester Prynne and Arthur Dimmesdale, the preacher in the community. Yet only Hester is convicted of the sin and forced to wear the scarlet letter A (= Adultery) on her chest. Hester, whose husband has apparently been lost at sea, never tells the name of her lover; Dimmesdale, in a profound lack of moral courage, does not confess till the end. Deceiving himself, he rationalizes his sin enough to stay silent about it and continue as the pastor; yet the sin eats away at him daily—the mark of divine discipline. How much better he would have fared if he had immediately confessed to his congregation and submitted to discipline. The dramatic contrast of Dimmesdale's silence about his own sin and the openly acknowledged sin of Hester is a remarkable story. She lives in the lonely isolation that the self-righteous community imposes upon her; however, she is not consumed from within.

Bible: Psalm 51. This psalm is David's full confession of sin.

Divine discipline is inevitably painful.

Poetry: "Easter Wings," by George Herbert. Herbert (1593–1633), who held prominent positions at a university and in government in England, gave it all up in 1630 and became a rector in the Church of England, where he spent his last few years in a small parish. He was noted for his wonderful physical and spiritual care of his parishioners. Regarded as saintly, he wrote religious poetry, which is widely read. In this pattern poem (1633), Herbert examines the discipline of the Lord:

> Lord, who createdst man in wealth and store,
> Though foolishly he lost the same,
> Decaying more and more,
> Till he became
> Most poore:
> With thee
> Oh let me rise
> As larks, harmoniously,
> And sing this day thy victories:
> Then shall the fall further the flight in me.
>
> My tender age in sorrow did beginne:
> And still with sicknesses and shame
> Thou didst so punish sinne,
> That I became
> Most thinne.
> With thee
> Let me combine
> And feel this day thy victorie:
> For, if I imp my wing on thine
> Affliction shall advance the flight in me.

The Lord Thwarts a Shrewd Counselor

Big Idea *When his repentant servants humbly submit to his discipline, the Lord protects and provides.*

Understanding the Text

The Text in Context

After leaving Jerusalem in the face of Shimei's curse, David faced the imposing power of Absalom, now buttressed by the defection of Ahithophel. This next literary unit describes how the Lord uses Hushai's advice to thwart Ahithophel and Absalom. In the middle of this unit we read that the Lord "had determined to frustrate the good advice of Ahithophel in order to bring disaster on Absalom" (2 Sam. 17:14). This key statement provides a framework for understanding all that transpires in chapters 16–17. It also sets the stage for the realization of the Lord's purpose as recorded in chapter 18. Ironically, while this statement bodes well for David (he will be delivered from Absalom's threat on his life), it also reminds us that the Lord's earlier judgment announcement against David is relentlessly materializing, as does Absalom's violating David's concubines (2 Sam. 16:21–22; cf. 12:11–12). Yes, the Lord will spare David, as he has done before when Saul was chasing him. But in the

process David will also pay the third installment of his self-imposed penalty.

At the end of this literary unit, allies bring provisions for David (cf. 2 Sam. 16:1). Like the king of Moab (1 Sam. 22:3–4), allies in Transjordan come to his aid (2 Sam. 17:27–29). This link to an earlier account of God's provision bodes well for David.

Historical and Cultural Background

When Absalom violates his father's concubines (16:21–22), it is a declaration that he has usurped his father's throne. Kings would sometimes take another king's concubines as tribute and as a sign of their lordship. For example, the Assyrian king Sennacherib took the concubines ("women of the palace") of both the Babylonian ruler Merodach-Baladan (*COS*, 2:301) and the Judahite king Hezekiah (*COS*, 2:303).

Interpretive Insights

16:16 *Long live the king!* Absalom understands himself to be the referent of

Hushai's statement of acclamation. Hushai certainly intends for Absalom to interpret his words in this way, but the reader of the story recognizes dramatic irony in the ambiguity of the statement.[1] Hushai does not say, "Long live King Absalom," as one might expect (see 1 Kings 1:25, 31, 34, 39).[2] Instead he uses the shorter, more ambiguous form of acclamation (see 1 Sam. 10:24; 2 Kings 11:12). In his own mind, David, not Absalom, is "the king."

16:18 *the one chosen by the* LORD, *. . . his I will be.* Hushai seemingly declares his loyalty to Absalom (note how he prefaces his statement with "No"). Yet his reference to "the one chosen by the LORD," while flattering Absalom, is a subtle reminder

to the reader that Hushai is really loyal to David, whom the Lord has chosen to be king (1 Sam. 16:1–12; 2 Sam. 6:21), not to Absalom, whom the story never describes as being the Lord's chosen.[3] Hushai's deceiving Absalom is all part of the Lord's plan to "bring disaster" on this usurper (see 17:14) and illustrates how God typically deals with

In Israel the houses, including David's palace, would have had flat roofs. Absalom pitches a tent on the roof so that all can see him with David's concubines. This drawing of David's palace in Jerusalem (a reconstruction that incorporates the existing archaeological structures) shows its flat roof and elevated location in the city.

deceivers (22:27). Indeed, the one who has used deception against his father (13:23–27; 15:7–9) has now become the deceived.

16:22 *he slept with his father's concubines in the sight of all Israel.* Ahithophel urges Absalom to violate David's concubines and thereby proclaim himself the rightful ruler.[4] When Israel hears of this bold action, they will know that Absalom has indeed rebelled against his father. Seeing their leader's brazen attitude, Absalom's supporters will be emboldened to follow his lead and bring the coup to its completion. This reprehensible act fulfills Nathan's prophecy (12:11–12), reminding the reader that Absalom's rebellion, though not endorsed by the Lord (see 17:14), is providentially part of the Lord's discipline of David for his sin with Bathsheba.[5] David himself seems to understand this (see 16:11–12).

17:2 *then all the people with him will flee.* Ahithophel projects his own readiness to shift allegiance upon David's followers, but they are far more loyal than he realizes or perhaps can appreciate (cf. 15:19–37; 17:15–22).[6]

I would strike down only the king. Ahithophel's advice demonstrates an appalling lack of respect for God's anointed king and a lack of fear for the Lord himself. Ahithophel's description of David as "the king" is telling and self-condemnatory, even if he only intends to use the expression in a referential way. His attitude toward the Lord's anointed (David) stands in contrast to the respect that David has shown the Lord's anointed (Saul). Ahithophel is ready to "strike down" (*nakah*) the king, while David has refused to let Abishai "pin" (*nakah*) Saul to the ground (1 Sam. 26:8).

Indeed, when David cut off just a corner of Saul's robe in the cave, he was "conscience-stricken" (1 Sam. 24:5; Hebrew, "the heart of David struck him [David] down").

17:11 *as numerous as the sand on the seashore.* Strategically, Hushai's advice makes sense, since such a force will be seemingly invincible. The proposal also plays on Absalom's vanity, since it depicts all Israel as rallying around him. But literarily there are ominous echoes for Absalom. Three times before in the Former Prophets a military force has been described in this way (Josh. 11:4; Judg. 7:12; 1 Sam. 13:5). In each case the expression is used of a foreign army that is then soundly defeated by the Lord's chosen leader (Joshua, Gideon, Saul).

17:14 *For the Lord had determined to frustrate the good advice of Ahithophel.* The Lord answered David's prayer (cf. 2 Sam. 15:31). The narrator's description of Ahithophel's advice as "good," in contradiction to Hushai's characterization of it as "not good" (17:7), reminds the reader that Absalom is a victim of divine deception (see the comment above on 16:18).

17:19 *His wife took a covering.* This episode is similar to an incident that occurred at Jericho when the Israelites were invading the land under Joshua.[7] If the many intertextual links are by design, then they contribute to the characterization of the main figures in the story. The respective spies correspond to one another, as do Rahab and the anonymous woman of Bahurim (vv. 17–20). Since the spies eventually report to David (v. 21), as the Israelite spies did to Joshua (Josh. 2:24), David and Joshua correspond, while Absalom, who sent the spies, is linked with the king of Jericho. In other words, David is on the Lord's side in this matter, while Absalom is cast in the role of the enemy.

17:23 *hanged himself.* There is poetic justice here: The one who has pitilessly advised his new master to strike David dead (17:2–3) now is dead himself, and the vocal chords that have uttered such brazen advice are crushed. The Lord has answered David's prayer when he frustrates Ahithophel's counsel; now in his providence the Lord takes this potentially dangerous foe off the playing field entirely. Ahithophel's self-destruction foreshadows what is about to happen to his new master, who will also die with his feet dangling in the air (18:9–15).

Jonathan and Ahimaaz had the dangerous task of bringing messages to David from Hushai. With the help of a woman in Bahurim, they eluded Absalom's men by hiding in a camouflaged well. Wells were often lined with stones, like the one shown here from Tel Goded, which would have provided hand and toe holds.

17:27 *When David came to Mahanaim.* This literary unit closes as the preceding one began, with David's receiving provisions (cf. 16:1). His supporters, who are from east of the Jordan, are foils for Absalom, "all the men of Israel," and David's nephew Amasa, who are trying to kill their rightful king (vv. 24–25).[ᵘ]

Theological Insights

Though it may seem incongruous, in this and the preceding episodes, David experiences both the discipline and the deliverance of God simultaneously. David understands Shimei's insulting treatment and false accusations as the discipline of God (16:10–11). Absalom's humiliating

treatment of David's concubines, in fulfillment of Nathan's prophecy (16:22; cf. 12:11–12), is also punishment from God. David submits to this divine discipline (cf. 15:25–26) but also looks to God for vindication (16:12; cf. 15:31). The Lord does vindicate and protect David, but ironically, in delivering David from Absalom's attack on his life (cf. 17:2–3), the Lord will force David to make the third installment of his self-imposed penalty. Though that payment is made in the next episode (18:1–17), the narrator informs us of its inevitability in this passage (17:14).

This account also nicely illustrates how divine sovereignty and human agency sometimes work together in the outworking of the divine purpose. In a previous episode, David asked the Lord to frustrate Ahithophel's advice (15:31). The Lord providentially began to answer his prayer by sending Hushai to meet David (15:32). In this episode we see Hushai doing his best to counteract Ahithophel's advice, illustrating how God sometimes answers prayer and works out his purposes through secondary causes. But there is more to the story than meets the eye. Indeed, as we read the advice of the two counselors, it is quite apparent that Ahithophel's plan is superior; even the narrator admits this (17:14). But in the end the Lord is manipulating the minds of Absalom and his men, causing them to prefer the desperate, inferior plan offered by Hushai, because he has already determined to bring disaster upon Absalom (17:14). This is reminiscent of the account of Eli's sons, who rejected their father's warning because the Lord had by that time decided to kill them (1 Sam. 2:25; see as well 1 Kings 12:15).

Teaching the Text

The Lord vindicates his humble, chosen servants when they are unjustly threatened. David is vulnerable in the face of Absalom's well-orchestrated and unexpected revolt. Though David's suffering is disciplinary, the Lord does not abandon him. Various individuals come to his aid and even risk their lives on his behalf. Most important, the Lord himself intervenes, causing Absalom to make an unwise decision that will prove to be disastrous.

Illustrating the Text

The Lord will vindicate those who humble themselves before his discipline.

Literature: *Sir Gawain and the Green Knight*. The author of this powerful Middle English poem is unknown. In it Sir Gawain begins his rise to greatness when he takes a challenge given by an ominous figure known as the Green Knight. Throughout the poem Gawain is tested and found truthful, until the third day of a gift-giving game, when his flaw emerges. Told that the belt he has been given can save his life, he does not admit to the returning lord that he has received it because he wants it to protect himself. The next day Gawain faces his fate with the Green Knight, who will hold him accountable. The Green Knight assaults Gawain three times, the third time grazing his neck with a sword. Then the Green Knight tells Gawain the first two blows are for the first two nights, when Gawain was honest, and the third blow is for the last night, when he was dishonest. However, says the Green Knight, Gawain's untruth is "no amorous work, nor wooing either, but because ye loved your life,—the less I blame you."

Gawain feels shame and admits his deed by showing the knight the belt, saying, "Lo! There is the deception, foul may it fall! . . . Now am I faulty and false, and a coward have ever been. From treachery and untruth ever come sorrow and care. Here I confess to you, knight, that my conduct is all faulty. Let me but please you now, and after I shall beware." The Green Knight commends his confession and gives him back the belt, which will serve as a humbling reminder to Gawain of his failure.[9]

Poetry: "The Man Watching," by Rainer Maria Rilke. In this poem (1920), translated by Robert Bly, Rilke (1875–1926), a very compelling poet, writes about the Angel who wrestled with characters in the Old Testament. To be beaten by such an angel was something to be proud of, to be strengthened by: paradoxically, this was growth by defeat. After an experience of discipline, Ken Gire quotes this poem and writes,

> According to the biblical story, Jacob, after wrestling till dawn, finally did walk away with God's blessing. But he walked with a limp. And he walked that way the rest of his life. Would I? . . . In dislocating my hip, God had taught me to cling. In making me limp, He had taught me to lean. . . . Not on my own two legs, but on Him.[10]

"O Absalom, My Son, My Son!"

Big Idea *The Lord's discipline, once decreed, is inescapable and just; it often brings great sorrow in its wake.*

Understanding the Text

The Text in Context

As the previous episode came to an end, David was in serious danger. But the preceding episode made it clear that David was not alone and that the Lord, while using Absalom as an instrument in his discipline of David, is going to bring about Absalom's defeat (17:14). This episode tells how that happens. The Lord halts Absalom's coup in its tracks, but in the process David pays the third installment of his self-imposed fourfold penalty (cf. 12:6). Nathan's prophecy continues to echo through the story as the sword continues to rip through David's house (cf. 12:10).

David's response to the loss of his son is heart wrenching yet also symptomatic of his failed leadership. Joab's rebuke and warning raise the issue of David's continuing support. Despite the failure of Absalom's coup, will Israel continue to support David? The stage is set for the conclusion of David's story, which will focus on his attempt to maintain his throne.

Historical and Cultural Background

Following Absalom's death, David weeps bitterly and appears to be ungrateful for the sacrifice his soldiers have made (19:1–4). Joab confronts him and accuses him of misplaced priorities: "You love those who hate you and hate those who love you" (v. 6). This is not empty rhetoric or hyperbole. Joab uses the terms "love" and "hate" in their covenantal sense of loyalty/disloyalty. David's response suggests that he is more loyal to the disloyal Absalom than he is to his faithful soldiers. A good illustration of the use of love/hate terminology in this sense can be seen in Amarna letter 286, where Abdi-Heba of Jerusalem asks the pharaoh's commissioner, "Why do you love the Apiru but hate the mayors?" (*COS*, 3:237).

Interpretive Insights

18:2 *David sent out his troops.* For the first time since 13:27, the narrator describes David as sending (*shalah*). In chapter 11 the narrator portrays David as possessing absolute sovereignty: he sent people where he willed (vv. 1, 3–4, 12, 27) and by a mere message accomplished his desires (vv. 6, 14). But he used his power to satisfy his lust and cover up his crime. In chapter 13 he continued to exercise his authority over others, but now it backfired on him as the Lord providentially brought to pass the fulfillment of his self-imposed penalty. He first sent Tamar to her brother Amnon's house, where she was raped; then he sent Amnon to his brother Absalom's sheepshearing, where he was murdered (see the comments above on 13:7, 27). Now he sends out his army to confront Absalom, giving them clear instructions not to harm the young man (v. 5). But once again David has, with his royal command, set in motion events that will bring him sorrow and culminate in the fulfillment of Nathan's prophecy (12:11–12). David has abused his royal authority; now the Lord is using that very royal authority as an instrument in his discipline of David.

18:5 *Be gentle with the young man Absalom for my sake.* David's reference to Absalom as a "young man" (see also vv. 29, 32) suggests that he is willing to overlook his son's actions as youthful indiscretion. Once again we get a hint of David's inability to hold those closest to him accountable for their behavior, including his sons (see the comment

Key Themes of 2 Samuel 18:1–19:8

- David pays the third installment of the self-imposed penalty for his crimes: Absalom is defeated and killed, ironically by Joab, who has been instrumental in Uriah's death.
- When David mourns Absalom's death, Joab warns him that he might lose the support of the army.

above on 13:21; cf. 1 Kings 1:6). Absalom's youth is no excuse for his behavior. Indeed, the narrator uses the same term (*na'ar*) of Eli's sons: "This sin of the young men was very great in the LORD's sight" (1 Sam. 2:17).

18:6 *to fight Israel.* Israel is cast in the role of the enemy, emphasizing the widespread support Absalom has gathered (see 15:6, 13; 16:15; 17:14, 24, 26) and David's vulnerability.

18:7 *the casualties that day were great.* The Hebrew text reads, "and there was a great defeat in that day." There may be a sad echo of Israel's defeat in the days of Eli. In 1 Samuel 4:17 the messenger announced to Eli that Israel had suffered "heavy losses" (Hebrew, "a great defeat"). These are the only two texts where this expression (*maggepah gedolah*) occurs in the Former Prophets.[1]

The battle between David's troops and the armies of Israel commanded by Absalom took place in the forest of Ephraim. This may be the large wooded area on either side of the Jabbok River, in modern Jordan. Shown here is the Jabbok River with its forested banks.

18:9 *the mule he was riding kept on going.* According to tradition (Josephus; the Talmud), his hair becomes entangled in the branches, but the text stops short of saying this specifically.[2] Since Absalom's mule is his royal mount (see 2 Sam. 13:29), the incident has symbolic significance: just as Absalom has lost his mule, so he is about to lose his kingship.[3]

18:14 *plunged them into Absalom's heart.* David's past failures have come back to haunt him. When Joab murdered Abner, David rebuked Joab but did not punish him for his crime (3:22–39). Now the unpunished murderer Joab has taken the life of another unpunished murderer, one who is near and dear to David's heart. David learns the hard way that it is dangerous to let hardened, unrepentant murderers go unpunished. It was also Joab who with calculating and cold-blooded efficiency carried out David's orders to have Uriah killed. He did so because he was committed to doing what was in the political interests of his king (11:14–25). Now this same Joab disregards David's orders and kills David's son with calculating and cold-blooded efficiency because, once again, he is committed to doing what is politically advantageous for David. David has let emotion and sentiment cloud his vision, but Joab knows that David can be safe only if and when Absalom is dead.[4]

18:15 *struck him and killed him.* It is perhaps appropriate that the account of Absalom's death contains echoes of both Uriah's death and Amnon's murder. David instructed Joab to withdraw from Uriah during the assault on the city so he would be "struck down and die" (11:15). The verbs (*nakah* and *mut*) are the same ones used by the narrator here in verse 15 to describe

how Joab's men finish off Absalom. As he planned Amnon's murder, Absalom commanded his men to "strike Amnon down" and "kill him" (13:28). Again the verbs are the same ones used to describe how Absalom, who ordered his men to kill his brother, meets his own demise at the hand of Joab's men. The intertextual links convey the notion of poetic justice, for both David and Absalom.

18:16 *Then Joab sounded the trumpet.* This is the second time that Joab is described as blowing a trumpet to signal the end of a military victory (cf. 2:28). Ironically, both times he led David's forces against the armies of "Israel" (cf. 2:17, 28, with 18:7, 16). The first time he defeated the pro-Saul Benjamite forces led by Abner, but on this second occasion the opposition has been led by David's very own son. What was strictly intertribal conflict has now become intrafamily strife that threatens to shred the national unity David has achieved.

18:17 *a large heap of rocks.* Undoubtedly Joab considers this form of burial fitting because Absalom is an accursed enemy (see Josh. 7:26; 8:29; 10:27) whose burial place will be a reminder of the destiny of all rebels.[5] There is an echo here of two incidents recorded in Joshua 7–8. After Achan was executed, Israel "heaped up a large pile of rocks" over him (Josh. 7:26). According to Joshua 8:29, after the king of Ai was hanged (*talah*) on a tree (cf. 2 Sam. 18:9), the soldiers threw his corpse (Hiphil of *shalak*) down (cf. 2 Sam. 18:17) and "raised a large pile of rocks" over it. These are the only three passages in the Old Testament that mention "a pile of rocks" (*gal-'abanim*), and in each case the adjective "large" (*gadol*) is added for good measure.

The intertextual linking casts Absalom in the role of a rebellious Israelite (Achan) who disgraced and jeopardized the covenant community and a foreign enemy (the king of Ai) who died a humiliating death.[6]

18:18 *He named the pillar after himself.* The juxtaposition of this notation (v. 18) with the description of Absalom's burial place (v. 17) is significant in at least a couple of ways. Absalom does indeed die without a son to carry on his name, a fitting end for a rebel.[7] His dishonorable burial also cancels out his earlier attempt to glorify himself beyond the grave.

18:19 *that the LORD has vindicated him by delivering him from the hand of his enemies.* The reports of the army's victory delivered by Ahimaaz and the Cushite messenger serve as a foil for David's sorrowful response to the news of Absalom's death.[8] The messengers' words provide one perspective: the Lord has delivered David from his enemies (v. 19), who have lifted their hand against him (v. 28) and risen up against him (vv. 31–32). From this perspective, Absalom was his father's mortal enemy. David's response reflects another perspective: by grieving the loss of his son (v. 33), David is, perhaps subconsciously, focusing on the event as divine discipline. After all, Absalom

becomes the third installment of David's self-imposed fourfold penalty for his crime against Uriah (cf. 12:6). In the different responses we are reminded of the two dimensions of the event: divine deliverance and divine discipline.

18:33 *He went up to the room over the gateway and wept.* The description of David's response to the news of Absalom's death echoes an earlier scene, when David went up the Mount of Olives, "weeping as he went" (15:30). On that first occasion he mourned because Absalom was threatening his throne and his life. Now ironically he is mourning the death of this one who has threatened him. But perhaps the two events are linked, for David must be sensing in both the disciplinary hand of God (cf. 15:26; 16:11). Yet Fokkelman comments on the tragic reality: "David should have realized that he could not retain both, the throne and his son. Retention of one really presupposes the loss of the other."[9]

If only I had died instead of you. Earlier David expressed his hope that the Lord would repay him good instead

This monument in the Kidron Valley is known as Absalom's Tomb. For centuries pilgrims to this site would throw rocks at it to show contempt for David's rebellious son. While tradition tries to link it to the pillar of Absalom mentioned in 2 Samuel 18, this structure was built during the first century AD, probably for a wealthy family to mark the site of their family tombs.

of (*tahat*) the ruin that Shimei predicted for him (16:12; cf. 16:8). But now that the Lord has delivered David from ruin and death, he wishes that he had died "instead of" (*tahat*) Absalom.[10] David is focusing on divine discipline, not divine deliverance.

19:4 *cried aloud.* Tamar's vindication continues here (see the comments on 13:31). Following her rape, she wept aloud (*za'aq*, 13:19); now David cries out (*za'aq*, 19:4 [5 MT]) over the death of his son.

O my son Absalom! O Absalom, my son, my son! The repetition of David's cry of anguish (cf. 18:33) draws attention to the depth of David's grief. This mirrors the earlier repetition of his command not to harm Absalom (18:5, 12) and of his question regarding Absalom's well-being (18:29, 32).[11]

19:8 *the Israelites had fled to their homes.* This is tragically ironic, for on an earlier occasion Israel fled to their homes following a defeat by a foreign army, the Philistines (1 Sam. 4:10). But now they do so after an unsuccessful coup against their rightful king. Once more there is an echo of that earlier defeat, when Eli's sons were killed (see comments on 18:6–7).

Theological Insights

The outworking of divine justice is the main theological theme that emerges in this episode. Through the device of literary allusion, the narrator depicts Absalom as getting what he deserves (see the comments on 18:15, 17 above). But the focal point is David, whose sorrow amid victory and deliverance betrays his awareness that divine discipline has engulfed him yet again. Once more the narrator utilizes literary allusion to show that David's earlier crimes and failures are coming back to haunt him. Reverberations of the murder of Uriah are heard in the description of Absalom's death at the hand of Joab (cf. 18:15), and an echo of Tamar's pain can be heard in David's mournful scream (cf. 19:4). The account is a sober reminder to all who read it that God is just and holds sinners accountable for their actions.

Teaching the Text

1. *The Lord's discipline, once decreed, is inescapable.* The prophet Nathan announced David's punishment: the sword would not depart from David's house, and the Lord would bring calamity on David from within his own household (12:10–12). David himself even imposed his own penalty: fourfold payment for the "lamb" he stole (12:6). He paid the first two installments when the infant died and when Absalom murdered Amnon. In this episode we read of the third installment as Joab, who played an important role in David's murder of Uriah, ruthlessly kills Absalom. David has commanded his three generals to spare Absalom's life, but in the providence of God Joab, not Abishai or Ittai, receives the report of Absalom's whereabouts and, in his typical fashion, does what he deems to be in David's best interests.

2. *The Lord's discipline, even when tempered by his salvation, can be painful.* From the perspective of David's army, the Lord has saved the king from the mortal threat mounted by his enemies (see 18:19, 28, 31). Indeed, David's family has been spared (19:5). But amid this great victory, David recognizes the disciplinary hand of God and feels the pain of losing his son. His

body shakes physically when he receives the news of Absalom's death, and he expresses his wish that he could have died instead of his son (18:33). Five times he shouts out Absalom's name, and eight times he cries out "my son" (18:33; 19:4). David has been forgiven, and the Lord has protected him in answer to his prayer, but he still needs to face the inevitable and painful consequences of his past deeds.

Illustrating the Text

Divine discipline is inescapable.

Film: *Duel*, directed by Steven Spielberg. Based on a short story by Richard Matheson (b. 1926), this film (1971) is Spielberg's (b. 1946) feature film debut. In it a terrified motorist, played by Dennis Weaver, is driving his Valiant auto on a remote and lonely road in the mountains when he realizes he is being chased and stalked by the unseen driver of a tanker truck, a 1955 Peterbilt 281. Although the film deserves watching for its powerful treatment of human fear in the face of the unknown, it also serves as a metaphor for the relentlessness of persistent pursuit, a metaphor also for God's action in our lives.

Poetry: "The Hound of Heaven," by Francis Thompson. A brilliant but tortured poet who struggled a lifetime with addiction to opium, even living as a street person, Thompson (1859–1907) writes about the pursuing God as "the hound of heaven." Well-known lines from that poem (1893) are as follows:

> I fled Him, down the nights and
>   down the days;
> I fled Him, down the arches of the
>   years;
> I fled Him, down the labyrinthine
>   ways
> Of my own mind; and in the mist
>   of tears
> I hid from Him, and under running
>   laughter.
> Up vistaed hopes I sped;
> And shot, precipitated,
> Adown Titanic glooms of chasmèd
>   fears,
> From those strong Feet that fol-
>   lowed, followed after.
> But with unhurrying chase,
> And unperturbèd pace,
> Deliberate speed, majestic instancy,
> They beat—and a Voice beat
> More instant than the Feet—
> "All things betray thee, who betray-
>   est Me."

Divine discipline is inevitably painful.

See the "Illustrating the Text" section of 2 Samuel 16:1–14.

The Return of the King
Brings Turmoil in the Kingdom

Big Idea *The consequences of sin can be persistent, even when the Lord's repentant servants do their best to promote unity and the Lord's faithful covenantal promise is fulfilled.*

Understanding the Text

The Text in Context

The previous episode ended with David's mourning the death of Absalom as if he were not grateful for what his men had accomplished on his behalf. Joab warned him that he was jeopardizing the loyalty of the troops, who had risked their lives for him. David presented himself to his loyal followers, and they came before him in a show of support. However, the Israelite tribes, who had supported Absalom, have fled to their homes. So as the story continues, two important questions surface: How will David respond to those who have opposed him? Will Israel renew its allegiance to David so that national unity can be restored? This next episode answers these questions: in an effort to solidify his rule and restore national unity, David extends favor to all, including enemies as well as friends. While Judah welcomes David back, the Israelite tribes vacillate. They argue among themselves (19:9–10) and then with Judah (19:41–43). Sheba the Benjamite even

organizes a rebellion against David that foreshadows the eventual secession of the Israelite tribes (20:2; cf. 1 Kings 12:16).[1] The saga continues in 1 Kings. (Thus 2 Samuel 21–24 does not continue the story; these chapters are an epilogue to the book and summarize David's reign.)

Interpretive Insights

19:9 *The king delivered us.* Though the Israelite tribes acknowledge that they threw their support to Absalom and "anointed" him, they refer to David, not his dead son, as "the king" and contemplate restoring his rule (v. 10).

19:23 *You shall not die.* Later, on his deathbed, David is not so merciful. He advises Solomon to make sure Shimei dies violently (1 Kings 2:8–9). This makes one wonder about David's motives in sparing Shimei now. He may be afraid of the Benjamites, who have turned out in large numbers. However, it is more likely that this pardon is designed to communicate to Benjamin and the northern tribes his willingness to let bygones be bygones. If David can pardon Shimei, then certainly he will welcome them back as his supporters.

19:43 *the men of Judah pressed their claims even more forcefully than the men of Israel.* The tribal unity sought by David is in serious jeopardy, despite his efforts to promote reconciliation.

20:1 *a troublemaker named Sheba.* The narrator leaves no room for a sympathetic view of the Benjamite rebel Sheba. He labels him a "troublemaker" (*'ish beliya'al*). Abigail used this same expression to describe her husband, Nabal (1 Sam. 25:25), and Shimei falsely accused David of being such a person (2 Sam. 16:7). Similar phrases are used of Eli's sons (1 Sam. 2:12), Saul's critics (10:27), and Nabal (25:17).

20:2 *all the men of Israel deserted David to follow Sheba.* Sheba, a Benjamite, exploits the hostility between Israel and Judah (cf. 19:41–43). This incident foreshadows the eventual division of the kingdom after Solomon's death. In fact, Sheba's words are repeated by the Israelites on that later occasion when they declare their independence from the Davidic dynasty (see 1 Kings 12:16).

Key Themes of 2 Samuel 19:9–20:26

- In contrast to the Israelite tribes, Judah welcomes David back.
- Despite David's attempts to promote reconciliation and peace, tribal jealousy and opposition to David persist.
- In fulfillment of Nathan's prophecy, violence continues to taint the royal court.
- In fulfillment of the Lord's covenantal promise, he preserves David's throne.

20:3 *They were kept in confinement till the day of their death, living as widows.* By including this detail, the narrator reminds us of Absalom's crime against his father (16:21–22), foretold by Nathan. In God's providence this is a fitting punishment for David's adultery (2 Sam. 12:11–12), the consequences of which continue to haunt him.

20:10 *Amasa died.* Nathan prophesied that the sword would never depart from David's house (12:10). In fulfillment of that prophecy, David's son Absalom murdered his brother Amnon, and later Joab, David's nephew, murdered Absalom. The narrator now records another bloody incident that stains David's house. We are not told of Joab's motives, but we can certainly

As David returns to Jerusalem he is met by loyal countrymen from Judah and questionably supportive men from the other tribes of Israel at the fords of the Jordan River. The Jordan River was wider and deeper in ancient times than it is today, and its banks are surrounded by dense, thorny thickets or eroded hills, as shown in this picture. Jordan River crossings took place at several fords, where sandbars and topography made traveling easier.

David's Sisters and Their Children

According to 17:25, Amasa is the son of Abigail (not David's wife), who is Zeruiah's sister. Zeruiah is the sister of David and the mother of Joab. With help from 1 Chronicles 2:16–17, we can reconstruct the family tree as follows:

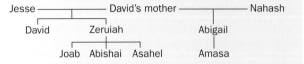

Joab and Amasa are cousins; both are David's nephews. According to 2 Samuel 17:25, Abigail's father is Nahash, not Jesse. This suggests that Abigail is the half sister of David and Zeruiah. Apparently Nahash was married to David's mother before or after her marriage to Jesse.

make an educated guess. He is undoubtedly jealous of Amasa, his replacement as David's general (20:4–5). He probably also distrusts Amasa, who has served as Absalom's general (17:25), and regards him as a threat to both the king's and his own well-being.

20:16 *a wise woman called from the city.* The reference to a wise woman invites comparison to an earlier incident involving a wise woman (14:1–22). During Absalom's exile, Joab hired a wise woman to persuade David to grant Absalom amnesty. The wise woman, encouraged by Joab, argued that David should give priority to the well-being of a guilty individual rather than implement justice. David's decision to do so led to disaster when Absalom rebelled against his father. On this later occasion a wise woman and her fellow citizens refuse to give priority to a dangerous individual (see 20:22).[2] This wise woman is a literary foil for Joab and David, who could have avoided a great deal of turmoil if they had not indulged Absalom following the murder of Amnon.

When Sheba takes refuge inside the fortified city of Abel Beth Maakah, the attacking troops under Joab build a siege ramp in order to batter down the walls. As they start to damage the walls, a wise woman from the city asks to speak to Joab. When she discovers the reason for the attack, she has Sheba executed, which saves the city from destruction. This Assyrian relief shows a siege ramp and a battering ram at the walls of Lachish (palace at Nineveh, 700–692 BC).

20:23 *Joab was over Israel's entire army.* The episode concludes with a list of David's cabinet members within the royal court. This is the second such insert in the narrative (see 8:16–18). There are two striking features of this second list when compared to the first: (1) Despite Joab's bloody deeds and temporary demotion, when all is said and done, he remains in charge of David's army, a testimony to the king's failure to implement justice, especially when close family members are involved. (2) By the end of his reign David has a supervisor of forced labor (20:24), an office that is not mentioned in the earlier list. Just as the list of David's wives foreshadowed trouble (3:2–5; 5:13–16), so this addition to the cabinet is ominous. David's polygamy, while perhaps not technically violating the law (cf. Deut. 17:17), sets a bad precedent for his son Solomon, who blatantly breaks God's command (1 Kings 11:1–8). Although the organization of forced labor may not be oppressive in David's time, it sets a dangerous precedent for Solomon and Rehoboam, who eventually expand this workforce in an oppressive manner (see 1 Kings 4:6; 5:13–14; 12:1–18), violating the principle that the king must not elevate himself above his countrymen (see Deut. 17:20). The oppressive policies of Solomon and Rehoboam lead to the division of the kingdom. In fact, Adoram (also called Adoniram), David's supervisor, continues in this position under Solomon (1 Kings 4:6; 5:14) and Rehoboam. When Rehoboam sends him out to retrieve the rebellious northern workforce, the Israelites stone him to death (1 Kings 12:18).

Theological Insights

The primary theological theme of this episode is the reliability of the Lord's word. On the one hand, the Lord preserves David's throne, in fulfillment of the covenantal promise he made through Nathan (2 Sam. 7:16). On the other hand, the persistent consequences of David's crimes continue to play themselves out. The civil unrest caused by Absalom's coup continues to threaten the nation's unity, and Nathan's prophecy

David's Return to the City

Why does the narrator inform us of the three encounters as David returns to the city? At least two reasons come to mind: (1) We are reminded of David's vulnerability. David has loyal friends like Barzillai (and apparently Mephibosheth), but he also has people (like Ziba) within his sphere of influence whose main concern is to promote their own interests. He also has outright enemies (like Shimei) who curse him one minute and then the next minute act as if they are loyal subjects. David can never be completely sure who is truly loyal. (2) David's response to all three of these individuals demonstrates his beneficence and his desire to unify God's people. He pardons an outright enemy, restores to favor one whose loyalty is not entirely certain (at least from his perspective), and offers a tried-and-true loyal subject a home in his royal palace. One would think that Israel will embrace such a beneficent king, but the northern tribes are restless and prone to go their separate way (see 2 Sam. 19:40–20:22).

that the sword will not depart from David's royal court (2 Sam. 12:10) continues to ring true. For the exiles the sustaining of the Davidic throne generates hope as they read the account, but the reality of God's discipline in David's experience also resonates with them: they know all too well from their own experience how persistent the consequences of sin can be.

Teaching the Text

1. *The consequences of sin can be persistent*. As in the preceding episode, we see again that the disciplinary consequences of sin can linger. The prophet Nathan announced David's punishment: the sword will not depart from David's house (2 Sam. 12:10). David has already lost two sons by the sword; in this episode he loses a nephew at the hands of another nephew. As in the case of Absalom (18:14–15), the vivid, detailed account of Joab's violent assault on Amasa draws attention to this reality

Ehud and Joab: Similarities and Differences

There are parallels between Joab's assassinations of Abner and Amasa and Ehud's assassination of the Moabite king Eglon, recorded in Judges 3:12–30. Both Ehud and Joab employ deceit to kill their victims. Joab asks to speak with Abner in private and then kills his unsuspecting victim (2 Sam. 3:27; cf. Judg. 3:19). Later he kills Amasa with a left-handed sword thrust as he grabs Amasa's beard with his right hand as if to kill him (2 Sam. 20:9–10). The description of how Joab has strapped his sword to his side (2 Sam. 20:8) is very similar to the description of Ehud given in Judges 3:16.[a] The significance of the link between Ehud and Joab is not so much in the similarity of the actions themselves (the description of which merely establishes a parallel), but rather in the contrast between the objects of those actions. Ehud killed a foreign oppressor and delivered Israel; Joab of Judah struck down a Benjamite (Abner), escalating the conflict between Judah and Benjamin, and now he kills one of his own relatives (his cousin Amasa). Ehud killed to liberate a nation; Joab's killing is strictly to promote his own interests.[b]

[a] G. T. K. Wong, "Ehud and Joab," 399–403. On parallels between Ehud's assassination of Eglon and Joab's murder of Amasa, see Cartledge, *1 and 2 Samuel*, 627.
[b] See Chisholm, "Ehud: Assessing an Assassin," 280–81.

(20:10, 12). It is as if the narrator, speaking for the divine Author of the story, wants us to see, smell, and feel sin's consequences as we see Amasa's intestines spill out on the ground and watch him wallowing in his own blood in the middle of the road, before finally being dragged aside and covered.

2. *Even as the Lord's discipline persists, the Lord's faithful promise to his chosen servant remains reliable.* Even as more blood is poured out within David's royal court and his nation is in danger of being torn apart around him, the Lord preserves his throne. Shimei begs for mercy, addressing David as "my lord the king" (19:20). Mephibosheth, whose loyalty has been in question since Ziba's report (16:1–4), and faithful Barzillai address him in this same way (19:26, 35 [27, 36 MT]). The rebel Sheba challenges David's authority but ends up dead and headless, as Joab returns to "the king" in Jerusalem (20:22). David himself expresses his awareness that his royal position has been restored (19:22), and the episode concludes with a list of the members of his royal court (20:23–26), as if we have returned to a more successful time in David's career (cf. 8:15–18). When the Lord delivered his covenant promise to David, he emphasized that David's throne, in contrast to Saul's, would endure (7:15–16), and this promise proves to be reliable.

Illustrating the Text

Sin's consequences are persistent.

Christian Biography: "Johnny Cash's Song of Redemption," by Ted Olson. In this

Joab feigned a kiss as he grasped Amasa's beard and used his opposite hand to thrust the dagger that killed his rival. The Assyrian soldier on this Nineveh palace relief has grabbed a prisoner's beard as he prepares to stab him with a dagger (700–692 BC).

piece Ted Olson talks about Johnny Cash's (1932–2003) long journey to God. His was a hard-lived life; he was often drug addicted; he left his wife and family for June Carter; he was subject to the temptations of his lifestyle. Cash never denied the pleasures of sin, but he also showed their persistent consequences. Finally, as Olson puts it,

> he found his way out of the cave, determined to get clean and sober. He made a good start, and he's been honest about the slips and relapses along the way—and not just with drugs. "They just kind of hold their distance," he told *Rolling Stone*. "I could invite them in: the sex demon, the drug demon. But I don't. They're very sinister. You got to watch 'em. They'll sneak up on you. All of a sudden there'll be a beautiful little Percodan laying there, and you'll want it."
>
> "The connection with God makes it all worth it," he said. "The greatest joy of my life was that I no longer felt separated from Him. Now he is my Counselor, my Rock of Ages to stand upon."[3]

God's promises are good even when he must discipline his chosen servants.

Inaugural Address: Abraham Lincoln. Abraham Lincoln's (1809–65) second inaugural address (March 4, 1865) expresses the spirit of the above principle in the following passage, delivered near the end of the American Civil War:

> Fondly do we hope—fervently do we pray—that this mighty scourge of war may speedily pass away. Yet, if God wills that it continue until all the wealth piled by the bondsman's two hundred and fifty years of unrequited toil shall be sunk, and until every drop of blood drawn with the lash shall be paid by another drawn with the sword, as was said three-thousand years ago, so still it must be said "the judgments of the Lord are true and righteous altogether."

Poetry: "Who Am I?," by Dietrich Bonhoeffer. Bonhoeffer (1906–45) was a German pastor, scholar, and martyr, and is mentioned earlier in connection with 2 Samuel 2:1–5:5. The camp doctor who saw Bonhoeffer die said that he had "hardly ever seen a man so entirely submissive to the will of God." In this poem, found in his *Letters and Papers from Prison*, Bonhoeffer's reflection echoes David's submission as he calls himself a "hypocrite" and "woebegone weakling" but affirms that he knows he belongs to God.[4]

The Structure and Function of 2 Samuel 21–24

These final chapters of 2 Samuel are an epilogue. They are arranged in a mirror structure, in which the elements in the second half of the literary unit thematically correspond to those of the first half, but in reverse order, creating a mirror effect:[1]

A   Saul's sin and its atonement: David as royal judge (21:1–14)

B   The mighty deeds of David's men (21:15–22)

C   David's song of thanksgiving (22:1–51)

C′   David's final words (23:1–7)

B′   The mighty deeds of David's men (23:8–39)

A′   David's sin and its atonement: David as royal priest (24:1–25)

The structure of the epilogue corresponds to the course of David's career as it unfolds in 1–2 Samuel. Section A (21:1–14), with its contrast between David and Saul, supplements 1 Samuel 15–2 Samuel 4, which demonstrates that David, not Saul, was the rightful king of Israel and that David was not responsible for the death of Saul and his descendants. On the contrary, David always sought to honor Saul and his family. Sections B (21:15–22) and B′ (23:8–39) correspond to 2 Samuel 5–10, which describe David's military victories. Section A′ (24:1–25) is thematically parallel to 2 Samuel 11–20, which describes David's moral failure and punishment. Sections C (22:1–51) and C′ (23:1–7) are poetic texts

that give a theological commentary on the career of David.[2]

The epilogue highlights the major themes of David's career: his divine election and superiority to Saul, his success in battle, and God's willingness to restore him to favor following acts of sin and times of chastisement. The events and poems included here epitomize and provide a microcosm of David's career and character.

The two poems (sections C and C′) appear to have been composed toward the end of David's life (see 22:1; 23:1). However, the events recorded in these chapters do not necessarily occur after the incident described in 2 Samuel 20. The narrative of David's career resumes in 1 Kings 1.

Second Samuel 22, which also appears with slight variations in Psalm 18, is a royal thanksgiving psalm. Several of its features reflect the position and activities of a king. David has participated in foreign wars (vv. 38–43) and exercised rule over defeated nations (vv. 44–46). He is the Lord's anointed king and the recipient of the Lord's covenantal promises (v. 51). In the first part of the song, David expresses his confidence in and allegiance to the Lord (vv. 2–3) and thanks the Lord for delivering him from mortal danger when he cried out for help (vv. 4–20). An assertion of his innocence, an affirmation of God's justice, and a generalized declaration of praise follow (vv. 21–32). In the next major unit of the song, David thanks the Lord for empowering him in battle (vv. 33–46). In the concluding verses (47–51) he praises the Lord in more general terms. There are several verbal links between the introductory, central, and concluding declarations of praise (vv. 2–3, 31–32, 47–51). These serve to form a thematic bracket around the two major sections of the song and the song as whole.

The much shorter second poem (23:1–7) is titled "the last words of David" (v. 1). It begins with a divine oracle that the Lord's Spirit has spoken through David (vv. 2–4). This is followed by David's response, which reflects on God's covenantal commitment to him (vv. 5–7). The reference to David as the Lord's "anointed" (v. 1) links this poem with the one that immediately precedes it (cf. 2 Sam. 22:51).

The poems are thematically central to the epilogue. They emphasize that (1) the Lord is the true source of the king's military successes (cf. 21:15–22; 23:8–39), (2) faithfulness is essential to enjoying the Lord's favor (cf. 22:21–25 and 23:3 with 21:1–14 and 24:1–25), and (3) the Lord's covenantal promises to David will be fulfilled despite human weakness and failure (cf. 22:51 and 23:5–7 with 21:15–17 and 24:1–25).

In combination with Hannah's song (1 Sam. 2:1–10), these poems also form a thematic framework for the books of Samuel. David reiterates several important themes from Hannah's Song: The Lord is the incomparable protector of his people (1 Sam. 2:2, 2 Sam. 22:32; 23:3) and rules the world with absolute justice, bringing low proud enemies and exalting his humble followers (1 Sam. 2:3–10; 2 Sam. 22:21–28). He appears in theophanic royal splendor to bring deliverance and victory to his king by destroying his enemies (1 Sam. 2:10; 2 Sam. 22:4–20). Hannah, viewing her experience as typical of God's intervention for his people, looked forward to what the Lord would do for Israel through his chosen king. David, being that king and having experienced the Lord's intervention in remarkable ways, looks back and sees the fulfillment of Hannah's expectation. The Lord has raised David to great heights (see esp. 2 Sam. 22:44–46) and guaranteed the fulfillment of his covenantal promise (22:51; 23:5–7).

Blood Vengeance in Gibeah

Big Idea *Sin sometimes has devastating consequences: God's justice must be satisfied.*

Understanding the Text

The Text in Context

As noted above, this first episode in the book's epilogue corresponds thematically to the lengthy section 1 Samuel 15–2 Samuel 4, where the narrator's primary focus is to demonstrate David's superiority to Saul and absolve David of any wrongdoing in the death of Saul and his sons. In this episode the point is clear: Saul's crimes, not any wrongdoing on David's part, are responsible for the demise of his offspring. Saul is portrayed as one who violated the covenant with the Gibeonites and was guilty of shedding innocent blood. By way of contrast, David is depicted as one through whom the Gibeonites receive the justice owed to them, yet also as one who does his best to honor Saul and his family.

Historical and Cultural Background

The Gibeonite treaty, which Saul violated, was protected by an oath and its accompanying "curses" (see esp. Josh. 9:20). Saul's crime has brought famine upon the land. Though not mentioned in Joshua 9, famine is a typical treaty curse in West Semitic treaties.[1] McCarter discusses a paral-

lel to this incident in Hittite literature from the fourteenth century BC.[2] The Hittites suffered from a plague for several years. When the Hittite king inquires of the storm-god, he is told that his father has violated a peace treaty with the Egyptians. The Hittite king laments that the sins of his father have fallen upon him. He confesses this sin to his god, presents sacrifices, and offers to make compensation for the transgression.

Interpretive Insights

21:1 *there was a famine.* Israel made a treaty with the Gibeonites in the time of Joshua, promising them that they would not harm them or take their lives as long as the Gibeonites kept their part of the bargain and served Israel as laborers (Josh. 9). Saul violated the treaty.

sought the face of the Lord. The expression "seek the face" refers to seeking the Lord's favor. Sometimes, as here, the petitioner desires the Lord's mercy (cf. 2 Chron. 7:14; Ps. 27:8; Hosea 5:6).

his blood-stained house. In contrast to David, whom the Lord has restrained from shedding the blood of Nabal and his house (1 Sam. 25:22, 26, 33), Saul's house is guilty of shedding the blood of the Gibeonites.

because he put the Gibeonites to death.
Killing innocent people was typical of
Saul, who also ordered the death of David
(1 Sam. 19:1, 15) and the priests at Nob
(22:17–18).

21:2 *Saul in his zeal.* Saul's attempt to
annihilate the Gibeonites was motivated
by nationalistic zeal, but as usual his zeal
extended beyond the limits of God's revealed will (see 1 Sam. 15).

21:3 *How shall I make atonement?* The
narrator depicts David as one who seeks to
make atonement so that blessing may be
restored to Israel, in contrast to Saul, who
brought bloodguilt upon his house and a
curse upon his nation.

21:6 *seven of his male descendants.* Saul
certainly killed more than seven of the
Gibeonites (v. 5), but the number seven has
symbolic significance throughout the ancient Near Eastern world, suggesting completeness and
fullness.[3] Apparently, as
far as the Gibeonites are
concerned, the execu-
tion of seven of Saul's
descendants will be
adequate compensa-
tion for what he has
done to them. Ap-
propriately the execu-
tion will take place in
Gibeah, Saul's home-
town. David complies
with their request,
yet it is apparent that he
himself is innocent of killing
Gibeonites. If Shimei has this incident in
mind when he accuses David of bloodguilt
against Saul's house, the narrator here
makes it clear that Shimei's accusation is

> ### Key Themes of 2 Samuel 21:1–14
>
> - Saul's crimes bring disaster to seven of his descendants, but David is not culpable in their death.
> - God's justice is satisfied only when Saul's sin against the Gibeonites is avenged.
> - As he has always done, David seeks to honor Saul and his family.

not grounded in fact (see the comment on
2 Sam. 16:8 above).[4] He goes on to show
that David keeps his promise to Jonathan
(21:7) and seeks to honor Saul and his offspring (vv. 11–14).

21:7 *The king spared Mephibosheth son
of Jonathan.* In choosing which of Saul's
descendants to hand over to the Gibeonites,
David spares Mephibosheth out of loyalty
to Jonathan and Saul (see 1 Sam. 20:15–
16, 42; 24:21–22). So even in an account
where David, for the well-being of the nation and in accordance with divine justice,
is forced to hand over seven
of Saul's descendants to
the Gibeonites, he does
his best to be faithful to
promises he has made.

21:9 *who killed them
and exposed their bod-
ies on a hill before the
LORD.* The addition of
"before the Lord" (cf.
v. 6) indicates the ritualistic and legal nature of
the execution and sug-
gests that the Gibeonites

> Saul's treaty violation brought famine to the land of Israel as
> God's judgment, even though Saul was dead. David's actions
> with the Gibeonites restore God's favor, and the rains return. In
> the plague prayers (shown here) of King Mursili, the Hittite king
> offers sacrifices and asks for mercy for an offense committed
> by his father, hoping that the plague, which they perceived as
> punishment, would stop.

David chooses to hand over the two sons whom Saul fathered by his concubine Rizpah (2 Sam. 3:7), as well as five of Saul's grandsons born to his daughter Merab. The Hebrew text in verse 8 says that Saul's daughter Michal gave birth to these five sons with her husband Adriel son of Barzillai the Meholathite. However, according to 1 Samuel 18:19, it was Merab, not Michal, who married Adriel. Furthermore, 2 Samuel 6:23 states that Michal had no children. Two Hebrew manuscripts, many LXX manuscripts, and the Peshitta read "Merab" here.

are offering the victims in the presence of the Lord, the guarantor of the treaty. The bodies are not buried but are left exposed as a sign of dishonor (1 Sam. 17:44, 46; Ps. 79:2; Jer. 16:4).

21:10 *she did not let the birds touch them by day or the wild animals by night.* The execution takes place in April–May (time of the barley harvest), and the victims' mother protects the corpses until the rains come, signaling that the famine/drought is over (see v. 1) and that the Lord has restored his favor. We are not certain how long the vigil lasts. The fall rains do not come until October–November, but perhaps the Lord causes it to rain earlier. Why does the narrator inform us of Rizpah's actions? He probably wants to honor her and her memory by recording her radical example of motherly devotion. It is likely that he also wants to remind his audience of the tragic consequences of Saul's sinful actions, which bring death and suffering to his family.

21:14 *God answered prayer in behalf of the land.* This probably refers primarily to the restoration of rain in seasonal regularity after its disruption (v. 1). This is an important note: it demonstrates that the Lord has taken up the Gibeonites' cause and that justice has been served. Rather than committing wrongdoing against the house of Saul, David has been the Lord's instrument in carrying out justice and restoring divine blessing.

Theological Insights

In this episode David, with the Lord's approval, allows the Gibeonites to execute seven of Saul's male descendants because of Saul's crimes against that city. Is it just for God to punish children for the sins of their ancestors? The Old Testament teaches that individuals do sometimes suffer the consequences of their forebears' deeds. The Lord warns his enemies that their sin

David handed over seven male descendants of Saul to the Gibeonites, who "killed them and exposed their bodies on a hill before the LORD" (2 Sam. 21:9). Pictured on this Assyrian relief are prisoners impaled on pikes so their bodies are exposed for all to see (palace at Nineveh, 700–692 BC).

will have negative consequences for their families through three or four generations (Exod. 20:5; 34:7; Num. 14:18). Dathan's, Abiram's, and Achan's innocent children died along with their sinful parents (Num. 16:27, 32 [apparently Korah's sons were spared: Num. 26:11]; Josh. 7:24). The Lord also took the lives of four of David's sons because of his sin against Uriah (2 Sam. 12:5–6, 10; cf. 12:14–15; 13:28–29; 18:15; 1 Kings 2:25). Though Jeremiah anticipates a day when God's judgment will operate on a strictly individual basis, he assumes that God has judged the children for their ancestors' sins in the past (31:29–30; cf. Lam. 5:7). However, the Old Testament law says a son should not be executed for his father's sin (Deut. 24:16; cf. 2 Kings 14:6). Ezekiel 18 seems to suggest that God himself abides by this principle and judges a person on the basis of the person's own actions, not those of the parents.

How can this apparent contradiction be harmonized? In each case in which children are punished for their parents' sin, direct rebellion against God is in view. (The Israelites made a solemn oath before God that they would live in peace with the Gibeonites [Josh. 9:18–20].) Because of the principle of corporate solidarity, the sovereign God of the universe has the freedom to judge a couple's descendants when divine authority has been directly challenged, but God does not allow humans—being finite and prone to injustice and excessive vengeance—that same freedom in civil cases.

Ezekiel 18 deals with a somewhat different situation. Here the hypothetical children in the illustrations are actively pursuing evil or righteousness in their daily lives. These exiles can rest assured that their fore-

bears' character will not negate their own behavior, for better or worse. For Ezekiel's generation, this is the important principle to recognize. They are not mere victims of God's judgment on their fathers and mothers. They too are sinners and need to take personal responsibility for their own actions. God in his grace has preserved them. He has given them opportunity to repent of their evil and to do what is right. Through the prophet Ezekiel, God assures the exiles that he will reward a proper response, regardless of their ancestors' shortcomings.

Teaching the Text

1. *God is just and holds people accountable for crimes they commit against others.* The Israelites made a treaty of peace with the Gibeonites that must not be violated, because it has been sealed with an oath in the Lord's name (Josh. 9:15, 18). At the time this treaty was made, the leaders of the nation recognized that divine wrath would fall on them if they violated the terms of the agreement (v. 20). Saul, in his misguided nationalistic zeal, violated the treaty by trying to destroy the Gibeonites (2 Sam. 21:2). The Lord, in his role as guarantor of the treaty, does not side with Israel in this matter, but he sides with the Gibeonites,

because their treaty rights have been violated. He punishes Israel for Saul's crimes (v. 1) and restores divine favor only when justice has been served and Saul's actions have been avenged to the satisfaction of the Gibeonites (vv. 6, 14). This episode is a reminder that God is just. He takes up the cause of the victims of injustice and will eventually punish those who perpetrate crimes against others. In the case of the Gibeonites, divine justice is executed shortly after the crime is committed. We know from Scripture and experience that this is not always the case, yet we can be confident that justice, sooner or later, will be served (Pss. 11:4–6; 58:10–11; 73:17–20).

2. *The consequences of sin can pursue an individual beyond death and bring horrific suffering to those who are innocent.* One of the great tragedies that attended Saul's failure and demise was the death of his son Jonathan, who exhibited so many admirable qualities and swore his allegiance to David. Jonathan would have made an ideal king or a superb second-in-command for David. But this was not to be: he ended up dying with his father at Mount Gilboa. Yet the consequences of Saul's sins follow him even beyond the grave. His crimes against the Gibeonites demand vengeance: two of his sons and five of his grandsons need to pay the price. Sin always has collateral damage, and in this case his own daughter Merab, who lost five of her sons, and his concubine Rizpah, who lost her two sons, are innocent victims. The heart-wrenching portrait of Rizpah's trying to keep the birds and wild animals from devouring the decaying carcasses of her sons is a vivid reminder of the unforeseen consequences of sin.

Illustrating the Text

God's justice is sometimes harsh.

Quote: *Life Together,* **by Dietrich Bonhoeffer.** In this classic exploration of life in

Rizpah mourned the death of her sons and stood vigil over their slain bodies so that scavenging birds and wild animals would not consume them, bringing further disgrace. Vultures pecking slain warriors are depicted on many Assyrian reliefs, like the one shown here from Nimrud (865–860 BC).

Christian community, Bonhoeffer (1906–45) discusses the hardness of God and the way Christian community should model it:

> Reproof is unavoidable. God's Word demands it when a brother falls into open sin.
>
> The practice of discipline in the congregation begins in the smallest circles. Where defection from God's word imperils the family fellowship and with it the whole congregation, the word of admonition and rebuke must be ventured. Nothing can be more cruel than the tenderness that consigns another to his sin. Nothing can be more compassionate than the severe rebuke that calls a brother back from the path of sin. It is a ministry of mercy; an ultimate offer of genuine fellowship when we allow nothing but God's Word to stand between us and succoring. . . . God's judgment is helpful and healing: . . . it serves a person. He who accepts the ministry of God's judgment is helped.[5]

Sin has unforeseen and persistent consequences, including the collateral damage it inflicts on innocent parties.

Literature: *Too Late the Phalarope*, by Alan Paton. Paton (1903–88) was a South African author and leader of anti-apartheid movements. In this novel (1953), whose strange name belies its importance and fascinating theme, Paton presents us with a compelling protagonist, Pieter van Vlaanderen, who seems to have it all but is a divided soul. He is a good-looking and respected person, a natural leader, an athlete, and more. Yet he has within him a darkness—an anger born of his father's rigid handling of him—that he will not discuss with anyone. Those who see its shadows do not confront him about it. As a result his complex emotions fester, leading him to sexual sin, clearly done because of his self-loathing. Everyone around him is destroyed, as is so often the case today when sexual sin (pornography, adultery, homosexual behavior) invades a marriage or a family. This novel has powerful effects on those who read it, especially on men.

Pieter's aunt, the novel's narrator, understands Pieter best:

> And if I write it down, people may know that he was two men, and that one was brave and gentle; and they may know, when they judge and condemn, that this one struggled with himself in darkness and alone, calling on his God and on the Lord Jesus Christ to have mercy on him. Therefore when the other Pieter van Vlaanderen did not entreat, this one entreated; and when the other did not repent, this one repented; and because there is no such magic, this one, the brave and gentle, was destroyed with him.[6]

Human Experience: Any number of stories exist about drunken drivers who think they are "just buzzed" and yet in driving end up destroying the lives of others.

David's Mighty Men

Big Idea *The Lord enables his chosen servants to accomplish their God-given tasks by providing them with the support they need.*

Understanding the Text

The Text in Context

As noted above, in the concentric structure of the epilogue are two matching units (21:15–22 and 23:8–39) that focus on David's mighty men. The epilogue reflects and summarizes David's career as outlined in 1–2 Samuel. These units correspond to 2 Samuel 5–10, which describes David's military victories. They also form a ring around the epilogue's central poetic texts (22:1–51 and 23:1–7). In the first of these poems, David reflects on his career as Is-

rael's warrior king and acknowledges that the Lord is his protector (2 Sam. 22:2–3, 31, 47). Time after time the Lord rescues him from death (22:4–20) and vindicates him before his enemies (22:21–29). The Lord energizes David for battle, enabling him to defeat his foes and extend his empire so that Israel experiences security (22:30–51). But David does not fight alone. He has several loyal and effective warriors who serve him well and through whom the Lord protects the king and defeats Israel's enemies. Their efforts are commemorated in the epilogue's reports of their exploits.

Interpretive Insights

21:15 *he became exhausted.* The narrator gives this detail to emphasize that David is vulnerable. This fact becomes especially alarming when we read in verse 16 that one of the Philistine warriors, a particularly imposing and well-armed soldier, has targeted David.

Once again, David is fighting against the Philistines (2 Sam. 21:15). Here is a close-up view of a Philistine warrior from the Egyptian reliefs at Medinet Habu (twelfth century BC).

21:17 *But Abishai son of Zeruiah came to David's rescue.* On two other occasions David's nephew Abishai, who helped his brother Joab murder Abner (2 Sam. 3:30), has volunteered to kill individuals whom he perceived as enemies of David (1 Sam. 26:8; 2 Sam. 16:9). Both times David reprimanded him; but in the context of war with the Philistines, his services were welcome! The verb used here (*'azar*) means to provide aid or support, especially to one who is in a challenging or even precarious position (see, e.g., its use in Josh. 10:6; 1 Sam. 7:12).

he struck the Philistine down and killed him. The narrator's description of Abishai's deed echoes David's victory over the Philistine champion Goliath (1 Sam. 17:50).

the lamp of Israel. This is the only place in the Old Testament where this expression is used.[1] A lamp guides one in the darkness so that one can walk without stumbling and lead others along (see Job 29:3), so here it may be a metaphor for David's leadership, which his men regard as essential for Israel's well-being.[2] Since a lamp is a symbol of physical life and prosperity (Job 18:6; 21:17; Prov. 13:9; 20:20; 24:20), it is possible that they view David as an agent of divine blessing for the nation.

21:21 *he taunted Israel.* The same verb (*harap*) appears in 1 Samuel 17, where the Philistine champion defied (*harap*) Israel and its armies (vv. 10, 25–26, 36, 45). Like David when he killed the Philistine, Jonathan fought on behalf of the Lord's covenant community, defending the honor of the nation and its God against the defiance of the enemy.

21:22 *they fell at the hands of David and his men.* The preceding account identifies David's four soldiers (Abishai, Sibbekai, Elhanan, and Jonathan) as the ones who killed the four Gittite warriors. But here the narrator gives David partial credit for the exploits of his men, emphasizing that they fought on his behalf.

23:10 *struck down the Philistines.* The narrator's description of Eleazar's and Shammah's (vv. 11–12) victories over the Philistines echoes the exploits of David their king (cf. 2 Sam. 5:25; 8:1).

The LORD brought about a great victory that day. Here and in verse 12 the narrator attributes the extraordinary exploits of two of David's mighty men to the Lord. As he has done on earlier occasions, the Lord has accomplished a great victory on behalf of his people (cf. 1 Sam. 11:13; 19:5).

23:16 *he poured it out before the LORD.* The king refuses to drink the water, because the men have risked their lives to get it. He will not treat this water (which, in his eyes, symbolizes their blood) lightly (v. 17). It deserves to be poured out before the Lord in honor of those who have demonstrated such allegiance to their king.

Theological Insights

Undoubtedly the narrator includes this account of the exploits of David's men to honor their memory and to inspire later generations with their bravery and loyalty. But these records also have a theological dimension. The Lord chose David to be the "lamp of Israel" (21:17b). When the enemy taunts Israel (21:21) and threatens

Who Killed Goliath?

According to 2 Samuel 21:19, Elhanan killed Goliath the Gittite. This seems to contradict 1 Samuel 17, where David is said to have killed this Philistine warrior (cf. 17:4, 23; see also 1 Sam. 21:9; 22:10). To complicate matters, 1 Chronicles 20:5 states that "Elhanan son of Jair killed Lahmi the brother of Goliath the Gittite." Various solutions have been proposed: (1) Identify David with Elhanan. (2) View Goliath as a title, not a proper name, so that a different Goliath is in view in 2 Samuel 21:19. (3) Regard verse 19 as textually corrupt and use 1 Chronicles 20:5 as a guide to reconstructing the original text. (4) Propose that verse 19 preserves the truth and that the name Goliath was erroneously attached to the originally unnamed Philistine champion killed by David. Of these options, the first and second appear strained and unlikely. The third or fourth approach seems preferable, but each has its problems.[a]

[a] For detailed discussion of this problem, see Chisholm, *Interpreting the Historical Books*, 175–77.

to destroy its leader (21:16), brave and loyal supporters rally to his aid (21:17a). By divine providence these men become defenders of the Lord's covenant community and his chosen king. Two times the narrator attributes the extraordinary achievements of David's men to the Lord (23:10, 12), placing their deeds in line with earlier victories that he has accomplished through Saul and David (1 Sam. 11:13; 19:5).

Teaching the Text

A primary theme emerges from the accounts of David's mighty men: *When the Lord gives his chosen servants a task to do,* *he provides support to aid them in their endeavors.* As the Lord's chosen king, David was responsible for national security. In the hostile environment in which ancient Israel existed, this meant that David must fight the wars of the Lord. Beginning with his victory over Goliath, he did so quite effectively. After becoming king of united Israel, he experienced great success in his campaigns against the surrounding nations (see 2 Sam. 8; 10). However, as David makes very clear in the lengthy poem that appears in 2 Samuel 22, he often faced death on the battlefield and was dependent on the Lord's protection for survival and success. In the accounts of David's mighty men, we discover that these brave and loyal soldiers were often the instruments of divine protection for David. The Lord gave David a challenging and dangerous task to do, and he did not leave David alone. Behind the remarkable exploits of David's men, one can see the Lord himself. On at least two occasions recorded here, Israel's armies retreated, but a lone warrior stood his ground and defeated the Philistines. But these individuals did not stand alone: the narrator informs us that the Lord "brought about a great victory" (23:10), much like he had done for another solo Philistine killer (cf. Judg. 15:18).

David's mighty men were brave and loyal soldiers who supported and protected their king. This Assyrian relief shows the king in his chariot with Assyrian troops stationed in front and his bodyguards following behind (palace at Nineveh, 640–620 BC).

Illustrating the Text

God supports those to whom he assigns challenging tasks, often through the actions of dedicated and loyal helpers.

Story: *Yearning: Living between How It Is and How It Ought to Be,* by Craig Barnes. Barnes is the president of Princeton Theological Seminary, where he is also a professor of pastoral ministry. Barnes tells the story of the church in which he was involved while living in Madison, Wisconsin, trying to set up a program for children and teenagers at risk for dropping out of the public school system. The church's Young Life group provided weekly tutoring at first, but the challenges went beyond academic needs. They began to look at all the agencies and political and educational systems that, as Barnes put it, "needed to be lobbied and manipulated" to meet their desired goals. Then those involved realized they were not working to "bring these kids and their families into our understanding of a loving community." In the learning process the church expanded its relationships with community organizations who shared their concern. "Soon," he writes, "'Project Opportunity' was launched," and fifty relationships were "made around the same model, with other churches coming on board to work on a common ministry of building relationships."[3]

Personal Stories: Many churches today provide a way for their teenagers to go on missions trips to build buildings, work with orphans, to do appointed tasks that would take a great deal of time and effort without the work of a group. With the present refugee situation, some churches annually send leaders and workers to provide instruction for women on how to sew or do things that

David's "Thirty" Men

Second Samuel 23:24 identifies "the Thirty" as David's most elite warriors, in addition to those already mentioned. One expects the list to include thirty names, but apparently at least thirty-three warriors are listed. Verses 24–31 name sixteen warriors, while verses 33–39a appear to list thirteen. Verse 32b is problematic and in Hebrew reads, "Eliahba the Shaalbonite, the sons of Jashen, Jonathan." (Contrary to the NIV, the MT does not indicate that this Jonathan is the son of Shammah, whose name appears at the beginning of v. 33.) At least four more individuals seem to be included here (we do not know how many of Jashen's sons are in view). If so, then the complete list includes at least thirty-three warriors. Perhaps the contingent originally included thirty warriors and was later expanded while retaining its original name. Another possibility is that these individuals were not all part of "the Thirty" at the same time.

Verse 39b suggests that the entire list numbers thirty-seven. This may count six of them as Jashen's sons, or it may refer to all the warriors named in the chapter, not just those in verses 24–39a. If the latter, this is problematic since five warriors are specifically mentioned in verses 8–23. Adding them to those listed in verses 24–39a, we arrive at a total of at least thirty-eight. However, the Shammah of verses 11 and 33 appears to be the same person.

might lead to their starting businesses, certainly to care for themselves in a better way.

Christian Organization: The Salvation Army. The Salvation Army began with William Booth in 1865. Leaving his pastorate behind, he began ministering to street people and the disenfranchised, thinking that then he would place these converts in churches. However, what he discovered was that the Victorian church of his day was not interested in accommodating these people. So began the East London Christian Mission, thereby starting a ministry that would in time become worldwide. The Salvation Army spread to America and around the world, providing an array of services to all kinds of people, also operating thousands of service units during World War II. The Salvation Army continues its work around the globe.[4]

"The LORD Is My Rock"

Big Idea *The Lord protects his chosen servants from those who oppose them and enables them to accomplish the tasks he has commissioned them to do.*

Understanding the Text

The Text in Context

This lengthy thanksgiving song, in which David praises the Lord for delivering him from death and for empowering him in battle, encapsulates the most important theological themes that emerge from the preceding narrative of David's career. (For fuller discussion, see above: "Additional Insights: The Structure and Function of 2 Samuel 21–24.")

Historical and Cultural Background

The theophanic depiction of the Lord as descending in the storm clouds, thundering from the sky, and hurling his lightning bolts (vv. 8–16) has numerous parallels in ancient Near Eastern literature. Identical

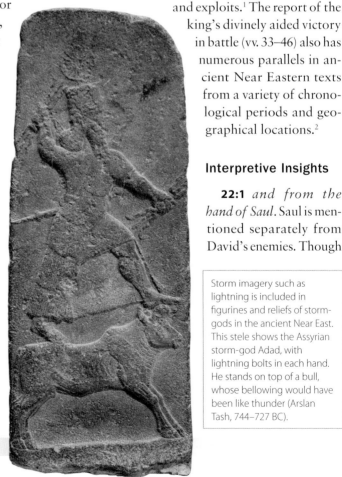

or similar imagery can be found in texts depicting storm deities (esp. the Canaanite god Baal), and also in royal annals in which warrior kings associate elements of the storm with their military prowess and exploits.[1] The report of the king's divinely aided victory in battle (vv. 33–46) also has numerous parallels in ancient Near Eastern texts from a variety of chronological periods and geographical locations.[2]

Interpretive Insights

22:1 *and from the hand of Saul.* Saul is mentioned separately from David's enemies. Though

> Storm imagery such as lightning is included in figurines and reliefs of storm-gods in the ancient Near East. This stele shows the Assyrian storm-god Adad, with lightning bolts in each hand. He stands on top of a bull, whose bellowing would have been like thunder (Arslan Tash, 744–727 BC).

Saul treated David as his enemy (1 Sam. 18:29) and regarded him as such (19:17; 24:19), David did not reciprocate. His men considered Saul to be David's enemy (24:4; 26:8), but David did not view Saul this way (2 Sam. 4:8–12).

22:2–3 *my rock.* David uses nine metaphors in verses 2–3 to depict the Lord as his protector and Savior. This heaping up of synonyms is for emphasis. Three of these terms were used earlier in 1 Samuel to describe the places where David found safety from Saul: "rock" (v. 2, *selaʿ*: 1 Sam. 23:25, 28), "fortress" (v. 2, *metsudah*: 1 Sam. 22:4–5; 24:22 [23 MT]), and "rock" (v. 3, *tsur*: 1 Sam. 24:3 [2]). The term translated "rock" in verse 3 (*tsur*) refers to a rocky cliff that is relatively inaccessible and would provide safety for one being pursued. David uses it in his introductory, central, and concluding declarations of praise (vv. 3, 32, 47). Of the nine images used in verses 2–3, it is the only one that appears in all three sections. This suggests that it is the dominant metaphor for God in this poem. Hannah also uses this metaphor for the Lord (1 Sam. 2:2).

the horn of my salvation. The horn of an ox underlies this metaphor (Deut. 33:17; 1 Kings 22:11; Ps. 92:10), which depicts military strength.[3] Hannah celebrates that the Lord has exalted her "horn," and she anticipates the day when the Lord will exalt the "horn of his anointed" (1 Sam. 2:1, 10). David, the king who has brought Hannah's expectation to realization, regards the Lord as his horn—that is, as the source of his strength that delivered him from those who opposed him.

22:5 *The waves of death.* David envisions the assaults of his enemies as ener-

Key Themes of 2 Samuel 22

- The Lord protects David and delivers him from those who seek his life.
- The Lord is just and vindicates his loyal followers.
- The Lord energizes David for battle and enables him to defeat the nations that oppose him.

gized by Death itself, which is depicted here as raging water and personified as a hunter (v. 6). In ancient Israelite thought, Death is not a static condition but a dynamic power that threatens the harmony of life and even life itself.

torrents of destruction. The Hebrew term translated "destruction" is *beliyaʿal*, the same word used to characterize two individuals who treated David with the utmost contempt: Nabal (1 Sam. 25:17, 25) and Sheba (2 Sam. 20:1). While the term is used here as an epithet for Death, it may echo the incidents in which these individuals opposed David. These hostile opponents (cf. v. 1) were agents of Death, which was determined to overwhelm David and claim him as its victim.

22:6 *the snares of death.* David personifies Death as a hunter who uses snares to trap his victims. The metaphor is appropriate since the psalms sometimes use such imagery to describe the evil plots of enemies (see Pss. 140:5; 141:9).[4] Here David views all of the attacks upon his life by the "hunters" (his human enemies) as one powerful assault by the "Hunter" (Death).

22:14 *The LORD thundered from heaven.* Hannah anticipated the Lord's thundering against his enemies in conjunction with the empowering of his chosen king (1 Sam. 2:10). David's theophanic description of the Lord's intervention on his behalf utilizes this same image.

22:15 *routed them.* The verb *hamam,* "to rout," is used in several accounts of the Lord's victories over his enemies (Exod. 14:24; Josh. 10:10; Judg. 4:15; 1 Sam. 7:10). Its use here links David's deliverance with the Lord's mighty historical deeds on behalf of Israel.

22:17 *he drew me out of deep waters.* The Lord reached down and delivered David from the surging waters of Death (cf. v. 5), proving his sovereign power over life and death, a fact that Hannah affirmed (cf. 1 Sam. 2:6).

22:25 *The Lord has rewarded me according to my righteousness.* David attributes his deliverance to his righteousness, which he defines in terms of a commitment to obey the Lord's commands (v. 22–23). When he stood before Saul, after sparing the king's life a second time, David affirmed that the Lord "rewards everyone for their righteousness and faithfulness" (1 Sam. 26:23). On that occasion David claimed to be innocent of trying to kill Saul, and he appealed to God for vindication (v. 24). The Lord did indeed vindicate him shortly thereafter.

22:26 *To the faithful you show yourself faithful.* Hannah declared that the Lord "will guard the feet of his faithful servants" (1 Sam. 2:9). The "faithful servants" (*hasidim*) are those loyal to the Lord. David uses this same word here as he describes how the Lord proves to be faithful to his loyal followers.

22:27 *but to the devious you show yourself shrewd.* Here the NIV does not adequately capture the idea being expressed. A better reading would be "You prove to be deceptive to one who is perverse" (AT). The point is that God sometimes uses de-ception to thwart the purposes of those who are morally and ethically corrupt. The word translated "devious" (*'iqqesh*) refers to those who are morally "twisted," or perverse. The Proverbs frequently use the term of evil men and their words, thoughts, and actions (Prov. 2:15; 8:8; 11:20; 17:20; 19:1; 22:5; 28:6). Their actions are the antithesis of just and upright behavior (8:8; 11:20; 19:1; 28:6). As one reflects on David's career, one can detect the providential "deceit" of God at work on David's behalf on several occasions (1 Sam. 16:2–3; 19:11–17; 2 Sam. 16:16–19; 17:7–14).[5]

22:28 *to bring them low.* The theme of the Lord's debasing (*shapal*) the proud also appears in Hannah's song (1 Sam. 2:7; cf. v. 3).

22:30 *I can scale a wall.* The translation "scale" is inadequate; the Hebrew verb (*dalag*) means "leap, spring" (cf. Song 2:8–9; Isa. 35:6). To emphasize the military superiority that God has provided, David describes himself as leaping over the wall of the enemy's city.[6]

22:31 *The Lord's word is flawless.* In this context the Lord's "word" is his oracular promise of protection and victory (vv. 33–46; cf. Ps. 12:5–7). Here David alludes to the numerous occasions when he inquired of the Lord and received a reliable oracle of victory or protection (1 Sam. 23:2, 4–5, 10–12; 30:8; 2 Sam. 5:19).[7]

22:32 *And who is the Rock except our God?* Like Hannah (1 Sam. 2:2), David affirms that the Lord is the incomparable protector of his people. Both use the metaphor of the "rock" to depict the Lord in this role (see the comment above on vv. 2–3). In both cases their affirmation is based on the Lord's ability to bring down the proud and exalt his humble followers (1 Sam. 2:3–10; 2 Sam. 22:28).

22:35 *He trains my hands for battle.* David depicts the Lord as training him in the art of warfare and as giving him a special protective shield (v. 36). In this way he makes it clear that his military prowess found its source in the Lord's supernatural enablement.[8]

22:44 *the attacks of the peoples.* The Hebrew text has "my people." Here David refers to attacks by his own countrymen rather than by foreigners. He most likely alludes to his conflicts with the Benjamite supporters of Saul (2 Sam. 2:8–3:1), his own son Absalom and his Israelite followers (2 Sam. 15–18), and Sheba (2 Sam. 20). In all of these cases large segments of the nation opposed David (2:8–9; 15:6, 13; 20:2).

22:45 *foreigners cower before me.* The historical background for the imagery of verses 44–46 can be found in 2 Samuel 8 and 10 (see esp. 8:9–10 and 10:19).[9]

22:47 *The Lord lives!* By affirming that the Lord "lives," David emphasizes his active presence and intervention, rather than the philosophical notion of his existence. The parallel line demonstrates this, for David identifies the Lord as "the Rock" (that is, protector; see the comment on vv. 2–3 above) and his "Savior." There is an echo here of

David's Claim to Be Righteous

In verses 21–25 David appears to claim moral perfection and unwavering allegiance to the Lord's covenant demands. But surely, given his moral failures and shortcomings, David is not claiming to be innocent in an absolute sense. David speaks here in general terms, using covenant terminology that derives from a context where only two extremes (loyalty and disloyalty) exist. As he reflects on his life, he asserts that loyalty to the Lord has characterized his attitudes and actions. Three observations support this interpretation: (1) The heading (v. 1) and style of the song indicate that David is generalizing about his experience. In verses 4–20 he treats his many narrow escapes as if they were one great event in which he experiences divine deliverance. In verses 33–46 he describes his numerous battles as if they were one decisive conflict. (2) Later in the Former Prophets, reflection on David's career casts him in the role of a loyal, even paradigmatic, follower of the Lord (1 Kings 3:3, 6, 14; 9:4; 11:4, 6, 33–34, 38; 14:8; 15:3, 5, 11; 2 Kings 14:3; 16:2; 18:3; 22:2). (3) In portraying attitudes toward the Lord, the psalms consistently speak of two groups, the righteous and the wicked. In this song these two groups are clearly differentiated (vv. 26–28). Though David at times failed to walk in accordance with God's covenant, he demonstrated in his attitudes and actions an allegiance to the Lord that was in contrast to the consistent anticovenant behavior of the wicked.

David's words before his battle with Goliath, when he expressed his disgust that the Philistine champion would defy the armies of the "living God" (1 Sam. 17:26, 36).

David is describing the Lord's protection when he refers to the Lord as his Rock. David pictures a rocky cliff that is relatively inaccessible and provides safety for one being pursued. He may be remembering the cliffs at En Gedi, shown here, where he went into hiding from Saul.

22:51 *he shows unfailing kindness to his anointed.* When the Lord made his special covenant with David, he promised that his "love" (*hesed*) would remain with David's dynasty (2 Sam. 7:15; cf. Ps. 89:28). Here David testifies that he has been the recipient of this "unfailing kindness" (*hesed*).

Theological Insights

The major theme of this song is the Lord's protection and deliverance. David opens the song by using nine different metaphors to assert that the Lord is his protector and Savior (vv. 2–3). In both the middle of the song and its conclusion he again calls the Lord his "rock" (vv. 32, 47). The song is filled with the vocabulary of protection and deliverance. David recalls that when he cried for help, he was "saved" from his enemies (v. 4). The Lord pulled him from the raging waters (v. 17) and "rescued" him from his powerful foes (v. 18). He led David into a "spacious place" as he "rescued" him (v. 20). The Lord characteristically saves the humble (v. 28) and "shields all who take refuge in him" (v. 31; cf. v. 3). Before battle the Lord gave him a "shield" of victory (v. 36). While David's enemies had no one to save them (v. 42), he experienced the Lord's deliverance to the fullest extent (vv. 44, 47, 49, 51).

Another prominent theme in the song is the Lord's supernatural enablement. Using hyperbole in some cases, David tells how he charged the enemy and even leaped over a wall with the Lord's help (v. 30). The Lord strengthened him (v. 40), giving him ability and skill (vv. 34–37) so that he was able to annihilate his enemies on the field of battle without stumbling (vv. 38–43). The Lord elevated David to a position of rulership over nations, some of which had not recognized the authority of Israel before David's reign (vv. 44–46, 48).

Because of the Lord's mighty acts on his behalf, David is convinced that the Lord is the incomparable King over all nations. He demonstrates his living presence by exercising his saving power on behalf of his people (v. 47). No other so-called god can begin to match the Lord's protective power (v. 32). In the thick of the battle, the Lord saves, but other gods do not (v. 42). The Lord is the "Most High" and exercises sovereign control over even the raging waters of chaos (vv. 14–16). As ruler of the nations, the Lord deserves their recognition and worship (v. 50). He controls the storm and uses it to subdue his enemies, including Death itself (vv. 5–20).

On the basis of his experience, David also asserts that the Lord is just and faithful. His assurances of victory are reliable (v. 31), and he keeps his covenant promises to his chosen servants (v. 51). The Lord rewards those who are loyal and obedient (vv. 21–27a) but opposes the wicked (v. 27b). In fact, his actions toward an individual are a mirror image of that person's deeds. Loyal followers find God to be faithful in his dealings with them. Wicked and deceptive rebels, who oppose divine authority and seek to destroy others, find the Lord to be a resolute and dangerous opponent, who frustrates and reverses their efforts and is not beyond using deceptive methods of his own to bring about their demise (v. 27b).

Teaching the Text

1. *Because the Lord is just, he protects and saves his loyal servants.* David celebrates the

All kings in the ancient Near East believed they fought on behalf of their gods. But David realized he was leading the armies of the living God (1 Sam. 16:26). This Assyrian relief shows the Assyrian god shooting arrows in battle as he flies in front of King Ashurnasirpal (palace at Nimrud, 865–860 BC).

Lord's protection and deliverance. Behind the faces of his many human enemies, he sees the power of Death, which the apostle Paul calls "the last enemy" (1 Cor. 15:26). But David affirms that the Lord is sovereign even over this powerful enemy and capable of delivering his people from its overwhelming, deadly waves and snares. For David, the Lord's salvation is an expression of his justice and faithfulness to his loyal followers. Because of their devotion to him, he vindicates them before their adversaries. For a fuller discussion of this theme, see our comments above under "Teaching the Text," for 1 Samuel 1:1–2:11.

2. *The Lord enables his chosen servants to accomplish the tasks he has commissioned them to do.* David is very much aware of the Lord's energizing power on the field of battle. Because he was God's chosen king, one of his primary tasks was to fight the Lord's battles against hostile enemies. He put his life on the line many times, but each time the Lord's assuring word of victory proved true, and David was able to conquer the enemies of God's covenant community. In the present era, the Lord's followers are commissioned to engage in spiritual conflict—not against flesh-and-blood enemies, but against "the spiritual forces of evil in the heavenly realms," which oppose God's church and its mission to proclaim the good news and produce new disciples of the risen Jesus (Eph. 6:12). The Lord provides the spiritual resources necessary to engage in this war against the Evil One (Eph. 6:10–18).

Illustrating the Text

The justice of God identifies with and vindicates his oppressed people.

See the *"Illustrating the Text" section of 1 Sam. 1:1–2:11.*

God will enable his people in spiritual warfare as they fulfill his commission to the church.

Hymn: "A Mighty Fortress Is Our God," by Martin Luther. The best-known hymn of Luther (1483–1546), this song (1527–29) has been called the "Battle Hymn of the Reformation." The third verse is particularly applicable:

> And though this world, with devils
>   filled, should threaten to undo
>   us,
> We will not fear, for God hath
>   willed His truth to triumph
>   through us:
> The Prince of Darkness grim, we
>   tremble not for him;
> His rage we can endure, for lo, his
>   doom is sure,
> One little word shall fell him.

Ruling in the Fear of the Lord

Big Idea *The Lord expects his chosen servants to promote righteousness and to find hope in his faithful promises.*

Understanding the Text

The Text in Context

This poem is titled "the last words of David" (v. 1). It begins with a divine oracle that the Lord's Spirit has spoken through David (vv. 2–4). This is followed by David's response, which reflects on God's covenantal commitment to him (vv. 5–7). The reference to David as the Lord's "anointed" (v. 1) links this poem with the one that immediately precedes it (cf. 2 Sam. 22:51). As noted above, these poems, as a tandem, form the pivot within the epilogue's concentric structure. They provide a theological summary of David's career and, together with Hannah's song (1 Sam. 2:1–10), a thematic framework for the books of Samuel. For a more detailed discussion, see above under "Additional Insights: The Structure and Function of 2 Samuel 21–24."

Historical and Cultural Background

The comparison of a righteous king to the light of the sun reminds one of Psalm 84:11, where the Lord, in his role as a just king who protects his people, is called a "sun and shield." The comparison of a king to the sun is common in ancient Near Eastern literature, where examples abound from Ugarit (in letters to the Hittite overlord) and Amarna (in letters to the pharaoh). The Assyrian kings Shalmaneser III, Ashurnasirpal II, and Esarhaddon use the epithet "sun" of themselves.[1]

In the ancient Near East, a righteous king was linked to the sun through the sun-god. One of the gods of both the sun and justice was Shamash. Kings who worshiped Shamash assumed the role as his administrator of justice. In this stele, Shamshi-Adad is shown wearing a maltese cross, a symbol of Shamash (temple of Nabu, Nimrud, 814 BC).

Interpretive Insights

23:1 *the man anointed by the God of Jacob.* As David reflects on his career and calling, he realizes that his divine election is foundational to all that he has accomplished; it defines his purpose as Israel's king.

23:3 *When one rules over people in righteousness.* The divine oracle speaks of the benefits of a righteous ruler. "Righteousness" refers here to morally upright behavior, which entails adherence to God's moral standards (22:21–25). Such behavior finds its source in the "fear of God," which is a humble, genuine respect for his moral authority and produces obedience (Deut. 6:2; 10:12). This description of the ideal king echoes the Deuteronomic regulations of kingship, which dictate that Israel's king is to study the law of the Lord "so that he may learn to revere [or, "fear"] the LORD his God" (Deut. 17:19).

23:4 *he is like the light of morning at sunrise.* The synonyms "light" (*'or*) and "brightness" (*nogah*) may signify divine deliverance and renewed blessing (Isa. 9:2 [9:1 MT]) associated with God's presence (Isa. 60:3; cf. v. 1). The brightness follows rain that produces vegetation, symbolizing divine blessing on the freshly watered earth. The righteous king is viewed here as the Lord's instrument of material and agricultural blessing for his people (cf. Pss. 72:1–7, 16; 144:12–14).

23:5 *he would not have made with me an everlasting covenant.* This is the only place in the Old Testament where the Davidic covenant is specifically called "everlasting," but its perpetual, irrevocable nature is stated elsewhere (2 Sam. 7:13, 16; Ps. 89:4, 28, 36–37). For fuller discussion of the na-

Key Themes of 2 Samuel 23:1–7

- The Lord expects David, as his chosen king, to promote righteousness.
- David places his hope in God's faithful covenantal promise.

ture of the Davidic covenant, see comments above on 2 Samuel 7.

arranged and secured in every part. This assertion is consistent with the notion that the covenant and its promises are irrevocable. The verb translated "arranged" (*'arak*) has a legal connotation here (cf. Job 13:18; 23:4; Ps. 50:21) and refers to the terms of the covenant being spelled out formally and clearly. The verb translated "secured" (*shamar*) apparently refers to the covenant's being guaranteed by the divine promise. Elsewhere to "keep a covenant" means to observe its terms and be faithful to the commitment it demands. Here the covenant is "secured" by God, the one who made it (cf. the previous line, which speaks of the Lord as the initiator of the covenant).

23:6 *evil men.* The term used here (*beliya'al*) carries the primary meaning of "worthless" and by extension "wicked, evil." David uses the term as a title for Death in the previous song (2 Sam. 22:5). The word normally follows and modifies "son(s)" or "man/men." Here it is used in isolation, but "sons" or "men" may be implied, or the term may be used collectively for all those who together embody this characteristic. In this context David has in mind those who oppose his rule.[2] In 1 Samuel 10:27 the word is used of those who opposed Saul, God's chosen king. It is also used to characterize Nabal and Sheba (1 Sam. 25:17, 25; 2 Sam. 20:1), both of whom treated David with disrespect and refused to honor him as the Lord's anointed.

Like the thorns described by David in verses 6–7, they both perished suddenly.

Theological Insights

This short poem makes an important contribution to our understanding of the Davidic covenant. The Lord chose David to embody the Deuteronomic ideal of kingship (Deut. 17:14–20). He was to promote righteousness and to fear the Lord, and in so doing to be an instrument of divine blessing for his people (vv. 3–4). At the same time, David could be confident in his covenantal relationship with the Lord, knowing that the divine promises had been formalized and secured (v. 5a). Thus David could expect to experience divine protection and blessing (v. 5b) and to see the demise of evil rebels (vv. 6–7). So, in short, the Davidic covenant demands that the chosen king promote God's moral standard; it also guarantees that obedience will be rewarded.

As God's chosen king, David was to set an example by fearing the Lord and promoting righteousness and justice. In Egypt, symbols of kingship were the crook and flail. In this relief from Abydos, the god Osiris is handing the crook and flail to the pharaoh, giving him the authority to rule (thirteenth century BC).

Teaching the Text

1. *The Lord expects his chosen servants to promote righteousness and to respect his authority.* David was to promote righteousness within the covenant community and serve as a model of one who respects the Lord's authority. But this is not a command that applies only to the king. The Lord expects the entire nation to fear him (Deut. 5:29; 6:2, 13, 24; 10:12, 20; 31:12–13); his chosen king is to lead the way. On such issues, nothing has changed in the present era. The Lord expects all of his chosen servants to live in a righteous manner and to respect his moral authority (Eph. 4:24; 5:8–10; 2 Tim. 2:22; 1 Pet. 2:17). This is especially true for those chosen to lead the church (1 Tim. 6:11; 2 Tim. 3:16–17). Yet in the present era genuine righteousness begins with faith in Jesus Christ (Rom. 1:17; Phil. 3:9), who frees his followers from slavery to sin and through his Spirit imparts the capacity to live in a righteous manner (Rom. 6:17–18; 14:17–18; Gal. 5:5).

2. *The Lord's chosen servants should place their hope in the Lord's faithful promise to David.* Despite his sins and failures, at the end of his life David still holds on to God's irrevocable covenantal promises, for he knows that ultimately God's purpose in choosing him will be realized. As a study of David's life illustrates, time after time God

demonstrates his faithfulness to David, even though he needs to discipline him severely. God's faithfulness to David gives all of his chosen servants reason to hope. In the end Jesus Christ fulfills the Davidic ideal, brings its promises to fruition, and destroys the enemies of his people (Rev. 3:7; 5:5; 22:16). Those who have chosen to follow him find safety (Rom. 8:31–39) and will experience the light of his kingdom (Rev. 21:23; 22:5).

Illustrating the Text

Fearing the Lord has important manifestations in our lives.

Literature: *The Wind in the Willows,* by Kenneth Grahame. In this classic children's tale (1908), one of the characters, "the Mole," has a supernatural experience, and a great awe falls upon him, "an awe that turned his muscles to water, bowed his head, and rooted his feet to the ground. It was no panic terror—indeed he felt wonderfully at peace and happy—but it was an awe that smote and held him, and without seeing, he knew it could only mean that some august Presence was very, very near."[3]

Biography: As told by Donald McCullough, in *The Trivialization of God* (1995). McCullough illustrates the importance of fearing the Lord with a story about Arturo Toscanini, one of the most acclaimed musicians of the late nineteenth and early twentieth centuries. The orchestra had just finished a superb performance of Beethoven's *Fifth Symphony* when the audience rose to its feet, clapping and shouting with delight. Toscanini, however, waved his arms violently for them to stop. Turning to the orchestra, he shouted, "You are nothing."

Pointing to himself, he shouted, "I am nothing." Then he said, "Beethoven is everything, everything, everything."[4]

Personal Stories: An African traveler says that when he was among a particularly savage tribe, his attention was drawn to their idol, stuck high upon a pole, as if seeming to convey the idea that the god could see around the country and every one of the people. The tribe believed that every act of dishonesty would be viewed by their god, and they would be known to be guilty of such acts and be punished accordingly. The effect of this faith was that no dishonest act was done within sight of this idol: the most valuable property was perfectly secure.

Confidence is the result of believing in the Lord's faithful promise to David.

Film: *Sophie Scholl: The Final Days.* This film (2005) is based on the true story of Sophia Magdalena Scholl (1921–43), a German student active within the White Rose nonviolent resistance group in Nazi Germany. She was convicted of high treason after being found distributing antiwar leaflets at the University of Munich with her brother Hans. They were both guillotined. Scholl is celebrated as one of the great German heroes who actively opposed the Third Reich during World War II.

Scholl's confidence in staying true to her principles was extraordinary; her religious faith was the key factor in her decision to oppose the Nazi regime unwaveringly, a decision that led to her death. Among her memorable quotes in the film are these words: "I will cling to the rope God has thrown me in Jesus Christ, even when my numb hands can no longer feel it."

David Brings a Plague upon Israel

Big Idea *When angered by sin, God may severely punish the sinners, but he is willing to relent from his judgment when sinners repent.*

Understanding the Text

The Text in Context

As noted above, this final episode in the book corresponds to 2 Samuel 21:1–14 in the concentric structure of the epilogue. In both episodes David successfully appeases God's anger. In the first instance Saul's sin against the Gibeonites prompts God's judgment; in the second instance God's anger at Israel, presumably due to some unidentified sin, is the catalyst for judgment. With its contrast between David and Saul, 2 Samuel 21:1–14 supplements 1 Samuel 15–2 Samuel 4, which demonstrates that David rather than Saul is the rightful king of Israel and that David is not responsible for the death of Saul and his descendants. Now 2 Samuel 24 supplements 2 Samuel 11–20, which describes David's moral failure and its negative consequences for the nation. Despite his sin and chastisement by the Lord, David remains the Lord's chosen servant and is not rejected as Saul was. In 2 Samuel 24 he sins and endures the horrible consequences of his action. But David successfully intercedes for the people, who are dying as punishment

*2 Samuel 23:8–39 is discussed with 21:15–22.

for his own sin, and his position as leader of the nation remains intact.

Interpretive Insights

24:1 *Again the anger of the* LORD *burned against Israel.* Only once before in 1–2 Samuel has the Lord's anger against his own people been mentioned. In 2 Samuel 6:7 his anger burned against Uzzah when he touched the ark. We are not told specifically why the Lord is angry with Israel on the occasion mentioned here in 2 Samuel 24. However, we should probably assume that his anger is prompted by sin. Elsewhere when the Lord's anger "burns" against his people, it is due to sin (see Exod. 32:10; Num. 11:33; 25:3; 32:13; Deut. 6:15; 7:4; 11:17; 29:27; Josh. 7:1; 23:16; Judg. 2:14, 20; 3:8; 10:7; 2 Kings 13:3; 23:26; Isa. 5:25). In all instances, blatant rebellion, usually in the form of idolatry, is the sin that prompts divine wrath.

he incited David against them. Would the Lord really punish sin by prompting more sin (cf. vv. 1 and 10)? This may seem unfair and contrary to God's holy nature, but the Bible shows that God sometimes judges sinners by inciting them to commit

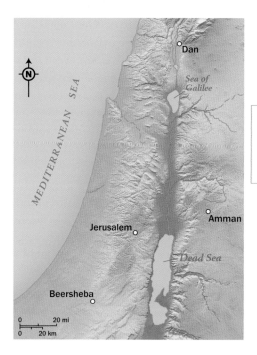

David was incited to take a military census and sent Joab and his commanders from "Dan to Beersheba." This phrase is used to describe the entire territory of the nation of Israel, even though the route Joab follows covers a more extensive geographical region.

more sin, which in turn prompts severe judgment. Sin can ignite a chain reaction that causes more sin and prompts more intense punishment until the sinner is destroyed. God sometimes deceives rebellious people by making them believe false prophetic messages (Jer. 4:10; see 1 Kings 22:23). As in the case of Saul, he sends spirits to torment sinful individuals and cause them to act in sinful ways (Judg. 9:23–24; 1 Sam. 16:14; 18:10; 19:9–10; see esp. 1 Sam. 26:19). According to Paul (2 Thess. 2:9–12), a time is coming when God will delude sinful people so that they will believe Satan's lies and self-destruct.

24:10 *I have sinned greatly in what I have done.* Most readers assume that David's military census is wrong because it is motivated by pride and/or reflects David's lack of faith in God's ability to protect the people. However, the matter may not be quite this simple. A military census

is permissible when ordered by the Lord (Num. 1:1–3) and when accompanied by a "ransom" payment given as a precautionary measure in the event that purity laws are violated (Exod. 30:12). Failure to make such payment could result in an outbreak of plague.[1] A military census activates the warriors who are counted and makes them subject to certain ritual purity laws governing military service (see, e.g., 1 Sam. 21:4–5; 2 Sam. 11:8, 11).[2] There is no indication in 2 Samuel 24 that David offers ransom payments to the Lord or that he is even aware of this legislation. By neglecting to collect these payments and then conducting a census that takes nearly ten months to complete, David creates a situation in which it is inevitable that such laws will be violated somewhere by someone, prompting the wrath of God.

For the second time in 1–2 Samuel, David confesses his sin (cf. 2 Sam. 12:13). Prior to David's confession before Nathan, the only individuals in the Former Prophets to say the words "I have sinned" are Saul (1 Sam. 15:24, 30; 26:21) and Achan (Josh. 7:20). However, David's earlier confession of his guilt, without any attempt to deny wrongdoing or to justify his actions, sets him apart from Saul (1 Sam. 13:11–12; 15:13–25). The same is true here. His conscience bothers him (2 Sam. 24:10; cf. 1 Sam. 24:5), and he spontaneously confesses, even adding the emphatic "very."[3]

I have done a very foolish thing. David's admission that he has acted foolishly is ironic, for it depicts David as Saul-like. Samuel accused Saul of acting foolishly when he refused to wait for the prophet and presumptuously offered a burnt offering (1 Sam. 13:13), and Saul admitted that he had acted foolishly in pursuing David as if he were a criminal (1 Sam. 26:21).

24:14 *for his mercy is great.* David decides that he would rather be punished directly by the Lord than be attacked by men, for the Lord is more merciful than human enemies. The Lord's "mercy," or compassion, is the tender love he feels for his people that moves him to pity their sinful, mortal condition and to show them mercy (Ps. 103:13–14). David appeals to God's tender love when he confesses his great sin, emphasizing his innate sinfulness and need for spiritual transformation (Ps. 51:1–10). This divine emotion is comparable to the love

David's action (taking a census) in response to God's anger results in punishment for the Israelites in the form of a plague. In the Sumerian text known as the Curse of Agade (pictured here), the people in the city of Agade suffer because of the god's response to the king's offense.

between blood brothers (Gen. 43:30) or to the love that a parent feels for a child (1 Kings 3:26; cf. Ps. 103:13). Yet God's compassion for his people surpasses that of a mother for her child (Isa. 49:15). Even so, in this case the Lord's mercy does not eliminate all consequences of sin: it simply causes the Lord to lessen the extent of his judgment (2 Sam. 24:15).

24:17 *When David saw the angel who was striking down the people.* If the events recorded in verses 17–25 occur *before* the incident described in verse 16, then the Lord's merciful decree is in response to David's intercession. However, if the verses are in chronological order, then the sequence is as follows: (1) The Lord relents from punishing Jerusalem (v. 16). (2) David, not being aware of the Lord's decision to relent, sees the angel and assumes that the destroyer is ready to invade the city. This prompts him to intercede for the people through prayer and offerings (vv. 17–25a). (3) The Lord, having already relented from further judgment, restores his favor (v. 25b).[4]

I . . . have done wrong. This is the same verb (ʿawah) used in 2 Samuel 7:14, where the Lord warns that wrongdoing on the part of the Davidic king will result in discipline. Yet he promises that he will not remove his love from him, as he did from Saul (v. 15). That proves to be the case here.

24:21 *that the plague on the people may be stopped.* A different word for the "plague" (*maggepah*) is used here (see also v. 25) than in verses 13, 15. This term is used of the plague that tormented the Philistines following the capture of the ark (1 Sam. 6:4), but in 1–2 Samuel it more often describes a mass slaughter of human beings (1 Sam. 4:17; 2 Sam. 17:9; 18:7). It appears that this term draws attention to the mass destruction of human life brought by the plague, whereas the word (*deber*) used earlier focuses more on the punitive nature of the plague.

24:25 *Then the* LORD *answered his prayer in behalf of the land*. This observation indicates that the Lord's anger has been appeased. It also provides a verbal link with the first episode in the epilogue (2 Sam. 21:14).

Theological Insights

This chapter is one of the most disturbing in the Bible because it depicts God as angry, deceptive, and unforgiving. It begins with the portrait of an angry God who incites his chosen servant David to sin by numbering the people. Later he wipes out a large number of Israelites for a sin that David, by his own admission, has committed. Yet in the midst of all this, David characterizes God as compassionate, a characteristic that, on the surface, seems nearly absent from this episode.

Several theological observations are in order: (1) David's suggestion that the Israelites are merely innocent "sheep" may be shortsighted, because verse 1 indicates that the Lord is angry with Israel, implying they have sinned. Each of the three options for judgment is designed to impact Israel negatively, suggesting that the Lord's primary purpose all along is to punish Israel.[5] (2) One sees the corporate dimension of David's relationship with Israel. Israel's sin prompts the Lord to incite Israel's king to do wrong, and the resulting punishment in turn negatively impacts all Israel. (3) Though compassionate, the Lord seemingly withholds forgiveness, even

The Parallel Account in 1 Chronicles 21

The parallel account in 1 Chronicles 21 makes no mention of the Lord's anger or involvement in prompting the census. Instead the text states, "Satan rose up against Israel and incited David to take a census of Israel" (v. 1). The word translated "Satan" in the NIV actually means "[an] adversary." It is used here *without* the Hebrew definite article (the). Elsewhere when it appears without the article, it usually refers to a personal or national adversary in the human sphere. (See 1 Sam. 29.4, 2 Sam. 10:22 [23 MT]; 1 Kings 5:4 [18]; 11:14, 23; Ps. 109:6. In Num. 22:22, 32 the angel of the Lord assumes the role of an adversary to Balaam.) When referring elsewhere to Satan, the noun has the article and is used as a title, "the Adversary" (see Job 1:6–9, 12; 2:1–4, 6–7; Zech. 3:1–2). In light of usage elsewhere, the adversary in 1 Chronicles 21:1 could well be a nearby nation whose hostility against Israel has incited or persuaded David to number the people so he can assess his military strength.

However, many versions (such as KJV, NIV, NRSV) prefer to take the noun in 1 Chronicles 21:1 as an isolated instance of a proper name and translate "Satan," perhaps because later revelation shows that inciting someone to sin is one of this evil spirit's favorite activities. Though it is far from certain that Satan is the referent here, some then try to use this passage to solve the problem of divine deception in 2 Samuel 24:1. In this approach 1 Chronicles 21:1 shows that Satan is the real culprit who incites David to sin. In this line of reasoning, 2 Samuel 24:1 indicates that God, because he is angered by Israel's sin, merely allows Satan to tempt David; and thus Satan, not God, is the real deceiver and instigator. However, arguing that God simply allows or permits Satan's activity hardly does justice to the demand of 2 Samuel 24:1, which depicts the divine deception as prompted by divine "anger" and makes no mention of any agent. Rather than being the key to solving the theological puzzle, 1 Chronicles 21:1 offers a more limited perspective of the episode by focusing on the instrument of divine deception. The best way to harmonize the two texts is to recognize the active role that both the Lord and his instrument of deception play in the event.[a]

[a] Chisholm, "Does God Deceive?," 22–23.

when David humbly confesses his foolish actions (v. 10). Perhaps the fact that the Lord relents can be interpreted as a form of forgiveness, but if so, then forgiveness in this case is merely a reduced sentence and punishment (see 2 Sam. 12:13–14, as well as Num. 14:13–35). If there is mercy here, surely it is a severe mercy. (4) Though it may seem antithetical to his character, God is not above using deception to facilitate his punishment of sin (see comments above on 2 Sam. 22:27). For further discussion of the theological dimensions of this passage, see below under "Teaching the Text."

Teaching the Text

1. *God's punishment of sin is sometimes very severe, even when sinners beg for forgiveness.* This episode mirrors the Bathsheba incident. David humbly confesses his sin but still suffers sin's painful consequences. The portrait of an angry and deceptive Deity who relents only after slaughtering a massive number of people is frightening in the extreme and does not tend to attract the reader to him. But if we assume, as we should, that God is justified in his response to Israel's sin, the divine perspective replaces our own as certain truths become clear: (1) God hates sin and is perfectly justified in punishing sinners in whatever way he deems appropriate.

(2) It is a testimony to God's patience and mercy that we do not read of such severe judgment more often in the pages of Scripture. (3) Realizing how sin activates divine anger and judgment, we gain a greater appreciation for what the outpouring of God's wrath upon his Son entailed.

2. *The Lord is compassionate and willing to soften his punishment when sinners approach him properly.* In the midst of this terrifying episode, it is surprising to hear David affirm that the Lord's "mercy is great" (24:14). After all, the Lord counters David's plea for forgiveness with three horrifying options for punishment and strikes down a huge number of Israelites. Yet in the face of this divine outburst, David places his faith in God's mercy, which is evident in God's willingness to relent from sending judgment in its full force. When David offers the appropriate sacrifices in the proper spirit, the Lord again hears the prayers of his people. One is reminded of Lamentations 3. Despite being surrounded by the sights and sounds of judgment and death (in the fall of Jerusalem), which he describes in graphic detail, the author can declare God's compassion (vv. 22, 32). Given the realities of human sin and divine holiness, human beings must see their mere survival as a sign of divine compassion. If God seems unduly harsh and cold in passages like 2 Samuel 24, it may be wise to recall Hosea 11, where God pulls back the curtain that cov-

The Lord commanded David to purchase the threshing floor, oxen, and threshing sledge of Araunah. David offered sacrifices to the Lord, and the plague was stopped. A threshing sledge sits at the edge of the threshing floor in this photograph.

ers his heart and gives us a glimpse of the emotional conflict he experiences when he is forced to punish his people. As God pours out his judgment upon his wayward people, his heart "is changed" within him and all his "compassion is aroused," prompting him to relent from sending his judgment with full force (vv. 8–9). Unlike human beings, who sometimes annihilate the object of their anger in blind rage, God is able to express his emotions in perfect balance, tempering his anger with compassion.

Illustrating the Text

God severely punishes sin and disciplines sinners through its consequences, even when they genuinely seek forgiveness.

Human Metaphor: Explain a scenario where a human being pushes another person off of a skyscraper and then is immediately and sincerely conscience-stricken. He or she can repent and receive forgiveness immediately, but the other person will still hit the pavement, there will still be a murder trial, and the offender will still face imprisonment or even the death penalty. Explore the ways in which this process will be affected and improved by repentance, and those ways in which God may choose to work through the natural consequences.

Testimony: This topic will strike very tender and wounded places in many hearts. Consider inviting someone to share a live, personal testimony about the way in which God has met them in the midst of grave consequences and faithfully led them through facing the music while also assuring them of forgiveness. Circumstances could include

recovery from drugs, imprisonment, marital unfaithfulness, pornography, fits of rage, and so on.

God is able to show wrath and mercy simultaneously and perfectly without violating his character.

Family Life / Parenting: Share a story about the way a parent can be moved and restrained by sincere compassion while also dispensing just consequences for their children's errors. Then simply ask, "How much more must our Father in heaven be able to do so?"

Gospel: This is a great place to point people to the cross and make an appeal for conversion. In the cross of Jesus Christ, we see a full revelation of the way God's unrestrained wrath against sin and undying compassion for human sinners coexist and find their final and complete satisfaction in one Savior.

Object Lesson: Use a pitcher of water, a very small glass, and a basin. Tell people the pitcher represents God's totally justified wrath against their personal sin. The small glass represents their capacity to stand up under that wrath; if it is filled to overflowing the person would be destroyed. Explain that nevertheless, for justice to be served, the whole pitcher must be poured out. Pour out a small portion of the pitcher into the small glass and then let the rest spill into the basin. Explain that the basin represents Christ, and that God's choice is to allow only a very small portion of the wrath we deserve to linger in this life as a means of disciplining us and drawing us to depend on him. We are spared the full, deadly flood because it fell on Christ instead, allowing us a chance to believe and be saved.

Notes

Introduction to 1 & 2 Samuel

1. See Chisholm, *Interpreting the Historical Books*, 80.

1 Samuel 1:1–2:11

1. See Polzin, *Samuel and the Deuteronomist*, 30–36.

2. See Chisholm, "Yahweh versus the Canaanite Gods," 176–79.

3. Polzin (*Samuel and the Deuteronomist*, 20–21) argues that the explanatory clauses here and in v. 6 reflect the perception of Elkanah and Peninnah, not necessarily the narrator's viewpoint.

4. See Cartledge, *1 and 2 Samuel*, 32.

5. See Polzin, *Samuel and the Deuteronomist*, 24.

6. Bodner, *1 Samuel*, 19.

7. This is the first time in the Hebrew Bible that the word *mashiah*, "anointed [one]," is used in a nominal manner to describe Israel's king. (The term is used as an adjectival modifier four times in Leviticus [4:3, 5, 16; 6:22] in the expression "the anointed priest.")

8. Bodner, *1 Samuel*, 27–28.

9. Koessler, *A Stranger in the House*, 59.

10. Coles, *The Story of Ruby Bridges*, 28.

1 Samuel 2:12–36

1. Klein, *1 Samuel*, 25.

2. Bodner, *1 Samuel*, 31.

3. See, e.g., McCarter, *I Samuel*, 81.

4. David G. Firth suggests that the prophecy actually has a dual referent. In addition to Zadok (the more distant fulfillment), Samuel, who functions as both prophet and priest, fulfills the prophecy in the more immediate future ("Narrative Repetition," 8). See as well Heller, *Power, Politics, and Prophecy*, 62–63.

5. Bodner, *1 Samuel*, 35.

6. Peter Taylor-Whiffen, "Shot at Dawn: Cowards, Traitors or Victims?," last updated March 3, 2011, http://www.bbc.co.uk/history/british/britain_wwone/shot_at_dawn_01.shtml.

7. Bunyan, *The Pilgrim's Progress*, 48.

1 Samuel 3

1. For a discussion of paneled structures in Hebrew narrative and an outline of 1 Sam. 3:4–14, see Chisholm, *Interpreting the Historical Books*, 50–52.

2. Bergen, *1, 2 Samuel*, 86.

3. McCarter, *I Samuel*, 98.

4. In the MT (Hebrew text) the verb "curse" is combined with a prepositional phrase, "for themselves." But this verb-preposition combination does not occur elsewhere in the Hebrew Bible. This verb usually takes a direct object, as in the alternate reading preferred above. An accidental mistake is possible since "God" in a purely consonantal Hebrew text would be *'lhym*, similar to "for themselves" (*lhm*). However, it is more likely that a scribe has deliberately altered the original reading "God" to "for themselves" in order to avoid the impropriety of making "God" the object of the verb. See McCarter, *I Samuel*, 96; Tsumura, *The First Book of Samuel*, 180; and Driver, *Notes on the Hebrew Text*, 44.

5. See McCarter, *I Samuel*, 98.

6. Boda, *A Severe Mercy*, 150.

7. Brontë, *Jane Eyre*, 386.

1 Samuel 4

1. Walton, *Ancient Near Eastern Thought*, 156.

2. For a convenient summary of biblical and extrabiblical evidence for the Philistines, see Howard, "Philistines."

3. On the dates proposed here, see Chisholm, "Chronology of Judges," 252.

4. McCarter, *I Samuel*, 108–9.

5. Bergen, *1, 2 Samuel*, 91; Arnold, *1 and 2 Samuel*, 95–96.

6. In the MT the two clauses are subject-fronted and juxtaposed, indicating simultaneous action and linking the two actions together temporally and conceptually.

7. If the chair does symbolize his authority, then his falling from it (v. 18) signifies the termination of his leadership. See Bodner, *1 Samuel*, 47.

8. Firth, "Narrative Repetition," 8.

9. Dillard, *Teaching a Stone to Talk*, 40–41.

1 Samuel 5

1. This kind of theological agenda is not unique to the Bible and reflects the cultural context in which the book of Judges originated and developed. In the Moabite Stone, King Mesha attributes Israel's victory over Moab to the anger of his god Chemosh. He then tells how Chemosh restored his divine favor and enabled him to defeat Israel once and for all. See COS, 2:137–38.

2. See Bluedorn, *Yahweh versus Baal*.

3. See Chisholm, "Yahweh versus the Canaanite Gods," 165–80.

4. Walton, *Ancient Near Eastern Thought*, 114–18.

5. For the latter view, see Feliu, *The God Dagan*, 302.

6. For a discussion of the OT and extrabiblical evidence pertaining to this deity, see Day, *Yahweh and the Gods*, 85–90.

7. Walton, *Ancient Near Eastern Thought*, 156.

8. Tsumura, *The First Book of Samuel*, 190.

9. See Klein, *1 Samuel*, 49; and Wiggins, "Old Testament Dagan," 269–72.

10. Klein, *1 Samuel*, 50.

11. McCarter, *I Samuel*, 120.

12. For a discussion of the competing views, see Klein, *1 Samuel*, 50–51.

13. Walton, *Covenant*, 65–66.

14. See Chisholm, "Polemic against Baalism," 267–68.

15. Lewis, *The Last Battle*, 33.

1 Samuel 6

1. Walton, *Ancient Near Eastern Thought*, 240.

2. Ibid., 249.

3. This summary of deductive divination is based on ibid., 249–63.

4. Ibid., 265.

5. Ibid., 259.

6. Milgrom, *Leviticus*, 50–51. See also Wenham, *Leviticus*, 106.

7. McCarter, *I Samuel*, 133.

8. Gordon, *1 and 2 Samuel*, 101.

9. The verb *kabed*, "harden" (v. 6), is used often of Pharaoh's hardening his heart (Exod. 8:15, 32; 9:7, 34); the relatively rare verb translated "dealt harshly" appears in Exod. 10:2 to describe how the Lord deals with the Egyptians; and in the exodus story "send . . . out" is used frequently of the Egyptians' sending away the Israelites.

10. Klein, *1 Samuel*, 57.

11. Bodner, *1 Samuel*, 57.

12. Such large numbers cannot be taken at face value in light of demographic analysis of ancient Palestine by modern archaeologists. See the population estimates for Palestine in the 13th–11th centuries BC given in Dever, *Who Were the Early Israelites?*, 97–98; idem, "Histories and Non-Histories," 77; Hess, *Israelite Religions*, 232. Without a doubt, 1 Kings 20:29–30 shows that numbers are either sometimes inflated in military accounts or have been misunderstood by later interpreters: after Israel kills 100,000 Aramaeans in battle, the rest of the Aramaean army flees to Aphek, where the town wall collapses and kills 27,000 of them—a preposterous claim if the figure is taken literally.

13. McCarter, *I Samuel*, 131.

14. Klein, *1 Samuel*, 60.

15. McCullough, *The Trivialization of God*, 114–15.

1 Samuel 7

1. Day, *Yahweh and the Gods*, 68–69, 131.

2. Chisholm, "Yahweh versus the Canaanite Gods," 180.

3. For Assyrian examples, see Grayson, *Assyrian Royal Inscriptions*, 2:134 (¶ 571), 145 (¶ 589), 161 (¶ 638), 166 (¶ 651); *ARAB*, 2:94 (¶ 171), 126 (¶ 253). The Egyptian king Ramesses III boasted that his battle cry was like that of the Canaanite storm-god Baal. See Edgerton and Wilson, *Historical Records of Ramses III*, 73, 100.

4. *ARAB*, 2:83 (¶ 155), 358 (¶ 925).

5. Polzin, *Samuel and the Deuteronomist*, 74.

6. Samuel's reference to Israel's Baal worship in 1 Sam. 12:10 is in a summary of the judges' period.

7. Klein, *1 Samuel*, 67.

8. This is one of the options offered by Gordon, *1 and 2 Samuel*, 107.

9. McCarter, *I Samuel*, 144. The practice of water libation is attested in the ancient Near East. Libations were offered as a drink to the gods, but it is not clear if that was Israel's understanding in this context. For fuller discussion, see *ZIBBCOT*, 2:303–4.

10. Moses's promise anticipates that God will raise up a line of prophets. Samuel was one of these in Israel's history. Jesus is the ultimate fulfillment of the promise.

11. In this regard, see Boda, *A Severe Mercy*, 150–51.

1 Samuel 8

1. Kitchen points out that all the features of kingship outlined by Samuel are attested in documents from these sites, including the presence of chariot warriors, conscription of males for military service and agricultural work, production of weapons by a class of craftsmen, the presence of large numbers of support staff in the royal palace, confiscation of land and produce by the crown, and taxation on crops and livestock (Kitchen, *Reliability of the Old Testament*, 95–96).

2. Gordon suggests that Samuel's "own little dynastic experiment," in which he appoints his own sons as heirs apparent to his position of judge (v. 1), may prompt the people to demand a dynastic royal institution like other nations (Gordon, *1 and 2 Samuel*, 109–10).

3. I owe this notion that the king is a surrogate palladium for the ark to Jonathan Walton, a graduate student at Wheaton College.

4. Klein, *1 Samuel*, 76. One detects the same kind of rhetoric in Ps. 51:4, where David, who has sinned against Uriah, nevertheless says to God, "Against you, you only, have I sinned."

5. McCarter, *I Samuel*, 157.

6. Klein, *1 Samuel*, 75.

7. See Evans, *The Message of Samuel*, 60. Bergen points out, "As Yahweh's true prophet, Samuel must first receive word from Yahweh before choosing a new king" (*1, 2 Samuel*, 118n11). However, one wonders why Samuel, knowing that the Lord intends to grant them a king, does not consult the Lord immediately.

8. See Polzin, *Samuel and the Deuteronomist*, 84.

9. The typical attitude is seen in a Phoenician inscription dating to the eighth or seventh century BC in which Azitawada boasts of his horses, shields, and armies that have been granted to him "by the grace of Ba'al and the gods" (*COS*, 2:149). With this divinely bestowed military might, he is able to make his land secure and crush the enemies of his people.

10. See Gerbrandt, *Kingship*, 190–91; Howard, "The Case for Kingship," 106–8.

11. O'Connell, *The Rhetoric of Judges*, 10, 268–304.

12. Wells, *No Place for Truth*, 183; as cited by Plantinga, *Not the Way*, 83.

13. Spurgeon, *Pictures from "Pilgrim's Progress,"* 171–72.

1 Samuel 9:1–10:8

1. See Long, *The Reign and Rejection of Saul*, 202.

2. See Bergen, *1, 2 Samuel*, 121–22.

3. In light of what later transpires, Exum calls the servant's words "darkly ironic" (*Tragedy and Biblical Narrative*, 158n23).

4. See Arnold, *1 and 2 Samuel*, 163, who reasons along similar lines.

5. Bergen, *1, 2 Samuel*, 123.

6. The expression "deliver from the hand of" (Hebrew, Hiphil of *yasha'* + *min* + *yad*) is not common. Before Judges, it occurs only in Exod. 14:30, and it appears only three times in 1–2 Samuel (1 Sam. 7:8; 9:16; 2 Sam. 3:18).

7. See Arnold, *1 and 2 Samuel*, 163–64, who reasons along similar lines.

8. Bergen recognizes the implications of the verb, but he views it as having a negative connotation in this case and depicting Saul as someone who will "hinder the welfare of the nation and act as a sort of barrier separating Israel from God's best for them" (*1, 2 Samuel*, 123).

9. Klein, *1 Samuel*, 83. A scribe's eye jumped from the first instance of "the LORD anointed you" to the second, accidentally omitting the words in between. See McCarter, *I Samuel*, 171.

10. See Long, *The Reign and Rejection of Saul*, 64; and Edelman, *King Saul in the Historiography*, 54. The expression "Do what your hand finds" occurs elsewhere only once, where it has a military connotation (see Judg. 9:33).

11. The MT of 10:5 reads "Gibeah of the God." This is the only place in the OT where a proper place name (Gibeah in this case) is qualified by the expression "the God." The phrase indicates that Gibeah belongs to God and thus highlights the fact that the Philistines are intruders, whom God intends to expel (see 9:16).

12. In three other instances in Judges, the Lord's Spirit empowers individuals (Othniel, Gideon, Jephthah) for battle, though the verb *tsalah* is not used (3:10; 6:34; 11:29).

13. Long, *The Reign and Rejection of Saul*, 63–64.

14. Defoe, *Robinson Crusoe*, 114, 176–77.

1 Samuel 10:9–27

1. For these parallels, see Dragga, "The Failure of Saul," 42–43; Chisholm, "The Role of Women," 47–48n34; Brooks, "Saul and the Samson Narrative," 21–22.

2. Lichtheim, *Ancient Egyptian Literature*, 2:41.

3. Ibid., 2:41–42.

4. Ibid., 2:39.

5. McCarter, *I Samuel*, 195.

6. Eslinger identifies the regulations as the "'monarchic constitution' that subordinates the monarchy to the theocracy" and serves as a sign of the Lord's "continuing supremacy" (*Kingship of God in Crisis*, 355). Klein (*1 Samuel*, 100) and Evans (*The Message of Samuel*, 73) suggest that the laws of kingship outlined in Deut. 17:14–20 are in view.

7. Fleming, *The Homesick Heart*, 37–38.

1 Samuel 11

1. For a convenient summary of biblical and extrabiblical evidence for the Ammonites, see Younker, "Ammonites."

2. Klein, *1 Samuel*, 102; see also McCarter, *I Samuel*, 198.

3. McCarter, *I Samuel*, 199.

4. Bergen, *1, 2 Samuel*, 135.

5. In Judg. 20:13 the Israelites demand that the criminals be handed over for execution. Benjamin's refusal to do so ignites the civil war. In 1 Sam. 11:12 the people make a similar demand as they express their desire to execute those who have failed to acknowledge Saul as king (cf. 10:27). But Saul refuses to seek vengeance and instead seeks to unite the people. See Polzin, *Samuel and the Deuteronomist*, 113.

6. The precise Hebrew phrase translated "as one man" occurs only nine times in the OT, three of which are in Judg. 20 (vv. 1, 8, 11). It is not a common idiom.

7. See Bodner, *1 Samuel*, 107.

8. The NIV understands the Hebrew noun (*melukah*) as referring to kingship, as the word does in 10:16 (Saul's recent election is in view), 25 (if the policies of Deut. 17:14–20 are the regulations in view), and 14:47 (note the following "over Israel"). However, another option is that the word refers here to the kingdom, or state. In this case the Lord is adjusting the Israelites' vision or casting a new vision of what the Israelite state will be, in contrast to what the people desire and Samuel has described earlier (cf. 8:11–18).

9. Long proposes a different explanation for the renewal of Saul's kingship. He suggests that there was a three-staged accession process in ancient Israel that included designation, demonstration (through military action), and confirmation. By his failure to take military action against the Philistine outpost (see our remarks on 10:7), Saul has "arrested" the process, which explains in part why some are less than enthusiastic about their new king. Saul's victory over the Ammonites, though not the demonstration originally envisioned by Samuel, "set the accession process back on track." For Long, then, the renewal of the kingship "served as a public recognition of this change in situation" (*The Reign and Rejection of Saul*, 227–28).

10. Steiner, *Real Presences*, 232.

1 Samuel 12

1. Klein, *1 Samuel*, 118.

2. McCarter, *I Samuel*, 218.

3. Lewis, *The Lion, the Witch and the Wardrobe*, chap. 4.

1 Samuel 13:1-15

1. The MT reads "Geba" in 13:3, but it is preferable to read "Gibeah" here in light of v. 2, which locates Jonathan and his troops in Gibeah, and in light of the reference to a Philistine garrison or prefect's being at Gibeah in 10:5. See Klein, *1 Samuel*, 122.

2. For discussion see McCarter, *I Samuel*, 222.

3. Evans, *The Message of Samuel*, 87; Bergen, *1, 2 Samuel*, 150.

4. One may wonder why it was wrong for Saul to offer sacrifices, when David (2 Sam. 6:17–18; 24:25) and Solomon (1 Kings 3:4) later do so. In Saul's case, Samuel clearly states that he, Samuel, would offer the sacrifice (1 Sam. 10:8). In David's case, in 2 Samuel 6 he works in conjunction with the priests (see 1 Chron. 15:26–27), and in 2 Samuel 24 he acts in response to the prophet's instructions (see vv. 11, 18). As for Solomon, it is reasonable to assume that he acted in concert with the priests (see 1 Kings 2:35; 8:3–5). Furthermore, by this point the Davidic king is exercising a priestly role in conjunction with the Davidic covenant (see Ps. 110:4), a privilege and status not granted to Saul.

5. Long, *The Reign and Rejection of Saul*, 90.

6. Long, *The Reign and Rejection of Saul*, 91.

7. McCarter argues that the expression refers to the Lord's will or purpose, not to some quality that David possesses. He translates, "a man of his own choosing" (*I Samuel*, 229). One can find support for this nuance of "heart" in 2 Sam. 7:21 and Ps. 20:4, where it refers to one's choice, will, or purpose. However, in 1 Sam. 13:14 the phrase modifies a noun ("man"), as it does in Jer. 3:15, where the Lord promises to give repentant Israel shepherds "according to" the Lord's "heart." In this case, a quality of the shepherds (their commitment to knowledge and understanding) is in view, as the following clause indicates. McCarter creates a false dichotomy; surely one chosen in the heart of the Deity would conform in his character and motives to the will of the Deity! For a helpful discussion of the interpretive issue, see Long, *The Reign and Rejection of Saul*, 91–93.

8. Arnold, *1 and 2 Samuel*, 198.

9. According to 1 Sam. 13:2, Saul's troops number three thousand, but by the time of his confrontation with Samuel, the number has dwindled to six hundred (v. 15). Furthermore, we discover from vv. 19–22 that the Israelite army is ill equipped for battle, due to the Philistines' domination of the iron industry.

10. Tozer, *An Anthology*, 189–90.

1 Samuel 13:16-14:23

1. On Jonathan as a foil for Saul in chaps. 13–14, see Long, *The Reign and Rejection of Saul*, 40–41.

2. Bodner, *1 Samuel*, 119.

3. In Exod. 28:4–6 and several other texts, an ephod appears to be a priestly or cultic garment. In some cases an ephod is used to obtain a divine oracle (1 Sam. 23:9; 30:7).

4. Gordon, *1 and 2 Samuel*, 136; Arnold, *1 and 2 Samuel*, 209.

5. See Bergen, *1, 2 Samuel*, 156.

6. See Gordon, *1 and 2 Samuel*, 137–38. Tsumura expresses a contrary view, but his argument is unconvincing (*The First Book of Samuel*, 365–66).

7. See McCarter, *I Samuel*, 239.

8. Cymbala, *Fresh Wind, Fresh Fire*, 11, 91, 184–85.

9. M. L. King Jr., "Letter from a Birmingham Jail," 399.

1 Samuel 14:24-52

1. Saul's actions in this chapter are in some respects reminiscent of Samson and Jephthah. Like Samson, Saul seems more concerned with personal vengeance than with accomplishing the Lord's purposes (14:24; see Judg. 15:7; 16:28). Like Jephthah, he makes a formalized statement of personal obligation that jeopardizes the life of his child. There is a technical distinction between a vow, which promises a gift to God in response to God's granting a request, and an oath, which commits one to a course of action in the name of God. For a comparison of Saul's oath with Jephthah's vow, see Exum, *Tragedy and Biblical Narrative*, 76.

2. Long, *The Reign and Rejection of Saul*, 130.

3. See McCarter, *I Samuel*, 247–48. For a contrary opinion, see Long, *The Reign and Rejection of Saul*, 125–28.

4. Long, *The Reign and Rejection of Saul*, 114–15.

5. Bodner, *1 Samuel*, 139.

6. Ibid., 140.

7. Long, *The Reign and Rejection of Saul*, 119–20.

8. Lewis, *Mere Christianity*, 168.

1 Samuel 15:1-22

1. For studies of the concept of the ban in the OT, see Niditch, *War in the Hebrew Bible*, 28–77; and Kaminsky, *Corporate Responsibility*, 78–93.

2. Niditch, *War in the Hebrew Bible*, 62.

3. Long, *The Reign and Rejection of Saul*, 142–43.

4. Ibid., 149.

1 Samuel 15:23-35

1. See Birch, *Rise of the Israelite Monarchy*, 82–83, 102–3.

2. Bodner, *1 Samuel*, 159.

3. For a fuller discussion and development of the contrast between these competing models, see Walton, *Genesis 1 as Ancient Cosmology*.

4. McCullough, *The Trivialization of God*, 93.

5. Lewis, *The Problem of Pain*, 40–41.

1 Samuel 16

1. Tsumura, *The First Book of Samuel*, 427.

2. Edelman, *King Saul in the Historiography*, 122; G. C. I. Wong, "Who Loved Whom?," 554–56. Tsumura (*The First Book of Samuel*, 432) contends that the following statement (that David becomes an armor-bearer) makes better sense if Saul is the subject of "loved," but David's loyalty to Saul nicely explains why he would be elevated to such an important post.

3. Moran, "Background of the Love of God."

4. Bergen, *1, 2 Samuel*, 184.

5. For more on these themes, see Chisholm, "Divine Hardening"; idem, "Does God Deceive?"

6. Guinness, *Prophetic Untimeliness*, 54.

1 Samuel 17

1. The structure of the Hebrew sentence in verse 14a (subject placed before a perfect verbal form) suggests this is a flashback, making a new paragraph. The Spirit first left Saul and then came upon David.

2. See Yadin, *The Art of Warfare*, 265.

3. See Hoffner, "A Hittite Analogue to the Contest of Champions?"

4. There are different traditions regarding Goliath's height. According to the MT, his height is six cubits and a span. A "cubit" is about eighteen inches (the distance between a man's elbow and the tip of his middle finger). The Hebrew word for "span" refers to the breadth of the open hand (from the tip of the thumb to the tip of the little finger), which is about nine inches (or a half a cubit). By this reckoning Goliath is nine feet nine inches tall. Some Greek manuscripts, Josephus, and the Qumran scroll from cave 4 have "four cubits and a span," or six feet nine inches. It is unclear whether one tradition is exaggerating for the sake of emphasis or the other tones down the story for the sake of credibility. See Hays, "Reconsidering the Height of Goliath"; Billington, "Goliath and the Exodus Giants"; and Hays, "A Response to Clyde Billington."

5. Gordon, *1 and 2 Samuel*, 154.

6. Goliath's armor and weapons reflect the Aegean origin of the Philistines but also give evidence of influence from Syria, Anatolia, and Egypt. See Tsumura, *The First Book of Samuel*, 442–44.

7. Edelman, *King Saul in the Historiography*, 126.

8. "Stood in awe" in 12:18 and "terrified" in 17:11 translate the same Hebrew expression, "feared greatly." Thus far in 1 Samuel, this expression appears only in these passages.

9. Scholars debate the referent of the Hebrew *kidon*. For the view that it is a scimitar, see McCarter, *I Samuel*, 292.

10. In the MT, v. 42a reads, "And the Philistine looked and saw David and despised him" (AT).

11. King and Stager, *Life in Biblical Israel*, 228–29.

12. Gordon, *1 and 2 Samuel*, 158; Edelman, *King Saul in the Historiography*, 133.

13. For a helpful study of the title "living God," see Mettinger, *In Search of God*, 82–91. He concludes that this title "demarcated Israelite thought from the conception of a dying and rising god whose cyclical biography reflected the vegetational seasons, and which was ubiquitous in Israel's surroundings. The characterization of YHWH as 'the living God' does not signify that fertility and agricultural abundance were his preeminent manifestations. Rather, the field of expression of 'the living God' was history" (90–91).

14. David's theology is not unique in its ancient Near Eastern context. Though well equipped with chariots and weapons, Assyrian kings emphasized that victory came from their gods and criticized enemy kings for placing their confidence in their weapons. See Meier, "The Sword," 170.

15. Yancey, *Reaching for the Invisible God*, 87–88.

1 Samuel 18

1. Moran, "Background of the Love of God."

2. See McCarter, *I Samuel*, 313.

3. Thompson, "The Significance of the Verb *Love*."

4. Gordon, *1 and 2 Samuel*, 160.

5. Tsumura, *The First Book of Samuel*, 478.

6. McCarter, *I Samuel*, 317.

7. It was common in the ancient Near East for victors to remove the heads, hands, and even genitals of their victims for the sake of casualty counts or as trophies of war.

8. According to the MT, David brings two hundred foreskins to Saul, but the LXX reads "one hundred" here, as requested by Saul (v. 25). Some prefer this reading because in 2 Sam. 3:14 David refers to the bride-price as one hundred foreskins. But that statement is technically correct: the price is one hundred foreskins. He decides to bring two hundred and thus is saying in effect: "I may be poor, but I'm an asset to have around!"

9. For an insightful discussion of the contrast between Saul and Jonathan, see Lozovyy, *Saul, Doeg, Nabal*, 141–47.

1 Samuel 19

1. For fuller discussion, see Miller, *The Religion of Ancient Israel*, 56; *TDOT*, 15:787–88.

2. See Wilson, *Prophecy and Society*, 103.

3. Edelman, *King Saul in the Historiography*, 144.

4. Bodner, *1 Samuel*, 203.

5. On the ancient Near Eastern background of the language, see McCarter, *I Samuel*, 322: in treaty contexts the idiom "do good" means the loyal actions of one party toward another.

6. On the hardening of Pharaoh's heart, see Chisholm, "Divine Hardening," 411–29.

7. Roseveare, *Living Sacrifice*, 20–21.

8. Ibid., 21.

9. Quoted in Morgan, *Near to the Heart of God*, March 16.

1 Samuel 20

1. The MT of v. 14 is difficult. By taking the problematic *lo'* in the first clause of v. 14 as *lu'*, "if" (in this case *'im*, "if," may be a clarifying gloss); the *lo'* at the beginning of second clause as an emphatic particle (cf. Ugaritic *lu*); and *lo'* at the beginning of the final clause as the particle *lu'*, "if"—we can thereby arrive at a reasonable interpretation of the passage, reflected in the following translation: "[v. 14] If I am still alive [and not killed by my father!], then certainly you must show me the covenantal loyalty of the LORD. And if I die, [v. 15] you must never cut off your covenantal loyalty from my house, not even when the LORD cuts off the enemies of David, each from upon the face of the ground" (AT).

2. Driver, *Notes on the Hebrew Text*, 166; McCarter, *I Samuel*, 337, 342.

3. In v. 26 the NIV portrays Saul as using the name "David" in his thoughts, but the MT uses only the pronoun, not David's name.

4. Newell, *A Martyr's Grace*, 82–84.

5. Ibid., 84.

1 Samuel 21:1–22:5

1. Ancient Near Eastern texts dating from various times and places mention the *habiru*. They (1) appear in both sedentary and nomadic roles; (2) are often viewed as foreigners, even though they cannot be defined in an ethnic sense; (3) are employed in a variety of jobs, including soldiers; and (4) were powerful enough in some cases to control political shifts in power.

2. In defending the actions of his disciples—who are violating Pharisaic rules by plucking, threshing, and eating grain on the Sabbath—Jesus appeals to this story (Matt. 12:3–4; Mark 2:25–26; Luke 6:3–4). Jesus may be referring to an alternate version, perhaps designed to protect David against charges of deception. Jesus places the story in the time of Abiathar and assumes that David really does need the bread for his companions.

3. As Steussy observes, "Evidently David no longer eschews the trappings of worldly military might" (*David: Biblical Portraits*, 72). Polzin puts a positive spin on this incident, suggesting that it symbolizes the "transfer of royal power from Saul to David" (*Samuel and the Deuteronomist*, 196–97). See as well Edelman, *King Saul in the Historiography*, 167–68.

4. Edelman, *King Saul in the Historiography*, 169.

5. The MT has a verb that apparently means "to mark, scribble," but some (based on the LXX) prefer the reading "hammered, knocked," or "spit." The latter makes excellent sense in light of the next statement, about saliva running down his beard.

6. The location of the stronghold mentioned in 22:4 is uncertain. Some argue that David, having left his parents in Moab, returned to Adullam (v. 1), which is called a "stronghold" in 2 Sam. 23:14. However, it is more likely that the stronghold was in Moab, because God's command in verse 5 ("go into") suggests David is outside Judah. See Bergen, *1, 2 Samuel*, 225–26, and Tsumura, *The First Book of Samuel*, 540.

7. Meier, "The Sword," 160–61.

8. Lewis, *The Lion, the Witch and the Wardrobe*, 51.

9. Bunyan, "The Returning Backslider," in *Christ a Complete Saviour*, quoted from http://ldolphin.org/backslide.html.

1 Samuel 22:6–23

1. On the parallels between the two incidents, see Polzin, *Samuel and the Deuteronomist*, 199. Saul uses emphatic language in telling Jonathan and Ahimelek that they must die (14:44; 22:16).

2. The phrase is used only here in 1–2 Samuel; the singular "priest of the LORD" is used of Ahijah in 1 Sam.14:3.

3. Exceptions to this include Deut. 20:13; Josh. 19:47; Judg. 18:27; 20:37, 48; 21:10. The Deuteronomic law pertains to a case in which a city refuses to accept an offer of peace; the Judges texts use the idiom ironically, applying, for purposes of contrast, the language of the original conquest to inappropriate or tragic military campaigns.

4. In the entire OT, only in these two verses do we find the precise Hebrew sequence used here, translated "from man (even) unto woman, from child even unto infant."

5. Evans, *The Message of Samuel*, 128.

6. Larsen, *The Company of the Creative*, 137–38.

7. Ibid., 137.

1 Samuel 23

1. Merton, *Essays of Thomas Merton*, 164.

1 Samuel 24

1. As translated in the NIV, the promise cited by David's men does not appear elsewhere. This translation, like that of most interpreters, assumes that the marginal reading of the Hebrew text, "enemy" (as opposed to plural, "enemies"), is correct and that the words "for you to deal with as you wish" are part of the promise. Syntactical parallels in the Hebrew text at Judg. 9:33 and 1 Kings 20:13 support this. However, if one reads with the Hebrew text, "enemies," it is possible to translate, "This is the day the LORD spoke of when he said to you, 'I will give your enemies into your hands,' so do to him as you wish." In this case, the final clause is an exhortation from the men to Saul, not part of the cited quotation from the Lord. One may then argue that the men are generalizing the Lord's words to David in 1 Sam. 23:4 (pertaining to the Philistines) and applying them here to Saul.

2. Apart from David's use of the title for Saul, the phrase "the LORD's anointed" appears only two other times: in 2 Sam. 19:21 (of David) and Lam. 4:20 (of the Davidic king).

3. Edelman, *King Saul in the Historiography*, 194.

4. The sole exception seems to be Gen. 29:11, where Jacob appears to cry tears of joy upon meeting Rachel.

5. Edelman, *King Saul in the Historiography*, 202.

6. Fénelon, *Let Go*, 13–14.

7. Teresa, *Works*, 288.

1 Samuel 25

1. For a positive assessment of David's actions in 1 Sam. 25, see Borgman, *David, Saul, and God*, 79–95.

2. Edelman, *King Saul in the Historiography*, 204.

3. Ibid., 204–5.

4. Bodner, *1 Samuel*, 262. On the literary parallels between Nabal and Saul, see Polzin, *Samuel and the Deuteronomist*, 205–15; and Biddle, "Ancestral Motifs," 626. Lozovyy (*Saul, Doeg, Nabal*, 67–70) acknowledges similarities but also points out several dissimilarities.

5. Gordon, *1 and 2 Samuel*, 183.

6. McCarter, *I Samuel*, 394.

7. In this regard, see Janzen's insightful study of Jephthah's vow: "Why the Deuteronomist Told."

8. Ten Boom, *Prison Letters*, 81.

9. Luther, *Devotions and Prayers*, 86.

1 Samuel 26

1. See Klein, *1 Samuel*, 256.

2. The verb *sut*, translated as "incited" in v. 19, is used elsewhere of a daughter's charming her father into giving her a gift (Josh. 15:18 = Judg. 1:14), of riches' enticing a man (Job 36:18), of an individual's persuading another person to follow a course of action (1 Kings 21:25; 2 Kings 18:32 = Isa. 36:18; 2 Chron. 18:2; 32:11, 15; Jer. 38:22; 43:3), of

a prophet's tempting people to worship idols (Deut. 13:6), and of Satan's inciting God to test Job (Job 2:3). When used with God as the subject, it refers to his drawing an enemy army away (2 Chron. 18:31), wooing people from destruction to blessing (Job 36:16), and enticing David to number the people (2 Sam. 24:1; cf. 1 Chron. 21:1, where this is attributed to one of Israel's adversaries).

3. David does not identify who should make this offering (26:19). Perhaps he is acknowledging, at least theoretically, that he has done something wrong, in which case Saul is God's instrument of discipline, and David is the one who should make the offering (see Bergen, *1, 2 Samuel*, 258). However, this seems unlikely, since David protests his innocence (vv. 18, 23–24) and Saul confesses to being in the wrong (v. 21). See Chisholm, "Does God Deceive?," 20.

4. For more on these themes, see Chisholm, "Divine Hardening"; idem, "Does God Deceive?"

5. Wagner, *Winning Words for Daily Living*, 241.

1 Samuel 27:1–28:2

1. McCarter, *I Samuel*, 416.

2. Edelman, *King Saul in the Historiography*, 232. For a different opinion, see Evans, *The Message of Samuel*, 148. She suggests that the primary reason David leaves the land is that he fears that one of his loyal supporters might kill Saul, jeopardize his position as future king, and set a precedent for assassination and rebellion. But David's motivation for leaving seems clear enough: he fears for his life!

3. See Bergen, *1, 2 Samuel*, 261–62.

4. McCarter, *I Samuel*, 413.

5. Gunn, *The Fate of King Saul*, 107; Edelman, *King Saul in the Historiography*, 235; Cartledge, *1 and 2 Samuel*, 313.

6. Edelman, *King Saul in the Historiography*, 240.

7. Havner, *All the Days*, 83.

8. Ford, *The Attentive Life*, 197.

1 Samuel 28:3–25

1. See *TDOT*, 1:130–34; Walton, *Ancient Near Eastern Thought*, 325. However, Jeffers rejects this interpretation and is content to say that an *'ob* simply "appears at times to be a tool, an instrument used to get in touch with the spirits of the dead" (*Magic and Divination*, 171).

2. See the discussion in Jeffers, *Magic and Divination*, 171–72.

3. For a translation of the text, see *COS*, 1:444. For bibliography and discussion, see Sparks, *Ancient Texts*, 222, who observes that the technique used in the Assyrian ritual involves drawing stones from a bag: a white stone means yes, a black stone means no. But "for the portent to be valid, the procedure had to be repeated three times with the same result; mixed results indicated no answer from the gods."

4. Bodner, *1 Samuel*, 298.

5. Meier, "The Sword," 160.

6. Bodner, *1 Samuel*, 300.

7. See Exum, *Tragedy and Biblical Narrative*, 24.

8. Torrey, *How to Pray*, 77–78.

9. Beichman, "Saddam's Mistake," *Washington Times*, April 13, 2003, http://www.washingtontimes.com/news/2003/apr/18/20030418-090922-5901r/.

1 Samuel 29–30

1. Edelman, *King Saul in the Historiography*, 252.

2. Bergen, *1, 2 Samuel*, 285.

3. Edelman, *King Saul in the Historiography*, 252–53.

4. Ibid., 260.

5. McCarter, *I Samuel*, 427–28.

6. Ibid., 427.

7. Edelman, *King Saul in the Historiography*, 265–66.

8. Bergen, *1, 2 Samuel*, 276.

9. Cartledge, *1 and 2 Samuel*, 333.

10. Edelman, *King Saul in the Historiography*, 272.

11. Klein, *1 Samuel*, 284.

12. Arnold, *1 and 2 Samuel*, 387.

13. Fitt, *The Shorter Life of D. L. Moody*, 81–84.

14. Ibid., 84–85.

1 Samuel 31–2 Samuel 1

1. McCarter, *II Samuel*, 64–65.

2. For a convincing refutation of this faulty view, see Arnold, *1 and 2 Samuel*, 412–14.

3. See our comments above on 1 Sam. 18, under "Historical and Cultural Background."

4. Edelman, *King Saul in the Historiography*, 285.

5. Sternberg, *The Poetics of Biblical Narrative*, 498.

6. The men of Jabesh Gilead probably intend to honor Saul by burying him under a tamarisk tree, since it may be viewed as sacred (see Gen. 21:33) and is associated with his kingship (1 Sam. 22:6). See Edelman, *King Saul in the Historiography*, 292.

7. See Berlin, *Poetics and Interpretation*, 80; Edelman, *King Saul in the Historiography*, 301–3.

8. Gordon, *1 and 2 Samuel*, 208.

9. Milton, *Paradise Lost*, book 1, lines 36–49, 70–74.

10. Donne, *The Works of John Donne*, 3:574–75.

11. Peterson, *Leap over a Wall*, 115, 116, 119.

2 Samuel 2:1–5:5

1. Niehaus, *Ancient Near Eastern Themes*, 34–50.

2. Such consulting in the narrator's portrayal of David is important: see Arnold, *1 and 2 Samuel*, 419–20.

3. Bergen, *1, 2 Samuel*, 310.

4. Bergen, *1, 2 Samuel*, 318.

5. Bonhoeffer, *Letters and Papers*; as cited in Cowan and Guinness, *Invitation to the Classics*, 350.

6. Peterson, *Leap over a Wall*, 130.

7. Bonhoeffer, *Letters and Papers*, 351.

2 Samuel 5:6–25

1. Edgerton and Wilson, *Historical Records of Ramses III*, 45.

2. Bergen, *1, 2 Samuel*, 320.

3. See Anderson, *2 Samuel*, 84.

4. McCarter, *II Samuel*, 141–42.

5. Anderson, *2 Samuel*, 93. The parallel in 1 Chron. 14:12, careful to avoid any appearance of evil, says that David and his men burn these idols (not carrying them off, as in 2 Sam. 5:21).

6. Dorsett, *A Passion for Souls*, 241–42.

7. Laird, Baker, and Landrum, *They Called Me Mama*, back cover.

2 Samuel 6

1. The ark was in Philistine territory for seven months (1 Sam. 6:1). According to 1 Sam. 7:2, it was in Kiriath Jearim for twenty years, but this cannot refer to the entire time period between its arrival in Kiriath Jearim and David's retrieving it: this period, which includes Saul's reign and the early part of David's, is longer than twenty years. The chronological notation in 1 Sam. 7:2 refers to the time that elapsed between the ark's arrival in Kiriath Jearim and the incident recorded in 1 Sam. 7:2–15.

2. The NIV of 2 Sam. 6:7 refers to Uzzah's negligence or irreverence. However, the word so translated (*shal*) is used only here in biblical Hebrew, so its meaning is uncertain. Perhaps it is cognate with Akkadian *shullu*, "impudence" (*HALOT*, 1502). The parallel text in 1 Chron. 13:10 lacks this word and reads, "because he reached out his hand over the ark" (AT). The LXX of 2 Sam. 6:7 also omits the word.

3. McCarter, *II Samuel*, 154.

4. Arnold, *1 and 2 Samuel*, 460–61. According to 2 Sam. 21:8 MT, Michal bore five sons to Adriel son of Barzillai. However, the reading "Michal" is probably an error here; some textual witnesses read "Merab" (as in the NIV), the name of Saul's other daughter. This is clearly correct since 1 Sam. 18:19 tells us that Merab, not Michal, married Adriel.

5. Dawn, *A Royal "Waste" of Time*, 152–53.

6. Tozer, *The Knowledge of the Holy*, 104–5.

2 Samuel 7

1. For the ancient Near Eastern context, see Niehaus, *Ancient Near Eastern Themes*, 71.

2. On royal grants and OT covenants, see Weinfeld, "The Covenant of Grant," 189–93.

3. Knoppers, "Royal Grants and the Davidic Covenant."

4. Ibid., 682–83.

5. In cases in the Bible where the grant-type covenant does appear to provide the background, there is typically a reference to the recipient's loyalty or behavior that is worthy of a reward (see Gen. 22:16–18; Num. 25:10–13; Josh. 14:8–9).

6. Arnold, *1 and 2 Samuel*, 473.

7. See ibid., 479–80.

8. On the ancient Near Eastern background of this metaphor, see McCarter, *II Samuel*, 207.

9. See Anderson, *2 Samuel*, 127, translating as "singled out" here.

10. See Bergen, *1, 2 Samuel*, 344. Jacob, after receiving the Lord's promise, does not immediately embrace it, but promises allegiance to God only if the Lord meets certain conditions that he, Jacob, lays down (Gen. 28:20–22). There is no such hesitation or bargaining on David's part: he fully embraces the promise.

11. This discipline may even entail the Davidic–Solomonic kingdom being territorially diminished. In 1 Kings 11:11–13, 31–39 (esp. v. 38) the Lord tells Jeroboam I that if he obeys the Lord, he can have a dynasty like David's—thus implying that the territorial limitations of the Davidic–Solomonic empire can be a perpetual condition.

Additional Insights

1. See Oswalt, *Isaiah: Chapters 40–66*, 438–39; Motyer, *The Prophecy of Isaiah*, 453–55; and Kaiser, "Kindnesses Promised to David," 96–97.

2. Eaton, *Festal Drama*, 87–88.

3. Blenkinsopp, *Isaiah 40–55*, 370.

2 Samuel 8–10

1. Gordon, *1 and 2 Samuel*, 243.

2. McCarter, *II Samuel*, 247.

3. McCarter (ibid., 243) suggests a slight alteration of 2 Sam. 8:3 MT (from *lehashib*, "to return," to *lehoshib*, "to place") and translates "to leave his stela."

4. Bergen, *1, 2 Samuel*, 348.

5. The MT actually has "chariots" as the object of the verb "hamstring," suggesting that this refers to dismantling the chariots (Anderson, *2 Samuel*, 132; Cartledge, *1 and 2 Samuel*, 467). It seems more likely that "chariots" is used here by metonymy for the horses that pull them. See McCarter, *II Samuel*, 249.

6. Bergen, *1, 2 Samuel*, 350.

7. Polzin, *David and the Deuteronomist*, 90.

8. Anderson (*2 Samuel*, 140) prefers to see "God" as an idiomatic superlative here and translates "utmost consideration" (139). But the near parallel with 1 Sam. 20:14, where *hesed* is also collocated with *'asah*, "do," favors taking the expression in the way we have suggested. See Gordon, *1 and 2 Samuel*, 248.

9. For a concise summary of David's dealings with Zobah (cf. 8:3–6) and the Aramaeans, see Pitard, *Ancient Damascus*, 89–95.

10. In a Phoenician inscription dating to about 700 BC, Azatiwada praises Baal for giving him "horse upon horse, and shield upon shield" (*COS*, 2:149).

11. See *NIDOTTE*, 3:234–35.

2 Samuel 11

1. On this last point, see McCarter, *II Samuel*, 290.

2. Ibid., 286.

3. Sternberg, *The Poetics of Biblical Narrative*, 214.

4. Bathsheba is still in the early stages of her first trimester of pregnancy. The period of mourning is likely seven days in length (Gen. 50:10; 1 Sam. 31:13). See McCarter, *II Samuel*, 288.

5. The Lord regards David's marriage to Bathsheba as an act of theft after the act of murder. See 2 Sam. 12:9.

6. See the Reformed theologian Packer on God's omniscience (*Concise Theology*, 31–32).

2 Samuel 12

1. Arnold, *1 and 2 Samuel*, 532.

2. Nathan uses a prophetic entrapment technique to get David to pronounce his own sentence. (See 1 Kings 20 for another example of this prophetic strategy.)

3. Exum, *Tragedy and Biblical Narrative*, 129.

4. Fokkelman (*Narrative Art and Poetry*, 93) links the two texts in his chart but does not explain the significance of the correlation.

5. Arnold, *1 and 2 Samuel*, 538.

6. Marshall, *The Prayers of Peter Marshall*, 25.

2 Samuel 13

1. See Polzin, *David and the Deuteronomist*, 137–38.

2. Bergen, *1, 2 Samuel*, 380.

3. Fokkelman, *Narrative Art and Poetry*, 104.

4. Ibid., 112.

5. See McCarter, *II Samuel*, 319. Based on 13:21 LXX, McCarter translates, "But he did nothing to chasten his son Amnon, because he loved him since he was his first-born" (315).

6. Exum, *Tragedy and Biblical Narrative*, 145.

7. Fokkelman, *Narrative Art and Poetry*, 125.

8. Arnold, *1 and 2 Samuel*, 565.

9. MacDonald, *Creation in Christ*, 75.

2 Samuel 14:1–15:12

1. See Weinfeld, *Social Justice in Ancient Israel*.

2. Perhaps the three sons die prematurely since 2 Sam. 18:18 says that Absalom has no heir when he erects his monument.

3. For further discussion of the narrator's characterization of Absalom here, see Fokkelman, *Narrative Art and Poetry*, 151.

4. See Cartledge, *1 and 2 Samuel*, 559.

5. Later, after Absalom's death, the Israelites refer to him as the "one whom we anointed to rule over us" (19:10).

6. Lewis, *Surprised by Joy*, 229.

7. Reprinted in Rottenberg, *The Structure of Argument*, 261–62.

2 Samuel 15:13–37

1. Gordon (*1 and 2 Samuel*, 273) sees the primary contrast as being with Ahithophel.

2. Arnold, *1 and 2 Samuel*, 581.

3. McCarter, *II Samuel*, 377; Fokkelman, *Narrative Art and Poetry*, 191; Bergen, *1, 2 Samuel*, 406.

4. Fokkelman, *Narrative Art and Poetry*, 193.

5. Frangipane, *This Day We Fight!*, 28.

2 Samuel 16:1–14

1. The events recorded in 21:1–14 may have occurred prior to Absalom's revolt.

2. Polzin, *David and the Deuteronomist*, 158.

3. The MT in 2 Sam. 16:12 reads "will see my iniquity," probably referring to "iniquity done [by Shimei] against me." A marginal reading in the MT has "my eye," perhaps meaning "my tears." However, some Hebrew manuscripts and ancient versions read "my suffering" (cf. NIV, "my misery"), which makes better sense. (In Hebrew the words "my iniquity," "my eye," and "my suffering" are almost identical in spelling.) David is not so much hoping for divine justice as he is for divine mercy.

4. Yancey, *Reaching for the Invisible God*, 188–89.

5. Editorial, http://www.christianitytoday.com/ct/2006/april/12.28.html.

2 Samuel 16:15–17:29

1. McCarter, *II Samuel*, 384.

2. Anderson, *2 Samuel*, 213; Fokkelman, *Narrative Art and Poetry*, 206.

3. Bergen, *1, 2 Samuel*, 410. Hushai also describes "the one chosen by the LORD" as being the choice of the people and Israel (16:18). Absalom undoubtedly thinks in terms of what has just happened in Hebron (15:10–12), but Hushai has in mind the events recorded in 2:4 and 5:1–3.

4. See 1 Kings 2:21–22, where Solomon, upon hearing that Adonijah wanted to marry Abishag, the last woman to sleep with David (1 Kings 1:1–4), concluded that the request was equivalent to asking for his father's throne. Thus 2 Sam. 12:8 seems to indicate that David took Saul's wives when he became king. McCarter, *II Samuel*, 384.

5. Arnold, *1 and 2 Samuel*, 587.

6. McCarter, *II Samuel*, 386.

7. See ibid., 388–89; Gordon, *1 and 2 Samuel*, 282.

8. See Arnold, *1 and 2 Samuel*, 593.

9. *Sir Gawain and the Green Knight*, 4.16.

10. Gire, *Windows to the Soul*, 111–13.

2 Samuel 18:1–19:8

1. The phrase occurs only one other time in the entire OT (2 Chron. 21:14).

2. McCarter, *II Samuel*, 406.

3. Ibid.

4. Fokkelman, *Narrative Art and Poetry*, 246–47.

5. McCarter, *II Samuel*, 407.

6. Bergen, *1, 2 Samuel*, 422.

7. The statement in 18:18 seems to contradict an earlier note that Absalom has three sons (14:27). The text does not harmonize the two passages, but some theorize that the sons may have died, and hence their names are not given. For discussion of the problem, see McCarter, *II Samuel*, 407.

8. On the contrasting perspectives, see Fokkelman, *Narrative Art and Poetry*, 257.

9. Ibid., 262.

10. Ibid., 265.

11. Polzin (*David and the Deuteronomist*, 188) states: "We have sympathy for David not just because the narrator makes doubly sure we know about the king's worry over Absalom, but also because the story manages to make David's double cry of grief . . . the climax of a steady buildup of tension."

2 Samuel 19:9–20:26

1. McCarter, *II Samuel*, 431.

2. McCarter, *II Samuel*, 431.

3. Olsen, "Cash's Song," http://www.christianitytoday.com/ct/2003/november/4.60.html?start=2.

4. Bonhoeffer, *Letters and Papers* (1972), 348.

Additional Insights

1. Several interpreters have recognized this structure. For a summary and bibliography, see Arnold, *1 and 2 Samuel*, 616.

2. For an insightful study of how the material in the epilogue relates to the depiction of David's career given in the preceding narrative, see Satterthwaite, "David in the Books of Samuel." He correctly contends that there is ambiguity and tension in the narrative of David's career and in the epilogue: "David as king has fallen short of the ideal represented by" the poetic texts in 1 Sam. 2:1–10; 2 Sam. 22; and 23:1–7 and "has been subject to God's judgment." He adds, "The ideal remains intact, but the tension between David's Thanksgiving / David's Last Words and the preceding narrative remains unresolved" (64).

2 Samuel 21:1–14

1. See, e.g., the treaty between Ashurnirari V and Mati'ilu (¶ 4), the vassal treaties of Esarhaddon (¶ 56), and the treaty between KTK and Arpad (I.A), in *ANET*, 532–33, 534–41, 659–61, respectively.

2. McCarter, *II Samuel*, 444; cf. Cartledge, *1 and 2 Samuel*, 639.

3. Bergen, *1, 2 Samuel*, 445.

4. The events recorded in 21:1–14 may have occurred earlier in David's reign, prior to Absalom's revolt.

5. Bonhoeffer, *Life Together*, 107.

6. Paton, *Too Late the Phalarope*, 11.

2 Samuel 21:15–22; 23:8–39

1. Though the exact phrase "lamp of Israel" occurs only here, the image of a lamp is associated with the Davidic dynasty in 1 Kings 11:36; 15:4; 2 Kings 8:19; 2 Chron. 21:7; Pss. 18:28; 132:7.

2. Bergen, *1, 2 Samuel*, 448–49.

3. Barnes, *Yearning*, 176–77.

4. See http://www.salvationarmy.org/ihq/history.

2 Samuel 22

1. For numerous parallels, see Chisholm, "Study of Psalm 18 / 2 Samuel 22," 160–62, 166–67, 170, 172–79, 181–83, 190–92, 196.

2. These include the Sumerian ruler Shulgi (2094–2047 BC), the Egyptian Pharaoh Ramesses II (1290–1224 BC), the Assyrian king Ashurnasirpal II (883–859 BC), the Moabite king Mesha (830 BC), and the Assyrian ruler Sargon (721–705 BC). See ibid., 41–44. Two of these texts appear in COS, 2:32–40 (Ramesses II), 137–38 (Mesha).

3. For ancient Near Eastern parallels, see Chisholm, "Study of Psalm 18 / 2 Samuel 22," 135–36.

4. Several of the Amarna letters use the "ensnared bird" motif to illustrate intense oppression and threats by enemies; see ibid., 155n3.

5. In a well-meaning attempt to protect the character of God, some have watered down the force of verse 27b. Some regard the statement as reflecting the evildoer's perception of God's actions or interpret it to mean that God simply gives the evildoers over to pursue their self-destructive behavior. But these interpretations fail to adequately reflect the active and direct nature of the divine response envisioned here. The Lord can and sometimes does use deception to thwart evildoers and bring about their demise (see, e.g., 1 Kings 22; Ezek. 14:4–11). In such cases the victims of divine deception have forfeited their right to the truth, and God's action should be viewed as retributive justice. As Alexander states, "The same course of proceeding which would be perverse in itself or towards a righteous person, when pursued towards a sinner becomes a mere act of vindicatory justice" (*The Psalms Translated*, 81). On the subject of divine deception in the OT, see Chisholm, "Does God Deceive?"

6. Similar hyperbolic descriptions appear in the Assyrian annals of Ashurnasirpal II and of Sargon. See Chisholm, "Study of Psalm 18 / 2 Samuel 22," 229–30. Ashurnasirpal claims that his warriors "flew" like a bird against a mighty citadel that "had the form of a mountain peak." Sargon reports that his army jumped across the Lower Zab River as if it were a mere "ditch."

7. Such oracles are well attested in ancient Near Eastern royal literature; see ibid., 241–42.

8. Ancient Near Eastern art and literature depict kings as receiving training in warfare from their gods, and several texts describe gods as giving special weapons to a king before battle. See ibid., 253, 260–61.

9. For ancient Near Eastern parallels to this motif, see ibid., 280–81.

2 Samuel 23:1–7

1. For numerous examples, see Chisholm, "Study of Psalm 18 / 2 Samuel 22," 131.

2. Gordon, *1 and 2 Samuel*, 311.

3. Grahame, *The Wind in the Willows*, 135.

4. McCullough, *The Trivialization of God*, 115–16.

2 Samuel 24

1. It is not clear if Exod. 30:12 refers only to censuses ordered by the Lord, as in Num. 1:1, or makes room for censuses taken by Moses apart from a divine command.

2. McCarter, *II Samuel*, 513–14.

3. For helpful thoughts on the contrast between Saul and David in this regard, see Arnold, *1 and 2 Samuel*, 645.

4. See Cartledge, *1 and 2 Samuel*, 707–8, 711.

5. The second potential punishment (24:13) seems to be directed at David himself, but if David is pursued by enemies, surely this will have a negative impact on all Israel.

Bibliography

Recommended Resources

Anderson, A. A. *2 Samuel*. Word Biblical Commentary. Dallas: Word, 1989.

Arnold, Bill T. *1 and 2 Samuel*. NIV Application Commentary. Grand Rapids: Zondervan, 2003.

Bergen, Robert D. *1, 2 Samuel*. New American Commentary 7. Nashville: Broadman & Holman, 1996. Reprint, 2002.

Bodner, Keith. *1 Samuel: A Narrative Commentary*. Sheffield: Sheffield Phoenix, 2009.

Cartledge, Tony W. *1 and 2 Samuel*. Smyth & Helwys Bible Commentary. Macon, GA: Smyth & Helwys, 2001.

Firth, David G. *1 and 2 Samuel*. Apollos Old Testament Commentary. Downers Grove, IL: IVP Academic, 2009.

Klein, Ralph W. *1 Samuel*. Word Biblical Commentary. Waco: Word, 1983.

McCarter, P. Kyle, Jr. *I Samuel*. Anchor Bible. Garden City, NY: Doubleday, 1980.

———. *II Samuel*. Anchor Bible. Garden City, NY: Doubleday, 1984.

Tsumura, David Toshio. *The First Book of Samuel*. New International Commentary on the Old Testament. Grand Rapids: Eerdmans, 2007.

Additional Works Cited

Alexander, Joseph A. *The Psalms Translated and Explained*. Edinburgh: Andrew Elliot, 1864.

Barnes, M. Craig. *Yearning: Living between How It Is and How It Ought to Be*. Downers Grove, IL: InterVarsity, 1992.

Barthélemy, D., D. W. Gooding, J. Lust, and E. Tov. *The Story of David and Goliath: Textual and Literary Criticism*. Göttingen: Vandenhoeck & Ruprecht, 1986.

Berlin, Adele. *Poetics and Interpretation of Biblical Narrative*. Sheffield: Almond, 1983.

Biddle, Mark E. "Ancestral Motifs in 1 Samuel 25: Intertextuality and Characterization." *Journal of Biblical Literature* 121 (2002): 617–38.

Billington, Clyde E. "Goliath and the Exodus Giants: How Tall Were They?" *Journal of the Evangelical Theological Society* 50 (2007): 489–508.

Birch, Bruce C. *The Rise of the Israelite Monarchy: The Growth and Development of 1 Samuel 7–15*. Missoula, MT: Scholars Press, 1976.

Blenkinsopp, Joseph. *Isaiah 40–55*. Anchor Bible. New York: Doubleday, 2002.

Bluedorn, Wolfgang. *Yahweh versus Baal: A Theological Reading of the Gideon–Abimelech Narrative*. Journal for the Study of the Old Testament: Supplement Series 329. Sheffield: Sheffield Academic Press, 2001.

Boda, Mark J. *A Severe Mercy: Sin and Its Remedy in the Old Testament*. Winona Lake, IN: Eisenbrauns, 2009.

Bonhoeffer, Dietrich. *Letters and Papers from Prison*. Edited by Eberhard Bethge. Translated by R. H. Fuller. London: Fontana, 1959. Reprint, New York: Collier/Macmillan, 1972.

———. *Life Together*. San Francisco: Harper, 1954.

Borgman, Paul. *David, Saul, and God: Rediscovering an Ancient Story*. Oxford: Oxford University Press, 2008.

Botterweck, G. Johannes, and Helmer Ringgren, eds. *Theological Dictionary of the Old Testament*. 15 vols. Grand Rapids: Eerdmans, 1974–2006.

Brontë, Charlotte. *Jane Eyre*. Edited by Michael Mason. New York: Penguin, 1996.

Brooks, Simcha S. "Saul and the Samson Narrative." *Journal for the Study of the Old Testament* 71 (1996): 19–25.

Brown, Francis, S. R. Driver, and Charles A. Briggs. *The New Brown, Driver, Briggs, Gesenius Hebrew and English Lexicon*. Peabody, MA: Hendrickson, 1979.

Brueggemann, Walter. *David's Truth in Israel's Imagination and Memory*. 2nd ed. Minneapolis: Fortress, 2002.

Bunyan, John. *The Pilgrim's Progress*. 1678. Slightly abridged. Chicago: Moody, 2007.

Chisholm, Robert B., Jr. "The Chronology of the Book of Judges: A Linguistic Clue to Solving a Pesky Problem." *Journal of the Evangelical Theological Society* 52 (2009): 247–55.

———. "Divine Hardening in the Old Testament." *Bibliotheca sacra* 153 (1996): 410–34.

———. "Does God 'Change His Mind'?" *Bibliotheca sacra* 152 (1995): 387–99.

———. "Does God Deceive?" *Bibliotheca sacra* 155 (1998): 11–28.

———. "Ehud: Assessing an Assassin." *Bibliotheca sacra* 168 (2011): 274–82.

———. "An Exegetical and Theological Study of Psalm 18 / 2 Samuel 22." ThD diss., Dallas Theological Seminary, 1983.

———. "How a Hermeneutical Virus Can Corrupt Theological Systems." *Bibliotheca sacra* 166 (2009): 259–70.

———. *Interpreting the Historical Books: An Exegetical Handbook*. Grand Rapids: Kregel, 2006.

———. "The Polemic against Baalism in Israel's Early History and Literature." *Bibliotheca sacra* 150 (1994): 267–83.

———. "The Role of Women in the Rhetorical Strategy of the Book of Judges." In *Integrity of Heart, Skillfulness of Hands*, edited by C. H. Dyer & R. B. Zuck, 34–49. Grand Rapids: Baker, 1994.

———. "When Prophecy Appears to Fail, Check Your Hermeneutic." *Journal of the Evangelical Theological Society* 53 (2010): 561–77.

———. "Yahweh versus the Canaanite Gods: Polemic in Judges and 1 Samuel 1–7." *Bibliotheca sacra* 164 (2007): 165–80.

Christianity Today. "Before the Next Sex Scandal." Where We Stand. 50, no. 4 (April 2006): 28–29.

Clendenen, E. Ray. "Textlinguistics and Prophecy in the Book of the Twelve." *Journal of the Evangelical Theological Society* 46 (2003): 385–99.

Coles, Robert. *The Story of Ruby Bridges*. New York: Scholastic, 1995.

Colson, Chuck. *Born Again*. Old Tappan, NJ: Chosen/Revell, 1976.

Cowan, Louise, and Os Guinness, eds. *Invitation to the Classics*. Grand Rapids: Baker, 1998.

Cymbala, Jim. *Fresh Wind, Fresh Fire: What Happens When God's Spirit Invades the Heart of His People*. Grand Rapids: Zondervan, 1997.

Dawn, Marva J. *A Royal "Waste" of Time: The Splendor of Worshiping God and Being Church for the World*. Grand Rapids: Eerdmans, 1999.

Day, John. *Yahweh and the Gods and Goddesses of Canaan*. Journal for the Study of the Old Testament: Supplement Series 265. Sheffield: Sheffield Academic Press, 2000.

Defoe, Daniel. *The Life and Surprizing Adventures of Robinson Crusoe, of York, Mariner*. Boston: Houghton Mifflin, 1895. First published 1719 by W. Taylor.

Dever, William G. "Histories and Non-Histories of Ancient Israel: The Question of the United Monarchy." In *In Search of Pre-Exilic Israel*, edited by John Day, 65–94. London: T&T Clark, 2004.

———. *Who Were the Early Israelites and Where Did They Come From?* Grand Rapids: Eerdmans, 2003.

Dillard, Annie. *Teaching a Stone to Talk*. New York: Harper & Row, 1982.

Donne, John. *The Poetical Works of Dr. John Donne: With a Memoir*. Boston: Little, Brown, 1864.

———. *The Works of John Donne*. Edited by Henry Alford. Vol. 3. London: John W. Parker, 1839.

Dorsett, Lyle. *A Passion for Souls*. Chicago: Moody, 1997.

Dragga, Sam. "In the Shadow of the Judges: The Failure of Saul." *Journal for the Study of the Old Testament* 38 (1987): 39–46.

Driver, S. R. *Notes on the Hebrew Text and the Topography of the Books of Samuel*. Reprint, Eugene, OR: Wipf & Stock, 2004.

Eaton, J. H. *Festal Drama in Deutero-Isaiah*. London: SPCK, 1979.

Edelman, Diana. *King Saul in the Historiography of Judah*. Journal for the Study of the Old Testament: Supplement Series 121. Sheffield: Sheffield Academic Press, 1991.

Edgerton, William F., and John A. Wilson. *Historical Records of Ramses III: The Texts in Medinet Habu*. 2 vols. Chicago: University of Chicago Press, 1936.

Eslinger, Lyle M. *Kingship of God in Crisis: A Close Reading of 1 Samuel 1–12*. Sheffield: Almond, 1985.

Evans, Mary J. *The Message of Samuel*. The Bible Speaks Today. Leicester, UK: Inter-Varsity, 2004.

Exum, J. Cheryl. *Tragedy and Biblical Narrative*. Cambridge: Cambridge University Press, 1992.

Feliu, Lluís. *The God Dagan in Bronze Age Syria*. Translated by W. G. E. Watson. Leiden: Brill, 2003.

Fénelon, François. *Let Go: To Get Peace and Real Joy*. Springdale, PA: Whitaker House, 1973.

Firth, David G. "'Play It Again, Sam': The Poetics of Narrative Repetition in 1 Samuel 1–7." *Tyndale Bulletin* 56 (2005): 1–17.

Fitt, Arthur Percy. *The Shorter Life of D. L. Moody*. In *The D. L. Moody Collection*, edited by James S. Bell Jr. Chicago: Moody, 1997.

Fleming, Jean. *The Homesick Heart: Longing for Spiritual Intimacy*. Colorado Springs: NavPress, 1995.

Fokkelman, J. P. *Narrative Art and Poetry in the Books of Samuel*. Vol. 1. Assen: Van Gorcum, 1981.

Ford, Leighton. *The Attentive Life: Discerning God's Presence in All Things*. Downers Grove, IL: Inter-Varsity, 2008.

Foster, Richard J. *Celebration of Discipline: The Path to Spiritual Growth*. New York: Harper & Row, 1978.

Foxe, John. *Foxe's Book of Martyrs*. 1563. Edited by William Byron Forbush. Giant Summit Books. Grand Rapids: Baker, 1978.

Frangipane, Francis. *This Day We Fight! Breaking the Bondage of a Passive Spirit*. Revised and expanded ed. Grand Rapids: Chosen, 2010.

Gerbrandt, G. E. *Kingship according to the Deuteronomistic History*. Society of Biblical Literature Dissertation Series 87. Atlanta: Scholars Press, 1986.

Gire, Ken. *Windows to the Soul*. Grand Rapids: Zondervan, 1996.

Golding, William. *Lord of the Flies: A Novel*. London: Faber, 1954.

Gordon, Robert P. *1 and 2 Samuel: A Commentary*. Grand Rapids: Zondervan, 1986.

Grahame, Kenneth. *The Wind in the Willows*. Magnet Books. London: Methuen Children's Books, 1978.

Grayson, Albert Kirk. *Assyrian Royal Inscriptions*. 2 vols. Wiesbaden: Otto Harrassowitz, 1972–76.

Guinness, Os. *Prophetic Untimeliness: A Challenge to the Idol of Relevance*. Grand Rapids: Baker Books, 2003.

Gunn, David. *The Fate of King Saul*. Journal for the Study of the Old Testament: Supplement Series 14. Sheffield: JSOT Press, 1980.

Hallo, William W., and K. Lawson Younger, eds. *The Context of Scripture*. 3 vols. Boston: Brill, 2003.

Hamilton, Bethany, with Sheryl Berk and Rick Bundschuh. *Soul Surfer: A True Story of Faith, Family, and Fighting to Get Back on the Board*. New York: Pocket Books / MTV Books, 2004.

Havner, Vance. *All the Days*. Old Tappan, NJ: Revell, 1976.

Hays, J. Daniel. "The Height of Goliath: A Response to Clyde Billington." *Journal of the Evangelical Theological Society* 50 (2007): 509–16.

———. "Reconsidering the Height of Goliath." *Journal of the Evangelical Theological Society* 48 (2005): 701–14.

Heller, Roy L. *Power, Politics, and Prophecy: The Character of Samuel and the Deuteronomistic Evaluation of Prophecy*. Library of Hebrew Bible / Old Testament Studies 40. New York: T&T Clark, 2006.

Hess, Richard S. *Israelite Religions: An Archaeological and Biblical Survey*. Grand Rapids: Baker Academic, 2007.

Hoffner, Harry A. "A Hittite Analogue to the David and Goliath Contest of Champions?" *Catholic Biblical Quarterly* 30 (1968): 220–25.

Howard, David M., Jr. "The Case for Kingship in Deuteronomy and the Former Prophets: A Review of G. E. Gerbrandt's *Kingship according to the Deuteronomistic History*." *Westminster Theological Journal* 52 (1990): 101–15.

———. "Philistines." In *Peoples of the Old Testament World*, edited by A. J. Hoerth, G. L. Mattingly, and E. M. Yamauchi, 231–50. Grand Rapids: Baker, 1994.

Janzen, David. "Why the Deuteronomist Told about the Sacrifice of Jephthah's Daughter." *Journal for the Study of the Old Testament* 29 (2005): 339–57.

Jeffers, Ann. *Magic and Divination in Ancient Palestine and Syria*. Leiden: Brill, 1996.

Kaiser, Walter C., Jr. "The Unfailing Kindnesses Promised to David: Isaiah 55:3." *Journal for the Study of the Old Testament* 45 (1989): 91–98.

Kaminsky, Joel S. *Corporate Responsibility in the Hebrew Bible*. Journal for the Study of the Old Testament: Supplement Series 196. Sheffield: Sheffield Academic Press, 1995.

Kessler, John. "Sexuality and Politics: The Motif of the Displaced Husband in the Books of Samuel." *Catholic Biblical Quarterly* 62 (2000): 409–23.

King, Martin Luther, Jr. "Letter from a Birmingham Jail." In *Encounters: Connecting, Creating, Composing*, by William R. Epperson et al. Dubuque, IA: Kendall/Hunt, 1994.

King, Philip J., and Lawrence E. Stager. *Life in Biblical Israel*. Louisville: Westminster John Knox, 2001.

Kitchen, K. A. *On the Reliability of the Old Testament*. Grand Rapids: Eerdmans, 2003.

Knoppers, Gary N. "Ancient Near Eastern Royal Grants and the Davidic Covenant: A Parallel?" *Journal of the American Oriental Society* 116 (1996): 670–97.

Koehler, Ludwig, and Walter Baumgartner. *The Hebrew and Aramaic Lexicon of the Old Testament*. Revised by W. Baumgartner and J. J. Stamm. Translated and edited by M. E. J. Richardson. 2 vols. Boston: Brill, 2001.

Koessler, John. *A Stranger in the House of God: From Doubt to Faith and Everywhere in Between*. Grand Rapids: Zondervan, 2007.

Laird, Margaret Nicholl, with Raymond B. Buker and Phil Landrum. *They Called Me Mama*. Chicago: Moody, 1975.

Larsen, David L. *The Company of the Creative: A Christian Reader's Guide to Great Literature and Its Themes*. Grand Rapids: Kregel, 1999.

Lawton, Robert B. "1 Samuel 18: David, Merob, and Michal." *Catholic Biblical Quarterly* 51 (1989): 423–25.

Lewis, C. S. *The Last Battle*. Vol. 7 of The Chronicles of Narnia. New York: Collier, 1956.

———. *The Lion, the Witch and the Wardrobe*. Vol. 1 of The Chronicles of Narnia. 1950. Reprint, New York: Harper Trophy, 1978.

———. *Mere Christianity*. New York: Collier, 1960.

———. *The Problem of Pain*. New York: Macmillan, 1962.

———. *Surprised by Joy: The Shape of My Early Life*. New York: Harcourt, Brace & World, 1955.

Lichtheim, Miriam. *Ancient Egyptian Literature*. 3 vols. Berkeley: University of California Press, 1976.

Long, V. Philips. *The Reign and Rejection of King Saul: A Case for Literary and Theological Coherence*. Society of Biblical Literature Dissertation Series 18. Atlanta: Scholars Press, 1989.

Lozovyy, Joseph. *Saul, Doeg, Nabal, and the "Son of Jesse": Readings in 1 Samuel 16–25*. Library of Hebrew Bible / Old Testament Studies 497. New York: T&T Clark, 2009.

Luckenbill, Daniel David. *Ancient Records of Assyria and Babylon*. 2 vols. Chicago: University of Chicago Press, 1926–27.

Luther, Martin. *Devotions and Prayers of Martin Luther*. Translated by Andrew Kosten. Grand Rapids: Baker, 1965.

MacDonald, George. *Creation in Christ*. Edited by Roland Hein. Wheaton: Harold Shaw, 1976.

———. *The Wise Woman: A Parable*. London: Strathan, 1875.

Marshall, Peter. *The Prayers of Peter Marshall*. New York: McGraw Hill, 1954.

McCullough, Donald. *The Trivialization of God: The Dangerous Illusion of a Manageable Deity*. Colorado Springs: NavPress, 1995.

McKenzie, Steven L. *King David: A Biography*. New York: Oxford University Press, 2000.

Meier, Samuel A. "The Sword: From Saul to David." In *Saul in Story and Tradition*, edited by C. S. Ehrlich and M. C. White, 156–74. Tübingen: Mohr Siebeck, 2006.

Merton, Thomas. *The Literary Essays of Thomas Merton*. New York: New Directions, 1984.

Mettinger, Tryggve N. D. *In Search of God: The Meaning and Message of the Everlasting Names*. Philadelphia: Fortress, 1988.

Milgrom, Jacob. *Leviticus*. Continental Commentaries. Minneapolis: Fortress, 2004.

Miller, Patrick D. *The Religion of Ancient Israel.* Louisville: Westminster John Knox, 2000.

Milton, John. *The Complete Poetry and Essential Prose of John Milton.* Edited by William Kerrigan, John Rumrich, and Stephen M. Fallon. New York: Modern Library, 2007.

———. *Paradise Lost.* London: Peter Parker, 1667.

Moran, William. "The Ancient Near Eastern Background of the Love of God in Deuteronomy." *Catholic Biblical Quarterly* 25 (1963): 77–84.

Morgan, Robert J. *Near to the Heart of God: Meditations on 366 Best-Loved Hymns.* Grand Rapids: Revell, 2010.

Motyer, J. Alec. *The Prophecy of Isaiah.* Downers Grove, IL: InterVarsity, 1993.

Newell, Marvin J. *A Martyr's Grace.* Chicago: Moody, 2007.

Niditch, Susan. *War in the Hebrew Bible: A Study in the Ethics of Violence.* New York: Oxford University Press, 1993.

Niehaus, Jeffrey J. *Ancient Near Eastern Themes in Biblical Theology.* Grand Rapids: Kregel, 2008.

O'Connell, Robert H. *The Rhetoric of the Book of Judges.* Vetus Testamentum Supplements 63. Leiden: Brill, 1996.

Olsen, Ted. "Johnny Cash's Song of Redemption." *Christianity Today* 47, no. 11 (November 1, 2003): 60.

Osborn, John Jay, Jr. *The Paper Chase.* Boston: Houghton Mifflin, 1971.

Oswalt, John N. *The Book of Isaiah: Chapters 40–66.* New International Commentary on the Old Testament. Grand Rapids: Eerdmans, 1998.

Packer, J. I. *Concise Theology: A Guide to Historic Christian Beliefs.* Wheaton: Tyndale House, 1993.

Paton, Alan. *Too Late the Phalarope.* New York: Scribner, 1953.

Peterson, Eugene. *Leap over a Wall: Earthy Spirituality for Everyday Christians.* New York: HarperCollins, 1997.

Piper, John. *A Hunger for God: Desiring God through Fasting and Prayer.* Wheaton: Crossway, 1997.

Pitard, Wayne T. *Ancient Damascus.* Winona Lake, IN: Eisenbrauns, 1987.

Plantinga, Cornelius, Jr. *Not the Way It's Supposed to Be.* Grand Rapids: Eerdmans, 1995.

Polzin, Robert. *David and the Deuteronomist.* Bloomington: Indiana University Press, 1993.

———. *Samuel and the Deuteronomist.* San Francisco: Harper & Row, 1989.

Pratt, Richard L., Jr. "Historical Contingencies and Biblical Predictions." In *The Way of Wisdom: Essays in Honor of Bruce K. Waltke,* edited by J. I. Packer and Sven K. Soderlund, 182–203. Grand Rapids: Zondervan, 2000.

Prejean, Helen. *Dead Man Walking: An Eyewitness Account of the Death Penalty in the United States.* New York: Random House, 1993.

Pritchard, James B., ed. *Ancient Near Eastern Texts Relating to the Old Testament.* 3rd ed. Princeton: Princeton University Press, 1969.

Roseveare, Helen. *Living Sacrifice.* Chicago: Moody, 1979.

Rottenberg, Annette T. *The Structure of Argument.* 4th ed. Boston: Bedford / St. Martin's, 2003.

Satterthwaite, Philip E. "David in the Books of Samuel: A Messianic Hope?" In *The Lord's Anointed: Interpretation of Old Testament Messianic Texts,* edited by P. E. Satterthwaite, R. S. Hess, and G. J. Wenham, 41–65. Grand Rapids: Baker, 1995.

Sir Gawain and the Green Knight. Translated by W. A. Nielson. http://www.yorku.ca/inpar/sggk_neilson.pdf.

Sparks, Kenton L. *Ancient Texts for the Study of Scripture: A Guide to the Background Literature.* Peabody, MA: Hendrickson, 2005.

Spurgeon, C. H. *Pictures from "Pilgrim's Progress."* Pasadena, TX: Pilgrim Publications, 1973.

Steiner, George. *Real Presences: Is There Anything in What We Say?* Chicago: University of Chicago Press, 1989.

Sternberg, Meir. *The Poetics of Biblical Narrative.* Bloomington: Indiana University Press, 1987.

Steussy, Marti J. *David: Biblical Portraits of Power.* Columbia: University of South Carolina Press, 1999.

Ten Boom, Corrie. *Corrie ten Boom's Prison Letters.* Old Tappan, NJ: Revell, 1975.

Teresa. *The Complete Works of Saint Teresa of Jesus.* Edited by E. A. Peers. London: Sheed & Ward, 1946.

Thompson, J. A. "The Significance of the Verb *Love* in the David-Jonathan Narratives in 1 Samuel." *Vetus Testamentum* 24 (1974): 334–38.

Tiemeyer, Lena-Sofia. "Prophecy as a Way of Cancelling Prophecy—The Strategic Uses of

Foreknowledge." *Zeitschrift für die alttestamentliche Wissenschaft* 117 (2005): 329–50.

Tolkien, J. R. R. *The Lord of the Rings*. 3 vols. London: Allen & Unwin, 1954–55.

Torrey, R. A. *How to Pray*. Chicago: Moody, 2007.

Tozer, A. W. *A. W. Tozer: An Anthology*. Edited by Harry Verploegh. Camp Hill, PA: Christian Publications, 1984.

———. *The Knowledge of the Holy: The Attributes of God; Their Meaning in the Christian Life*. New York: Harper, 1961.

VanGemeren, Willem A., ed. *New International Dictionary of Old Testament Theology and Exegesis*. 5 vols. Grand Rapids: Zondervan, 1997.

Wagner, Charles U. *Winning Words for Daily Living*. Grand Rapids: Kregel, 1989.

Walton, John H. *Ancient Near Eastern Thought and the Old Testament: Introducing the Conceptual World of the Hebrew Bible*. Grand Rapids: Baker Academic, 2006.

———. *Covenant: God's Purpose, God's Plan*. Grand Rapids: Zondervan, 1994.

———. *Genesis 1 as Ancient Cosmology*. Winona Lake, IN: Eisenbrauns, 2011.

———, ed. *Zondervan Illustrated Bible Backgrounds Commentary: Old Testament*. 5 vols. Grand Rapids: Zondervan, 2009.

Weinfeld, Moshe. "The Covenant of Grant in the Old Testament and in the Ancient Near East." *Journal of the American Oriental Society* 90 (1970): 180–203.

———. *Social Justice in Ancient Israel and in the Ancient Near East*. Minneapolis: Fortress, 1995.

Wells, David. *No Place for Truth*. Grand Rapids: Eerdmans, 1993.

Wenham, G. J. *The Book of Leviticus*. New International Commentary on the Old Testament. Grand Rapids: Eerdmans, 1979.

Wiggins, Steve A. "Old Testament Dagan in the Light of Ugarit." *Vetus Testamentum* 43 (1993): 268–74.

Wilkerson, David. *The Cross and the Switchblade*. New York: B. Geis Associates / Random House, 1963.

Wilson, Robert R. *Prophecy and Society in Ancient Israel*. Philadelphia: Fortress, 1980.

Wong, G. C. I. "Who Loved Whom? A Note on 1 Samuel xvi 21." *Vetus Testamentum* 47 (1997): 554–56.

Wong, Gregory T. K. "Ehud and Joab: Separated at Birth?" *Vetus Testamentum* 56 (2006): 399–412.

Wurmbrand, Richard. *Tortured for Christ*. London: Hodder & Stoughton, 1967.

Yadin, Yigael. *The Art of Warfare in Biblical Lands*. Translated by M. Pearlman. London: Weidenfeld & Nicolson, 1963.

Yancey, Philip. *Reaching for the Invisible God: What Can We Expect to Find?* Grand Rapids: Zondervan, 2000.

Younker, Randall W. "Ammonites." In *Peoples of the Old Testament World*, edited by A. J. Hoerth, G. L. Mattingly, and E. M. Yamauchi, 293–316. Grand Rapids: Baker Books, 1994.

Image Credits

Unless otherwise indicated, photos, illustrations, and maps are copyright © Baker Photo Archive.

The Baker Photo Archive acknowledges the permission of the following institutions and individuals.

Photo on page 94 © Baker Photo Archive. Courtesy of the Aegyptisches Museum, Berlin, Germany.

Photos on pages 9, 13, 33, 39, 48, 52, 54, 102, 120, 135, 146, 148, 168, 173, 192, 227, 228, 230, 240, 254, 280, 283, 288, 290, 301, 302 © Baker Photo Archive. Courtesy of the British Museum, London, England.

Photos on pages 30, 166, 204, 245 © Baker Photo Archive. Courtesy of the Egyptian Ministry of Antiquities and the Museum of Egyptian Antiquities, Cairo, Egypt.

Photo on page 10 © Baker Photo Archive. Courtesy of the Eretz Museum, Tel Aviv, Israel.

Photo on page 117 © Baker Photo Archive. Courtesy of the Greek Ministry of Antiquities and the National Archaeological Museum, Athens, Greece.

Photo on page 242 © Baker Photo Archive. Courtesy of the Jordanian Ministry of Antiquities and the Amman Archaeological Museum.

Photos on pages 46, 99, 250, 296, 308 © Baker Photo Archive. Courtesy of the Musée du Louvre; Autorisation de photographer et de filmer. Louvre, Paris, France.

Photos on pages 124, 262 © Baker Photo Archive. Courtesy of the Oriental Institute Museum, Chicago.

Photo on page 105 © Baker Photo Archive. Courtesy of the Pergamon Museum, Berlin.

Photos on pages 44, 214, 220, 233 © Baker Photo Archive. Courtesy of the Skirball Museum, Hebrew Union College–Jewish Institute of Religion, 13 King David Street, Jerusalem 94101.

Photos on pages 66, 96, 100, 130, 287 © Baker Photo Archive. Courtesy of the Turkish Ministry of Antiquities and the Istanbul Archaeological Museum. Translation of inscription on page 100 from the Istanbul Archaeological Museum.

Photos on pages 213, 218 © Baker Photo Archive. Courtesy of the Turkish Ministry of Antiquities and the Museum of Anatolian Civilizations, Ankara, Turkey.

Additional image credits

Photo on page 269 © Deror avi, CC-by-sa-3.0.

Photo on page 21 © Dr. James C. Martin and the Israel Museum. Collection of the Israel Museum, Jerusalem, and courtesy of the Israel Antiquities Authority, exhibited at the Israel Museum, Jerusalem.

Photo on page 57 © Einsamer Schütze / Wikimedia Commons, courtesy of the Roemer-Pelizaeus Museum, Hildescheim, Germany.

Photo on page 24 © Fredduf / Wikimedia Commons, courtesy of the Louvre.

Photo on page 16 © Guillaume Blanchard / Wikimedia Commons, CC-by-sa-3.0, courtesy of the Louvre.

Photo on page 50 © Heretiq / Wikimedia Commons, CC-by-sa-2.5.

Photo on page 223 © Joeb07 / Wikimedia Commons.

Photos on pages 118, 260 © Kim Walton.

Photos on pages 69, 106, 123, 136, 165, 190, 196, 294 © Kim Walton, courtesy of the British Museum, London, England.

Photo on page 86 © Kim Walton, courtesy of The Eretz Israel Museum, Tel Aviv, Israel.

Photo on page 60 © Kim Walton, courtesy of the Turkish Ministry of Antiquities and the Istanbul Archaeological Museum.

Photo on page 41 © Kim Walton, courtesy of the Metropolitan Museum of Art, New York.

Photo on page 151 © Library of Congress Prints & Photographs Division, [reproduction number, LC-DIG-ggbain-17575].

Photo on page 126 © Library of Congress Prints & Photographs Division, Detroit Publishing Company Collection, [reproduction number, LC-DIG-ppmsca-01151].

Photos on pages 132, 171, 208 © Marie-Lan Nguyen / Wikimedia Commons, courtesy of the Louvre.

Photos on pages 83, 304 © Olaf Tausch / Wikimedia Commons, CC-by-3.0.

Photo on page 63 © Olaf Tausch / Wikimedia Commons, CC-by-3.0, courtesy of the Open Air Museum at Memphis, Egypt.

Photo on page 159 © Rémih / Wikimedia Commons, CC-by-sa-3.0.

Image on page 267 © Ritmeyer Archaeological Design.

Photo on page 177 © Todd Bolen / BiblePlaces.com.

Photo on page 258 © The Yorck Project / Wikimedia Commons.

Photos on pages 2, 36, 28, 112, 155, 239, 246 © Zev Radovan / www.BibleLandPictures.com.

Contributors

General Editors
Mark L. Strauss
John H. Walton

Associate Editor, Illustrating the Text
Rosalie de Rosset

Series Development
Jack Kuhatschek
Brian Vos

Project Editor
James Korsmo

Interior Design
Brian Brunsting

Visual Content
Kim Walton

Cover Direction
Paula Gibson
Michael Cook

Index

prophets, 36, 47, 66, 78, 110, 82–84, 184, 215, 242, 289, 314, 319. *See also* Nathan; Samuel: as prophet; Saul: among the prophets
and the Davidic king, 54, 84, 125, 222, 225, 229–30, 236
Prophets, the, 2, 42, 54, 107, 215, 225, 230, 289. *See also* Former Prophets; Isaiah; Jeremiah
psalms, 78, 132, 214, 215, 221, 224, 237, 242–43, 263, 264, 284, 297, 299, 302

Qumran, 15, 68, 70, 149, 317

Ramesses, 12, 63
Ramesses II, 63, 322
Ramesses III, 27, 34, 93, 206, 314
rebellion, 17, 74, 76, 80, 100, 102, 104, 185, 221, 240, 278–79, 281, 282, 304, 306
of Absalom, 200, 241, 250, 252, 256, 268, 274–75, 280
consequences of, 12, 42, 50–51, 55, 63, 84, 149, 194, 198, 199, 248, 289
God's response to, 14, 22, 78, 79, 81, 113–15, 186, 212–13, 219, 242, 300, 306–7
of Israel, 42, 53, 60, 75–78
against Saul, 110, 160, 167, 319
of Saul, 102, 104, 198, 221
Red Sea, 72, 77, 82, 84, 88, 89, 169
religion. *See* ancient Near East: religion in; gods; idolatry; pagan religion; worship
religious formalism, 96, 97. *See also* oath; oracle; sacrifice
and obedience, 30, 82, 98–103, 107, 166, 216
and Saul, 29, 92–93, 95, 98, 99, 105
repentance, 17, 24, 42–49, 78, 107, 242–43, 278, 289, 306, 311. *See also* confession of sin
of Israel, 38, 42, 89, 197, 316
and restoration, 186, 253, 264
and submission to God, 260, 264, 266
revelation, 18, 21, 155–56, 192, 216, 309. *See also* God: self-revelation of
of God's will, 18, 47, 138, 186, 287
of God's word, 11, 20–21, 47
prophetic, 20, 24, 28, 78, 123–24, 182, 184

sacrifice, 15, 16, 18, 22, 57, 74, 82–83, 98–103, 107, 113, 213–14, 241, 286, 287, 308, 310, 319. *See also* religious formalism
burnt offering, 40, 82, 94, 308
guilt offering, 35, 39
and Saul, 80, 82, 92, 95, 96, 104–5, 108, 172, 316
Samson, 9, 27, 32, 90, 119, 252
and David, 3, 112, 153, 232, 233, 248
and Samuel, 2–3, 10, 62–63

and Saul, 3, 56, 60, 62–63, 70, 72, 94–96, 232, 316
Samuel. *See also* Samson: and Samuel
anointing of David, 1–3, 8, 9, 12, 23, 44, 47, 63, 110, 113, 116, 144–45, 164
anointing of Saul, 1, 8, 24, 44, 56, 58, 75, 113, 164, 185
contrasted with Eli, 14–15, 18, 20, 21, 26, 44, 47
credentials of, 1, 8, 14, 20, 22, 44, 46, 47, 77–78
death of, 57, 164–65, 182–85
as deliverer of Israel, 3, 9, 44, 58, 62–63
as intercessor, 45–47, 53, 77–78, 82, 100
as priest, 20, 82, 84, 313
as prophet, 1, 8, 14, 20–25, 46, 47, 52, 57, 63–65, 74, 75, 77, 78, 80, 82–84, 107, 110, 113, 125, 136–37, 164–65, 182–85, 194, 195, 308
Saul. *See also* David: contrasted with Saul; Eli: and Saul; Samson: and Saul
abandoned by the Spirit, 110, 112, 113, 116, 123–24, 130, 172, 174, 198, 317
anointing of, 1, 8, 24, 44, 56, 58, 59, 71, 75, 113, 158–60, 162, 164, 166, 170–71, 178, 185, 197, 198, 268, 318
attempts to kill David by, 107, 113, 116, 123, 125, 128–31, 134, 137, 140, 146, 150, 155, 156, 160, 167, 170–72, 176, 179, 185, 198, 235, 239, 287
character flaws of, 62, 65, 72, 82, 86, 92, 156
death of, 62, 122, 161, 165, 171, 184, 185, 188–90, 194–98, 200–204, 208, 261, 284, 286, 306
as deliverer of Israel, 59, 62, 68, 70, 80, 92, 123, 152, 198, 201
disobedience by, 81, 83, 100, 106, 108, 131, 149, 150, 171, 185, 186, 206, 209
dynasty of, 1, 4, 14, 80–87, 98, 104, 108, 110, 137, 150, 185, 186, 195, 198, 221
empowered by the Spirit, 3, 59, 60, 62, 68, 70, 72–74, 80, 112, 114, 123, 131, 150, 174
as God's chosen ruler, 56–59, 63, 65, 68, 74, 84, 111–12, 158, 303
among the prophets, 60, 123–24, 128–29, 131, 142, 182
rejected by God, 8, 17, 30, 46, 57, 80, 84, 87, 101, 105, 106, 108, 111–14, 125, 131, 138, 148, 150, 154, 164, 167, 172, 174, 177, 182–83, 185, 189, 204, 232, 238, 306
and religious formalism, 29, 64, 92–93, 95, 98, 99, 105
sins of, 82, 83, 87, 105–6, 138, 158, 170, 172–74, 185, 196, 241, 284,

287, 288, 290, 306–7 (*see also* confession of sin: by Saul)
sons of, 161, 185, 189, 194–96, 198, 228, 261, 284, 286–88, 290, 306 (*see also* Jonathan: as Saul's son)
spear of, 124, 127, 128, 131, 137, 140, 146, 154, 170–71, 178, 196
tormented by evil spirit, 108, 110, 112–14, 116, 123–25, 130, 131, 150, 171, 174, 307
security, 35, 44, 64, 66, 74, 114, 143–44, 179, 232, 292, 315
as coming from God, 45, 48–49, 58, 60, 62, 68, 70, 72, 75–78, 89, 192, 220–21, 226, 230, 236
national, 20, 50, 54, 56, 58, 61, 76, 210, 220, 226, 229, 294
Septuagint, 22, 41, 59, 88, 93, 95, 119, 136, 149, 166, 201, 246, 288, 317, 318, 320, 321
shakab, 21, 234, 239, 241, 245
Shiloh, 3, 10, 14, 22, 23, 28, 34, 38, 215
sin, 48, 78, 95, 114, 156, 186–87, 221, 225, 276, 286, 310, 322. *See also* adultery; confession of sin; disobedience; idolatry; murder; rebellion
of Achan, 3, 94, 101, 105, 196, 241, 289, 307
of David, 2, 101, 218, 232–34, 236–45, 247–49, 253, 256, 261, 263, 268, 284, 289, 304, 306–8, 310, 314
of Eli and his sons, 15, 18, 22, 23, 28, 44, 149–50, 273
of the Israelites, 18, 27, 46, 57, 78, 102, 197, 215, 240, 243, 289, 309
of Saul, 82, 83, 87, 105–6, 138, 158, 170, 172–74, 185, 196, 241, 284, 286–88, 290, 306–7
Solomon, 4, 6, 168, 205, 209, 241–43, 263, 264, 278, 279, 281, 316, 320, 321
and appointment of Zadok, 14, 17, 149
as David's successor, 14, 58, 205, 218, 224
spirit, evil, 108, 110, 112–14, 116, 123–25, 130, 131, 150, 171, 174, 307
Spirit, Holy, 124, 128, 142, 182, 285, 302, 304
coming upon, 60–62, 70, 110, 112, 116, 123
empowerment by, 3, 59, 60, 62, 72–74, 80, 90, 114, 131, 150, 174, 315
and prophesying, 60, 131, 142, 182
withdrawal of, 110, 112, 113, 116, 123–24, 130, 172, 174, 198, 317
storm, 9, 11, 32–33, 44–49, 74–75, 117, 296–97, 300
storm-god, 11, 33, 45, 46, 286, 296, 314

tabernacle, 14, 18, 21, 23
Tamar, 244–48, 251, 254, 273, 276
Tel Dan, 44, 206–7, 220, 233
temple, 16, 34, 46, 83, 107, 209. *See also* worship center
of Dagon, 26, 32–34, 36, 212

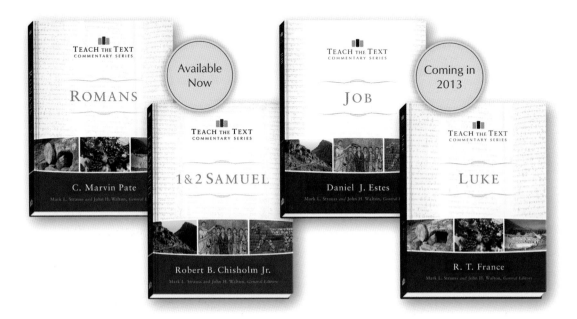